Volume XXX

Tennyson's Philological Medievalism

ISSN 2043-8230

Series Editors
Karl Fugelso
Chris Jones

Medievalism aims to provide a forum for monographs and collections devoted to the burgeoning and highly dynamic multi-disciplinary field of medievalism studies: that is, work investigating the influence and appearance of 'the medieval' in the society and culture of later ages. Titles within the series investigate the post-medieval construction and manifestations of the Middle Ages – attitudes towards, and uses and meanings of, 'the medieval' – in all fields of culture, from politics and international relations, literature, history, architecture, and ceremonial ritual to film and the visual arts. It welcomes a wide range of topics, from historiographical subjects to revivalism, with the emphasis always firmly on what the idea of 'the medieval' has variously meant and continues to mean; it is founded on the belief that scholars interested in the Middle Ages can and should communicate their research both beyond and within the academic community of medievalists, and on the continuing relevance and presence of 'the medieval' in the contemporary world.

New proposals are welcomed. They may be sent directly to the editors or the publishers at the addresses given below.

Professor Karl Fugelso	Professor Chris Jones	Boydell & Brewer Ltd
Art Department	Department of English	PO Box 9
Towson University	University of Utah	Woodbridge
3103 Center for the Arts	LNCO, Rm 3500	Suffolk IP12 3DF
8000 York Road	255 S Central Campus Drive	UK
Towson, MD 21252-0001	Salt Lake City	
USA	UT 84112	
kfugelso@towson.edu	USA	
	chris.s.jones@utah.edu	

Previous volumes in this series are printed at the back of this book

Tennyson's Philological Medievalism

Sarah Weaver

D. S. BREWER

© Sarah Weaver 2024

All Rights Reserved. Except as permitted under current legislation
no part of this work may be photocopied, stored in a retrieval system,
published, performed in public, adapted, broadcast,
transmitted, recorded or reproduced in any form or by any means,
without the prior permission of the copyright owner

The right of Sarah Weaver to be identified as
the author of this work has been asserted in accordance with
sections 77 and 78 of the Copyright, Designs and Patents Act 1988

First published 2024
D. S. Brewer, Cambridge

ISBN 978 1 84384 661 1

D. S. Brewer is an imprint of Boydell & Brewer Ltd
PO Box 9, Woodbridge, Suffolk IP12 3DF, UK
and of Boydell & Brewer Inc.
668 Mt Hope Avenue, Rochester, NY 14620-2731, USA
website: www.boydellandbrewer.com

A CIP catalogue record for this book is available
from the British Library

The publisher has no responsibility for the continued existence or accuracy of URLs for
external or third-party internet websites referred to in this book, and does not guarantee
that any content on such websites is, or will remain, accurate or appropriate

For Mark

Contents

List of Illustrations	viii
Acknowledgments	ix
List of Abbreviations	x
Conventions Used in This Volume	xi
Timeline of Relevant Events and Publications	xii
Introduction: Tennyson's Philological Literary Language	1
1 "Between the chaos and the cosmos of human speech": Seeking the Source of Meaning	28
2 "The people whose tongue we speak": Anglo-Saxons as Linguistic Ancestors	61
3 Removing the Veil of Custom and Familiarity	118
4 "All that men have been doing and thinking and feeling": Evoking and Invoking the Past	168
Conclusion	223
Bibliography	229
Index	242

Illustrations

Figures

1	A table of Grimm's Law in one of Tennyson's notebooks. MS Eng 952 (Notebook 37), Houghton Library, Harvard University.	35
2	A page of Tennyson's copy of *The History of the Anglo-Saxons* by Sharon Turner, showing marginal notes. TRC/AT/2238, Lincolnshire Archives, Lincoln, UK.	73
3	Frontispiece of Rasmus Rask's *Grammar of the Anglo-Saxon Tongue*, edited by Benjamin Thorpe.	125
4	A page of Tennyson's notebook glossary. MS Eng 952 (Notebook 4), Houghton Library, Harvard University.	126
5	A page of Tennyson's notebook rhyme lists. MS Eng 95210, Houghton Library, Harvard University.	176

Tables

1	Dictionaries owned by Tennyson or his father.	15
2	Dictionaries that Tennyson consulted but did not own.	16
3	Grammars and editions of Anglo-Saxon texts listed in Bosworth's 1838 dictionary, in order of publication date.	87
4	Early versions of lines 259–263 of *Beowulf*.	93
5	Alliteration placement on the stressed syllables in a long line of Old English poetry.	100
6	Alliteration patterns in *In Memoriam*.	219

The author and publisher are grateful to all the institutions and individuals listed for permission to reproduce the materials in which they hold copyright. Every effort has been made to trace the copyright holders; apologies are offered for any omission, and the publisher will be pleased to add any necessary acknowledgment in subsequent editions.

Acknowledgments

My husband Mark Rubin has lived with this project at every stage, through the thrills of discovery and the agonies of revision. This book was made possible by his unfailing support and that of my parents, James and Cheryl. I cannot thank them enough.

I also wish to thank Heather Glen and Michael Hurley for reading early drafts and asking the right questions to move the project in fertile new directions. I'm likewise grateful to Richard Dance for encouraging my exertions in Old English, and to Simon Keynes for sharing his expertise on J.M. Kemble, as well as the archival material he has personally collected related to Kemble. In addition, the staff at the Tennyson Research Centre and Lincolnshire Archives were a great help when I needed to consult the libraries of the Tennyson family.

For their encouragement throughout the research and writing process, I offer personal thanks to Ian Felce, Philip Sidney, Nadine Tschacksch, Laura Grimwood, Ewan Jones, and Phyllis Weliver.

At Boydell & Brewer, Caroline Palmer has my heartfelt gratitude for her help and patience.

Abbreviations

BB	Balin and Balan
CA	The Coming of Arthur
G	Guinevere
GE	Geraint and Enid
GL	Gareth and Lynette
HG	The Holy Grail
LE	Lancelot and Elaine
LT	The Last Tournament
MG	The Marriage of Geraint
MV	Merlin and Vivien
OED	*Oxford English Dictionary*
PA	The Passing of Arthur
PE	Pelleas and Ettarre

Conventions Used in This Volume

THE WORD *PHILOLOGY* has applied to an enormous range of academic practices; when referring to philology, I include any scholarly endeavors related to uncovering the history of either single words or languages generally. By "new philology," I mean the systematic study of historical and comparative linguistics that developed in continental Europe in the first decades of the nineteenth century and were subsequently adopted in Britain. The matter of whether to call the language of the Anglo-Saxons "Old English" is still under debate.[1] I have chosen to use the label when referring to the language of the Anglo-Saxons, and hence their vernacular texts. On a practical level, it provides variety of terminology. It also reflects the fact that the figures I discuss generally argued for continuity of cultural inheritance, though they themselves nearly always employed the term "Anglo-Saxon" or simply "Saxon."

Placing Tennyson's poetry in the context of interconnected movements such as Anglo-Saxonism, philology, folklore, and dialect studies requires citing a wide range of writers and scholars without spending a great deal of time with them individually. Every effort has been made to aid the reader in keeping track of these figures via periodic reminders of their relevance to the discussion. In addition, dates are provided for all works as they appear throughout, so that the reader may orient themselves within the overlapping nineteenth-century contexts in which I discuss Tennyson's oeuvre. However, the reader may also find it helpful to make use of the provided timeline. As for the corpus itself, all poems are cited from the three-volume Christopher Ricks edition. The facts relating to Tennyson's ownership of certain books is taken from *Tennyson in Lincoln: A Catalogue of the Collections in the Research Centre* and the online catalogue of the Lincolnshire Archives.[2] Unless otherwise noted, all definitions and etymologies come from the online *Oxford English Dictionary*, accessed between 2010 and 2023. Finally, because this book discusses so many single words, I have adopted the practice of referring to them using italics rather than cluttering the page with an overabundance of quotation marks.

---

[1] E.J. Christie, "'An Unfollowable World': *Beowulf*, English Poetry, and the Phenomenalism of Language," *Literature Compass* 10, no. 7 (2013): 519.

[2] Nancie Campbell, *Tennyson in Lincoln: A Catalogue of the Collections in the Research Centre*, vol. 1, 2 vols. (Lincoln: Tennyson Society, 1971).

Timeline of Relevant Events and Publications

1701	Thomas Benson, *Vocabularium Anglo-Saxonicum*.
1772	Edward Lye, *Dictionarium Saxonico et Gothico-Latinum*.
1780s	William Jones gives lectures to the Asiatick Society of Bengal, proposing a parent language from which Sanskrit, Latin, Greek, and other languages descended.
1786	John Horne Tooke, *Diversions of Purley*. Enduringly popular. Argued that all words can be traced back to sensation.
1795	Oxford's Rawlinson professorship of Anglo-Saxon established, though appointees are not especially active in the subject.
1799–1805	Sharon Turner, *History of the Anglo-Saxons*. Idealizes Anglo-Saxon society and includes excerpts from *Beowulf* and other Old English texts.
1809	Tennyson born.
1817	Rasmus Rask, *Angelsaksisk Sproglaere*. An Anglo-Saxon grammar in Danish.
1819	Jacob Grimm, *Deutsche Grammatik*. Proposes a system to explain sound-change patterns (Grimm's Law).
	Walter Scott, *Ivanhoe*.
1820s	Julius Charles Hare reforms teaching at Trinity College, Cambridge, emphasizing close reading.
1822	Grimm, *Deutsche Grammatik* expanded second edition.
1823	Joseph Bosworth, *The Elements of Anglo-Saxon Grammar*.
1826	John Josias Conybeare, *Illustrations of Anglo-Saxon Poetry*.
1827	*Poems by Two Brothers*.
	Tennyson comes up to Trinity College, Cambridge.
	Julius and Augustus Hare, *Guesses at Truth, By Two Brothers*.
1828	Watermark date of the notebook in which Tennyson created a glossary of Old and Middle English words and translated a few lines of *Beowulf*.

Timeline of Relevant Events and Publications

1829 (Summer) Kemble goes to Germany and studies continental comparative philology, returning to England later that year.

1830 *Poems, Chiefly Lyrical.*

Benjamin Thorpe (ed.), *A Grammar of the Anglo-Saxon Tongue* by Rasmus Rask

(July) The "Spanish Adventure" of the Cambridge Apostles.

Thomas Wright comes up to Trinity College, Cambridge.

1831 (February) Tennyson leaves Cambridge.

Kemble returns to Cambridge from Spain, tutors Wright in Anglo-Saxon.

(August) Arthur Hallam's review of *Poems, Chiefly Lyrical.*

1832 *Poems.*

1833 (April) Kemble, "Review of Cædmon's Metrical Paraphrase" in the *Gentleman's Magazine*. Asserts that continental methods are superior to those of British medievalists.

(September) Arthur Hallam dies.

J.M. Kemble, *The Anglo-Saxon poems of Beowulf, The Travellers, and The Battle of Finnesburh* (November letter to Tennyson: "I rejoice to say *Beowulf* is out").

(December) Tennyson writes to Kemble: "Some thoughts, vague ones, I have, of coming up to Cambridge and attending your lectures next term".

1834 Kemble delivers lectures at Cambridge on the "History of the English Language, First, or Anglo-Saxon Period".

(March) A pamphlet titled *The Anglo-Saxon Meteor* appears, insulting Kemble personally and professionally.

(April) Kemble, "Review of Analecta Anglo-Saxonica" in the *Gentleman's Magazine*. Denigrates the state of philology in Britain.

(December) Kemble again insults British medievalist scholarship in another review in the *Gentleman's Magazine*, titled "Oxford Professors of Anglo-Saxon."

1837 Kemble, *A Translation of the Anglo-Saxon Poem of Beowulf.*

1838 Joseph Bosworth, *A Dictionary of the Anglo-Saxon Language.*

1842 *Poems* (2 volumes).

Charles Edward Mudie begins lending books.

Philological Society of London formed.

1844 William Barnes, *Poems of Rural Life in the Dorset Dialect.*

	Timeline of Relevant Events and Publications
1846	Wright, *Essays on Subjects Connected with the Literature, Popular Superstitions and History of England in the Middle Ages.*
1849	Kemble, *The Saxons in England.*
1850	*In Memoriam.*
	Tennyson named poet laureate.
1851	Trench, *On the Study of Words.*
1855	*Maud, and Other Poems.*
	Trench, *English, Past and Present.*
1857	Kemble dies.
	Trench, *On Some Deficiencies in Our English Dictionaries.*
	Work begins on the *New English Dictionary*, predecessor to the *Oxford English Dictionary.*
1858	Bosworth appointed Rawlinson professor of Anglo-Saxon at Oxford.
1859	First set of *Idylls of the King.*
	Philological Society, *Proposal for the Publication of a New English Dictionary.*
	Trench, *A Select Glossary of English Words Used Formerly in Senses Different from Their Present.*
1861	Friedrich Max Müller gives popular lectures on language at the Royal Institution.
	Müller, *Lectures on the Science of Language.* Sells rapidly.
1862	William Barnes, *TIW*. Claims to trace the fifty Germanic roots of English.
1863	Müller gives second series of lectures.
	Watermark date of the notebook in which Tennyson wrote out a table of Grimm's Law.
1864	*Enoch Arden.*
	Müller, second series of *Lectures on the Science of Language.*
1867	Bosworth gives £10,000 to found an Anglo-Saxon professorship at Cambridge.
1868	Chair of Comparative Philology created at Oxford for Max Müller.
1869	*The Holy Grail and Other Poems.*
1871	"The Last Tournament".
1872	"Gareth and Lynette".
1875	*Queen Mary.*

1876	*Harold.*
	Hallam Tennyson, "The Song of Brunanburh".
1880	*Ballads and Other Poems*, which includes "The Battle of Brunanburh".
1885	*Tiresias and Other Poems*, containing the last idyll ("Balin and Balan").
1886	Trench dies.
1889	*Demeter and Other Poems.*
1892	Tennyson dies.
1908–1910	Eversley Edition of Tennyson's works published.

Introduction
Tennyson's Philological Literary Language

IN JANUARY 1857, Jane Carlyle had been feeling unwell. Emily Tennyson, whose husband was by this time a well-established literary figure, wrote with sympathy and invited her for a visit to the Isle of Wight. Flattered by the attention, Carlyle replied, "I feel both surprised and gratified, as if I were an *obsolete* word that some great Poet (Alfred Tennyson for example) had taken a notion to look up in the Dictionary."[1] This analogy is a telling one, and it captures many of the themes at the heart of this book. Jane Carlyle takes it as a given that poets are interested in unusual words, particularly those that have gone out of use. By citing Tennyson as an example of such a poet, she both pays the compliment of calling him great and suggests that he, too, was attracted to words that were strikingly antiquated.

This book builds upon the same foundation as Carlyle's letter. Specifically, it considers how Tennyson developed his style while intellectually engaged with two major movements of the nineteenth century: medievalism and philology. That he wrote medievalist poetry is not a matter of debate. Even had he composed nothing else deserving the name, his twelve *Idylls of the King*, published between 1859 and 1885, depicted Arthurian legend in lavish, exhaustive detail. Tennyson committed himself to writing a comprehensive version of the myth, going so far as to cite his sources in the Eversley Edition.[2] This book, however, argues for myriad medievalisms in Tennyson's writing, ranging in scale from narrative (such as in the *Idylls*) to single vowels.

The *Idylls of the King* are a case of what I call performative medievalism, an idea discussed further below. Other medievalist manifestations, which are the primary focus of this book, grew out of the poet's fascination with the history of the English language and those who have spoken it over the centuries. They are woven into the fabric of his verse, whatever the subject matter, from spare elegiac tone to alliterative patterns to the use of obsolete meanings of single words, and even his verb conjugations. These techniques that draw on language history I categorize as philological medievalism, and they are the result of the poet's many-faceted verbal curiosity. If the minute, scattered nature of this kind of medievalism suggests that it is hidden in plain sight, the unexpected inside the familiar, then that is exactly what Tennyson's linguistically attuned friends said about the epic histories within words. *Tennyson's Philological Medievalism* aims to show how his medievalism filtered down to the smaller scale of his stylistic choices.

---

[1] Hallam Tennyson, *Alfred Lord Tennyson: A Memoir*, vol. 1 (London: Macmillan, 1897), 417.
[2] The Eversley Edition is a multivolume set published by Macmillan from 1908–1910. Tennyson and his son Hallam collaborated on the notes for these volumes before the poet's death in 1892.

Tennyson's affinity for the archaic was fed not only by his early reading of Chaucer and other canonical authors but also by his substantial engagement with the Anglo-Saxon period as it was being studied and imaginatively reconstructed during his lifetime. That cultural rediscovery took place largely through attention to Anglo-Saxon language. As more and better transcriptions from medieval manuscripts became available, scholars came to better understand Old English grammar and more accurately identify the meaning of its words. This in turn equipped them to examine, compare, and publish more manuscripts. Medievalists and philologists – often the same individuals – enabled and enhanced each other's research; it is therefore essential to consider their work together. Moreover, Tennyson's relationship with antiquated language deserves particular attention in relation to the "new" philology that came to the fore during his youth.

Although many centuries and many cultures have pondered the origin of speech, rarely has the study of language history been laden with more supposed significance or been more widely discussed than in nineteenth-century Europe. Its importance was particularly emphasized in Germany and England, where it infiltrated every field of intellectual life and thence popular consciousness. Increasingly over the course of the century, philology was called upon to support an unrivalled variety of other fields of inquiry, and it enjoyed widespread currency among the educated classes. One's attitude toward, and approach to, philology located one along axes of other values. Other scholars have thoroughly elaborated the histories of language study and Anglo-Saxonism in England, and there is no need to repeat their efforts in detail. However, understanding the parallel development of philology and medievalism helps place Tennyson's linguistic experimentation in a broader context.

Philology and Anglo-Saxonism in England

The term *philology* has applied to a wide range of critical practices over time. Indeed, James Turner identifies its various ventures as the source of all of the now-distinct subjects that constitute the humanities.[3] To help unpack the meanings of *philology*, we might turn to the *Oxford English Dictionary* (henceforth the *OED*), where several definitions emerge from the Greek etymons that form the word, *philo* (liking for) and *logos* (word, speech). There we learn of a now-rare definition, "love of learning and literature," as well as one that implies a disproportionate love of one's own words. Among the possibilities, the following is the sense most relevant to the cultural milieu that is the focus of this book:

> The branch of knowledge that deals with the structure, historical development, and relationships of languages or language families; the historical study of the phonology and morphology of languages; historical linguistics. See also *comparative philology*.[4]

---

[3] James Turner, *Philology: The Forgotten Origins of the Modern Humanities* (Princeton: Princeton University Press, 2014), ix–x.
[4] *OED Online.* Oxford University Press. https://www.oed.com/dictionary/comparative_adj#8796911.

This process of appealing to the *OED* enacts the Victorian era's investment in the history of English, its enthusiasm for categorization, and its faith in the roots and history of a word to give shape to its meaning. Indeed, consulting an academic resource that can legitimately claim to be "the definitive record of the English language" is possible only because of the growth in linguistic scholarship that took place during the nineteenth century, the *OED* itself being a product of that same research.

Philology as linguistic analysis emerged in the early modern period in the form of Biblical exegesis – interpreting Scripture through close attention to the words of the word of God. It further developed as a way to enhance understanding of the Classics; by the late eighteenth century, it had come to denote a holistic method of understanding classical literature by putting it in context. As the nineteenth century approached, historical linguistics of a more objective, philosophically neutral type developed in symbiotic relationship with study of the medieval. In a feedback loop of academic interdependence, research on earlier forms of English unlocked the contents of medieval manuscripts, which in turn provided linguistic material for philologists to scrutinize. Previously, such texts had been considered useful only for proving political points.

Post-medieval interest in specifically Anglo-Saxon documents dates to at least the reign of Elizabeth I, at which time it was politically imperative to establish that there had been an ancient English church with its own distinct traditions.[5] It was this Renaissance hunt for evidence that gave old documents – so recently considered worthless – new value. Elizabeth's Archbishop of Canterbury, Matthew Parker, set about collecting manuscripts that had been scattered in the dissolution of the monasteries during her father's reign. Parker founded the Society of Antiquaries, published some of the texts that he had salvaged, and left a great deal more of them to Corpus Christi College, Cambridge.[6] Nearly three centuries later, this treasure trove became a major resource for Tennyson's Cambridge friend John Mitchell Kemble, who spent much of his time as an undergraduate probing the Corpus Christi holdings rather than attending to his university studies. His work as an Anglo-Saxonist was built upon meticulous examination of primary sources, paying much closer attention to their language than had been considered important in previous generations. But in Parker's time, being able to read Old English was little more than a necessary tool for extracting politically convenient historical data.

Scholarship in subsequent centuries gradually shifted focus to seeking historical facts in the language itself. The change took place slowly, however. From Parker onward, well into the nineteenth century, church history and legal history continued to be the primary motivation – or at least, justification – for studying Old English. As Kathryn Sutherland notes, "Evidence about the past ... gains consent by virtue

---

[5] Clare A. Simmons, *Reversing the Conquest: History and Myth in Nineteenth-Century British Literature* (New Brunswick: Rutgers University Press, 1990), 15.
[6] Alice Chandler, *A Dream of Order: The Medieval Ideal in Nineteenth-Century English Literature* (Lincoln: University of Nebraska Press, 1970), 13.

of its adaptability to a present need already inscribed within the historical inquiry."[7] Elizabethan researchers found evidence of peculiarly English ecclesiastical traditions because that was what they needed from the past. Similarly, the English Civil War of the 1640s spurred research into the history of English law, a project that would continue for at least two centuries.

Serious study of Anglo-Saxon language got underway at the turn of the eighteenth century, though scholars continued to justify it primarily as an instrument that enabled other projects. Anglo-Saxon studies, insofar as they existed, were the preoccupation of a handful of devotees, whose publications reveal two shifts in academic attitudes toward medieval texts. First, these scholars felt that such texts should be made available to more readers of their own time, which led to expanded publishing efforts. For example, among the so-called "nest of Saxonists" at Oxford, interested students had to share a single copy of William Somner's large and expensive 1659 dictionary, a fact that prompted them to create an abridged version (1701) that would be somewhat more affordable. Meanwhile, George Hickes published a massive Old English grammar – revised and expanded from an earlier effort – from 1703–1705, and a condensed version appeared six years after that.[8] These works became the basis for many that followed during the early decades of the eighteenth century. The second shift in perception that affected Anglo-Saxon studies was that medieval documents began to acquire antiquarian value as physical and aesthetic objects aside from any interest in the subject matter they contained. As a result, catalogues were made of extant manuscripts, and publications visually reflected their source material through typefaces that replicated historical handwriting.

Eighteenth-century publications were foundational to serious medievalist scholarship, but the desire to disseminate texts and the devotion to visual authenticity were fundamentally at odds with one another. The latter impulse dominated the century, and thus the resulting volumes were expensive and printed in small editions. As Clare A. Simmons explains:

> The very enthusiasm of the scholars compounded the difficulties [of printing]. Not content with only Anglo-Saxon type – the writing of the early scribes was believed to be a different alphabet, and hence a special font was believed to be necessary – many editors also chose to quote from Greek and Middle English sources, the latter usually being reproduced in Gothic type.[9]

---

[7] Kathryn Sutherland, "Editing for a New Century: Elizabeth Elstob's Anglo-Saxon Manifesto and Ælfric's St Gregory Homily," in *The Editing of Old English: Papers from the 1990 Manchester Conference*, ed. D.G. Scragg and Paul E. Szarmach (Cambridge: D.S. Brewer, 1994), 213–214.

[8] Michael Murphy, "Antiquary to Academic: The Progress of Anglo-Saxon Scholarship," in *Anglo-Saxon Scholarship: The First Three Centuries*, ed. Carl T. Berkhout and Milton McC. Gatch, A Reference Publication in Literature (Boston: G.K. Hall, 1982), 8, 10–11.

[9] Simmons, *Reversing the Conquest*, 22.

This differentiating practice was at work, for example, in Elizabeth Elstob's 1715 *Rudiments of Grammar for the English-Saxon Tongue*.[10] Elstob, along with her brother William, tried to make Anglo-Saxon texts more approachable. In fact, she presented her grammar as an introduction to the subject for young women, Old English being a less elite language to learn than those of the ancient classical world. In the interests of accessibility, she took the unprecedented step of translating into Modern English rather than Latin. It is therefore notable that even Elstob's textbooks, which otherwise prioritize helping the reader, employ lettering derived from medieval handwriting and retain other manuscript elements, such as decorative triangles of dots at the ends of sentences. Elstob made her typographical choices explicit in her grammar's guide to the Anglo-Saxon alphabet. It includes forms not familiar to readers: yogh (ȝ) for lower-case *g*; the runic wynn (ƿ) for the sound we now represent with *w*; ash (æ) for short *a*; thorn (þ) and eth (ð) for *th* sounds; and the Tironian scribal abbreviations for *that* and *and*. However, even letters that are common to both Old and Modern English are given in medieval form – most notably *r* and *s* with long descenders, but also *d*, *t*, and capital *G* and *M*, among others.[11]

This printing practice adds visual alienation to the challenges of grammatical changes wrought by the passage of time. It also reflects the fact that Elstob and her contemporaries considered the language – and the alphabet that represented it – essentially other, for all that they argued for continuity in legal and ecclesiastical traditions. The number and complexity of fonts multiplied as dictionaries such as Edward Lye's 1772 *Dictionarium Saxonico et Gothico-Latinum* (which Tennyson used) began to give genealogies for their words, indicating Meso-Gothic roots with specialized type. Published editions of manuscripts likewise reflected a developing appreciation for the aesthetic qualities of old works.[12] Consequently, this nascent Anglo-Saxonist revival stalled because of the expense of publishing by these standards.[13] The antiquarian impulse that prompted such printing styles proved enduring, moreover. Though interest in the texts themselves gradually superseded aesthetic priorities during the nineteenth century, imitative alphabets remained in use in many publications, leading Tennyson to use a medieval script when writing Old English phrases in his own notebook (discussed in Chapter 3).

The turn of the nineteenth century brought more literary productions that handled Anglo-Saxon subjects, including two well-reviewed works titled "Alfred,

---

[10] For more on Elstob's grammar, see Shaun Hughes, "The Anglo-Saxon Grammars of George Hickes and Elizabeth Elstob," in *Anglo-Saxon Scholarship: The First Three Centuries*, ed. Carl T. Berkhout and Milton McC. Gatch, A Reference Publication in Literature (Boston: G.K. Hall, 1982), 119–147.

[11] Elizabeth Elstob, *The Rudiments of Grammar for the English-Saxon Tongue* (London: W. Bowyer, 1715), 3.

[12] Elizabeth A. Fay, *Romantic Medievalism: History and the Romantic Literary Ideal* (Basingstoke: Palgrave, 2002), 12–13.

[13] Sarah H. Collins, "The Elstobs and the End of the Saxon Revival," in *Anglo-Saxon Scholarship: The First Three Centuries*, ed. Carl T. Berkhout and Milton McC Gatch (Boston: G.K. Hall, 1982), 116.

an Epic Poem," introducing historical figures to readers outside the ivory tower.[14] During the 1820s and 1830s, Old English grammars and editions of medieval texts began to appear in print with increasing regularity (see Table 3). Despite lingering antiquarianism, from the 1820s onward, research on the history of language and what it revealed about the history of humanity became more rigorous and more available to a broader audience in terms of both price and venue (for example, periodicals). These philological innovations complemented a shift in how the public perceived the Anglo-Saxons. During the nineteenth century, they came to identify that earlier society as cultural ancestors, a move that helped them craft a sense of what it meant to be English in the context of an expanding empire that brought them face to face with very different societies.

One of the most influential popularizers of this historical interpretation was Sharon Turner. His extremely successful *History of the Anglo-Saxons* (published 1799–1805) idealized the titular civilization, as other books had before it, but in much greater detail and at more length. He argued – and it is worth noting that it still needed arguing in the first years of the nineteenth century – that studying the Anglo-Saxons made just as much sense as reading about the "customs and transactions" of "uncultivated savages" around the world, which the British reading public already found interesting.[15] Writers including Walter Scott, William Wordsworth, and Samuel Taylor Coleridge liked Turner's history, and Wordsworth subsequently wrote twenty sonnets on Anglo-Saxon topics in the 1820s.[16] Medievalist utopianism offered a past in which government was small-scale and fair, all levels of society were connected to the land, and the average worldview had room for emotion and the supernatural, beyond cold reason.[17] This idealization extended to language, as well. Joseph Bosworth, who produced an Anglo-Saxon dictionary in 1838, observed that Anglo-Saxon had many dialects, and "with a free people it could not be otherwise." In other words, in a society where individual expression is the norm, the natural consequence is that forms of expression will proliferate.[18]

Idealizing the Anglo-Saxons, however, led to a narrative obstacle: how was the Norman Conquest to be incorporated into the story of England's progress? One common interpretation was that of the "Norman Yoke," as most memorably depicted in Walter Scott's novel *Ivanhoe* (1819): Norman political and social

---

[14] Lynda Pratt, "Anglo-Saxon attitudes?: Alfred the Great and the Romantic national epic," in *Literary Appropriations of the Anglo-Saxons from the Thirteenth to the Twentieth Century*, ed. Donald Scragg and Carole Weinberg, Cambridge Studies in Anglo-Saxon England 29 (Cambridge: Cambridge University Press, 2006), 138; Joseph Cottle, *Alfred: An Epic Poem in Twenty-Four Books* (London: Longman and Rees, 1800); Henry James Pye, *Alfred: An Epic Poem, in Six Books* (London: W. Bulmer, 1801).

[15] Quoted in Pratt, "Anglo-Saxon Attitudes?: Alfred the Great and the Romantic National Epic," 144.

[16] Chandler, *A Dream of Order*, 85; Donald Scragg, "Introduction. The Anglo-Saxons: fact and fiction," in *Literary Appropriations of the Anglo-Saxons from the Thirteenth to the Twentieth Century*, ed. Donald Scragg and Carole Weinberg, Cambridge Studies in Anglo-Saxon England 29 (Cambridge: Cambridge University Press, 2006), 13.

[17] Chandler, *A Dream of Order*, 102.

[18] Joseph Bosworth, *A Dictionary of the Anglo-Saxon Language* (London: Longman, Rees, Orme, Brown, Green, and Longman, 1838), xxxvi.

institutions had oppressed the good, free Anglo-Saxons, down to the level of their words and grammar. For example, Bosworth wrote, "Look at the [Modern] English [language], polluted by Danish and Norman conquests, distorted in its genuine and noble features ... to mould it after the French fashion, invaded by a hostile entrance of Greek and Latin words ... yet the old English principle is not overpowered."[19] This interpretation, with its emphasis on conquests and invasions, could easily lead to a linguistic nativism that favored the Germanic portion of the English lexicon; such rhetoric was very much alive in Tennyson's lifetime and among his acquaintances. However, a competing narrative also emerged – one that identified the very blending of multiple peoples as the key to England's strength.

Alongside historical narratives, interested readers also began to have access to medieval literature. Turner's history, for example, included excerpts from *Beowulf* and other Old English texts; it provided a crucial sampling of early literature for his readers, including Tennyson. Full editions of original material began to creep into publication in England in the 1820s. Meanwhile, the first two decades of the nineteenth century saw the development of important linguistic insights abroad. Rasmus Rask produced a Danish-language grammar of Old English, *Angelsaksisk Sproglaere* (1817); when it was translated into English in 1830, this work proved influential, to the extent that philological historian Hans Aarsleff credits the translation's publication as the exact moment when new philology was introduced to England.[20] Two years later, Jacob Grimm published his revolutionary *Deutsche Grammatik* (1819, expanded second edition 1822), in which he explained certain laws of sound change among the Indo-European languages. These volumes represented a new methodology for translating old documents and even reconstructing lost languages.

British scholars were slow to adopt the "new philology," as Chapter 1 explores more fully, but the simultaneous emergence of full textual editions and new linguistic laws reflects how complementary advances in linguistics and medieval studies made each other possible. In 1844, Tennyson's friend, the Anglo-Saxonist John Mitchell Kemble, wrote to Grimm:

> Here and there I meet with men both in and out of the universities who take up the study [of Anglo-Saxon] seriously and well, and I believe that in a very few years, we shall see a good sober, [sic] system of study to replace the dim, vague generalities with which we have been offended heretofore. What is most wanted, however, is the establishment of professorships at Oxford and Cambridge, to carry the war on.[21]

Up to the time of Kemble's letter, research on historical English language and culture had been only loosely connected with academic institutions. Old English gained a toehold for English studies at universities by requiring the same skills as studying dead classical languages did; more recent literature, in contrast, was considered

---

[19] Ibid., xxxix.
[20] Hans Aarsleff, *The Study of Language in England, 1780–1860* (Westport: Greenwood Press, 1979), 166.
[21] John Mitchell Kemble, *John Mitchell Kemble and Jakob Grimm; A Correspondence 1832–1852*, ed. Raymond A. Wiley (Leiden: Brill, 1971), 253.

unexaminable because taste could not be taught or tested. English began to establish itself as a university discipline in the 1820s through 1840s in the form of history and philosophy of language, including grammar and etymology, as well as training in speaking and composition.[22]

As for formal academic posts, Oxford's Rawlinson professorship of Anglo-Saxon had actually been established in 1795. Its appointees were not especially active in the subject for the position's first few decades, but Kemble was certainly aware of its existence. More than ten years before this letter to Grimm (1833–1834), he waged an epistolary war in the *Gentleman's Magazine* (discussed in Chapter 2) in which he raged against the more conservative methods of studying the Anglo-Saxons, of which he considered Oxford a stronghold. He wrote of one of his adversaries in the debate:

> I know not whether he has filled, does fill, or means to fill the Saxon Chair in that University; but from the specimen of his ability which he has supplied in these letters, I can assure him that he is worthy to take his place in the long list of illustrious obscures who have already enjoyed that cheap dignity.[23]

In point of fact, Kemble had at least considered applying to the position himself, asking Grimm if he would be willing to supply a letter of reference.[24] Why, then, did he say a decade later that "What is most wanted … is the establishment of professorships at Oxford and Cambridge," when he was very well aware of the chair at Oxford? The key seems to be that he hoped for academic positions dedicated to "a good sober, system of study to replace the dim, vague generalities" that had dominated the field previously. In other words, he felt that the ancient universities needed chairs guided by new-philological principles.

Officially, an Anglo-Saxon lectureship had been established at Cambridge even earlier, in 1640, but it was quickly abandoned. It wasn't until 1867 – more than twenty years after Kemble's letter to Grimm – that the university created a new Anglo-Saxon chair. It did so with the help of an endowment of £10,000 from Joseph Bosworth (author of the Old English dictionary mentioned above), who had held the equivalent post at Oxford.[25] Bosworth had the means to give this generous gift because his publications on the subject had earned as much as £18,000 – a powerful testimony to the readership that Anglo-Saxon topics gained as the century went on.[26]

---

[22] D.J. Palmer, *The Rise of English Studies: An Account of the Study of the English Language and Literature from Its Origins to the Making of the Oxford English School* (London: Published for the University of Hull by the Oxford University Press, 1965), 19–22.

[23] John Mitchell Kemble, "Oxford Professors of Anglo-Saxon," *The Gentleman's Magazine*, December 1834, 605.

[24] Daniel Thomas, "'Modest but Well-Deserved Claims': The Friendship of Samuel Fox and Joseph Bosworth and the Study of Anglo-Saxon in the Nineteenth Century," *Amsterdamer Beiträge Zur Älteren Germanistik* 78, no. 2–3 (August 30, 2018): 236; Kemble, *Correspondence*, 46.

[25] Aarsleff, *The Study of Language in England, 1780–1860*, 169; Henry Bradley and John D. Haigh, "Bosworth, Joseph," in *Oxford Dictionary of National Biography* (London: Smith, Elder, & Co., May 13, 2021).

[26] Bradley and Haigh, "Bosworth, Joseph."

It was in the midst of this growth of both Anglo-Saxonism and systematic philology that Tennyson developed as a poet, and these movements left their mark. The connection between Tennyson and Victorian language study has often been recognized, but as yet it has not been examined at length. In *Language and Structure in Tennyson's Poetry*, F.E.L. Priestley tracked an evolution from the poet's conventional, imitative early works to, in the 1830s, verse that experimented with sound and form and was "marked by a fondness for archaism and for affected diction;" however, Priestley did not recognize the influence of philology or medievalism in that shift.[27] W. David Shaw's analysis of *Tennyson's Style* identifies some of the same techniques described in this book, but his work is primarily descriptive; to the extent that he traces influence, he looks to poetic predecessors, such as Milton and the Romantics.[28] Donald S. Hair's book on *Tennyson's Language* maps the landscape of the period's language theories in order to inform his reading of the poet's ideas about magical names and the importance of speech and vows – a more thematic take on Tennyson's verse and its relationship to speech.[29] Elizabeth Hirsh, like Hair, commented on the priority the poet gave to speech over written language, especially in *In Memoriam*.[30]

Approaching closer to my methodology, Hair's article on "Soul and Spirit in *In Memoriam*" focuses on the philological work being done by specific lexical units, finding that the etymologies of *soul* and *spirit* distinguish their usage in Tennyson's masterwork.[31] Alan Sinfield also examined Tennyson's use of language in the latter's *magnum opus*. In introducing *The Language of Tennyson's In Memoriam*, he describes three possible approaches to analyzing poetic language: a scholar may study forms of language that poetry generally uses; forms used habitually or distinctively by a poet (or group); or significant, unusual uses in a single work. It is the last category that Sinfield undertakes for Tennyson's elegy in particular.[32] The present volume embraces both the second and third categories – that is, I look at linguistic devices that Tennyson favored generally, as well as those employed to effect within specific poems. Richard Marggraf Turley[33] and Patrick Greig Scott have produced articles that come closest to my approach, emphasizing (in Scott's words) "Tennyson's own view of language, and ... the kinds of linguistic awareness he might have expected of his readers" because of the period's enthusiasm for philology.[34] However, the length constraints of the article format necessarily restrict them to offering representative

---

[27] F.E.L. Priestley, *Language and Structure in Tennyson's Poetry*, The Language Library (London: Deutsch, 1973), 25.

[28] W. David Shaw, *Tennyson's Style* (Ithaca: Cornell University Press, 1976).

[29] Donald S. Hair, *Tennyson's Language* (Toronto: University of Toronto Press, 1991).

[30] Elizabeth A. Hirsh, "'No Record of Reply': In Memoriam and Victorian Language Theory," *English Literary History* 55, no. 1 (1988): 133–134.

[31] Donald S. Hair, "Soul and Spirit in 'In Memoriam,'" *Victorian Poetry* 34, no. 2 (July 1, 1996): 175–191.

[32] Alan Sinfield, *The Language of Tennyson's In Memoriam* (Oxford: Basil Blackwell, 1971), 3–4.

[33] Richard Marggraf Turley, "Tennyson and the Nineteenth-Century Language Debate," *Leeds Studies in English*, no. 28 (1997).

[34] Patrick Greig Scott, "'Flowering in a Lonely Word': Tennyson and the Victorian Study of Language," *Victorian Poetry* 18, no. 4 (1980): 371.

examples from a few of the best-known works – specifically, "Œnone," "The Palace of Art," and "The Princess." This is not to dismiss Scott's or Turley's efforts; on the contrary, their articles reveal how rich a seam of material is to be found on this subject within Tennyson's oeuvre.

More recently, Chris Jones's *Fossil Poetry* deals with the same cultural circumstances as does *Tennyson's Philological Medievalism* – namely, the nineteenth century's pervasive and often conflicting philological attitudes. As part of his large-scale study of linguistic nativism in nineteenth-century poetry, Jones devotes a chapter to "Tennyson's Anglo-Saxon," demonstrating that the poet engaged with Old English language and literature to an extent previously underestimated, and for a great deal of his long career.[35] The present volume, particularly Chapter 2, is in conversation with Jones's; it builds on the same historical background but emphasizes different elements and adds new research to the story of the myriad manifestations of Tennyson's medievalism.

Of necessity, for example, I cover some of the same biographical ground in establishing Tennyson's relationship with philological endeavors; to avoid doing so would be to leave out context that is crucial to recognizing how he conceived of the history of the English language and its speakers. However, I do not attempt to duplicate Jones's comprehensive survey of nineteenth-century Anglo-Saxon scholars, for example; instead, I refer to key researchers and their work selectively, focusing on identifying which sources the poet could have drawn upon at various points in time. Similarly, it would be negligent to ignore or gloss over Tennyson's translation of the Anglo-Saxon poem "The Battle of Brunanburh," for which Jones provides insightful context and analysis. But whereas Jones gives more history surrounding nineteenth-century conceptions of Anglo-Saxon poetic structure, I am more concerned with Tennyson's individual word choices. Our work is thus complementary.

As the survey above makes clear, research on Tennyson's language and style has largely concentrated on *In Memoriam*, with Turley and Scott contributing observations on "Œnone," "The Palace of Art," and "The Princess." When attention has been paid to his Anglo-Saxonism, it has focused on his overtly medievalist poems. The present volume expands on the work of earlier publications by mapping more extensively certain traits within Tennyson's poetry more generally. The chapters that follow unpack how Tennyson's knowledge of English language history is embedded in his style, his word choices, and his masterful construction of ambiguities. As a full-length study of a single writer, this book has the space to consider his philologically informed style across the entirety of his career and in greater depth than a single article or chapter can do. Before proceeding to those particulars, however, it is worth pausing to firmly establish the premise upon which we are to proceed.

Tennyson's Philological Knowledge

This book takes as its basis a number of historical and biographical facts – namely, that the upper and middle classes of nineteenth-century England became increasingly interested in the origins of words and the evolution of languages; that Tennyson

---

[35] Chris Jones, *Fossil Poetry: Anglo-Saxon and Linguistic Nativism in Nineteenth-Century Poetry* (Oxford: Oxford University Press, 2018), 237.

was exposed to medieval texts and contemporary philological theories through the books that he read and the acquaintances he made as a student at Cambridge and beyond; that his knowledge of historical English, though amateur, was extensive; and that this knowledge influenced his word choices and his prosody. In seeking his philologically derived techniques, such as using an obscure meaning of a word, two potential objections arise: how do we know that Tennyson knew a particular sense and intended to employ it, and how likely were his readers to recognize his linguistic cleverness *in situ*?

To a large extent, the former question is more important than the latter. If we can be reasonably confident of an intentional philological wordplay, it helps us to understand Tennyson's poetry better, no matter how many nineteenth-century readers did or did not notice it. The following chapters supply evidence that Tennyson brought a philological medievalist mindset to composing poetry. Once that is granted, then even if a particular example was not consciously crafted to be unusual, it can still testify to his general method, especially if it stood out to his readers. Reader knowledge is difficult to gauge, especially given the breadth of society that knew at least some Tennyson. Nevertheless, there is sufficient reason to believe that his expected audience was familiar with contemporary theories about historical language, as discussed further below.

Reconstructing Tennyson's philological knowledge requires confronting several risks inherent to biography. This is especially the case given his disgust for public inquisitiveness about the man behind the writing:

> He said ... that the desiring anecdotes and acquaintance with the lives of great men was treating them like pigs to be ripped open for the public; that he knew he himself should be ripped open like a pig; that he thanked God Almighty with his whole heart and soul that he knew nothing, and that the world knew nothing, of Shakespeare but his writings; and that he thanked God Almighty that he knew nothing of Jane Austen, and that there were no letters preserved either of Shakespeare's or Jane Austen's.[36]

Accordingly, the poet and his son Hallam controlled the available information about his personal life and, to an extent, his creative process. Much of what we know about the latter are denials of influence or defensive explanations meant to deflect criticism. We can learn from short comments that "The Talking Oak" was an experiment in giving voice to nature, or that "Tithonus" was a "pendant" to "Ulysses"; but Tennyson wrote no essays on the poet's function in society, as others did, and he was a notoriously bad correspondent whose letters were brief and businesslike.

At the largest scale, the philosophies that informed the nineteenth-century investment in philology and Anglo-Saxon studies can help to illuminate Tennyson's writing, but we must beware of reading his verse in search of dogma, for he was reticent to offer the public any information outside the text of his poems, much less an articulated theory of poetic style. "They are always speaking of me as if I were a writer of philosophical treatises," Tennyson complained, and the warning

---

[36] Quoted in Christopher Ricks, *Tennyson*, 2nd ed., Masters of World Literature (London: Macmillan, 1989), 160–161.

is fitting here.[37] Other candidates for similar studies benefit from having expressed more explicit ideological premises for their work. The story of Gerard Manley Hopkins's philological fascination, for example, leaps out from the lines of his sprung rhythm and dense mouthfuls of nonstandard vocabulary. In examining his style, a researcher is aided by the existence of Hopkins's letters and his lectures on poetic theory.[38] Likewise, an examination of William Morris's transmutations of Icelandic sagas can proceed with the assurance that the endeavor was but one expression of a didactic cultural agenda that grounded itself in a well-known medievalism.[39] It is much more difficult to locate an equivalent stylistic program in Tennyson's work. Nevertheless, an impressive array of scholars have concurred, each from the perspective of his or her own research, that this poet's style is characterized by a marked affection for "words for their own sake," as J.F.A. Pyre put it.[40]

Another means of tracing the shape of Tennyson's philological medievalism lies in considering the work of two of his Cambridge acquaintances: John Mitchell Kemble, who became a pioneering Anglo-Saxon scholar, and Richard Chenevix Trench, who went on to write popular works on philology as well as influencing the Philological Society. Through the former, Tennyson became ever more aware of the Germanic branch of English etymology, as well as Old English poetry. Kemble, with whom the poet was especially friendly in the years immediately following university, is an ideal prism through which to view the various elements that contributed to a rising national fascination with the ancient peoples of Britain. A passionate advocate for the "new philology" practiced by the Grimms and other continental scholars, he is informative both through his invectives against common but misguided practices, and through the subtler assumptions behind his own assertions. Like Kemble, Tennyson saw in the Anglo-Saxons a cultural heritage that superseded genealogical descent. Some of his poems directly handle themes relating to that heritage. Even more importantly, his early exposure to Old English verse equipped him to use similar techniques in his own poetics, as seen in his attraction to compounds and alliteration.

Trench's work was broader and more broadly accessible, aimed at educating the public about the importance of studying the accumulated social history behind words and registers. He also cited three linguistic tasks performed by a poet, which encapsulate Tennyson's philological-medievalist techniques as identified in this book:

> [T]he old and the familiar will often become new in his hands; ... he will give the stamp of allowance ... to words ... which hitherto have lived only on the lips of the multitude, or been confined to some single dialect and province; ... he will enrich his native tongue with words unknown and non-existent before.[41]

---

[37] Quoted in Ricks, 210.

[38] See, for example, Cary H. Plotkin, *The Tenth Muse: Victorian Philology and the Genesis of the Poetic Language of Gerard Manley Hopkins* (Carbondale: Southern Illinois University Press, 1989).

[39] See Ian Felce, *William Morris and the Icelandic Sagas*, Medievalism 13 (Cambridge: D.S. Brewer, 2018).

[40] J.F.A. Pyre, *The Formation of Tennyson's Style: A Study, Primarily, of the Versification of the Early Poems*, Studies in Language and Literature 12 (Madison: University of Wisconsin Press, 1921), 225.

[41] Richard Chenevix Trench, *On the Study of Words*, 7th ed. (John W. Parker, 1856), 116–117.

Tennyson showed how archaic usages can transform the impact of old and familiar words, and he constructed his diction so as to bring out a word's etymological metaphor. He gave "the stamp of allowance" to items from his storehouse of old words, gleaned from sources that span centuries, by working them into his poems as verbal antiques. And he exercised his poet's right to invent or re-invent words. Combining these skills, his compositions took advantage of English's layered history by applying the effects of register made possible by its mixture of sources.

We must be cautious, of course, not to conflate the views of Tennyson's friends with his own. For example, Tennyson wrote in an 1855 letter to Charles Richard Weld:

> I do not believe in [the Celtic deity Teutates] being Mercury any more than I believe that Woden and Thor are Mars and Jupiter but in the old unlearned days when men thought themselves most learned and knew but little Latin and less Greek they used to confuse and transubstantiate the Classic and Barbaric Divinities at pleasure.[42]

Kemble, who was anything but unlearned, had devoted a lengthy chapter of *The Saxons in England* (1849) to reconstructing the pagan Germanic pantheon, equating them with gods of the classical world – including Thor as Jupiter (though he found Tíw, not Woden, to be the equivalent of Mars).[43] Likewise, we cannot ignore Tennyson's remark that Trench, one of the great popularizers of philology, was "a bold truehearted Idoloclast – yet I have no faith in any one of his opinions."[44]

It is not my intention to suggest that reading Kemble's and Trench's writings provides a straightforward key to their friend's poetry, nor that theirs were the only opinions on linguistic matters with which Tennyson engaged. Nevertheless, their work deserves more attention than it has yet received in this context. Both men appear regularly in Tennyson scholarship, but often as peripheral phantoms whose mere existence, and perhaps a choice quotation or two, serve as evidence of the poet's linguistic acuity. An investigation of their attraction to the history of English provides insight into the ideas that their cohort at Trinity College discussed, debated, promoted, and absorbed into their own work. As members of the semi-secret society known as the Cambridge Apostles, and as acolytes of their tutor Julius Charles Hare (and through him of Coleridge and German philosophy), Kemble, Trench, and Tennyson formed part of a group that took words seriously, contributing to Tennyson's understanding of language at an important stage in his poetic development.

Within individual poems, approaching the text on the scale of single word choices is a familiar practice for any critic trained since New Criticism emphasized its importance, reinforcing close reading as a means of unpacking the valences of connotation that surround each lexical unit. Paul de Man wrote that

---

[42] Alfred Tennyson, *The Letters of Alfred Lord Tennyson*, ed. Cecil Y. Lang and Edgar Finley Shannon, vol. 2 (Oxford: Clarendon, 1982), 134.

[43] John Mitchell Kemble, *The Saxons in England: A History of the English Commonwealth Till the Period of the Norman Conquest*, vol. 1 (London: Longman, Brown, Green & Longmans, 1849), 340.

[44] Alfred Tennyson, *The Letters of Alfred Lord Tennyson*, ed. Cecil Y. Lang and Edgar Finley Shannon, vol. 1 (Oxford: Clarendon, 1982), 71.

the late-twentieth-century "turn to theory occurred as a return to philology," and indeed it is a major concern of this book to identify instances of word choices that are noteworthy for their effect at a local level.[45] Nevertheless, in expanding the task to tens of thousands of lines of poetry, there are also methodological dangers to emphasizing the proverbial trees rather more than the forest – that is, the poem as a whole. A critic with an eye to etymology – and the online *OED* at her elbow – must beware of overeagerness in listening for Tennyson's linguistic echoes.

Unless a contemporary reader commented on a particular phrase, the job of identifying it as sounding arcane to the Victorian ear is often a matter of weighing probabilities. Furthermore, it is entirely possible to create valences of potential meaning at any point in any poem simply by delving into the various definitions provided by a dictionary. There is some exploratory value in the practice, which can reveal William Empson's third type of ambiguity: "Two ideas, which are connected only by being both relevant in the context, can be given in one word simultaneously. This is often done by reference to derivations."[46] The process reminds the investigator of the fluid nature of words that have had many historical meanings and may still hold vastly different possible definitions; this is especially notable in poetry, where hidden meanings are expected and sought out. However, the exercise can quickly become absurd, especially given that Tennyson cannot be expected to have known every former or alternative meaning of every word he employed. Empson acknowledged the danger on the first page of *Seven Types of Ambiguity*, writing, "In a sufficiently extended sense any prose statement could be called ambiguous."[47] In this way, we might "discover," for example, that when the speaker of "Break, break, break" misses "the touch of a vanished hand," he is saying that the hand has "become worthless or vain" (11), which is clearly the opposite of the poem's emotional thrust.

A catalogue of such discoveries may demonstrate the ingenuity of the critic, but it is not conducive to the aim of this book, which is to trace how Tennyson expressed in his poetry his interest in the history and mechanics of the English language. Accordingly, I have been cautious in identifying noteworthy diction. As a guiding principle, it is useful to employ Alan Sinfield's proposition that a word is "poetically significant" if it adds to the web of structured meanings in the poem that contains it.[48] I have therefore looked for instances in which the context helps define the term in question, lending support to the additional meanings I find there. For innovations, when Tennyson's use is the first or only cited example in the *OED*, it is remarkable enough to merit mention, as with the words *reboant* and *peaky*. The same principle applies to Tennyson innovating the part of speech for which he employs a word. For example, he provides the only cited example of using *nard* as a verb (to anoint with ointment, "Lover's Tale" 671) and *dully* as an adjective ("Palace of Art" 275). Likewise, if Tennyson's usage seems to be absent from the *OED* entirely, I have felt confident in including it, as when he glossed *fold* as "cloud" in "The Two Voices" (192).

[45] Paul de Man, *The Resistance to Theory*, Theory and History of Literature 33 (Minneapolis: University of Minnesota Press, 1986), 24.
[46] William Empson, *Seven Types of Ambiguity*, 3rd ed. (London: Hogarth, 1984), 102.
[47] Empson, 1.
[48] Sinfield, *The Language of Tennyson's In Memoriam*, 5.

Contemporary dictionaries, particularly those Tennyson owned, can be useful in checking which meanings he could have known, though he often knew more than his earliest dictionaries, thanks to his extensive reading from previous centuries. Even so, he was clearly interested in what dictionaries had to offer, because he owned a good many and consulted several more. His notes in a homemade glossary of Old and Middle English, for example, copied some entries verbatim from secondary sources (see Chapter 3 for more details). Table 1 lists the dictionaries that Tennyson (or in one case, his father) owned, ordered by publication date. In addition, there is evidence that Tennyson consulted the works listed in Table 2.

Table 1 Dictionaries owned by Tennyson or his father.

Editor	Title	Year
Nathan Bailey	*An Universal Etymological English Dictionary*	1st ed. 1721, father's copy not dated
Rasmus Rask, trans. Benjamin Thorpe	*A Grammar of the Anglo-Saxon Tongue*	1830
Samuel Johnson	*A Dictionary of the English Language*	1831
Charles Richardson	*A New English Dictionary*	1836–1837
Joseph Bosworth	*A Dictionary of the Anglo-Saxon Language* Replaced Edward Lye's (see below) as the standard volume. Contains a preface and a revised version of Bosworth's 1826 *Essentials of Anglo-Saxon Grammar*, which summarized the work of Grimm and Rask.	1838 Gift 1844
Noah Webster, revised by Chauncey A. Goodrich	*An American Dictionary of the English Language*	1854 Gift 1855
John Camden Hotten	*The Slang Dictionary; or, the vulgar words, street phrases, and "fast" expressions of high and low society*	1864
John Greaves Nall	*An Etymological and Comparative Glossary of the Dialect and Provincialisms of East Anglia*	1866
Edward FitzGerald	*Sea Words and Phrases Along the Suffolk Coast*	1869
W.D. Parish	*A Dictionary of the Sussex Dialect and Collection of Provincialisms in Use in the County of Sussex*	1875
W.W. Skeat	*A Concise Etymological Dictionary of the English Language*	1882
W.W. Skeat	*An Etymological Dictionary of the English Language*	1882

| J.A.H. Murray | *A New English Dictionary; founded on the materials collected by the Philological Society* A–Boz | 1884–1887 |
| W.H. Long | *A Dictionary of the Isle of Wight Dialect, and of Provincialisms Used in the Island* Hallam Tennyson appears in the list of subscribers. | 1886 |

Table 2   Dictionaries that Tennyson consulted but did not own.

Editor	**Title**	**Year**
Thomas Benson	*Vocabularium Anglo-Saxonicum* An abridged student edition of William Somner's 1659 *Dictionarium Saxonico-Latino-Anglicum*	1701
John Urry and Timothy Thomas	Glossary in *The Works of Geoffrey Chaucer* Although Thomas created the glossary after Urry's death, Tennyson cites it in his notebook as "Urry's Glossary".[49]	1721
Edward Lye	*Dictionarium Saxonico et Gothico-Latinum*	1772
Thomas Tyrwhitt	Glossary in *Poetical Works of Geoffrey Chaucer in Fourteen Volumes*	1782

A fuller reconstruction of nondictionary references that Tennyson drew upon for his homemade glossary of old and obsolete words is available elsewhere and need not be replicated here,[50] but the sheer number of lexicographical works in these two tables attests to his enthusiasm for words. It also represents a significant monetary as well as intellectual investment in philology. Drips of ink and occasional doodles in the margins of his copies show that, at the very least, some of them lay open to various pages near his work surface. Moreover, he was interested in the origins of his words throughout his career. His notebook glossary demonstrates his research as a young man; at the end of his life, his Eversley Edition annotations often include etymologies for the words he is glossing. For example, his note for *charlatan* as used in *In Memoriam* – and explained decades later – shows an enduring commitment to knowing the biographies of his terms: "From Italian *ciarlatano*, a mounteback; hence the accent on the last syllable."[51]

[49] Alfred Tennyson, *The Harvard Manuscripts: Notebooks 1–4 (MS Eng 952)*, ed. Christopher Ricks and Aidan Day, vol. 1, Tennyson Archive (New York: Garland, 1987), 239.
[50] Sarah Weaver, *Tennyson's Notebook Glossary and Rhyme Lists*, Tennyson Society Monographs 17 (Lincoln: Tennyson Society, 2019), 43–44.
[51] Alfred Tennyson, *Enoch Arden and In Memoriam*, Eversley Edition, vol. 3 of *The Works of Alfred Lord Tennyson*, ed. Hallam Tennyson (London: Macmillan, 1909), 260.

The Eversley Edition glosses themselves help identify phrases that Tennyson or his son thought readers might need help interpreting, though he was not very happy about providing that assistance. In his introduction to the notes, the poet grumbled about the task of annotating his work, saying he did not know what information he should supply. For example, he asked, "Shall I write what dictionaries tell to save some of the idle folk trouble?"[52] Whatever his reluctance to come to the aid of "idle folk," Tennyson's comment shows that he knew that his readers might not know all the words he used. Letters, memoirs, and reviews occasionally discuss specific lexical choices, thereby helping locate words that struck Victorian readers as unusual. Chapter 3 delves into Tennyson's use of historical meanings and the inherent metaphors of his words, but first let us consider how much philological knowledge it is fair to assume in his readers.

Tennyson's Philological Readership

Philology – its scientific discoveries and the often less-than-scholarly conclusions derived from them – appeared in a wide range of nineteenth-century books and essays, and even fiction. In the wake of the new philology of the 1820s, for example, *Middlemarch*'s Mr. Casaubon, who resists academic innovation and plods on with his massive "Key to all Mythologies," is introduced as a figure to be satirized. Indeed, Seth Lerer sees Casaubon and other elements of George Eliot's novel as influenced by the popular writing of Julius Charles Hare, the tutor or mentor of many at Trinity College, Cambridge, including the young Tennyson[53] (Chapter 1 discusses Hare further). By midcentury, the "science of language" and the implications of its findings were an unavoidable presence in the reading material of the educated British population – as was Tennyson's verse. There was, I contend, a great deal of overlap in the presumed readership of *In Memoriam* and Trench's *On the Study of Words*, published the following year. This becomes clear through examining the readership of Tennyson's books alongside that of the periodicals in which they were advertised or in which his poems were printed.

Edgar Finley Shannon has demonstrated that the 1842 *Poems* was "reviewed by periodicals of all types and complexions, by daily and weekly newspapers, by literary weeklies, by magazines, both secular and religious, by student publications, by the great quarterly reviews, and by organs of all parties catering to all classes of readers from lords to laborers."[54] As this quotation implies, there is evidence that his poetry also began to appear in lectures to the working classes.[55] Those readers were was less likely to be reading about the latest philological claims, because philology was not generally aimed at them. The great overlap lay with middle-class readers.

---

[52] Alfred Tennyson, *Poems I*, Eversley Edition, vol. 1 of *The Works of Alfred Lord Tennyson*, ed. Hallam Tennyson (London: Macmillan, 1908), 333.

[53] Seth Lerer, "Middlemarch and Julius Charles Hare," *Neophilologus* 87, no. 4 (n.d.): 654.

[54] Edgar Finley Shannon, ed., *Tennyson and the Reviewers: A Study of His Literary Reputation and of the Influence of the Critics Upon His Poetry, 1827–1851* (Cambridge: Harvard University Press, 1952), 79.

[55] James Tozer, "Tennyson's Popularity," *Tennyson Research Bulletin* 10, no. 4 (November 2015): 373.

Jim Cheshire has shown that the publisher Moxon "found a market for poetry with the emerging middle class," with Tennyson's books as his main product; the 1842 collection was Moxon's "first real success with contemporary poetry and helped him break into the middle-class market." This market of readers for Tennyson – and, as we shall see, philology – was growing, thanks to the rapid expansion of the reading public generally: it quadrupled in size between 1830 and 1901. Cheshire concludes that "Tennyson's early poetry extended his readership to a level that allowed it to surge in response to *Idylls of the King* [beginning in 1859] and *Enoch Arden* [1864]."[56] By P.G. Scott's reckoning, too, when *Enoch Arden* was published, it made "an impact on the whole of the reading public."[57] Cheshire's calculations indicate a slightly earlier starting point for Tennyson's large-scale popularity, but most assessments concur that by sometime in the middle of the century, Tennyson was very widely read. His 1850 appointment to poet laureate, moreover, cemented his position as a writer well known to the public. This was also when Trench and other popularizers of new philology began to publish on the subject.

The prices of Tennyson's books indicate a middle-to-upper-class audience for new copies, generally in the range of five to seven shillings, which was a significant purchase for a middle-class reader.[58] (For a full list of Tennyson's first editions and their prices, see June Steffensen Hagen's impressive work.)[59] Table 3 lays out the prices of key Anglo-Saxonist publications from the first thirty-odd years of the century; it shows that certain grammars and texts could be had for a price equivalent to a book of Tennyson's verse, though the cost for larger or more academic volumes could be much higher. On the other hand, Trench's books were more affordable, which – combined with his engaging style – enabled his ideas to spread: they cost between three and four shillings.[60]

Even for those not inclined or able to spend a significant portion of their income on buying a book, there were other venues for being exposed to both Tennyson's verse and the latest theories about the history of language. The overlap of assumed readership emerges when we examine the contents of the *Athenaeum*, the *Examiner*, and the catalogues of Mudie's Select Library. According to Cheshire, Moxon placed most of his advertising for Tennyson in the *Athenaeum* and the *Examiner*. At a minimum, this indicates that Moxon thought these periodicals catered to the type of reader who might be attracted to Tennyson's verse. Indeed, whether he knew it or not, the former publication was intimately tied to the Cambridge Apostles. In 1828,

---

[56] Jim Cheshire, *Tennyson and Mid-Victorian Publishing: Moxon, Poetry, Commerce* (London: Palgrave Macmillan, 2016), 93, 6, 11.

[57] Patrick Greig Scott, *Tennyson's Enoch Arden: A Victorian Best-Seller*, Tennyson Society Monographs 2 (Lincoln: Tennyson Society, 1970), 2.

[58] Cheshire, *Tennyson and Mid-Victorian Publishing*, 92, citing Simon Eliot.

[59] June Steffensen Hagen, *Tennyson and His Publishers* (University Park: Pennsylvania State University Press, 1979), 186–187.

[60] "English: Past and Present," *Notes and Queries* 12, no. 297 (July 7, 1855); Richard Chenevix Trench, "Books Relating to the Society's Dictionary," in *On Some Deficiencies in Our English Dictionaries: Being the Substance of Two Papers Read Before the Philological Society, Nov. 5, and Nov. 19, 1857* (London: J.W. Parker and Son, 1857), 24; "A Select Glossary of English Words," *Publishers' Circular and General Record of British and Foreign Literature*, November 1, 1859.

while Tennyson's cohort was still at university, Trench wrote to Kemble that the *Athenaeum* was "entirely written by Apostles."[61] The periodical, which was less than a year old at the time of Trench's letter, had quickly been sold by its founder to a group of Cambridge Apostles, including F.D. Maurice and John Sterling.[62] Presumably as a result of this connection, it published a short, glowing review of Tennyson's poem "Timbuctoo" in 1829, before he had ever published a full volume of his own verse.[63]

According to *Athenaeum* historian Leslie A. Marchand, "The journal early became a depository for miscellaneous, scholarly and antiquarian information as well as a forum for the discussion of disputed matters of literary or historical interest." Philology was among the most discussed and disputed of matters both literary and historical as the century went on. Moreover, it made those topics accessible for middlebrow, middle-class readers: from 1831, an issue cost only 4d., a price point that other periodicals found it nearly impossible to compete with; in 1862, the price dropped to 3d. Its affordability, combined with a dedication to independent reviewing and articles written by subject-matter experts, earned the magazine a massive circulation. In short, "The high aim which the *Athenaeum* set for itself was to make literature, art, and science popular without stooping to 'popularize' them."[64] It described itself to potential advertisers as "the leading literary organ, and therefore circulating entirely among the best classes."[65] Reviews provided lengthy quotations in case readers could not afford the books themselves; thus, some portion of Tennyson's readership literally was the readership of the *Athenaeum*, when it reviewed his books. And it reviewed all of his books except for *Poems by Two Brothers* – published before the magazine existed – and *Poems, Chiefly Lyrical*, the first volume in which all poems were his own.

The *Athenaeum*'s "complete coverage of every cultural interest of the time" certainly included philology.[66] In the middle of the century, for example, the journal regularly published status reports on the progress of the *New English Dictionary* and the work of the Philological Society.[67] The *Athenaeum*'s "pleasant relations with Grimm in Germany" undoubtedly further strengthened its reporting of new-philological hypotheses. It featured contributions from prominent Anglo-Saxonists Thomas Wright and Frederic Madden and "frequent papers, letters, and reviews by Skeat, Furnivall, Sweet, and Trevelyan," as well.[68] It also reviewed linguistic publications by less famous writers, such as an 1854 book titled *Outlines of Comparative*

---

[61] W.C. Lubenow, *The Cambridge Apostles, 1820–1914: Liberalism, Imagination, and Friendship in British Intellectual and Professional Life* (Cambridge: Cambridge University Press, 1998), 212.

[62] Leslie A. Marchand, *The Athenaeum: A Mirror of Victorian Culture* (Chapel Hill: University of North Carolina Press, 1941), 5–6.

[63] "Timbuctoo," *Athenaeum*, July 22, 1829: 456.

[64] Marchand, *Athenaeum*, 58, 34, 81, 67.

[65] Quoted in Rosemary Scott, "Poetry in the 'Athenaeum': 1851 and 1881," *Victorian Periodicals Review* 29, no. 1 (Spring 1996): 24.

[66] Marchand, *Athenaeum*, 27.

[67] Richard W. Bailey, "'This Unique and Peerless Specimen': The Reputation of the *OED*," in *Lexicography and the OED*, ed. Lynda Mugglestone, Oxford Studies in Lexicography and Lexicology (Oxford: Oxford University Press, 2000), 226–227.

[68] Marchand, *Athenaeum*, 48, 58, 90.

Philology by M. Schele de Vere (the reviewer thought it tried to cover too much ground in too small a space).[69] An issue from the end of 1860 contains a review of an *Essay on the Origin of Language* by Frederic W. Farrar, a Cambridge Apostle from a little after Tennyson's time. The review begins by saying that Farrar's slim edition "cannot with justice be said to contain any new revelations on the origin of language" but subsequently endorses the book as "a very intelligent and useful exposition of the principal discoveries and conclusions" that have arisen from comparative philology.[70] In short, the *Athenaeum* considered its audience likely to be interested in both Tennyson's poems and the workings of language. In any case, a reader who came to its pages looking for one also encountered the other.

Moxon's other major venue of choice for advertising books of Tennyson's verse was the *Examiner*, which also regularly reviewed Tennyson's books of poetry.[71] Moreover, it was one of the periodicals in which Tennyson most often published his compositions directly – six poems in five years that spanned the midpoint of the century (1849–1854), by Kathryn Ledbetter's count.[72] This preference was likely strengthened by the early support and friendship of the magazine's cofounder, Leigh Hunt. In his role as self-appointed literary agent, Arthur Hallam contacted Hunt in 1831 to draw his attention to Tennyson as a poet; Hunt subsequently wrote a positive review of Tennyson's work.[73] Two years later, in the spring of 1833, Tennyson attended a supper party thrown by Moxon, where (according to Arthur Hallam) "he remained till three in the morning, and was delighted with Leigh Hunt who met him there, and exchanged compliments at a great rate."[74] That summer, Hunt joined a small group (including Moxon) for supper at Tennyson's rooms in London, the conversation again lasting well into the wee hours.[75] By 1837, the friendship had progressed to the point that the two had made plans to have tea together, on which occasion and Tennyson was to have "tumbled [Hunt's] books." The following year, Tennyson signed up for a subscription to help Hunt financially and asked the organizer how Hunt was doing, saying, "I have some books of his which ought to be returned." Ten years later (1847), letters show them having dinner together at the invitation of Tennyson (who was notoriously bad at keeping in touch with his friends).[76] They continued to correspond at least into the 1850s.[77]

---

[69] "Outlines of Comparative Philology; with a Sketch of the Languages of Europe, Arranged upon Philological Principles: And a Brief History of the Art of Writing. By M. Schele de Vere," *Athenaeum*, February 18, 1854, 212.

[70] "An Essay on the Origin of Language; Based on Modern Researches, and Especially on the Work of M. Renan. By Frederic W. Farrar, M.A. (Murray)," *Athenaeum*, December 8, 1860, 788.

[71] Shannon, *Tennyson and the Reviewers*, 169–174.

[72] Kathryn Ledbetter, *Tennyson and Victorian Periodicals: Commodities in Context*, The Nineteenth Century Series (Hampshire, England and Burlington, VT: Ashgate, 2007), 203.

[73] Robert Bernard Martin, *Tennyson: The Unquiet Heart* (Oxford: Clarendon Press, 1983), 140–141.

[74] Tennyson, *Letters*, 1982, 1:91.

[75] Martin, *Tennyson*, 180.

[76] Tennyson, *Letters*, 1982, 1:154, 167, 278.

[77] Tennyson, *Letters*, 1982, 2:192.

In addition to Moxon's promotion of Tennyson, *Examiner* advertisements from the mid-1840s include recurring notices for *The Classical Museum*, "a Journal of Philology" that described itself as taking over from the defunct *Philological Museum*.[78] *The Philological Museum* had been edited by Trinity tutor Julius Charles Hare, and Kemble had published an article "On English Præterites" in it. The *Examiner* provided a brief review praising the first issue of the successor publication (*The Classical Museum*), noting that alongside its main mission to "throw light on points of classical antiquity," it would also offer "occasional investigations of the early history and literature of our own country, which we are glad to see promised."[79] Other advertisements and reviews confirm that multiple parties believed that some subset of the *Examiner*'s readership was interested in philological and historical topics. We may see this, for example, in an 1849 advertisement by bookseller and printer John Russell Smith, who published several books related to dialect (including William Barnes's well-known *Poems of Rural Life*) as well as the work of the Archaeological Association[80] (of which Kemble was an active member). In the advertisement, Smith highlighted the availability of publications by the Camden Society.[81] The Camden Society had been founded a decade earlier (1838) to publish "such historical or literary documents as were yet inedited, and worthy of notice," by means of subscription. It rapidly became successful, gaining 1,250 members within two years and inspiring the formation of similar societies[82] – another indication of the burgeoning interest in the past more generally. One of the Camden's founders was Thomas Wright, a former student of Kemble's who had become estranged from his mentor but who nonetheless helped bring medieval texts into print.

The *Examiner* itself, beyond its advertisements, had high standards for language matters. It could be quite critical of subpar publications relating to linguistic topics, such as an 1844 book by Morgan Kavanagh entitled *The Discovery of the Science of Languages*; the reviewer explained in detail how the author's philological system was wrong.[83] *Upton's Physioglyphics* of the same year fared little better. The review begins by stating the core problem of etymological research – namely, that for every type of word except onomatopoeia, the connection between sound and sense seems to be arbitrary:

> There seems no reason why this animal should be called "dog" and that "cat" rather than any other name the human lips may pronounce. Compound words may be traced to their roots, and these roots may be pursued from one language to another, but the cause why the roots themselves exist remains unsolved.

---

[78] "Classical Museum," *Examiner*, May 4, 1844.
[79] "The Classical Museum," *Examiner*, June 24, 1843, 389.
[80] R.J. Goulden, "Smith, John Russell (1810–1894), Bookseller and Bibliographer," *Oxford Dictionary of National Biography*, September 23, 2004.
[81] John Russell Smith, "Choice, Cheap, and Useful Books," *Examiner*, July 8, 1843, 432.
[82] F.J. Levy, "The Founding of the Camden Society," *Victorian Studies* 7, no. 3 (March 1964): 295–297, 300.
[83] "The Discovery of the Science of Languages. By Morgan Kavanagh," *Examiner*, no. 1892 (May 4, 1844): 275.

(This is what Kemble called the "awful problem of the Cratylus," discussed in Chapter 1.) Mr. Upton, writes the *Examiner*'s reviewer, is one of those "enthusiasts who would thus pursue language to its most secret hiding-place" by claiming to locate the connection of signifier to signified by means of letter-by-letter essentialism.[84] It was an idea belonging to the old school of philological thought, and the reviewer had no patience for it.

The fact that many of the reviewed titles have slipped into obscurity does not especially matter; evidently, the *Examiner* frequently reviewed books that dealt with linguistic subjects. The existence of these reviews indicates that the editorship of the periodical presumed that such works would be of interest to its readers. The reviews themselves are presented in the voice of one familiar with the latest philological ideas, and they assume an audience that shares that familiarity – or at the very least might be interested in such topics. For example, an 1849 review of two grammar and etymology books by R.G. Latham reminds the reader, "Dr. Latham's original and valuable researches in philology have frequently been mentioned in this journal."[85] Similarly, the *Examiner* also reviewed the *Transactions of the Philological Society* as its issues appeared, Trench's *On the Study of Words* (1851) and *On Some Deficiencies in Our English Dictionaries* (1857), and similar books on language.

Further evidence of the expected similarity in readership of Tennyson and philology is to be found in the catalogues of Mudie's Select Library. For those who wished to read the books advertised or reviewed in periodicals such as the *Athenaeum* or the *Examiner*, circulating libraries made them available at an affordable price, and no institution more so than Mudie's. Charles Edward Mudie began lending books from his London shop in 1842, the same year that Moxon broke into to middle-class poetry market with Tennyson's two-volume *Poems*. The fee to borrow from Mudie's was a guinea a year, which Guinevere L. Griest shows to be "an astonishingly low rate" compared to other book lenders. Over the next two decades, the library grew rapidly, moving first to a bigger shop in 1852, then into a custom-built building in 1860. The business then expanded to branch locations and made arrangements to distribute books to book clubs and provincial libraries.[86] The period during which Mudie's established itself as a "leviathan" of the book world comprised the exact years in which Tennyson's readership was surging, his literary success indisputably established by the time *Enoch Arden* came out in 1864.

As its name suggested, Mudie's Select Library was selective in what it carried. Although it offered books on a wider range of subjects than its predecessors, the library chose works of good quality that were morally unobjectionable. The accessible price and good reputation meant that writers and publishers were anxious to see their books appear in the library's advertising. Such a mention not only promoted a publication to Mudie's subscribers, the endorsement would encourage other circulating libraries to follow suit.[87] In short, volumes on offer in its catalogues implic-

---

[84] "Upton's Physioglyphics," *Examiner*, September 21, 1844, 597.

[85] "Elements of English Grammar, for the Use of Ladies' Schools. By R.G. Latham, M.D.," *Examiner*, no. 2178 (October 27, 1849): 677.

[86] Guinevere L. Griest, *Mudie's Circulating Library and the Victorian Novel* (Bloomington: Indiana University Press, 1970), 17, 19–22.

[87] Ibid., 18, 20.

itly conformed with mainstream Victorian interests. It is therefore significant that advertisements for Mudie's regularly boasted that Tennyson's works were available to be borrowed, while books on language appeared in the catalogues.

An 1857 booklet, for example, lists Trench's *English, Past and Present* and *On the Study of Words*, as well as Schlegel's *Lectures on the Philosophy of Life and Philosophy of Language* and books with titles such as *Conversations on Language by Mrs. Marcet* (also listed as the author of "conversations" on other topics, such as the history of England, natural philosophy, and vegetable physiology), *The One Primeval Language* by Rev. C. Forster (three volumes), *Essays on Thought and Language* by B.H. Smart, *Language as a Means of Mental Culture* by C. Marcel (2 volumes), and *Outlines of the History of English Language* by Craik.[88] Similarly, an advertisement in the *Daily Telegraph* from 1865 listed Oxford professor Max Müller's *Lectures on Language* as among the "New Miscellaneous Books at Mudie's Library."[89]

From this survey, it is clear that the same type of readers were expected to be interested in both Tennyson and philology. It is with this assurance that the following chapters analyze the poet's style in the context of the Victorian conception of language history. Does it follow that his readers recognized his old words, old meanings, neologisms, etc.? Some certainly did; reviewers often pointed out these practices, thereby alerting other readers to his tendencies. Moreover, those who read Tennyson had every reason to come to him prepared to find the imprint of philological curiosity.

Echoes and Performance

This book considers how Tennyson's language and prosody emphasize echoes of earlier periods. Broadly speaking, those echoes could add depth to the sentiment being expressed, or they could act as surface effects in service of what I have termed performative medievalism. By "performative medievalism," I mean a type of artistic production that emphasizes outward forms of life in the Middle Ages – for example, clothing, social protocol, activities such as jousting, or period-specific verbal expressions – such that those trappings of a past time serve to re-create it, typically for the purpose of entertainment. It might also be called decorative medievalism or re-enactive medievalism. Although Tennyson sometimes employed this performative mode, I argue that he more often used his knowledge of historical English to revive history within the present as part of embracing the multilayered language of an alloyed populace. Linguistic medievalism certainly can be performative, however. Archaic words in an archaic context can act as a kind of set painting, and Tennyson used them as such in his medieval-themed poems.

For example, The Eversley Edition notes to "The Talking Oak" (written around 1837) tell the reader that a *spence* was "the monks' buttery."[90] The word provides a moment of time travel as the oak recalls the dissolution of the monasteries – that

---

[88] *Catalogue of New and Standard Works in Circulation at Mudie's Select Library*, 1857, 146, 17, 223, 52, 134, 93, 47.
[89] "Classified Advertising," *Daily Telegraph*, April 15, 1865, 7.
[90] Alfred Tennyson, *Poems II*, Eversley Edition, vol. 2 of *The Works of Alfred Lord Tennyson*, ed. Hallam Tennyson (London: Macmillan, 1908), 335–336.

is, when "bluff Harry [Henry VIII] broke into the spence" (47). The poem "The Day-Dream" (1842) tells the latter part of the Sleeping Beauty story, beginning with a description of the dormant castle. The characters establish the medievalist setting, from the maid-of-honor and page to the king and his barons. Smaller details further paint the picture, as in the lines, "Here droops the banner on the tower, / On the hall-hearths the festal fires" (13–14). When we read that "The mantles from the golden pegs / Droop sleepily" (19–20), *mantles* helps place the story in the Middle Ages. (The prince also wears a glittering mantle.) Sunbeams shine "through the Oriel" window, the architectural detail further setting the scene (34). When the spell is broken, the king exclaims, "'By holy rood'" and then "'pardy,'" the latter of which the Eversley Edition glossed (*par dieu*), quoting *Hamlet* for reference.[91]

When medieval words or words for medieval things accumulate in proximity to each other, and especially if they do so in a poem with a matching setting, they add to that setting and bring their historical context with them. In poems that are *not* explicitly medievalist, Tennyson's use of arcane vocabulary instead creates a sense that echoes from medieval society reverberated through his own day. Echoes are an appropriate metaphor here. Beyond the fact that they are common in Tennyson's work,[92] they share the substance of the initial utterance, but they are a fainter, slightly altered version of the original. This is very much how patriotic philologists like Kemble conceived of the relation between Modern English and Old English. As an analogy for poetic influence, echoes also describe the subtlety of the effect Anglo-Saxon literature had on Tennyson. It is the task of this book to identify those historical linguistic echoes.

Tennyson's Philological Medievalism uses philology to highlight certain characteristics of the poet's style and to argue for its intellectual importance to him. The linguistic curiosity of his century provided the poet with a way of understanding his words; nineteenth-century philology, in turn, can help us understand what he did with those words. At times, I attempt large-scale analysis, such as a breakdown of *In Memoriam*'s alliterative patterns; however, this work does not belong to the schools of distant reading or computer-aided corpus linguistics. The research set forth in the following pages assumes that its chief purpose is to contribute to an understanding and appreciation of Tennyson's particular talents and choices.

It is hardly surprising that *In Memoriam* has been the subject of most philologically oriented Tennyson scholarship to date; in addition to being the poet's most famous and acclaimed work, it invites such attention through its carefully crafted ambiguity regarding its central concerns. The elegy rewards philologically grounded investigation, and it stands as a capstone to his poetic development. For this reason, *Tennyson's Philological Medievalism* draws primarily on the poetry spanning from his earliest efforts through *In Memoriam*, including drafts, alternate versions, and unpublished poems. This is not to suggest that Tennyson ceased to write philologically after 1850; on the contrary, that year represents a point at which his historically informed poetic techniques were fully realized. Although they continued to feature

---

[91] Ibid., 2:346.
[92] Seamus Perry, *Alfred Tennyson*, Writers and Their Work (Tavistok: Northcote House, 2005), 29.

in poems both celebrated and obscure for the rest of Tennyson's career, I discuss later works more selectively. For example, the laureate chose the events leading up to the Norman Conquest as the topic of his play *Harold*, and thus it provides valuable insight into his perception of the Anglo-Saxons. The *Idylls of the King* feature in Chapter 4 as examples of poems that mostly (but not entirely) emphasize a performative medievalism in contrast to the philological resonance of linguistic archaisms.

As a poet laureate who held the position for forty-two years, Tennyson was, in Linda Dowling's phrase, "a revered institution in his own right."[93] When studying philology, which shared with complementary sciences a claim to the honor of being part of a gentleman's common knowledge, we can better understand its impact by examining it in relation to so eminent a figure, especially one whose craft was to be a master of words. Conversely, poetry that is known to reflect contemporary concerns – from Lyell's geology to the charge of the Light Brigade – will certainly reward the reader who brings to it an eye and ear for philology.

The first chapter begins by mapping the landscape of nineteenth-century philology to demonstrate that Tennyson's long-recognized penchant for outmoded words and usages had serious theoretical stakes. Although philosophers have, for millennia, grappled with how language relates to reality and the human mind, improvements in the methodology of historical and comparative linguistics combined with the Victorian mania for categorization to produce scores of publications on the history of English and related languages, while age-old theoretical questions simultaneously gained urgency in the context of other scientific breakthroughs. Thanks to the work of writers and lecturers who made accessible the implications of these new discoveries, linguistic history became a matter of importance to an unprecedentedly broad swath of the population.

Using Plato's *Cratylus* as a roadmap to the major philosophical concerns behind language theory, Chapter 1 shows how they came into sharper focus in the nineteenth century by interacting with developments in other scientific fields. Simultaneously, poets continued to be important figures in the theory of language; understanding their privileged position in the writings of Trench and others helps illuminate Tennyson's sense of himself as a craftsman of language. This chapter concludes by surveying some linguistic themes that play out in Tennyson's verse. The mystery of communication was an ongoing fascination for him, and he explored the intersection of sound and meaning throughout his career. His curiosity about the mechanics of language sometimes found expression in playfulness, especially as a young poet experimenting with its effects. Later poems, most notably *In Memoriam* and the *Idylls of the King* (both treated in Chapter 4), explore more urgently the impossibility of communicating without distortion, as well as the weakness of words in controlling actions.

Chapter 2 explores Tennyson's Anglo-Saxonism. It first introduces the major scholars of his day and examines their attraction to primitivism alongside their desire to find cultural continuity. It then discusses Tennyson's two direct translations from Old English poetry before considering the echoes of Anglo-Saxon style

---

[93] Linda Dowling, *Language and Decadence in the Victorian Fin de Siècle* (Princeton: Princeton University Press, 1986), 124.

in his original compositions. The chapter argues that, although he was far from wishing to turn back the clock, Tennyson nonetheless drew on some of the features of Old English poetic style.

Chapter 3 examines in depth the various practices that emerged from Tennyson's knowledge of historical English. It discusses his predilection for archaic words and pronunciation, his fondness for dialect and compounds, and his use of literal etymological meanings that reveal a word's inherent metaphor. This chapter most dramatically underlines the procedural difficulties of a project such as this one, which is complicated by the subtlety and dispersion of the phenomena it tracks. The 2,000 pages in Christopher Ricks's comprehensive edition of Tennyson's poems, which include notebook scribbles, extensive footnotes, and variora, offer an overwhelming wealth of material. Confronting the task of gathering single-word examples spread across an enormous corpus, the problem is akin to sifting – and arranging into sensible order – particular grains of sand on a beach. Faced with this analogy, it is heartening to adopt Trench's outlook when he affirmed that words are "not, like the sands of the sea, innumerable disconnected atoms, but growing out of roots, clustering in families, connecting and intertwining themselves with all that men have been doing and thinking and feeling."[94] In this case, my task has been to discern some ways in which philology intertwined with what Tennyson was doing and thinking and feeling, often manifesting in his choice and arrangement of words.

Chapter 4 reveals Tennyson's sensitivity to the anthropological layers of the English language by discussing his selection of vocabulary with reference to etymological origin. Its scope thereafter is both narrower and broader than those that precede it. Instead of tracing single word choices across a vast corpus, it considers the effects of Tennyson's historically minded techniques in the context of two major works, *Idylls of the King* and *In Memoriam*. The poems that comprise the Arthurian collection stand in opposition to the subtleties and dark puns with which *In Memoriam* abounds. Where the elegy offers us evocative words that refuse to describe the afterlife precisely, the *Idylls* present words that are overwhelmingly and concretely worldly through their antiquarian medievalism. They use archaisms decoratively to a far greater extent than much of the corpus, but in so doing they illustrate an aesthetic appreciation that is always a part of the allure of archaic words. Scholarly material concerning *In Memoriam* has filled many books, but the poem's presence here must necessarily be limited. I therefore focus on three elements relating to philology. First, it is a poem deeply concerned with communication. Second, the calibrated ambiguity of the language at crucial moments reflects the Cambridge Apostles' speculative attitude that no single doctrinal assertion could encompass complex spiritual truths. Finally, I consider how it shares some of its structural components with Old English elegy. In ending with these two major monuments of Tennyson's oeuvre, I bring to bear the individual insights of earlier chapters, showing the interplay of the various techniques that the poet favored.

With the luxury of space afforded by a full-length monograph, it is possible to bring together – and expand upon – characteristics that have been identified in the style of the pre-eminent Victorian poet. By then considering these components

---

[94] Trench, *On the Study of Words*, 27.

together, we can place them in relation to one another and the larger intellectual context of Tennyson, his friends, and his society. Finally, this process allows us to see his writing as a constant engagement with the past, which – through words – is still alive in the present. That is the work of this book.

1
"Between the chaos and the cosmos of human speech": Seeking the Source of Meaning

ALFRED TENNYSON CAME of age in the midst of the explosive growth in popularity of both Anglo-Saxonism and philology, and he did so among men who were to be responsible for advancing both fields. The beginning of his poetic career coincided with a shift in how linguistic study was pursued, from a system that began with a philosophical stance and proceeded to look for evidence, to a process that began with observation and comparison. The conclusions that researchers drew from this methodological change aroused both anxiety and excitement and provoked wide-ranging debate over what language revealed about the human condition. Understanding that debate is crucial to understanding Tennyson's attitude toward his own words.

The appeal of philology fell broadly into two types, each offering something reassuring to its adherents. One was primarily etymological: it was the search for originary linguistic units inside modern English words, which have suffered both encrustation and erosion during their centuries in use. This approach promised truth invested in words and insight into mankind's origins. Such insight, in turn, could support narratives of human history that described either degeneration from a highly inflected language of pre-Babelian clarity, or positive progression from animalistic grunts to articulacy. The goal for philologists of this school was to find the original human language in which "every syllable signified" and words were more evocative of sensory experience.[1] The other motivation for philological inquiry was more sociological. It investigated the mass of changes that have taken place in a language, focusing on the process of change itself. This version of philology used words to illuminate the lives and minds of those who spoke them. Generally, the first approach characterized early scholars, while the second was developed by the so-called new philologists. However, both inclinations are evident in the writings of those curious about linguistic history in the nineteenth century, and they are inextricably bound up with questions about how language conveys meaning.

---

[1] Turley, "Tennyson and the Nineteenth-Century Language Debate," 128.

Language Theory

Paul de Man described theories about the nature of language as "a set of unresolved tensions powerful enough to have generated an infinitely prolonged discourse of endless frustration."[2] Even the briefest survey of writing on the subject will confirm this assessment. Yet despite its irreconcilable contradictions, the operation of speech has provoked curiosity among writers ranging from ancient Greek philosophers to modern-day children's-book authors. As Leslie Stephen observed, each person experiences in miniature the mental development undergone by the whole species;[3] the miracle of articulacy therefore has a personal draw beyond its large-scale implications.

In the search for authoritative expression, the first recourse is usually to history; the urge to find a word's true or precise meaning by means of its etymology is an old and enduring one. In the twenty-first century, newspaper columns and blogs frequently bemoan the degradation of the English language caused by texting and instant messaging, their rhetoric unknowingly resurrecting 300-year-old narratives of linguistic – and therefore cultural – decay. The same arguments were alive among the literary men and women of Tennyson's day. For a thorough account of the development of language theory leading up to the middle of the nineteenth century, Hans Aarsleff's landmark book *The Study of Language in England, 1780–1860* is indispensable; in brief, the late eighteenth and early nineteenth centuries abounded with speculative etymologies that were little more than imaginative word associations. Tennyson's friend, the Anglo-Saxonist John Mitchell Kemble, complained in 1832 that the grammarians of England, though capable, "all have more or less wandered into speculations upon the nature of language itself, and suffered themselves to be led away by fanciful and groundless resemblances into the wildest etymological errors."[4]

Many of these etymologists were following in the footsteps of John Horne Tooke's *Diversions of Purley* (1786), a book that proved enduringly popular, partly because it merged philology and philosophy to argue that all words can be traced back to sensation in Lockean fashion. So great was Horne Tooke's influence that his ideas held sway in England well into the 1830s (when Kemble grumbled about it). For example, when historian Sharon Turner laid out his method of inquiring into Anglo-Saxon language in 1799–1805, he wrote, "I shall follow the steps of the author of the Diversions of Purley, and build upon his foundations." Indeed, Turner describes the linguistic progress of early English thus: "The primitive nouns expressing sensible objects, having been formed, they were multiplied by combinations with each other. They were then applied to express ideas more abstracted."[5] Even as Turner wrote these words, however, a new approach was developing on the continent – one that

---

[2] de Man, *The Resistance to Theory*, 13.
[3] Quoted in Dennis Taylor, *Hardy's Literary Language and Victorian Philology* (Oxford: Clarendon Press, 1993), 220.
[4] John Mitchell Kemble, "Specimens from the Chronicle of England by Lajamon, the Monk of Severn," 1832, Kemble Box, Trinity College Cambridge, 2.
[5] Sharon Turner, *The History of the Anglo-Saxons*, 2nd ed., vol. 2 (London: Longman, Hurst, Rees, and Orme, 1807), 448, 455.

would revolutionize both the practice of comparative philology as a whole and perceptions about the history of English in particular.

The foundations of the new system were laid halfway around the world and moved slowly through Europe toward Britain. While Horne Tooke's ideas were being introduced and circulated in England, an English judge in India was paving the way for what would become the "new philology" that eventually dominated the field. Sir William Jones originally studied Sanskrit in order to understand the history of local law, but he had a love of his new home and a talent with languages that led him to translate Indian literature – Tennyson drew on Jones's work for a number of his early poems – and to form the Asiatick Society of Bengal to bring together people with similar interests. In his annual speeches to the society, and in its journal, Jones set out some of the key tenets of nonspeculative language comparison. Most importantly, he explained that the new system was to deal only with facts and evidence and leave aside the question of mind. By doing so, it would reveal unintuitive connections. Whereas Horne Tooke had found evidence to support his presupposed philosophical stance, Jones urged approaching languages observationally, only later extrapolating the implications of the evidence one found. Jones was also the first to suggest that there might be a parent language from which Sanskrit, Latin, Greek, and other languages descended – what is now known as Proto-Indo-European.[6]

Jones delivered these discourses in the 1780s, the same decade in which Horne Tooke published *The Diversions of Purley*. Though Horne Tooke remained the uncontested philological authority in England for the next fifty-odd years, Jones was an inspiration to German scholars. The Berlin Academy had already begun engaging with the language debates in the second half of the eighteenth century by setting the topics of their essay prizes accordingly, and the winning essays hinted at developing Romantic ideals. The 1750 winner, for example, stated that language is a democracy and store of human knowledge, including historic errors of understanding.[7] It was an idea that would eventually resound through Victorian linguistic study, as when Tennyson's friend Richard Chenevix Trench described language as "a storehouse of so much unconscious wisdom."[8] German Romanticism embraced the model of language development that depicted it as an organism, and thinkers of this school appreciated that it was controlled by the general population of speakers. No ruler could force a language to behave in a certain way, because it adapts to the interactions of daily life. Furthermore, the study of etymology and comparative philology was inescapably historicist, and German Romanticism relied on the notion that history, if properly understood, could replace philosophy.[9]

In 1819, Jacob Grimm gave a boost to the new system when he published the first volume of his *Deutsche Grammatik*, or German grammar. This work, most notably in its revised second edition (1822), proposed a set of rules that described how sounds within words change over time. These sound-change laws explained,

[6] Aarsleff, *The Study of Language in England, 1780–1860*, 13, 88, 119–133.
[7] Ibid., 143–152.
[8] Trench, *On the Study of Words*, 28.
[9] J.W. Burrow, "The Uses of Philology in Victorian England," in *Ideas and Institutions of Victorian Britain: Essays in Honour of George Kitson Clark*, ed. Robert Robson (London: Bell, 1967), 185–186, 200.

for example, why English has *what* and *father* and while the Latin equivalents are *quod* and *pater*. Though others had noted some of the same sound changes, Grimm expanded the observations into a systematic schema known to this day as "Grimm's Law."[10] Like Jones, Jacob and his brother Wilhelm had first familiarized themselves with older forms of German in order to research the history of law; that work then led them into serious study of linguistic principles, the mythology of the Germanic peoples, and folklore. These interrelated interests often occurred together in the writings of British scholars as they took up Grimm's methods. Kemble, for example, delved deeply into grammatical history but also published a massive set of Anglo-Saxon charters and eventually turned to archaeology.

As Kemble's participation attests, one of the early toeholds of the so-called "new philology" that Grimm advanced was at Trinity College, Cambridge, thanks in large part to Julius Charles Hare, who taught and mentored members of Tennyson's circle. Hare was both well known and intellectually influential in the mid-nineteenth century. Elected a Fellow of Trinity in 1818 (the year before Grimm's grammar came out), and taking up a Classical lectureship there in 1822, Hare helped reform the college's teaching in alignment with the principles behind new philology. As a result of German academic historicism, teaching of the Classics had begun to expand at the turn of the century, from imparting a knowledge of literature in isolation to taking account of the cultures of antiquity more generally. This method emphasized minute study of the languages of ancient Greece and Rome in order to illuminate the societies in which they were spoken.[11]

Bringing this pedagogy to his Cambridge students, Hare incorporated what we would recognize as close reading into his teaching at Trinity in the 1820s. Frederick Denison Maurice, a former student of Hare's and an alumnus of the Cambridge Apostles debating society from slightly before Tennyson's time, recalled it this way:

> The lecturer [Hare] seemed most anxious to impress us with the feeling that there was no road to the sense which did not go through the words. He took infinite pains to make us understand the force of nouns, verbs, participles, and the grammar of the sentences. We often spent an hour on the strophe or anti-strophe of a chorus ... You will think that so much philological carefulness could not have been obtained without the sacrifice of higher objects. How could we discover the divine intuitions of the poet, while we were tormenting ourselves about his tenses? I cannot tell; but it seems to me that I never learnt so much about ["Antigone"], about Greek dramatic poetry generally, about all poetry, as in that term.[12]

Hare's approach to classical literature was evidently grounded in linguistic detail. He also believed in teaching students by guiding them toward making their own discoveries.

Following his own philosophy that "one's business [as a teacher] is much more to excite than to infuse," Hare developed critical-thinking skills in his students,

---

[10] Turley, "Tennyson and the Nineteenth-Century Language Debate," 126.
[11] Burrow, "The Uses of Philology in Victorian England," 181–182.
[12] Frederick Denison Maurice, *The Life of Frederick Denison Maurice: Chiefly Told in His Own Letters*, ed. Frederick Maurice, vol. 1 (London: Macmillan, 1884), 53.

never directly telling them, for example, the moral of a narrative.[13] He took the same approach when he wrote, with his brother Augustus, *Guesses at Truth, By Two Brothers*. This two-volume collection of aphorisms and short essays proved to be a popular success, going through roughly twenty editions from its first publication in 1827 (the year Tennyson came up to Cambridge) through the start of the twentieth century.[14] In the preface to *Guesses at Truth*, Hare warns that if he is "addressing one of that numerous class, which reads to be told what to think, let me advise you to meddle with the book no further. You seek to buy a house ready furnished; do not come to look for it in a stone-quarry." Instead, he says, read it "if you are building up your opinions for yourself, and want only to be provided with materials."[15] For Hare, his fragmentary book was an antidote to what he called "mechanical reading" because it continually forces the reader to construct opinions from the raw material of evocative statements.[16]

Though *Guesses* went through many editions, its general format remained the same. It comprises short statements and analogies describing human nature in general; commentary on contemporary society, such as deficiencies in how the poor laws were administered; and lengthier passages (rarely more than ten pages long) usually concerning matters of theology, morality, poetry, and language. Each section is visually separated from its neighbors by a horizontal line in the first edition, and later by a blank line. The range of subject matter means that the book can change topics abruptly to startle readers out of passive reading habits; indeed, Hare tends to separate longer arguments by inserting short statements between them. For example, one group of fragments relates to originality in poetry; it is followed by reflections on what creates a civilized "national mind," after which several sections discuss the growing tendency to use plural pronouns as a cheap means of gaining authority or showing respect. Other groupings include analyses of Shakespeare scholarship, rules for coining new words and writing clearly, and the relative importance of using a language according to its history. Elsewhere, after several essays concerning Shakespeare and the elements of good poetry, the reader encounters the sentence, "I like the smell of a dunged field, and the tumult of a popular election."[17] These dictums are often provocative in their isolation. As in the preceding example, there may be little or no further explanation as to how disparate elements are connected. Hare adds to the effect by citing his sources very specifically – which was not standard practice – thereby drawing attention to the fact that he is providing but a fragment of someone else's writing as part of the patchwork of his own argument, which is itself only one "guess at truth" in a scrapbook of many.

For Hare, splintered texts were the best way to try to glimpse (in his own words) the "harmonious universe bursting forth from the jarring and fragmentary chaos of

---

[13] N. Merrill Distad, *Guessing at Truth: The Life of Julius Charles Hare (1795–1855)* (Shepherdstown: Patmos Press, 1979), 42–44.

[14] Lerer, "Middlemarch and Julius Charles Hare," 653.

[15] Julius Charles Hare, *Guesses at Truth, by Two Brothers: Two Series in One Volume* (London: George Routledge & Sons, n.d.), v.

[16] Quoted in Distad, *Guessing at Truth*, 72.

[17] Hare, *Guesses at Truth, by Two Brothers: Two Series in One Volume*, 163.

hollow realities."[18] The idea that the fragmentary can better approximate truth than traditional rhetoric would have resonated with Tennyson; it is a common theme in his poetry, as Chapter 4 examines more deeply. In addition, Seth Lerer has argued that *Guesses* "provided readers ... with a ready digest of researches," especially German philosophy and philology, which were largely inaccessible to most English readers both because few could speak German and because German scholarship was treated with suspicion and therefore not widely circulated.[19]

Hare's influence was felt at Trinity, especially among the members of the Conversazione Society, commonly known as the Cambridge Apostles, who counted Tennyson among their members – officially for a short time, but unofficially for the rest of his life.[20] Most of the Apostles felt that the weekly meetings of this tight-knit speculative debating society constituted the most valuable education they had received while at university. The society's principles, as well as its friendships, remained deeply important to them throughout their lives. Collectively, the group was inclined toward Germanic ideas, sometimes filtered through Coleridge, whom they admired, and sometimes imbibed from Hare, who taught many of the members. For example, Edward FitzGerald reminisced in later life about his and Tennyson's "college days, when the German school, with Coleridge, Julius Hare, etc., to expound, came to reform all our Notions."[21] Indeed, it became standard practice for Apostles to travel to Germany, and letters between them eagerly exchange ideas picked up during continental travel.[22]

One aspect of the Apostles' Germanic affinity was a historicist approach to all intellectual pursuits, especially languages – another trait they shared with Hare. Their mentor promoted linguistic ideas, for example, as the editor of a short-lived Cambridge journal called the *Philological Museum*, the stated focus of which was "to illustrate the language, the literature, the philosophy, the history, the manners, institutions, mythology, and the religion of ancient Greece and Rome," with occasional forays into "the philology of modern languages." In the inaugural issue (1832), Hare contributed an article of more than seventy pages "On the Names of the Days of the Week."[23] Tennyson's glossary of old vocabulary, made during his university years (the notebook is watermarked 1828), shows a particular interest in words for "times of day, months, and seasons;"[24] it is impossible to know for sure whether the poet's interest in such terminology was inspired directly by Hare's, but it is likely that the same ideas were under discussion among his cohort.

Three decades later, Richard Chenevix Trench – also an alumnus of Trinity and the Apostles – suggested that Hare's philological teaching method for texts of

---

[18] Julius Charles Hare, *Guesses at Truth: Second Series*, 2nd ed. (London: printed for Taylor and Walton, 1848), 95.
[19] Lerer, "Middlemarch and Julius Charles Hare," 656.
[20] Though his official membership was brief – he was too shy to read essays in front of the group – Tennyson remained so close to the Apostles that most considered him an honorary member, which status they officially bestowed on him many years later.
[21] Tennyson, *Poems I*, 368.
[22] Lubenow, *The Cambridge Apostles*, 110.
[23] Julius Charles Hare, ed., *The Philological Museum*, vol. 1 (Cambridge: J. Smith, 1832), iv, 1–72.
[24] Jones, *Fossil Poetry*, 241.

the ancient world could be applied English literature. Under pressure to complete their education swiftly, Trench observed, the number of young men able to delve into Latin and Greek was shrinking at midcentury; in lieu of those studies, he proposed that "the *decomposition*, word by word, of small portions of our best poetry and prose ... to be followed by a reconstruction, of some small portions of a great English Classic" could compensate for the absence of classical studies.[25] Trench's proposal carries strong echoes of Hare's influence. It also reflects how philology helped English literature gain legitimacy during the nineteenth century as a subject of formal study.[26]

Both Trench and his fellow Apostle John Mitchell Kemble went on to make philology an important component of their lifeworks. Kemble spent time studying with the Grimms and carried on a scholarly correspondence with Jacob, sharing his own discoveries in Old English with his German counterpart while publishing as many medieval texts as he could. Trench published several popular books in the 1850s that transmitted to the public the excitement of what could be uncovered through philological undertakings. Trench's works mark the moment at midcentury when the ideas behind new philology were finally gaining broader acceptance, but Tennyson's circle had adopted them early. Kemble wrote to Grimm in 1834, although probably with his customary flair for exaggeration, "There is no Cambridge man unacquainted at least with your name" – undoubtedly with Hare's assistance. That same year, Kemble delivered a series of lectures at Cambridge on the "History of the English Language, First, or Anglo-Saxon Period," in which he planned to introduce his audience to the new philology in more depth. He was "full of confident hope" for this project because "the moment is arrived in England for it, and people are already becoming conscious that a new power is at work among them."[27]

That "new power" was not yet widespread in its influence, but it caught Tennyson's attention as well as that of his friends, and his interest in language history continued unabated for the rest of his life. Tennyson's diary from an 1846 trip on the continent, for example, records that he "talk[ed] about language with Germans."[28] Nearly two decades after that, now in his mid-fifties, he copied a table of Grimm's Law into one of his notebooks (see Figure 1).[29] His table traces variations in nine sounds through eight languages. Rasmus Rask had suggested some sound changes in an 1818 treatise on the origin of Old Norse and Icelandic,[30] but this was not Tennyson's source. Apart from the unlikelihood of his being able to access a copy of, and understand, a Danish-language essay on linguistics, Tennyson explicitly titles his table "Grimm's Law." It is possible that he read Grimm's original German

---

[25] Richard Chenevix Trench, *A Select Glossary of English Words Used Formerly in Senses Different from Their Present*, 2nd ed. (London: John W. Parker and Son, 1859), vi.
[26] Palmer, *The Rise of English Studies*, 22–26.
[27] Kemble, *Correspondence*, 50, 49.
[28] Hallam Tennyson, *Memoir*, 1:232.
[29] Alfred Tennyson, *The Harvard Manuscripts: Notebooks 28–39 (MS Eng 952)*, ed. Christopher Ricks and Aidan Day, vol. 4, Tennyson Archive (New York: Garland, 1987), 215.
[30] Kate Burridge, "Nineteenth-Century Study of Sound Change from Rask to Saussure," in *The Oxford Handbook of the History of Linguistics*, ed. Keith Allan (Oxford: Oxford University Press, 2013), 141–165.

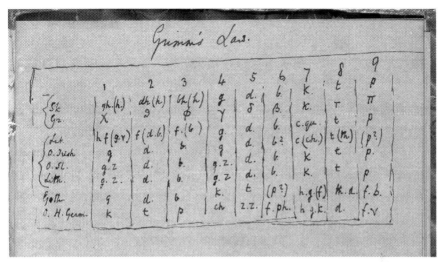

Figure 1 A table of Grimm's Law in one of Tennyson's notebooks. MS Eng 952 (Notebook 37), Houghton Library, Harvard University.

text or became familiar with its arguments during his time at Cambridge via his friends there, as Chapter 2 demonstrates; however, the notebook table does not directly map onto anything equivalent in the *Deutsche Grammatik*'s discussion of *lautverschiebung* (sound change).[31] Instead, it exactly matches the "General Table of Grimm's Law" in Friedrich Max Müller's second series of *Lectures on the Science of Language*, published in 1864.[32] Müller, like Trench, gave lectures that conveyed the exciting discoveries about society that could be extrapolated from deep linguistic research. Tennyson's handwritten table is the first item in his notebook, which is watermarked 1863. The subsequent pages contain drafts of "Lucretius" (written 1865–1868), "Northern Farmer, New Style" (written around 1865), and *Balin and Balan* (written 1872–1874). This evidence indicates that Tennyson read Müller's lectures soon after they appeared and was still engaged enough with comparative grammar that he copied out a highly technical schema for future reference.

Müller was arguably the greatest popularizer of new philology to the Victorian public. Originally from Germany, he moved to England in 1846 to pursue work on Sanskrit and soon settled in Oxford, where he eventually became professor of modern languages and then the first professor of comparative philology.[33] The popularity of philology continued to expand over the middle decades of the century

---

[31] Jacob Grimm, *Deutsche Grammatik* (Göttingen: Dieterichsche buchhandlung, 1822), 584.

[32] Friedrich Max Müller, *Lectures on the Science of Language: Delivered at the Royal Institution of Great Britain in February, March, April, & May, 1863*, vol. 2, Second Series (Longman, Green, Longman, Roberts, and Green, 1864), 222.

[33] John R. Davis and Angus Nicholls, "Introduction – Friedrich Max Müller: The Career and Intellectual Trajectory of a German Philologist in Victorian Britain," in *Friedrich Max Müller and the Role of Philology in Victorian Thought*, ed. John R. Davis and Angus Nicholls (London: Routledge, 2018), 6–8.

(Trench's accessibly written books sold well in the 1850s); Müller tapped into, and fed, this general fascination when he gave a series of lectures on the science of language to the Royal Institution in April and May of 1861. As historian James Turner describes it, the lectures "drew an immense crowd from London's intelligentsia ... and, when published a couple months later, a large readership. Reviewers cheered ... The book went through three editions in the first year." [34] The *Publishers' Circular* announced the publication of the lectures by noting that the original events had "attracted ... much attention among the learned and fashionable audiences of the Royal Institution."[35] No doubt pleased by the response, the Royal Institution asked Müller to give second lecture series, which he delivered in 1863 and published in 1864.[36] It was from the printed edition of this second series that Tennyson copied Grimm's Law.

Müller's books were expensive, costing twelve shillings for the first series[37] and eighteen shillings for the second[38] – far more than Trench's, which cost between three and four shillings. The fact that they sold so well speaks to the fact that, by the 1860s, "the science of language" had infiltrated nearly every field of inquiry and entered the public consciousness. This swelling interest in the history of words was more than academic, for exciting – and sometimes unsettling – implications accompanied the study of how languages function. Writers such as Horne Tooke had begun with a philosophical argument and "uncovered" (or created) their etymologies accordingly. While the new philology did not deny its own philosophical ramifications, it emphasized understanding linguistic facts first, then assessing what they indicated. By following an inductive rather than a deductive methodology, Victorian linguists were forced to confront age-old philosophical questions with a new urgency; the conclusions to which their findings pointed had repercussions for how human beings could understand themselves, and how a poet like Tennyson understood his craft.

"The awful problem of the 'Cratylus'": Philosophical Matters

The first known text to treat the origin of language is Plato's *Cratylus*, a text familiar to the classically educated of nineteenth-century Europe, including Tennyson and his friends. In this dialogue, Hermogenes and Cratylus ask Socrates to settle a dispute over the nature of naming. The titular Cratylus argues "that a name is not whatever people call a thing by agreement ... but that there is a kind of inherent correctness in names, which is the same for all men." Hermogenes, for example –

---

[34] Turner, *Philology*, 244.

[35] "Literary Intelligence," *Publishers' Circular and General Record of British and Foreign Literature: Containing a Complete List of All New Works Published in Great Britain, and Every Work of Interest Published Abroad*, July 16, 1861, 298.

[36] Turner, *Philology*, 244.

[37] "New Works Published from the 16th to the 31st of December," *Publishers' Circular and General Record of British and Foreign Literature: Containing a Complete List of All New Works Published in Great Britain, and Every Work of Interest Published Abroad*, December 31, 1861, 699.

[38] *General List of Works, New Books and New Editions, Published by Messrs. Longmans, Green, Reader, and Dyer* (London: Longmans, Green, Reader, and Dyer, 1865), 5.

"born-of-Hermes" – has been misnamed according to his colleague, and this mistake is separate from usage: "your name is not Hermogenes, even if all mankind call you so." Hermogenes, in contrast, believes that "whatever name you give to a thing is its right name" and that "no name belongs to any particular thing by nature, but only by the habit and custom of those who employ it and who established the usage."[39]

Socrates works concessions from both sides, but Cratylus's essentialist view receives a fuller defense. Speaking to the conventionalist Hermogenes, Socrates likens his linguistic relativism to the idea that reality is actually different for each person who perceives it – a theory too extreme for any of the participants. Because "things have some fixed reality of their own, not in relation to us nor caused by us," and because "actions also are performed according to their own nature," then the action of naming must have a certain correctness to it, as well; therefore "the instrument which the nature of things prescribes must be employed." In other words, if we accept that there exists an objective reality, then things should be named according to their natures. Indeed, the whole purpose of naming is to "teach one another something, and [to] separate things according to their natures." How, then, are such correct names to be created? Socrates posits name-makers (ονοματουργου) or lawgivers (νομοθετης) equivalent to artisans who "must discover the instrument [i.e., word] naturally fitted for each purpose and must embody that ... not in accordance with [their] own will, but in accordance with its nature." What follows is a series of etymological explorations, some more serious than others, concluding that "a name ... is a vocal imitation of that which is imitated" (that is, onomatopoeia). Although most of the text argues in favor of Cratylus's position, he is forced in turn to concede that convention plays a role in language; it is impossible, for example, to capture the nature of numbers. Furthermore, if a name-maker were to mislabel something because he misunderstood its nature, convention would nevertheless entrench the false designation through usage.[40]

Plato's *Cratylus* comments on the three biggest problems in the theory and practice of philology. First, there is only so far into history that etymology can be pushed in order to find the original names. From a practical perspective, "on account of the lapse of time it may be impossible to find out about the earliest words." Second, the world continues to change, and therefore even names are not an immutable source of truth. Finally, the mechanism by which the name-maker links sound to signified object or idea remains a mystery: Socrates admits, "How realities are to be learned or discovered is perhaps too great a question for you or me to determine." The dialogue ends inconclusively by reflecting, "surely no man of sense can put himself and his soul under the control of names, and trust in names and their makers to the point of affirming that he knows anything; nor will he condemn himself and all things and say that there is no health in them, but that all things are flowing like leaky pots."[41]

---

[39] Plato, "Cratylus," in *Cratylus; Parmenides; Greater Hippias; Lesser Hippias*, trans. H.N. Fowler, vol. 4, Plato in Twelve Volumes (Cambridge, MA: Harvard University Press, 1977), 7, 9–11.
[40] Ibid., 17, 21, 23, 27, 135, 175.
[41] Ibid., 129, 187, 191.

These concerns run through the publications of Tennyson's contemporaries, inflected by the desires and fears of their own time. For the poet himself, they fed the common authorial concern that words may never be able to convey experience satisfactorily. Richard Marggraf Turley finds, for example, that Tennyson's poems written in the 1830s "point out entrenched anxieties regarding language" – a result of conversations with the Cambridge Apostles.[42] As the following chapters demonstrate, those uncertainties prompted the poet to pay close attention to his word choices and, in turn, force his readers to pay attention to them, as well. Turley and other critics tend to conclude that Tennyson's poetic resistance to philological anxieties were futile and ultimately failed. However, the entire philological endeavor – especially for the Victorians – was attractive precisely because it seemed to offer a means of identifying some kind of origin, either of human language or of the English people.

Correct Naming

A large part of philology's appeal lay in its potential to locate a word's authentic, original, primary, or uncomplicated meaning. The desire for precision, indeed, motivated philologists from disparate methodological schools. William Whewell, Master of Trinity College and Tennyson's tutor, thought there could be such a thing as a mathematically precise language, and the idea of "algebraic" language appears in other philological musings, as well, though few thought it truly possible or even desirable anymore.[43] Assuming that Plato's imagined name-makers mapped reality onto sound, then identifying those basic units of signification – whether we call them names, elements, roots, or morphemes – can help us accurately employ the words they subsequently constructed. William Barnes, a dialect poet and sometime historian whom we will encounter again in later chapters, introduced his 1862 book on English's "Teutonic" roots by explaining their practical value: "It seems to me that through a knowledge of the stem-building of English from its primary roots we should win a more accurate use of English words, and more correct definitions of such words in our dictionaries."[44] Trench similarly advocated understanding etymology as a means of improving the exactness of one's speech.[45]

Sometimes the yearning for powerful original meaning was explicit in the motivations of philological scholars, particularly those who approached their research within the framework of orthodox Christianity. In the Christian tradition, Adam named the animals by understanding the nature of each; he is the Platonic name-giver of the Bible, surpassed only by God, who spoke the universe into being. In one of the most mystical and poetic passages of the New Testament, the Gospel of John begins by describing Christ's place in the Trinity as the Word: "In the beginning was the Word, and the Word was with God, and the Word was God ... And the Word

---

[42] Turley, "Tennyson and the Nineteenth-Century Language Debate," 123.

[43] Hair, *Tennyson's Language*, 28; Hare, *Guesses at Truth, by Two Brothers: Two Series in One Volume*, 80.

[44] William Barnes, *TIW: Or, A View of the Roots and Stems of the English as a Teutonic Tongue* (London: John Russell Smith, 1862), xviii.

[45] Trench, *On the Study of Words*, 148.

was made flesh, and dwelt among us ... full of grace and truth."[46] Tennyson alluded to this passage in *In Memoriam*: "And so the Word had breath, and wrought / With human hands the creed of creeds" (xxxvi.9). Trench wrote in 1841 regarding Jesus's parables: "They belong to one another, the type and the thing typified, by an inward necessity," a phrase reminiscent of Cratylus's essentialist argument for language. Trench also asserted that Christ had made words new.[47]

By the time new philology came to prominence, its practitioners generally acknowledged that searching for a language in which a word represented one and only one object or idea was a futile venture, and the idea of a linguistic golden age had largely ceased to be taken literally. Nevertheless, it remained an attractive concept. Tennyson opposed the relativism that proposed that reality is only as it seems to each person, the very philosophy that Plato had used as an analogy to the linguistic relativism that constituted a conventionalist model of language.[48] It is not surprising, therefore, that the poet was curious about the mechanism of correct "naming" – that is, finding the best word for a thing or idea. After all, if language rests only upon convention, convention can fail. Tennyson expressed this concern in the context of his grief for Arthur Hallam, in the following lines:

> I could not tell it: if I could
> Yet every form of mind is made
> To vary in some light or shade
> So were my tale misunderstood.   ("Whispers" 13–16)

The gap between individual minds is always a potential threat to literary productions, whose authors therefore seek out "the [word] naturally fitted for each purpose," to borrow Plato's phrase. Yet Plato had also recognized that naming cannot remain static in a dynamic world; new philology was built on this very fact.

The Origin of Language

As an examination of *Cratylus* makes clear, curiosity about language – how words acquire significance and authority, how they are formed, the relation of signifier to signified – has always led to consideration of the origin and nature of humanity itself. Where did language come from? Did it develop from random animalistic noises that people learned to control, or did God provide it? If the latter, did humanity enter the world with a hardwired vocabulary, or merely the ability to speak? The Anglo-Saxonist and lexicographer Joseph Bosworth wrote in 1838 that "the first grasp decides all the rest" of a given language's development – but how did that first grasp come about?[49]

Kemble called the conundrum "the awful problem of the 'Cratylus'" in a letter to Grimm in 1840, writing that he had "a Platonic veneration for language as the

---

[46] John 1.1–14.
[47] Richard Chenevix Trench, *Notes on the Parables of Our Lord* (London: Pickering & Inglis, 1953), 14, 24.
[48] Isobel Armstrong, *Victorian Poetry: Poetry, Poetics and Politics* (Abingdon: Routledge, 1993), 41.
[49] Bosworth, *A Dictionary of the Anglo-Saxon Language*, xxxviii.

divine organon of the *Logos* in man," but where did the power of language originate? "Drive it as you will," he wrote, "turn it as you may, the ultimate basis of language is – something congenital with man, inseparable from his nature, potential and underdeveloped perhaps, but still there." Twelve years later (1852), he wrote to Grimm after reading the latter's "Über den Ursprung der Sprache" and summarized the paradox that every language historian encounters when contemplating humanity at the earliest stages of verbal development:

> I cannot conceive man to exist without speech, nor can I quite get over the difficulty of its first commencement: ce n'est que le premier pas qui coûte:[50] but the power, and will to make this first step seems quite as difficult to comprehend, as the assumption that man brought his language ready made into the world, or at least so much of it as involved its own development and progress.[51]

Müller, writing in the 1860s, was equally convinced that thought and language were impossible to separate. Yet more succinctly, geologist Charles Lyell quoted William Humboldt in 1863: "Man is man only by means of speech, but in order to invent speech he must be already man."[52] There was no clear solution to such questions in the nineteenth century, any more than there had been in ancient Greece. However, they took on a new resonance in this period as similar questions arose in other fields of inquiry, such as the geology of Lyell and others.

For the Victorians, fascination with etymology was one aspect of a wide-ranging search for origins – linguistic, national, cultural, and biological. In fact, philology was woven into many other forms of such inquiry. Since language is (in Trench's words) "the amber in which a thousand precious and subtle thoughts have been safely embedded and preserved,"[53] it is unsurprising that one of the most common comparisons was between etymological research and the work of a geologist,[54] especially in the case of English with its layers of different source languages.[55] The simile reflects the idea that language has preserved the thoughts of past generations as fossils; it also shows a simultaneous understanding that the medium is constantly though imperceptibly changing. In 1851, Trench described the preservative capability of words thus:

> [J]ust as in some fossil, curious and beautiful shapes of vegetable or animal life, the graceful fern or the finely vertebrated lizard, such as now, it may be, have been extinct for thousands of years, are permanently bound up with the stone, and rescued from that perishing which would have otherwise been theirs – so in words are beautiful thoughts and images, the imagination and the feeling of past ages, of men long since in their graves, of men whose very names have perished, these, which would so easily have perished too, preserved and made safe for ever.[56]

---

[50] "it is only the first step that counts" (my translation).
[51] Kemble, *Correspondence*, 193, 310.
[52] Charles Lyell, *The Geological Evidences of the Antiquity of Man, with Remarks on Theories of the Origin of Species by Variation* (London: John Murray, 1863), 468.
[53] Trench, *On the Study of Words*, 25.
[54] Taylor, *Hardy's Literary Language and Victorian Philology*, 282.
[55] Trench, *On the Study of Words*, 68–69.
[56] Ibid., 4–5.

He further calls language fossil ethics, fossil history, and fossil poetry, borrowing the last phrase from Ralph Waldo Emerson, who wrote in 1844: "As the limestone of the continent consists of infinite masses of the shells of animalcules, so language is made up of images, or tropes, which now, in their secondary use, have long ceased to remind us of their poetic origin."[57]

The geological metaphor is especially notable given the contemporary developments in that field and in biology. Indeed, Stephen G. Alter argues that language history provided the "way to put the argument" for evolution,[58] expanding on Gillian Beer's contention that language theory provided Darwin with a "thought model" and that ever since, "evolutionary theory and language theory ... have drawn upon each other's evidences, and, even more, upon each other's metaphors."[59] Darwin published *The Origin of Species* in 1859, at the end of the decade in which Trench had published several philological books. In *Origin*, Darwin argues that species classification should be structured on a genealogical model ("like a pedigree"), illustrating his point "by taking the case of languages." He writes that a genealogical model would be the only possible one in mapping out the world's languages, especially if "all extinct languages, and all intermediate and slowly changing dialects, had to be included;" and as with languages, so with species.[60] Lyell published *The Geological Evidences of the Antiquity of Man* four years later, in 1863 – just as Müller was delivering his second series of popular lectures on philology. In *Geological Evidences*, Lyell drew a parallel between Darwinian natural selection in biology and the evolution of languages. Chapter 23, titled "Origins and Development of Languages and Species Compared," offers a prolonged analogy between philology and the study of species evolution. Since languages change more quickly, Lyell writes with a touch of envy, it is easier to describe their development convincingly. Nonetheless, he imagines the objections that an illiterate crowd would raise to theories of language development – objections paralleled in the debate over gradual evolution in species. He then outlines how a philologist would go about proving his thesis.

First, a linguist on such a mission would point out that no language is more than a thousand years old, as demonstrated by the impossibility of understanding texts from the early Middle Ages. Next, he would show that the geographical locations of sister languages bear witness to the influence of an earlier tongue, even if there is no written proof of its existence. The enormous quantity of mostly ephemeral new words coined for technical or slang use seems random, but as with biological mutations, "there are nevertheless fixed laws in action, by which, in the general struggle for existence, some terms and dialects gain the victory over others."[61] The letters that remain in the spelling of a word despite no longer being pronounced are

---

[57] Ralph Waldo Emerson, "The Poet," in *Essays and Lectures*, ed. Joel Porte, The Library of America (New York: Literary Classics of the United States, 1983), 457.

[58] Stephen G. Alter, *Darwinism and the Linguistic Image: Language, Race, and Natural Theology in the Nineteenth Century*, New Studies in American Intellectual and Cultural History (Baltimore: Johns Hopkins University Press, 1999), 15–19.

[59] Gillian Beer, "Darwin and the Growth of Language Theory," in *Open Fields: Science in Cultural Encounter* (Oxford: Clarendon Press, 1996), 103, 95.

[60] Charles Darwin, *On the Origin of Species: A Facsimile*, ed. Ernst Mayr (Cambridge, MA: Harvard University Press, 1964), 22.

[61] Lyell, *Geological Evidences*, 463.

like vestigial organs. Finally, gaps are to be expected in a subject of which no one consciously makes a record.

Twelve years after *Origins*, and eight years after Lyell's *Evidences*, Darwin set about making explicit the implications of evolutionary theory for the human race in *The Descent of Man* (1871). Unsurprisingly, language is a crucial element of his argument, for "[t]he formation of different languages and of distinct species, and the proofs that both have been developed through a gradual process, are curiously the same." Darwin stated that "no philologist now supposes that any language has been deliberately invented; each has been slowly and unconsciously developed by many steps." (This statement was not quite accurate, though language's continuation through stages of unconscious development was agreed to be a given.) When it came to "the origin of articulate language," he concluded that "language owes its origin to the imitation and modification ... of various natural sounds, the voices of other animals, and man's own instinctive cries."[62] This is a version of the Platonic theory of onomatopoeic imitation, stripped of much of its conscious agency and all of the prophetic qualities of the name-maker.

Müller dismissively called this the "bow-wow theory" of linguistic origins, and he worked hard to discredit it.[63] Religious apologists who disliked Darwin's and Lyell's model of human development but accepted the new method of philological research had to address the origin of the urge to speak. In *The New Cratylus* (1839), John William Donaldson – a philologist who studied at Trinity College shortly after Tennyson's cohort – posited a compromise that reconciled Christian narrative and the mounting evidence for language evolution: God gave the *ability* to invent words, but not the words themselves.[64] Like Emerson, Donaldson considered primitive man to be a natural poet.[65] Trench went further in his book *On the Study of Words* (1851), asserting that it was impossible for the ability to lie dormant; early humans were not only capable of speaking but felt compelled to do so. It was thus "the not merely possible, but the necessary, emanation of the spirit with which [man] had been endowed. Man makes his own language, but he makes it as the bee makes its cells, as the bird its nest."[66] In a later edition, Trench drove the point home: "he cannot do otherwise."[67] Tennyson anticipated Trench's comment in section xxi of *In Memoriam*, when the speaker states, "I do but sing because I must, / And pipe but as the linnets sing" (23–24). He cannot do otherwise.

In the face of unknowable origins and an unstable linguistic present, amateurs and scholars alike often resort to etymology for firm definitions, but its comfort is short-lived, because each component of a word has components of its own. As *Cratylus* points out, etymological curiosity can never be fully satisfied, for truth recedes vanishingly into the past. Plato writes, "[I]f a person asks about the words by means of which names are formed, and again about those by means of which those words

---

[62] Charles Darwin, *The Descent of Man, and Selection in Relation to Sex*, vol. 1 (New York: D. Appleton, 1871), 53–57.
[63] Turner, *Philology*, 244–245.
[64] Hair, *Tennyson's Language*, 19.
[65] Burrow, "The Uses of Philology in Victorian England," 192.
[66] Trench, *On the Study of Words*, 17.
[67] Quoted in Hair, *Tennyson's Language*, 140.

were formed, and keeps on doing this indefinitely, he who answers his questions will at last give up; will he not?" Though unlikely to be achieved in practice, the etymologist's ideal goal would be to discover "the names which are the elements of the other names and words" – the original syllables that signified simple ideas, and which became the building blocks for all other compound ideas and metaphors – that is, words.[68]

Because the first sounds of human utterance were unrecoverable, roots took their place as the simplest identifiable units of meaning. This is what William Barnes claimed to have identified in his book *TIW* (1862). The work lists what Barnes considered to be the fifty Germanic roots of the English language and a variety of basic ideas stemming from them through the mechanism of suffixes. Around the same time, Müller highlighted the immense importance of roots in the preface to the fifth edition of his *Lectures*, though he sidestepped the issue of how they came to exist. Addressing a large readership, and explicitly hoping to interest amateurs as well as eminent thinkers, he emphasized:

> All words ... whether in English or in Sanskrit, encumbered with prefixes and suffixes and mouldering away under the action of phonetic corruption, must in the last instance be traced back, by means of definite phonetic laws, to ... roots. These roots stand like barriers between the chaos and the cosmos of human speech.[69]

Roots could be discovered, and the very metaphor of roots promised stability; in Linda Dowling's words, Müller made them "the mystic nexus between mind and matter."[70] Though Müller, like Plato, was unable to say where they came from, roots at least partially satisfied the intellectual craving for origins. They still left open the question of whether to interpret subsequent language change as progress or decline. New philology's solution to that riddle was to place value on what could be learned by studying change itself.

The Anthropology of Language Change

It is a recurrent theme in philological writing, especially by the middle of the nineteenth century, that there has been order to the apparent chaos of language all along; linguists merely reveal the hidden system. As Kemble described it, part of the satisfaction of philological study was the perception of "regularity where all seemed irregular, of law where all was confusion, of irrefragable necessity where all assumed the appearance of caprice."[71] The same might be said of the search for medieval origins for cultural keystones, and indeed the pursuits were complementary. Bosworth, in his Anglo-Saxon dictionary (1838), rebuffed the fear that language change led to "the curse of Babel" by asserting that rules of change exist and are systematic. Therefore, "every language is of necessity what it is, and it is not in the power of fancy or

---

[68] Plato, "Cratylus," 129, 131.
[69] Friedrich Max Müller, *Lectures on the Science of Language: Delivered at the Royal Institution of Great Britain in April, May, & June 1861*, 5th ed. (London: Longmans, Green, 1866), ix.
[70] Dowling, *Decadence*, 71.
[71] Kemble, "Lajamon," 4.

choice to obey or disobey these laws."[72] Müller in the 1860s likewise declared that language "is regulated by its own invariable laws, which, even when we are not able fully to understand them, must yet be admitted to exist."[73]

Turner's 1805 *History of the Anglo-Saxons* had contained an early hint of the change-based approach that was to be the hallmark of new philology. The set of chapters on Anglo-Saxon language begins by stating the difficulty of "explain[ing] the history of any language" after centuries of modification. The best we can do, Turner says, is classify types of words and "trac[e] these to their elementary sources." So far, so Platonic. He continues:

> We shall perhaps be unable to discover the original words with which the language began, but we may hope to trace the progress of its formation, and so of the principles on which that progress has been made.[74]

Turner's generation of linguists tended to focus more on the search for "elementary sources," but new philology stressed the value of "trac[ing] the progress" of a language. Its devotees mapped out a more complete diagram of linguistic family trees than ever before, at the same time that the disciplines of geology, biology, ethnography, archaeology, and anthropology provided new data to complement the contemplation of origins. In parallel with linguistic history, these disciplines examined how people, societies, animals, ecosystems, and the landscape morph over time, which unsettled many assumptions about the stability of those systems.

Philology's intersection with many intellectual areas becomes apparent in the similes used to describe words and how they alter. Whewell (the Master of Trinity who believed in the possibility of algebraic language) wrote:

> The English language is a conglomerate of Latin words, bound together in a Saxon cement; the fragments of the Latin being partly portions introduced directly from the parent quarry, with all their sharp edges, and partly pebbles of the same material, obscured and shaped by long rolling in a Norman or some other channel.[75]

Trench compared individual words to men, in that their births and deaths should be recorded, and that if we wish to understand what they are, we should know what they have been.[76] Furthermore, he often described the adoption of loan words as a type of naturalization process for English citizenship.[77] In Trench's writings from the 1850s, words are also like tokens that, once cleaned, reveal themselves to be precious coins (an archaeological image), and "tools which, themselves the result of the finest mechanical skill, do at the same time render other and further triumphs

---

[72] Bosworth, *A Dictionary of the Anglo-Saxon Language*, xxxviii.
[73] Quoted in Turner, *Philology*, 245.
[74] Turner, *History of the Anglo-Saxons*, 1807, 2:448.
[75] Quoted in Taylor, *Hardy's Literary Language and Victorian Philology*, 282.
[76] Richard Chenevix Trench, *On Some Deficiencies in Our English Dictionaries: Being the Substance of Two Papers Read Before the Philological Society, Nov. 5, and Nov. 19, 1857*, 2nd ed. (London: John W. Parker and Son, 1860), 29, 41, 43; Richard Chenevix Trench, *English, Past and Present*, 2nd ed. (John W. Parker, 1855), 194.
[77] Trench, *English, Past and Present*, 27, 59, 95; Trench, *Deficiencies*, 15, 31.

of art possible."[78] As for English specifically, Trench likens it to a body, describing the Saxon portion as "its joints, its whole *articulation*, its sinews and its ligaments." The next sentence compares English to a building, with Anglo-Saxon elements as mortar that binds the bricks or stones of Latinate vocabulary.[79]

The findings from philology's cognate fields lent the metaphor of roots an even stronger allure than it had previously possessed, but they also confirmed another problem that Plato had identified: the world changes, and so words may cease to be "correct" – that is, to mean what they originally did. Tennyson evidently pondered this problem into his old age. In his play *Queen Mary* (1875), the future Queen Elizabeth I likens the fragility of history's truth to the alteration of a word:

> But truth of story …
> Is like a word that comes from olden days,
> And passes thro' the peoples: every tongue
> Alters it passing, till it spells and speaks
> Quite other than at first.[80]

The fact that language is constantly undergoing incremental changes, shifting sounds and altering meanings, raised the specter of autonomous speech that, rather than helping people express themselves, operates according to its own laws. Lyell remarked that "Even when a language is regarded with superstitious veneration as the vehicle of divine truths and religious precepts [i.e., holy scripture], and which has prevailed for many generations, it will be incapable of permanently maintaining its ground."[81]

It is noteworthy that Lyell labels faith in the truth of the linguistic medium "superstitious," given that such faith was foundational to early philology and continued to underpin later versions unconsciously. New philology took as its concern the mechanics of change, an approach that easily could have amplified concern over language's lack of stability. However, its more diplomatic advocates – Trench and Müller in particular – worked to domesticate the concept of unconscious linguistic change by positioning it as a positive. Once the principles of change were identified, they said, those principles provided glimpses into human history. In Kemble's words, "[T]he spirit of a people is to be traced in the formation of their language, and … their history has no trifling connection with their tongue."[82] In this new context, philology promised to use the very changes of a language to illuminate matters both specific and general; it had the potential to explain the workings of an individual mind and the movements of whole races.

With their lectures and publications, Müller and Trench helped philology to capture the public imagination. Specifically, they knew how to communicate effectively the many implications of philology's findings and its connection to topics that were

---

[78] Trench, *On the Study of Words*, 26, 99–100, 123.
[79] Trench, *English, Past and Present*, 21–22.
[80] Alfred Tennyson, "Queen Mary," in *Queen Mary and Harold*, Eversley Edition, vol. 8 of *The Works of Alfred Lord Tennyson*, ed. Hallam Tennyson (London: Macmillan, 1908), 118.
[81] Lyell, *Geological Evidences*, 464.
[82] Kemble, "Lajamon," 6.

very much on the minds of the Victorian public, describing linguistic discoveries as a source of awe and excitement rather than fear. By Müller's own admission, the major challenge of preparing linguistic lectures for a general audience was "the dryness of many of the problems which I shall have to discuss. Declensions and conjugations cannot be made amusing." Nevertheless, he argued that the grand story of human history shines through the minutiae of philological parsing:

> The study of words may be tedious to the school-boy, as breaking of stones is to the wayside labourer, but to the thoughtful eye of the geologist these stones are full of interest – he sees miracles in the high road, and reads chronicles in every ditch. Language, too, has marvels of her own, which she unveils to the inquiring glance of the patient student. There are chronicles below her surface, there are sermons in every word.[83]

This passage employs the by-then common geological analogy for language, but crucially, Müller writes that philological study uncovers "marvels" and "sermons." In their eminently quotable descriptions, Müller and Trench allowed for wonder as well as anthropological insight.

The same kind of domesticating move is evident in "A Study in Scarlet," the story that introduced Sherlock Holmes to the public in 1887. The detective comments to Dr. Watson:

> Do you remember what Darwin says about music? He claims that the power of producing and appreciating it existed among the human race long before the power of speech was arrived at. Perhaps that is why we are so subtly influenced by it. There are vague memories in our souls of those misty centuries when the world was in its childhood.[84]

Darwin had actually posited that "some early progenitor of man, probably used his voice largely … in singing" for the purposes of mating. Holmes transforms Darwin's hypothesis of animalistic imitation into a dreamlike concept of "memories in our souls" of "misty centuries." It can be an appealing notion, that the minds of our ancestors subtly influence us whenever we participate in expression that we inherited from them. For Holmes, this means music; for others, the resonances of a word's biography echo the past through the mouths of modern speakers.

By shifting the scholarly dialogue away from origins and toward the process of change, new philologists could also navigate two competing interpretations of human civilization – one of progress, one of decay. For the geologist Lyell, linguistic evolution paralleled biological evolution as a positive progression from simple perception of the world to increasing precision. "As civilisation advances," he wrote, words become more specific in meaning. As the process continues:

> The farther this subdivision of [word] function is carried, the more complete and perfect the language becomes, just as species of higher grade have special organs,

---

[83] Müller, *Lectures*, 5th ed., 2–3.
[84] Arthur Conan Doyle, "A Study in Scarlet," in *Sherlock Holmes: The Complete Novels and Stories*, vol. 1 (New York: Bantam, 2003), 39.

such as eyes, lungs, and stomach, for seeing, breathing, and digesting, which in simpler organisms are all performed by one and the same part of the body.[85]

Corroborating this view, archaeological discoveries concerning early human society had put an end to the idea of a golden age.[86] Yet there remained the fact of lost inflections and dead languages of apparently better exactitude.

Trench described both processes – innovation and corrosion – going forward at the same time in a dynamic system. His favorite image for a living language was "a tree in which the vital sap is yet working, ascending from its roots into its branches; and as this works, new leaves are being put forth by it, old are dropping away and dying."[87] Organic metaphors were especially attractive in light of the Romanticism that had spurred the continental branch of philological study; Müller, steeped in German Romantic language theory throughout his education, likewise described language change as a natural process.[88] Trench further wrote that even the death of a language was a natural process – and it was not permanent. Languages, he wrote, "have their youth, their manhood, their old age, their decrepitude, their final dissolution ... [O]ut of their death a new life comes forth ... [T]hey must have had the germs of death, the possibilities of decay, in them from the very first."[89] In this vibrant model, language was less a subject for valuative judgment and more a window into the lives of past populations. Because words have been "connecting and intertwining themselves with all that men have been doing and thinking and feeling from the beginning of the world till now," there was a decidedly anthropological bent to studying their adaptations over time.[90]

Moreover, words actually preserved ancient ideas and could endure long beyond the physical artifacts of the past. Trench makes the point in his *Select Glossary of English Words Used Formerly in Senses Different from Their Present* (1859). The book's entire purpose is to show the differences between current and former meanings of certain words. Yet the "revised and improved" second edition (published the same year as the first) bears the motto *Res fugiunt, vocabula manent* on the title page: Things flee, words remain.[91] With the help of philological research, words that remain can reveal themselves as archives of thought.

The question of what information old words may contain was central to philologists in the middle of the nineteenth century, but the same ideas were under consideration in the previous decades, as well. An unpublished sonnet by Tennyson from about 1830 considered whether we can ever understand ancient mindsets:

> The constant spirit of the world exults
> In fertile change and wide variety,
> And this is my delight to live and see

---

[85] Lyell, *Geological Evidences*, 468.
[86] Burrow, "The Uses of Philology in Victorian England," 202.
[87] Trench, *English, Past and Present*, 37.
[88] Turner, *Philology*, 245.
[89] Trench, *English, Past and Present*, 98.
[90] Trench, *On the Study of Words*, 27–28.
[91] Trench, *A Select Glossary*.

Old principles still working new results.
Nothing is altogether old or new (5)
Though all things in another form are cast,
And what in human thought is just and true
Though fashioned in a thousand forms will last.
But some high-thoughted moods and moulds of mind
Can never be remodelled or expressed (10)
Again by any later century,
As in the oldest crusts of Earth we find
Enormous fossilbones and shapes imprest
Of ancient races that have ceased to be.

The octave expresses a positive attitude toward change, which is "fertile" both because there is much change in the world and because it produces many "new results" and thus is pregnant with possibilities. The multiple meanings available within a single word choice enhance the poem's theme, a technique Tennyson would continue to develop over the course of his career. Other words reflect the paradox that the poem considers. With the most basic knowledge of Latin or etymology, we may notice the oxymoron of "The constant spirit of the world exults." The spirit of the world is *constant*, from Latin meaning standing firm, yet it *exults*, with a literal sense of leaping out. The same tension becomes apparent when we take the first two lines together: "The constant spirit … exults / In … change." One definition of *constant* is "Remaining ever the same in condition, quality, state, or form; invariable, fixed, unchanging, uniform." How can something unchanging change its form and remain constant? That is the philosophical question posed here, and Tennyson explores it through the clash of individual words as well as in the poem's argument.

The sonnet structure also echoes the same apparent contradictions, with the sestet dampening the positive tone of the first eight lines. Despite the fact that "nothing is altogether new," a culture has psychological qualities that cannot be "remodelled or expressed / Again by any later century." Two possible reasons for this suggest themselves, and they are closely connected: either the feeling is impossible to communicate due to its very nature, or there is not language to do so. In the last three lines, Tennyson introduces the image of fossils for ideas that cannot be reshaped by later centuries. As we have already seen, it became common to describe language as a fossil record and historical linguistics as a means of identifying bygone "moods and moulds of mind."

As comparative philologists reconstructed the roots and branches of the Proto-Indo-European language tree, a corresponding map of human migration began to emerge. Ethnologists therefore especially valued philological insights.[92] Those insights held the promise of settling once and for all whether human beings had a single origin (suggesting some version of Eden) or developed in several independent groups. Kemble, for example, concluded that "the connection of [Indo-European] languages argues a connection of race," supporting a Biblical single-origin model.[93]

[92] Burrow, "The Uses of Philology in Victorian England," 188.
[93] John Mitchell Kemble, "History of the English Language, First, or Anglo-Saxon Period" (J. & J.J. Deighton, 1834), 20.

Unsurprisingly, philology's anthropological extrapolations also contributed to an ongoing construction of cultural identity that grounded itself in the traditions – real or imagined – of the Anglo-Saxons. It was not until the nineteenth century that Old English began to be appreciated for its own virtues, while simultaneously Anglo-Saxonist scholarship came to be of interest to the broader educated population. By the time Tennyson came up to Cambridge, the Anglo-Saxons were widely considered the founding fathers of British society,[94] a position that made them a possible solution to the desire for origins in England, while the matter of human origin remained occluded. At the same time, shedding light on language's fluidity raised an ancient question: what does a word mean if it has meant many things? And what is a poet's role in the making of meaning?

The Poet as Language Maker

As a basis for linguistics, the pseudo-mystical importance of a word's original metaphor might have proved intellectually unsustainable, but its emotional appeal remained strong. Because early speakers pieced words together from the simplest building blocks of idea-syllables, etymology promised to uncover the metaphor that constituted their fusion. Thus, Trench wrote (borrowing from German philosopher Jean Paul) that "All language is in some sort ... a collection of faded metaphors."[95] In nineteenth-century language theory, therefore, the poet held a uniquely privileged position. Plato's imagined name-maker was a kind of poet, and in turn, contemporary poets kept language alive. The Cambridge Apostles were Shelley enthusiasts, and it seems likely that they would have read his *Defence of Poetry* when it was published in 1840. In it, Shelley writes of early speakers:

> Their language is vitally metaphorical; that is, it marks the before unapprehended relations of things and perpetuates their apprehension, until the words which represent them become, through time, signs for portions or classes of thoughts instead of pictures of integral thoughts; and then if no new poets should arise to create afresh the associations which have been thus disorganized, language will be dead to all the nobler purposes of human intercourse.[96]

All language, Shelley suggests, is poetry, at least when it is first pieced together. Poets, like early language-makers, must show the rest of mankind how to perceive the world in new ways.

Not long after Shelley's essay appeared in print, another poet-theorist expressed almost identical ideas. Emerson saw the poet as a kind of prophet, not least when creating new language. In a near-paraphrase of *Cratylus*, he writes that "the poet is the Namer, or Language-maker, naming things sometimes after their appearance, sometimes after their essence, and giving to every one its own name and not another's." He continues:

---

[94] Scragg, "Introduction," 5.
[95] Quoted in Hair, *Tennyson's Language*, 11.
[96] Percy Bysshe Shelley, "A Defence of Poetry," in *Shelley's Poetry and Prose*, ed. Donald H. Reiman and Neil Fraistat, 2nd ed., Norton Critical Edition (New York: Norton, 2002), 512.

> The poets made all the words, and therefore language is the archives of history … For, though the origin of most of our words is forgotten, each word was at first a stroke of genius, and obtained currency, because for the moment it symbolized the world to the first speaker and to the hearer. The etymologist finds the deadest word to have been once a brilliant picture. Language is fossil poetry.[97]

If every word, when coined, was a poetic metaphor, then it follows that etymology can help uncover the poetics of everyday words. Trench offered the same premise in his philological writing seven years later, stating:

> Many a single word … is itself a concentrated poem, having stores of poetical thought and imagery laid up in it … The image may have grown trite and ordinary now; perhaps through the help of this very word may have become so entirely the heritage of all, as to seem little better than a commonplace; yet not the less he who first discerned the relation, and devised the new words which should express it … this man was in his degree a poet – a maker, that is, of things which were not before.[98]

Seen through the correct prism, that is, a single word could show itself to contain a poetic metaphor. Emerson's influence on Trench is obvious when we compare the latter's much-quoted passage above with the American's statement, "It does not need that a poem should be long. Every word was once a poem. Every new relation is a new word."[99] So similar were their descriptions that the phrase "fossil poetry" is often erroneously attributed to Trench, despite his having credited it to "a popular American writer."[100]

Further emphasizing the vividness of early language, Emerson draws attention to the physical origin of many words, making his point by means of a typical appeal to etymology:

> Every word which is used to express a moral or intellectual fact, if traced to its root, is found to be borrowed from some material appearance. *Right* means *straight*; *wrong* means *twisted*. *Spirit* primarily means *wind*; *transgression*, the crossing of a *line*; *supercilious*, the *raising of the eyebrow*. We say the *heart* to express emotion, the *head* to denote thought; and *thought* and *emotion* are words borrowed from sensible things, and now appropriated to spiritual nature. Most of the process by which this transformation is made, is hidden from us in the remote time when language was framed.

In this paragraph, Emerson performs the standard philological ritual: appealing to roots and noting the metaphorical nature of early usage. "As we go back in history," he writes later, "language becomes more picturesque, until its infancy, when it is all poetry."[101]

---

[97] Emerson, "The Poet," 457.
[98] Trench, *On the Study of Words*, 5–6.
[99] Emerson, "The Poet," 455.
[100] Trench, *On the Study of Words*, 4.
[101] Emerson, "The Poet," 20, 22.

Tennyson first read Emerson in 1841, upon being given a copy of his collected essays from that year by American publisher Charles Stearns Wheeler, with whom Tennyson was negotiating for distribution of his own work. Although the essay "The Poet" was still being written at this time, Emerson had already articulated its main concepts elsewhere. Tennyson acknowledged the gift in a letter to the publisher, writing:

> I am much obliged to you for the volume of Emerson's Essays. I had heard of him before and I know that Carlyle rates him highly. He has great thoughts and imagination, but he sometimes misleads himself by his own facility of talking brilliantly.[102]

A similar distrust of a "facility of talking brilliantly" has, of course, featured in critiques of Tennyson's work since the late nineteenth century. His "finest verbalism" (in Walt Whitman's phrase) has aroused suspicions that his poems do not mean much of anything or are in fact deceptive, while Emerson strays from scholarly philology into mystical abstractions that lead some distance from his task of describing a poet's function.[103]

Tennyson's equivocation indicates that he was somewhat skeptical of Emerson's more outlandish claims for the figure of the poet-prophet. Nevertheless, the Englishman was surrounded by a discourse dedicated to the notion that words had once embodied vivid imagery. His friend Kemble, for example, admonished fellow Cambridge Apostle William Bodham Donne: "'*Language in its spontaneous period is sensuous*', which golden law write up in any Etymological Dictionary you possess."[104] In "The Old Chieftain," a primitivist poem from the 1827 volume *Poems by Two Brothers*, Tennyson equates bygone physical and verbal strength, hinting at an early interest in the potency of old words. The chieftain begins his speech: "When my voice was high, and my arm was strong" (5). Not only did the chieftain's song rally his men to battle, the army is portrayed as irresistible because it has the "united powers / Of battle and music" (13–14). When he recalls that "each word that I spake was the death of a foe," he suggests there was a time when speech was indivisible from the thing spoken of.

As with the old chieftain, etymological nostalgia for the former vividness of now-faded metaphors implies infirmity in modern speech, which requires a remedy. Now that language is old, Trench describes three valuable tasks for poetry:

> Extending the domain of thought and feeling, [the poet] will scarcely fail to extend that also of language … It is not merely that the old and the familiar will often become new in his hands; that he will give the stamp of allowance … to words … which hitherto have lived only on the lips of the multitude, or been confined to some single dialect and province; but he will enrich his native tongue with words unknown and non-existent before – non-existent, that is, save in their elements.[105]

---

[102] Tennyson, *Letters*, 1982, 1:193.
[103] Perry, *Alfred Tennyson*, 1–3.
[104] Frances M. Brookfield, *The Cambridge "Apostles"* (New York: AMS Press, 1973), 178–179.
[105] Trench, *On the Study of Words*, 116–117.

For Trench, as for Emerson, a poet was a Platonic name-maker. Plato's name-maker perceived the nature of things, while Shelley's poet perceives relations between things; each then forges a vehicle – either a word or a poem – to convey the idea (or relation) to others. In doing similar communicative and imaginative work, poets will naturally coin new words – "enrich [their] native tongue" – in the process.

This book aims to show that Tennyson wrote poetry that performed all three of Trench's tasks and was motivated to do so by his interest in philology. In fact, he did his job as a language-maker so well that the editors of the *OED* contacted Tennyson to check the usage of some of his words.[106] According to historian Simon Winchester, "The exchange of letters between [editor J.A.H.] Murray and the ennobled poet figures prominently in the Dictionary's public archives; and the *OED*'s notes ... take on a rare personal tone by writing that it is all explained 'as Tennyson tells us.'"[107] In fact, Tennyson was one of several literary figures upon which the dictionary relied. The public prospectus for the project explained its guiding principles and asked for help from volunteer readers. Those interested in working on eighteenth- and nineteenth-century literature could help by contributing:

> a careful analysis of the works of any of the principal writers, extracting all remarkable words, and all passages which contain definitions or explanations, or which, by reason of their intrinsic merit, are specially eligible as illustrative quotations. We have not given a list of these writers, as their names must be familiar to all; but Wordsworth, Scott, Coleridge, Southey, Tennyson, Ruskin, Macaulay, and Froude may be mentioned as pre-eminently important.

A list of the works "already undertaken" for analysis shows that Tennyson's works had already been claimed.[108]

The list of supposedly obvious writers is informative. At the very least, it gives a glimpse of the canon as understood by the leaders of the Philological Society. It also demonstrates the reciprocal relationship between authors and linguistic authority. Those who are recognized as "the principal writers" of a period lend legitimacy to any way they used their language; at the same time, these examples suggest what kind of style was considered good writing – for mid-nineteenth-century lexicographers, at least. As Romantic poets, Wordsworth, Coleridge, and Southey wrote from a commitment to the plain language of everyday people. Scott's enormous fame rested on historical fiction. Tennyson's philological style is the subject of the rest of this book. Consciously or not, the Philological Society recommended writers whose work was interested in the past while simultaneously representing their own moment in time.

According to the online version of the *OED* (as of early 2023), Tennyson is "The 32nd most frequently quoted source ... with a total of 6450 quotations (about 0.17%

---

[106] See, for example, Alfred Tennyson, *The Letters of Alfred Lord Tennyson*, ed. Cecil Y. Lang and Edgar Finley Shannon, vol. 3 (Oxford: Clarendon, 1982), 337.

[107] Simon Winchester, *The Meaning of Everything: The Story of the Oxford English Dictionary* (Oxford: Oxford University Press, 2003), 146.

[108] Philological Society, *Proposal for the Publication of a New English Dictionary* (London: Trübner, 1859), 6, 29.

of all *OED* quotations)." These quotations show Tennyson employing words in several ways. Eighty-nine percent of his quotations help illustrate an existing meaning; this in itself indicates that he used words in a context that makes their meaning clear (making them valuable as dictionary examples). It was a technique that he also employed when using words innovatively, as Chapter 3 explores. Tennyson's most quoted texts, in order, are "The Princess," *In Memoriam*, "Enid," "Maud," *Enoch Arden*, "Aylmer's Field," "Elaine," *Becket*, "Gareth and Lynette," and *Harold*. They lean toward medieval subject matter, and future research might fruitfully investigate the kind of words for which the *OED* judged Tennyson to be a good source.

The following chapters elaborate some of the ways in which Tennyson drew on the history of his words to enhance – and sometimes complicate – their effect in his work. One of his methods was to look back to literal meanings as defined by etymons. Although he was too inclusive to wish to return to an imagined purer speech, he was invested in the "living powers" (to borrow Coleridge's phrase) that constituted his vocabulary.[109] He was also endlessly fascinated by the mechanism by which words convey meaning.

Tennyson's Liminal Language

New philology assertively portrayed itself as a science, breaking from its literary past,[110] as we may see in the protestation of the *OED*'s chief editor, J.A.H. Murray: "I am not a literary man … I am a man of science, and I am interested in that branch of Anthropology which deals with the history of human speech."[111] But the history of the English language was inevitably of interest to those whose craft lay in weighing their words and deciding how to arrange them to intended effect. Poetry's implied density of meaning makes fertile ground for considering the question of where meaning lurks.

In his book on *Tennyson's Fixations*, Matthew Rowlinson identifies "the place of voice" as one of that poet's obsessions, prominent enough in his verse to merit its own chapter. Rowlinson's emphatically Freudian readings unfortunately isolate Tennyson's linguistic curiosity from its philosophical and philological context; however, we need not agree that "The Skipping-Rope" and "The Hesperides" produce "language as autoerotic repetition" in order to find that Tennyson's poetry exhibits a fixation with speech.[112] Throughout his career, he drew attention to the mystery of how language works through dense repetition of words, sounds, homonyms, and

---

[109] Samuel Taylor Coleridge, *Essays on His Times in The Morning Post and The Courier*, ed. David V. Erdman, vol. 2, The Collected Works of Samuel Taylor Coleridge 3 (London: Routledge & Kegan Paul, 1978), 249.

[110] Alter, *Darwinism and the Linguistic Image*, 80.

[111] Quoted in K. M. Elisabeth Murray, *Caught in the Web of Words: James A.H. Murray and the Oxford English Dictionary* (New Haven: Yale University Press, 1995), 292.

[112] Matthew Rowlinson, *Tennyson's Fixations: Psychoanalysis and the Topics of the Early Poetry*, Victorian Literature and Culture Series (Charlottesville: University Press of Virginia, 1994), 66.

puns, straining and sometimes nearly breaking language's communicative function in probing its boundaries.

The poem "The 'How' and the 'Why'" (published 1830) is a good example of this exploration. It reads like a nursery rhyme as its repetition accelerates its rhythm, which in turn makes it difficult to formulate answers to the philosophical questions that it asks. However, as often as repetition begins to establish an expectation, the poem alters its pattern, frequently through a change in question words – for example, from *what* to *why* to *whether*. The questions themselves are both philosophically fundamental and absurdly unanswerable ("Why round is not square?"); thus, it is appropriate that, through its manipulation of language, the poem asks the reader to consider the basic and unanswerable question of how the mind can transform a rush of sounds into units that form meaning. In the third stanza, important question words reverse the history of language by being framed as onomatopoeia: "The little bird pipeth – 'why? why?'" and "the black owl … chaunts 'how? how?'" (26, 30–31). The final stanza then juxtaposes theological questions – "What the life is? where the soul may lie?" – with mundane ones: "Why a church is with a steeple built; / And a house with a chimneypot?" (32–35). Consequently, the act of asking – of demanding to make sense of the world through words – becomes ridiculous.

The poem's mechanics also do their best to disrupt the reader's sense of linguistic order. The rhyme scheme and meter are irregular, which Christopher Ricks suggests is why (along with other early poems) it was never reprinted. In addition to the end-rhyme patterns, there are rhymes within single lines, which multiply the chiming – for example, "We laugh, we cry, we are born, we die" (8). Halfway through the second stanza, Tennyson builds an alternating chain with the rhymes and repetitions:

> The bulrush nods unto his brother (10)
> The wheatears whisper to each other:
> What is it they say? What do they there?
> Why two and two make four? Why round is not square?
> Why the rocks stand still, and the light clouds fly?
> Why the heavy oak groans, and the white willows sigh? (15)
> Why deep is not high, and high is not deep?
> Whether we wake or whether we sleep?
> Whether we sleep or whether we die?
> How you are you? Why I am I?
> Who will riddle me the *how* and the *why*? (20)

The end-rhymes are arranged in couplets, the last of which connects to the refrain ("Who will riddle me the *how* and the *why*?"). Line 16 complicates the pattern by first repeating line 15's end-rhyme ("sigh … high") and then inverting its own first half ("Why deep is not high, and high is not deep?"). Lines 17–18 also carry an end-rhyme into the middle of the next line, this time by repeating the entire phrase, "Whether we sleep." The latter half of that line ("or whether we die") then returns to the initial rhyme that began the chain. The poem's final two lines create a similar chain, which breaks the established refrain by inserting an additional, intermediate question word: "Who will riddle me the how and the what? / Who will riddle me the what and the why?" The result is a frustration of expected patterning, echoing the seeming chaos of language itself.

Yet more conspicuously, "Second Song" from the same volume pushes language toward pure onomatopoeia. It is addressed to an owl, and Tennyson puns on the bird's calls:

> I
> Thy tuwhits are lulled I wot,
> Thy tuwhoos of yesternight,
> Which upon the dark afloat,
> So took echo with delight,
> So took echo with delight, (5)
> That her voice untuneful grown,
> Wears all day a fainter tone.
>
> II
> I would mock thy chaunt anew;
> But I cannot mimick it;
> Not a whit of thy tuwhoo, (10)
> Thee to woo to thy tuwhit,
> Thee to woo to thy tuwhit,
> With a lengthen'd loud halloo,
> Tuwhoo, tuwhit, tuwhit, tuwhoo-o-o.

Despite the speaker's claim that he "cannot mimick" the owl, imitative sound dominates. The line "So took echo with delight," for example, literally echoes itself through immediate repetition. In lines 10–12, the linguistic crisis reaches its peak, for real words (a whit, to woo) pun on onomatopoeia (tuwhit, tuwhoo), and the complete repetition of tongue-twisting line 11 makes it yet more difficult to separate the sense from the nonsense. The poem foregrounds the potential for words, as Hare had put it three years earlier, to "lose their character, and from being the tokens and exponents of thoughts, become mere air-propelling sounds."[113] Even on the scale of stanza, each individual sentence makes little grammatical sense; indeed, the second stanza devolves into a fragmentary nonsentence starting in line 10.

Tennyson is not known as a writer of nonsense, but in these experimental early poems, he presses the boundaries of how far readers can keep sound and meaning united. They are relatively rare specimens; he would soon move toward more narrative constructs for his poems, but with a keen ear for how sound could distract from, or enhance, a line. In particular, he would point out phrases he had crafted to sound like what they were describing. For example, "The Golden Year" (from the mid-1840s) ends with the sound of an explosion: "I heard them blast / The steep slate-quarry, and the great echo flap / And buffet round the hills, from bluff to bluff" (74–76). The Eversley Edition comments that the final line is "Onomatopoeic. 'Bluff

---

[113] Julius Charles Hare, *Guesses at Truth, by Two Brothers*, 5th ed. (Boston: Ticknor and Fields, 1861), 478.

to bluff' gives the echo of the blasting as I heard it from the mountain on the counter side."[114] His Eversley Edition notes likewise comment on the line "In unremorseful folds of rolling fire" in "The Holy Grail" (written 1868), saying, "This line gives onomatopœically the 'unremorseful flames.'"[115]

Near the end of his career, Tennyson once again imitated birdsong in "The Throstle" (1889). The first stanza gives a sense of its style:

> "Summer is coming, summer is coming.
> I know it, I know it, I know it.
> Light again, leaf again, life again, love again,"
> Yes, my wild little Poet.

This poem's rhythm and repetition re-create the sound of the titular bird's call very effectively without blurring sound and sense the way he had in his early experiments. It is also an example of an ongoing theme in Tennyson's poetry: the almost-communicative sounds of nature. He calls the bird "my wild little poet," and his poems often suggest that nature is speaking just beyond human perception. "Before I could read," he recalled as an old man, "I was in the habit on a stormy day of spreading my arms to the wind and crying out, 'I hear a voice that's speaking in the wind.'"[116] The idea stayed with him all his life.

Angela Leighton has described Tennyson's lifelong obsession with "noises generally: the 'hum', the 'unknown tongues', the 'notes', which resonate outside articulate speech" – all of which grow out of his poetic straining to detect intention in the world around him.[117] A typical instance from the 1830s reads:

> Whate'er I see, where'er I move,
> These whispers rise, and fall away,
> Something of pain – of bliss – of Love,
> But what, were hard to say. ("Whispers" 9–12)

In this poem, as in many others, "Nature gives ... a hint of somewhat unexprest" (6, 8). Philology, then, complemented Tennyson's pre-existing preoccupation with liminal sounds. In "The Poet," Emerson strays beyond the bounds of philology, arguing that on a mystical level, every object in the world is symbolic and therefore linguistic: "Nature offers all her creatures to [the poet] as a picture-language ... [N]ature is a symbol, in the whole, and in every part."[118] Trench similarly wrote that nature is "the hieroglyphics of God" and the world a parable.[119] While Tennyson did not go so far, his poetry is replete with sounds of nature that poise on the edge of being

---

[114] Tennyson, *Poems II*, 337.
[115] Alfred Tennyson, *Idylls of the King*, ed. Hallam Tennyson, Eversley Edition, vol. 5 of *The Works of Alfred Lord Tennyson*, ed. Hallam Tennyson (London: Macmillan, 1908), 493.
[116] Hallam Tennyson, *Memoir*, 1:11.
[117] Angela Leighton, "Tennyson's Hum," *Tennyson Research Bulletin* 9, no. 4 (November 2010): 315.
[118] Emerson, "The Poet," 452.
[119] Trench, *Parables*, 16.

understood as language, especially in his early work. The speaker of his juvenile poem "Adeline," for example, asks the subject why she smiles, wondering:

> Hast thou heard the butterflies
> What they say betwixt their wings?
> Or in stillest evenings
> With what voice the violet woos
> To his heart the silver dews? (28–32)

The same poem imagines the heroine speaking "in the language wherewith Spring / Letters cowslips on the hill" (60–61).

One manifestation of Tennyson's fascination with the boundaries between speech, potential or near-speech, and mere sound is the prevalence of murmuring and buzzing in his poetry. The lyric "Come down, O maid" within "The Princess" asks the maid to descend to the valley where all sounds are sweet, citing the "murmuring of innumerable bees" – a line famous for how its sound reflects its sense. This murmuring combines with other natural sounds, as well as the shepherd's pipe and the call of children; murmurs join with human voice, but even the voices are inarticulate and nonspecific (children vaguely "crying"). In "Sense and Conscience," an early notebook draft poem, sense drugs conscience by driving him "to deep shades, / A gloom monotonously musical / With hum of murmurous bees" and a variety of other natural sounds, including waterfalls, winds, and doves (44–46).

The murmur or hum of bees in relation to human speech is especially noteworthy, for bees had been associated with linguistic skill for centuries and had been newly recast in philological narrative. Recall Trench's simile: "Man makes his own language, but he makes it as the bee makes its cells, as the bird its nest."[120] In fact, the bee simile was common as a representation of how language changes over time: like a beehive, the change is gradual and invisible to its inhabitants minute by minute. Lyell, for example, used the comparison in *Geological Evidences of the Antiquity of Man*.[121]

Trench and Lyell were drawing on very old precedent. "In the western tradition," writes Claire Preston, "honey stands for eloquence, immortality and sheer pleasure." The story of an infant being fed by bees and subsequently speaking words sweet as honey has been applied to Plato, Pindar, Sophocles, Xenophon, Vergil, Lucan, and St. Basil.[122] Tennyson used the same trope. He describes the title character of "Edwin Morris" (written 1839, reusing lines from a draft of "The Gardener's Daughter") as "A full-celled honeycomb of eloquence / Stored from all flowers" (26–27). A fantasy of baby Eleänore (1830) imagines "the yellow-banded bees" feeding her pure honey, after which she is "with the hum of swarming bees / Into dreamful slumber lulled" (22–30). Again, for the mysterious Adeline, "Some honey-converse feeds thy mind" (40). The ways in which Tennyson mentions bees, and more importantly his continued attraction to the effect of humming and murmuring, reveal a lifelong curiosity regarding the limits of signification.

---

[120] Trench, *On the Study of Words*, 17.
[121] Lyell, *Geological Evidences*, 469.
[122] Claire Preston, *Bee*, Animal (London: Reaktion, 2006), 11–13.

In his poetry, bees often hum as a counterpoint to human silence or absence: "the wild bee hummeth / About the mossed headstone" ("Claribel" [1830] 11–12), and similarly we hear of the peace over a grave: "Chaunteth not the brooding bee / Sweeter tones than calumny?" ("A Dirge" [1830] 16–17). The debate that rages in "The Two Voices" (written in the 1830s) considers how the world carries on without particular individuals: "Not less the bee would range her cells" if the speaker died (70). In the same fashion, "A Farewell" (written around 1837) imagines the brook at Somersby in Tennyson's absence, where trees will sigh and "here by thee will hum the bee" (11). Occasionally, the humans are active and the bees inactive, but again the speech of one sets off the silence of the other. In "Œnone," the eponymous heroine is the only waking thing, in contrast to the rest of nature, including "the golden bee," which is "lily-cradled" (28–29). As a general symbol of nature going silent, the "winter" portion of "The Window" song cycle (written 1866–1867) lists among the effects of frost, "the bees are stilled, and the flies are killed" (52). It is in "Lancelot and Elaine" (written 1858) that Tennyson makes an explicit simile between words and the buzz of bees:

> Her father's latest word hummed in her ear,
> …
> But she was happy enough and shook it off,
> As we shake off the bee that buzzes at us   (775, 779–780)

Several critics have identified carelessness toward speech as the catalyst of Camelot's undoing in the *Idylls*. When Elaine reduces her father's word to the buzzing of a bee, she dismisses it to the realm of noise which, at best, hints at sense.

In Memoriam also employs the analogy of men and bees to express the speaker's fraught relationship with faith. Section L asks for spiritual support when:

> my faith is dry,
> And men the flies of latter spring,
> That lay their eggs, and sting and sing
> And weave their petty cells and die.   (9–12)

As cited by Christopher Ricks, "William Allingham's *Diary* … makes it clear that Tennyson spoke of flies as bees."[123] This may have been an artifact of Lincolnshire dialect, which used the term *bees* to refer to flies, as Tennyson later did in "Northern Farmer, New Style" (published 1869).[124] The original drafts of "The Poet's Song" (1842) and "The Two Voices" (written 1833) bear this out, reading respectively, "The swallow stopt as he hunted the bee" (later changed to *fly*) (9) and "flies will weave their tinsel cells" (changed to "not less the bee would range her cells") (70). As is appropriate for this section of *In Memoriam*, the comparison here

---

[123] Alfred Tennyson, *The Poems of Tennyson*, ed. Christopher B. Ricks, 2nd ed., vol. 2, Longman Annotated English Poets (London: Longman, 1987), 178; William Allingham, *William Allingham: A Diary*, ed. H. Allingham and D. Radford (London: Macmillan, 1907), 312.

[124] George Edward Campion, *A Tennyson Dialect Glossary with the Dialect Poems* (Lincoln: Lincolnshire Association, 1969), 14.

works against a historic mythology of bees as pure or pious. Medieval tradition held that bees escaped Eden uncorrupted and were one of two species that could access heaven, while their hum and flight were associated with the soul's flight to heaven.[125] In contrast, Tennyson's speaker sometimes loses faith; in times of doubt, men seem to be only bees, whose work lacks wonder. Their cells are "petty," and their singing is followed by death rather than transcendence. The bees sing, but does the song mean anything? Here, uncertainty as to whether apian humming has meaning represents the question of whether man's words and actions have any larger significance in the world – a theological extension of his early exploration of the borders of noise and sense.

After Arthur Hallam's death, Tennyson's poems became especially concerned with messages unreceived or indecipherable. As discussed further in Chapter 4, it is a concern that runs throughout *In Memoriam*; it also affected Tennyson's poetry ever after, especially with regard to the potential latent communication within nature, which seems to await understanding. In section lxix of *In Memoriam*, the speaker "found an angel of the night ... The voice was not the voice of grief, / The words were hard to understand" (14, 19–20). A similar moment had appeared in "The Vision of Sin," at the end of which a voice (presumably of God) speaks from the heavenly mountain:

> At last I heard a voice upon the slope
> Cry to the summit, "Is there any hope?"
> To which an answer peal'd from that high land,
> But in a tongue no man could understand.   (219–222)

Languages that can give answers to spiritual mysteries are tantalizingly incomprehensible in Tennyson's poetry. The voices of nature likewise seem to speak just outside the ability of man to understand, while human utterance can become indistinct and therefore cease to be communication at all. Curious as he obviously was about the sources and limits of signification, philology equipped Tennyson to consider the matter. It also quite literally provided him with a vocabulary for his poetic work, as Chapter 3 demonstrates.

The importance that the Victorians assigned to philology may be seen in Kemble's syllabus for an 1834 lecture series on "History of the English Language, First, or Anglo-Saxon Period." The summary of the concluding lecture announces, "The aim of all Etymological researches is to make the observed similarity in [grammatical] forms, reveal ... how it springs from the similarity of thoughts." The final topic was to be, "Value of these enquiries, in the spiritual education of Man."[126] It is no wonder that Kemble elsewhere referred to the "metaphysical field of grammar,"[127] for new methods of pursuing historical linguistics granted "a new and mighty privilege, yet a difficult duty ... to the etymologist, who, if he be not a practical metaphysician,

---

[125] Preston, *Bee*, 76, 80, 120.
[126] Kemble, "History of the English Language," 20.
[127] Kemble, *Correspondence*, 193.

will be nothing at all."[128] His fellow Anglo-Saxonist Joseph Bosworth agreed that "a good etymologist is most likely to become the best metaphysician" because he seeks the "real and internal meaning" of words.[129]

That philology could serve many masters is evident in the fact that Darwin and Müller invoked it in correspondence with each other to argue for and against evolution, respectively.[130] It had a place equally in the study of theology and science, making it invaluable for those wishing to reconcile the two, such as Tennyson. In fact, the poet approved of Darwin's *The Descent of Man* and discussed with its author that evolution need not conflict with Christianity.[131] Elizabeth Hirsh writes that Tennyson was most sympathetic with "the school of language theory" that "tried hard to reconcile scientific and religious-humanist accounts of language."[132] New philology implied the possibility of a world in which "The hills are shadows, and they flow / From form to form, and nothing stands" while also regarding truths laid up in words with a reverence bordering on the religious (*In Memoriam* cxxiii.5–6). Even the Darwinian geologist Lyell admitted, upon considering the complexities of how language had developed by means of a vast array of people speaking to each other over millennia, "we cannot but look upon the result as a profound mystery."[133] Philology allowed Tennyson to inhabit the intellectual space between materialism and faith. For Müller, "roots stand like barriers between the chaos and the cosmos of human speech;"[134] Tennyson, the Victorian name-shaper, stood between fear and hope for language itself.

---

[128] John Mitchell Kemble, *John Mitchell Kemble's Review of Jakob Grimm's Deutsche Grammatik: Originally Set for the Foreign Quarterly Review but Never Published* (Binghampton, NY: CEMERS, SUNY-Binghampton, 1981), 40.
[129] Bosworth, *A Dictionary of the Anglo-Saxon Language*, clxiv.
[130] Burrow, "The Uses of Philology in Victorian England," 201.
[131] John Batchelor, *Tennyson: To Strive, to Seek, to Find* (London: Chatto & Windus, 2012), 291.
[132] Hirsh, "No Record of Reply," 233.
[133] Lyell, *Geological Evidences*, 469.
[134] Müller, *Lectures*, 5th ed., ix.

2

"The people whose tongue we speak": Anglo-Saxons as Linguistic Ancestors

THOUGH TRUTH MAY recede into the past for the etymologist, new-philological researchers could use their skills to reconstruct ancient societies. For nineteenth-century Englishmen and -women, one of the most appealing periods to investigate was the one that provided the core of their language and the supposed basis for their powerful nation: the time of the Anglo-Saxons. Strengthening their relationship with a specific past was one way that Victorians responded to their uncertainty about human origins, which other disciplines were stirring up. The Anglo-Saxons were situated at a convenient historical distance for this purpose – recent enough for there to be written records of them, but distant enough that there was room for primitivist imagination to flourish. As the Introduction discussed, study of Old English language had practical origins in the early modern period as a means of unlocking the contents of medieval documents for political purposes.[1] Yet the Anglo-Saxons failed to capture the popular imagination until the advent of what E.J. Christie has termed "philological nationalism."[2] Interest in all aspects of the Anglo-Saxons grew over the nineteenth century to the point of widespread popularity as their society came to be seen as foundational to English identity.[3]

For over 300 years, English history before the Norman Conquest had primarily been pressed into the service of establishing precedents for English ecclesiastical and legal practices. The first few decades of the eighteenth century produced important but little-read works by a "nest of Saxonists" at Oxford – self-taught scholars who instilled their zeal in a small group of students.[4] Enthusiasm for the Anglo-Saxons plateaued while neoclassical admiration reigned,[5] but by the mid-nineteenth century, they were widely considered the founding fathers of English society.

---

[1] Murphy, "Antiquary to Academic," 3–4.

[2] T.A. Shippey and Andreas Haarder, eds., *Beowulf: The Critical Heritage*, Critical Heritage Series (London: Routledge, 1998), 26–28; E.J. Christie, "'An Unfollowable World': *Beowulf*, English Poetry, and the Phenomenalism of Language," *Literature Compass* 10, no. 7 (2013): 521.

[3] Clare A. Simmons, "'Iron-Worded Proof': Victorian Identity and the Old English Language," *Studies in Medievalism* 4 (1992): 210.

[4] Murphy, "Antiquary to Academic," 8.

[5] Allen J. Frantzen, *Desire for Origins: New Language, Old English, and Teaching the Tradition* (New Brunswick: Rutgers University Press, 1990), 50–51.

Recovering and reclaiming them – their language, literature, and perceived cultural strengths – formed part of what Meredith Martin has aptly called the "cross-disciplinary project of nation making."[6] The manifestations of nineteenth-century Anglo-Saxonism included plays, poems, historical novels, and amateur scholarship, with King Alfred proving an especially attractive figure for the imagination, one who could be invoked for opposing sides of various political debates.[7]

Tennyson was well positioned to participate in the phenomenon as he developed his literary skill. He partook of the century's Anglo-Saxonist enthusiasm from its early stages. He studied Old English in depth as a young man, when resources for doing so were scarce, and he was still intrigued by Anglo-Saxon literature as an old man, when he translated the poem "The Battle of Brunanburh." Sometimes his interest took the form of explicit references to England's presumed ancestors or oblique allusions in his political poems. More often, his poetry resonates with what his Cambridge friend John Mitchell Kemble called "echoes from the deserted temples of the past" in his stylistic choices.[8] This chapter explores which qualities of the Anglo-Saxons Tennyson found attractive, how he interacted with their texts, and how their poetry helped shape the patterns of his own.

Tennyson and Victorian Anglo-Saxonists

Tennyson had an interest in pre-Conquest Britain from childhood onward. His father's library contained books on the island's history, some with Alfred's name inscribed in them, as well as Thomas Percy's *Reliques of Ancient English Poetry*, a ballad collection that helped popularize early British folk literature. Once Tennyson came up to Trinity College, Cambridge, his familiarity with Anglo-Saxon history and literature was enhanced by his friendship with the members of the Cambridge Apostles. As the previous chapter described, the Apostles became early adopters of Germanic scholarship and philosophy, placing them on the leading edge of the eventual Victorian enthusiasm for all things "Teutonic." They half-jokingly called Tennyson "Alfred the great" in reference to the most famous Anglo-Saxon king,[9] and Kemble sometimes spelled his friend's name with the Old English orthography "Ælfred."[10]

Even if Tennyson had encountered no other source of information about the Anglo-Saxons, his friendship with Kemble would have guaranteed ample exposure to their language and literature, which in turn affected his own. Tennyson's friend came from a distinguished theatrical family, who were attuned to the nuances of

---

[6] Meredith Martin, *The Rise and Fall of Meter: Poetry and English National Culture, 1860–1930*, 1st ed. (Princeton: Princeton University Press, 2012), 19.

[7] Suzanne C. Hagedorn, "Received Wisdom: The Reception History of Alfred's Preface to the Pastoral Care," in *Anglo-Saxonism and the Construction of Social Identity*, ed. Allen J. Frantzen and John D. Niles (Gainesville, FL: University Press of Florida, 1997), 96–99; Pratt, "Anglo-Saxon Attitudes?: Alfred the Great and the Romantic National Epic," 141.

[8] John Mitchell Kemble, *The Anglo-Saxon Poems of Beowulf, the Travellers Song and the Battle of Finnesburh*, vol. 1 (London: Pickering, 1835), xxxii.

[9] Tennyson, *Letters*, 1982, 1:73.

[10] Catharine Bodham Johnson, *William Bodham Donne and His Friends* (London: Methuen, 1905), 16.

words. His father, it was said, would have been an excellent philologist had he chosen to pursue the subject.[11] The seeds of Kemble's interest in language having been sown by his family, they were likely cultivated by his schoolmaster, Charles Richardson, who compiled the first English dictionary to employ historical illustrations.[12] (Tennyson later owned a copy.)

As an undergraduate at Cambridge, Kemble pursued his own interests instead of the prescribed coursework, developing his taste for Old English and metaphysics rather than mathematics and classics. He recalled, moreover, that his membership in the Apostles was the most valuable aspect of his time at university:

> To my *education* given in that society I feel that I owe every power I possess, and the rescuing myself from a ridiculous state of prejudice and prepossessions with which I came armed to Cambridge. From "the Apostles" I, at least, learnt to think as a *free man*.[13]

In 1829, conferral of his degree having been deferred because he had used his exams to denounce the required reading, Kemble traveled to Germany, where he familiarized himself with German academic methodology.[14] He returned to England armed with the innovative, systematic comparative techniques of continental philology and an evangelical ardor for them. It would take more than a decade for British philologists – all of them more or less self-taught – to accept this new way of reconstructing the history of their own language.[15] Kemble proved to be a pioneer in Anglo-Saxon studies. In between alienating most members the academic community by decrying their recalcitrance, he edited the first English publications of *Beowulf* – the Old English text in 1833 and a translation in 1837 – as well as publishing a two-volume history of the Anglo-Saxons, a pamphlet on their runes, six large volumes of their charters that remained authoritative for the better part of a century, editions of various other texts, and articles on archaeology.

Kemble's exuberance was not limited to academic forums; he was zealous in his political, social, and scholarly views all his life, whether expressing them in private letters, at the Cambridge Union debating society, or in print. When R.J. Tennant wrote to Tennyson describing an evening with the Apostles, he included the report that "Kemble got into a passion about nothing but quickly jumped out again," an event that was no doubt very common.[16] Indeed, his enthusiasm for whatever had seized his attention at the moment was always uncontainable; those in

---

[11] Bruce Dickins, "John Mitchell Kemble and Old English Scholarship," *Proceedings of the British Academy* 25 (1939): 51.
[12] E.G. Stanley, *Imagining the Anglo-Saxon Past: The Search for Anglo-Saxon Paganism and Anglo-Saxon Trial by Jury* (Cambridge: D.S. Brewer, 2000), 30.
[13] Quoted in Peter Allen, *The Cambridge Apostles: The Early Years* (Cambridge: Cambridge University Press, 1978), 8.
[14] Dickins, "John Mitchell Kemble and Old English Scholarship," 54–55.
[15] Richard Marggraf Turley, "Nationalism and the Reception of Jacob Grimm's Deutsche Grammatik by English-Speaking Audiences," *German Life and Letters* 54, no. 3 (July 2001): 234–252.
[16] Hallam Tennyson, *Memoir*, 1:44.

communication with him at all were bound to hear his latest harangue.[17] Sometimes this was a source of eye-rolling amusement bordering on annoyance, as when he decided that coffee and tea were unhealthy and therefore breakfast should be accompanied by wine or beer. Of this crusade, fellow Apostle J.W. Blakesley remarked that Kemble considered it so important in early 1830 that, "although he sent much good counsel to us [in a recent letter] concerning the conduct of our lives, he began and ended it by advice concerning the conduct of our breakfasts." Trench received a similar diatribe.[18]

If Kemble was so insistent on the rather trivial matter of breakfast beverages, his proselytizing of philology was impossible to avoid, for the history and languages of Germanic peoples occupied him to the point of obsession for most of his adult life. Letters between the Apostles show that he shared his knowledge of these subjects with his friends, who then continued to discuss his ideas within their circle. In 1832, Arthur Hallam reported to Tennyson:

> The last two days Kemble has been staying here. He has been very lively but he is so absorbed in Gothic manuscripts, that however conversation may begin he is sure to make it end in that. If one says "a fine day John" he answers "very true, and it is a curious fact that in the nine thousandth line of the first Edda, the great giant Hubbadub makes precisely the same remark to the brave knight Siegfried."[19]

Around the same time, Tennyson's brother Charles reported after a trip to London: "John Kemble is buried in Gothic manuscripts, and will only talk of Runes and Eddas, and of the brave knight Siegfried."[20]

Six months later (in early 1833), Hallam wrote to Kemble that he was attempting to acquire a copy of the latter's article "On English Præterites." By then, Kemble had already warned him about a needed emendation with such fervency that Hallam wryly assured his friend that he would "cheerfully … make with pencil or pen that important alteration of *swylce* for *swylke* on which the destinies of mankind may be reasonably supposed to depend."[21] In point of fact, Hallam was mistaken about the intended correction. Kemble's printed text attempts to correct a footnote in Frederic Madden's edition of *Havelok the Dane* (1828) in which Madden quotes *Beowulf*.[22] Kemble was working on his own edition of *Beowulf* at the time and so was well positioned to notice transcription errors. In his article, Kemble tried to emend Madden's text from *swyke* to *swylce* (replacing *k* with *lc*), but a typographical error had produced *swlyce* in the "corrected" text (reversing the *y* and *l* in Kemble's new word). It must have been an infuriating error for the meticulous Kemble, especially in the context of making a textual correction. He evidently shared his annoyance

---

[17] See, for example, Tennyson, *Letters*, 1982, 1:185.
[18] Richard Chenevix Trench, *Letters and Memorials*, ed. Maria Marcia Fanny Trench, vol. 1 (London: Kegan Paul, Trench, 1888), 49, 52.
[19] Arthur Henry Hallam, *The Letters of Arthur Henry Hallam*, ed. Jack Kolb (Columbus: Ohio State University Press, 1981), 646.
[20] Hallam Tennyson, *Memoir*, 1:102.
[21] Hallam, *Letters*, 738.
[22] Frederick Madden, *The Ancient English Romance of Havelok the Dane: Accompanied by the French Text* (London: W. Nichol, Shakespeare Press for the Roxburghe Club, 1828), 197.

with his friends. In Hallam's copy of the article, which was a gift from the author, the transposition of letters has been corrected by hand in the margin – presumably by Kemble.[23] Hallam's confusion should caution us against assuming that all the Apostles had equal expertise, but this exchange also shows that they regularly discussed philological ideas and their current projects. Kemble's projects were extensive, especially when it came to examining original documents. In 1834, five years after leaving Cambridge and two years after his friends reported him being "absorbed" and "buried" in manuscripts, he believed that he had "read through almost, if not every Anglo-Saxon MS in England."[24]

The letters and references that remain indicate that, certainly in the years immediately following university, Kemble and Tennyson were closer friends than many even within the Apostles. They dined and smoked together in London, and Kemble's letters to others would sometimes contain drafts of Tennyson's latest compositions. An 1832 gathering at Kemble's home saw Tennyson performing a series of imitations, including "a Teutonic deity."[25] At the beginning of 1833, Kemble wrote to Tennyson and included some comments – written in runes – about the latter's recent poems. Unfortunately, the poet's son excised the actual runic message when cutting and pinning together the draft materials for his memoir.[26] Although we do not have the rest of the letter, Tennyson was evidently meant to be able to decode the message, for Kemble playfully admonished, "Don't tell anyone what I have said above in the Runes!" At the end of the same year, Cambridge Apostle Stephen Spring Rice sent Tennyson (on Kemble's behalf) "to fill up your leisure hours a folio Saxo-Grammaticus … to be jammed into the bowl of your pipe."[27] In 1835, fellow Apostle John Moore Heath wrote a letter to accompany a package of books Tennyson had requested to borrow. Heath noted that he was including "a Teutonic song which Kemble has imported."[28]

In addition to Kemble sending Germanic reading to his friend, Tennyson was evidently aware of Kemble's latest efforts in the field. For example, he mentioned "vague" thoughts of attending Kemble's 1834 Cambridge lectures on "History of the English Language, First, or Anglo-Saxon Period," though it is unclear whether he ever did. And he was aware of Kemble's work on *Beowulf* before it was published; there is no explanation needed for the announcement, "I rejoice to say *Beowulf* is out" – and in reply, "I am heartily glad you have got *Beowulf* out."[29] Kemble gave Ten-

---

[23] John Mitchell Kemble, "On English Præterites," inscribed "Arthur H. Hallam from His Affectionate Friend. J. M. Kemble," 1833, collection of Simon Keynes, Trinity College Cambridge, 10.
[24] Kemble, *Correspondence*, 49.
[25] Tennyson, *Letters*, 1982, 1:74–77, xx.
[26] Philip L. Elliott, *The Making of the Memoir*, Tennyson Society Monographs 12 (Lincoln: Tennyson Society, 1995), 9.
[27] Tennyson, *Letters*, 1982, 1:86, 98–99. Saxo Grammaticus ("Saxo the learned") wrote the first history of the Danes, at the beginning of the thirteenth century. Interest in his writing increased greatly in the nineteenth century, including drawing connections between Saxo's ancient heroes and the figures of Anglo-Saxon and Norse literature. Saxo Grammaticus, *The History of the Danes*, 1980, 1:1; Saxo Grammaticus, *The History of the Danes*, 1980, 2:4.
[28] Tennyson, *Letters*, 1982, 1:128.
[29] Ibid., 101, 98–101.

nyson an inscribed copy of at least the second volume of this project, the translation published in 1837. Although the Anglo-Saxonist drifted away from of his old friends somewhat in middle age as his attention shifted to archaeology in the aftermath of a bitter divorce, he and Tennyson remained friendly enough that Kemble's last book was sent as a gift to the poet soon after its author had died in 1857.[30] More than fifty years later, Tennyson's son cited a charter from Kemble's edition in an Eversley note on the historical figure depicted in the poem "Godiva." The fact indicates both how authoritative Kemble's publications had become and that Hallam Tennyson, at least, was reading them with some care.[31]

Kemble, of course, was far from the only scholar working to decipher and disseminate texts from this period of English history. Indeed, with the growth of Anglo-Saxon studies over the course of the century, he was but one member of a new generation of medievalists. Some of them, such as rector-antiquarian Samuel Fox (now largely forgotten) and Oxford professor Robert Meadows White, adhered to traditional antiquarian approaches;[32] others, such as Benjamin Thorpe, joined Kemble in embracing new-philological techniques as a means of unpacking the content of long-neglected manuscripts. Confident to the point of arrogance in the superiority of his methods, Kemble clashed with most other medievalists of his day, but he had far more in common with them than he would have liked to admit. The dynamics between them – both unconscious agreement and explicit disputes – provide a means of mapping the field of Anglo-Saxonism in the middle of the century. He was both typical and iconoclastic, making him a useful point of entry into the debates and assumptions encountered by Victorians who were interested the history of the English nation and its language.

By 1833, when Kemble's *Beowulf* appeared in print, the Anglo-Saxons had acquired enough cultural capital that he ignited a war of words in the *Gentleman's Magazine* over the proper way to study them. The inciting incident was a review he wrote lauding his friend Benjamin Thorpe's edition of the medieval poet Cædmon's metrical paraphrase of Scripture. The review opens by regretting that, after the important work of early Anglo-Saxon scholars in England, "we contentedly suffered ourselves to be outstripped, in every direction, by our continental brethren." Those responsible for "put[ting] us in the right road" again in recent years hailed from other nations, and they were so good at Old English that they could correct manuscript transcriptions without ever having seen the originals. Kemble gives particular credit to Rask and Grimm, Reinhold Schmid's edition of Anglo-Saxon laws,[33] and N.F.S. Grundtvig's *Beowulf* emendations.[34] Only after asserting the superiority of continental scholars does Kemble turn to praising Thorpe's work, pointing out that

---

[30] Emily Tennyson, *Lady Tennyson's Journal*, ed. James O. Hoge (Charlottesville: University Press of Virginia, 1981), 113.

[31] Tennyson, *Poems II*, 344.

[32] Thomas, "'Modest but Well-Deserved Claims': The Friendship of Samuel Fox and Joseph Bosworth and the Study of Anglo-Saxon in the Nineteenth Century," 228–229, 237.

[33] Reinhold Schmid, *Die Gesetze Der Angelsachsen* (Leipzig: F.A. Brockhaus, 1832).

[34] Kemble refers to Grundtvig's "Danish paraphrase of Beowulf" – either "Om Bjovulfs Drape" (1817) or *Bjowulfs Drape* (1820). Kemp Malone, "Grundtvig as Beowulf Critic," *The Review of English Studies* 17, no. 66 (April 1941): 130.

Thorpe "has studied in this sound school of northern philologists" and implying that such study is the reason for his success.[35]

A flurry of angry letters from other medievalists appeared in the magazine for nearly two years afterward, both attacking and defending Kemble's statements about the flaws in the old methods of Anglo-Saxon research. A year after his first review, he provoked anger again in the course of reviewing Thorpe's *Analecta Anglo-Saxonica*, an anthology of Old English texts. In this second salvo, he noted that Thorpe's work was especially needed in England. He took the opportunity to observe that without the Danes and Germans and those who studied them, "we might still be where we were, with idle texts, idle grammars, idle dictionaries, and the consequences of all these – idle and ignorant scholars." National pride was at stake over who was doing the best work on Anglo-Saxon, and Kemble announced in no uncertain terms that it was not the English. In fact, he wrote, his countrymen of the old school had committed such gross errors in grammar that if those lazy mistakes had been "perpetrated by a boy in the second form of a public school," they would have rightly resulted in "a liberal application of ferula or direr birch" – that is, corporal punishment.[36]

In addition to the angry replies in the magazine, a pamphlet appeared a year after the first review, entitled *The Anglo-Saxon Meteor, or Letters in Defence of Oxford, treating of the Wonderful Gothic Attainments of John M. Kemble of Trinity College, Cambridge*. Written in the voice of an Oxford academic, it assaulted Kemble's integrity both personally and professionally.[37] He struck back with an article in the *Gentleman's Magazine* on "Oxford Professors of Anglo-Saxon," taking aim at the academic establishment that he saw as clinging to the antiquarian methods that had dominated the field for too long.[38] That such a sustained and pointed argument could take place so publicly, much of it in a popular magazine, speaks to a growing national investment in the ownership of Anglo-Saxon documents. These texts had been out of sight and out of mind for centuries. Now they were considered vital to understanding what it meant to be English, and their language was the way to understand them. Philology helped decipher Old English and offered evidence for continuity between the Anglo-Saxons and modern citizens. The stakes had been raised over the question of how to pursue linguistic research correctly.

Among those who agreed with Kemble on the superiority of the new-philological approach was Thomas Wright, who had been his student. Wright came up to Trinity College, Cambridge in 1830, the year that Kemble received his degree (after his hiatus abroad). Like Kemble, Wright devoted much of his time as an undergraduate to pursuing historical research of his own rather than his formal studies. Upon returning from forays in Germany (for academic purposes) and Spain (for political ones), Kemble tutored Wright in Anglo-Saxon topics, teaching his protégé for "several hours of the day for nearly three years." However, the relationship seems to

---

[35] John Mitchell Kemble, "Review of Cædmon's Metrical Paraphrase," *The Gentleman's Magazine*, April 1833, 329.
[36] John Mitchell Kemble, "Review of Analecta Anglo-Saxonica," *The Gentleman's Magazine*, April 1834, 392.
[37] Kemble, *Correspondence*, 9.
[38] Kemble, "Oxford Professors of Anglo-Saxon."

have soured at that point. During of the *Gentleman's Magazine* controversy of 1833–1834, Wright publicly defended the luminaries of the old school whose work had advanced Anglo-Saxon studies in their day, and he lashed out at Kemble's *Beowulf*, writing that in its pages, "We have no longer Anglo-Saxon but German Saxon."[39] Wright's insult to Kemble's (supposedly nonnative) style essentially confirms Kemble's original point that it was continental scholars – or Englishmen trained by them – who were doing most of the work on Old English texts, but it further divided the two men. By 1835, the rift between them had widened further. Kemble believed that his mentee had used a transcription of his while the elder scholar was away in Germany, without permission – and worse, that Wright had treated his subjects superficially, seeking the reputation and money to be gained from publishing rather than focusing on the quality of his scholarship.[40]

Wright took Kemble's disdain for jealousy; his former teacher denied it, saying he could hardly feel jealous toward someone whom he had trained from scratch and who had "utterly disappointed me by making none of the progress which I had a right to expect from him." Kemble dismissed Wright's publications as "crude notes" plagiarized from his instructor's ideas, saying that Wright had spun out several years of work based on "the scraps of knowledge he picked up from me at Cambridge, and upon transcripts stolen from my books, & used without restraint or acknowledgment." To Grimm he fumed:

> I had the pleasure of seeing my views travestied, my collections ill-used, and the whole subject on which I have long been working most groundedly and seriously, taken out of my hands, and miserably ill-treated in a flippant, superficial, wretched style, by a man who has not a thought on the subject but what he has picked up from me.

In short, "He is a literary pirate, and as ignorant as he is impudent."[41] Kemble certainly had a way with insults, his rhetoric sharpening the angrier he became. His lack of diplomacy, unsurprisingly, did no favors for his career or his relationships with other medievalists.

The irony of this feud is that Wright and Kemble shared academic passions and followed similar career arcs. After focusing on their personal intellectual interests at Cambridge, both men published prolifically, though Wright on a wider range of subjects and often much more cursorily. Both unsuccessfully sought academic positions; the *Oxford Dictionary of National Biography* notes that "temperamentally [Wright] does not seem to have been a very employable person," a statement that could have been applied equally to his former mentor.[42] Both of them joined or

---

[39] Quoted in Gretchen P. Ackerman, "J.M. Kemble and Sir Frederic Madden: 'Conceit and Too Much Germanism'?," in *Anglo-Saxon Scholarship: The First Three Centuries*, ed. Carl T. Berkhout and Milton McC. Gatch, A Reference Publication in Literature (Boston: G.K. Hall, 1982), 173.

[40] Kemble, *Correspondence*, 233, 140–141.

[41] Ibid., 141, 152, 112, 152.

[42] Michael Welman Thompson, "Wright, Thomas (1810–1877)," in *Oxford Dictionary of National Biography*, September 17, 2015.

helped found numerous learned societies, and both gravitated in later years toward archaeology.

Wright and Kemble did not even greatly disagree intellectually, though Kemble was a more diligent researcher. Indeed, Wright remained firmly aligned with the new philology long after he and Kemble fell out. In a book of medievalist essays that he published in 1846 – more than a decade after his former mentor had called him a "literary pirate" – Wright agreed that "It has been reserved for our own days, and (to our shame be it spoken) for foreigners, to revive the study of a language which must, on so many accounts, be interesting to Englishmen." He praised Grimm's system of language study and asserted, "it is by an appreciation of this system only that we can proceed in the Anglo-Saxon with any degree of security."[43]

Kemble was equally frustrated by Frederic Madden, whom he somewhat unfairly considered a rival, despite their philological views fundamentally aligning. Six years older than Kemble, Madden was self-taught in the literature of multiple languages from an early age. He matriculated at Oxford but did not have the resources to support himself to completion of a degree, instead gaining experience helping copy and catalogue manuscripts.[44] Kemble referred to Madden as "a good scholar" in his first letter to Grimm in 1832,[45] at which time Madden was working as assistant keeper in the department of manuscripts at the British Museum. (He was promoted to keeper in 1837.)[46] Despite his early praise, Kemble was not shy about publicly pointing out Madden's errors, and he considered the slightly older man a partisan of the old guard of antiquarians. Madden took seriously Kemble's critiques and improved his scholarship in response to them, but Kemble grew if anything more critical as the years went by. Part of his bitterness stemmed from jealousy over Madden's professional success: in addition to his position at the British Museum, Madden succeeded in seeking a knighthood, while Kemble struggled to receive formal recognition of his achievements.[47] Nevertheless, Madden set aside his pride when weighing in on the *Gentleman's Magazine* fracas. He wrote that "Mr. Kemble ... is in the right, and ... the old school of Saxonists ... did not study the language on those sound principles of grammar and analogy which have recently been pointed out to us by the Northern philologists."[48]

Among the Oxford professors of the previous generation whom Kemble railed against, a key figure was John Josias Conybeare. Conybeare was an Oxford alumnus who had received his BA in 1801. He was ordained the following year but returned to Oxford in 1808 as professor of Anglo-Saxon for four years. He went on to serve as professor of poetry, alongside his duties as a priest. As an academic, he published several papers on geology and many more on Anglo-Saxon texts. His *Illustrations*

---

[43] Thomas Wright, *Essays on Subjects Connected with the Literature, Popular Superstitions and History of England in the Middle Ages*, vol. 1 (London: John Russell Smith, 1846), 5, 7.
[44] Michael Borrie, "Madden, Sir Frederic (1801–1873)," in *Oxford Dictionary of National Biography*, August 10, 2023.
[45] Kemble, *Correspondence*, 21.
[46] Borrie, "Madden, Sir Frederic (1801–1873)."
[47] Ackerman, "J.M. Kemble and Sir Frederic Madden," 171.
[48] Quoted in ibid., 174.

70 *Tennyson's Philological Medievalism*

of Anglo-Saxon Poetry came out posthumously in 1826, edited by his brother[49] – a book Tennyson likely consulted. Conybeare had been dead for eleven years when the pamphlet *The Anglo-Saxon Meteor* made its vicious attack on Kemble and his work, but Kemble used him as a proxy for the Oxford establishment that he perceived as holding back the field of Anglo-Saxon studies. He later came to believe that the letters and pamphlet had not come from Oxford after all, "and I therefore regret the sledge-hammer style in which I belaboured poor Conybeare."[50]

Joseph Bosworth was a near-contemporary of Conybeare's but lived longer and therefore had more influence on the field. In 1823, Bosworth published an Anglo-Saxon grammar drawing on the works of major eighteenth-century predecessors George Hickes and Edward Lye. An abridged version of Bosworth's grammar came out a few years later, coinciding with Conybeare's *Illustrations* and around the time Tennyson and his friends were coming up to Cambridge. Bosworth's major contribution to the field was an Old English dictionary (1838), which Tennyson later owned. Bosworth was clearly familiar with the work of continental philologists, but he mostly drew conclusions based on his personal reading of his predecessors and the material he could access himself. He was appointed Rawlinson professor of Anglo-Saxon at Oxford in 1858. Nine years later, as described in the Introduction, he gave £10,000 to found an equivalent professorship at Cambridge. This was a gift made possible by the robust sales of his publications, further evidence of the growing interest in Anglo-Saxon subjects.[51]

When *The Anglo-Saxon Meteor* was published attacking him, Kemble suspected Bosworth of being its author, and he lashed out with typical ferocity. Once again, however, the animosity seems to have been one-sided. In the preface to his dictionary, for example, Bosworth noted that Kemble gave "an improved Saxon text" as compared to the parts of *Beowulf* that Conybeare had printed. And unbeknownst to Kemble, Bosworth wrote to a collaborator about the fight taking place in the press: "You will see how poor Kemble has been buffeted. Such angry squabbles do no good. I wrote one letter to compose the strife."[52]

With Bosworth, as with other scholars whose achievements define nineteenth-century Anglo-Saxonism, the rift with Kemble centered on the relative rigor of their work rather than any essential disagreement about the importance of understanding the Old English language and sharing the documents written in it. For those not as concerned with the degree of precision that Kemble demanded of his fellow researchers, the differences between these men did not rise to the level of ignoring any of their contributions. Tennyson was not pursuing philological study to the same degree as his friend, but he read widely and deeply about the history of his language. In fact, he owned or consulted books by most of the major scholars

---

[49] H.S. Torrens, "Conybeare, John Josias (1779–1824), Geologist, Antiquary, and Church of England Clergyman," in *Oxford Dictionary of National Biography*, September 28, 2006.
[50] Kemble, *Correspondence*, 108.
[51] Bradley and Haigh, "Bosworth, Joseph."
[52] Quoted in E.G. Stanley, "J. Bosworth's Interest in 'Friesic' for His Dictionary of the Anglo-Saxon Language (1838): 'The Friesic Is Far the Most Important Language for My Purpose,'" in *Aspects of Old Frisian Philology*, ed. Rolf H. Bremmer Jr, Geart van der Meer, and Oebele Vries (Amsterdam: Rodopi, 1990), 447.

who were bringing Old English into print. He was quite catholic in his medievalist self-education, making use of works by Anglo-Saxonists whom Kemble excoriated – another good reminder not to conflate their opinions overmuch. Precisely because he was not embroiled in the minutiae that occupied true experts, Tennyson seems to have understood better than his friend that although Kemble and his colleagues clashed over academic methodology, "they shared ... an attitude toward the past, which they saw in vital relationship to the present," as Allen J. Frantzen has put it.[53] It is the claim of this book that Tennyson likewise saw the past in vital relationship to the present, from the origins of single words to the enduring practices of government institutions. The following sections outline how he learned about the specifically Anglo-Saxon past and brought it into the present of his own poetry.

The work that first introduced the Anglo-Saxons to a large number of Britons was Sharon Turner's *History of the Anglo-Saxons*, published in the years straddling the turn of the nineteenth century (1799–1805). Turner's *History* went through many editions, disseminating the idea that the core strengths of England were to be found in Anglo-Saxon sociopolitical structures. It was the unrivalled authority on the subject until Kemble produced his own history, *The Saxons in England* (1849), his most broadly accessible work and the one for which he was best known in his own day.[54] Even then, Turner's *magnum opus* retained widespread respect. The usually quarrelsome Kemble cites Turner on only one occasion in his own two-volume effort, leaving his predecessor's reputation to continue undisturbed. Tennyson owned a later edition of Kemble's work, as well as a copy of the second edition of Turner (1807), in which the poet marked passages he apparently intended to reuse elsewhere.

Tennyson's overt depictions of Anglo-Saxon themes are fairly rare, but there is evidence that he considered writing a narrative poem about that society. Marginalia in his copy of Turner's *History* show the poet selecting specific passages for some kind of reuse. These passages, which Tennyson numbered 1–7, are taken from the story of the gradual conversion of the Anglo-Saxons to Christianity, with Turner's rendition paraphrasing the Venerable Bede's *Ecclesiastical History of the English People*. The episodes that Tennyson marked are as follows: Section 1 consists of one sentence noting that Gregory the Great was "one of the few popes whose character has been distinguished by sincere religion." Section 2 (making up thirty-three lines of body text in Turner's book) tells of Gregory seeing English youths for sale in Rome and beings struck by "their fair and beautiful countenances." When he learns they are called Angles, he cries, "Angles! that is to say, angels. They have angel countenances, and ought to join the angelic companies." Turner's narrative continues:

> The name of their province, Deira, was a consonancy that struck him: "De ira, from wrath! – Yes, from the wrath of God they must be plucked, and brought to the grace of Christ." ... [H]e heard that their king's name was Ella; and ... he exclaimed, "Alleluia! – they must sing Alleluias there in praise of their Creator."[55]

---

[53] Frantzen, *Desire for Origins*, 58.
[54] Dickins, "John Mitchell Kemble and Old English Scholarship," 68.
[55] Sharon Turner, *The History of the Anglo-Saxons* (Tennyson's copy), 2nd ed., vol. 2 (London: Longman, Hurst, Rees, and Orme, 1807), TRC/AT/2238, Lincolnshire Archives, Lincoln, UK, 432–434.

72 *Tennyson's Philological Medievalism*

Here Gregory performs a kind of wishful theological philology that must have appealed to Tennyson, because he employed it himself it in his play *Becket* (1884). Another character describes Becket carrying a cross thus: "As once he bore the standard of the Angles, / So now he bears the standard of the angels."[56]

The third and fourth sections Tennyson wanted to use (four lines and twenty-two lines long, respectively) comprise Gregory sending missionaries to England. The poet originally marked one long, contiguous section with the number 3, writing "turn" at the bottom of a page to indicate that the passage continued. However, he later crossed out two paragraphs and wrote "omit" in both the left and right margins next to them (see Figure 2). These paragraphs describe how the missionaries became frightened and turned back before Gregory ordered them to carry out the mission; it seems Tennyson wanted to simplify the narrative. The next two selected passages, which he has had to renumber after dividing the previous one, are short: single sentences of three lines each. They set up the story of the conversion of Northumbria, which began when King Edwin married the Christian princess of another kingdom.[57]

Section 7 (also renumbered) is considerably longer, measuring thirty-three lines of Turner's prose. It consists of the famous passage in which one of Edwin's ealdormen compares earthly life to the flight of a sparrow through the hall during a winter storm. Turner, like Bede before him, presents the ealdorman's speech as occurring after the pagan high priest has also advised converting to Christianity, pointing out that he (the priest) has been the most devoted follower of the old gods and yet has not benefited as much as others who were less pious – therefore the old gods are of no use. Tennyson has bracketed the printed words "The next speaker" (i.e., the ealdorman) and written in the margin, "One speaker." He evidently planned to put both arguments for conversion into the mouth of one character, probably once again to make the storytelling simpler. Turner's next paragraph reflects on how the ealdorman correctly identified "the great value of Christianity" as its "delightful assurance of a happy futurity." This paragraph is the last piece of marked text; after it, Tennyson has written "end" and underlined it twice.[58]

There is no way to know when Tennyson made these notes or why he did not follow through on the project, but its themes would have been at home in his oeuvre. Turner's concluding moral, that life is made meaningful by knowing there is an afterlife, was a point that Tennyson often made in personal conversation. As for the story, it offered fertile ground for what he did best. Tennyson wrote successful dramatic monologues and seems to have been especially drawn to writing in the voice of a historical or mythical figure, whether it be Ulysses, the Celtic queen Boudicëa, or the early Christian saint Simeon Stylites. The analogy of the sparrow in the hall would have provided scope for descriptions of both storm and revelry as part of an extended analogy. And because the story is one of conversion to Christianity, it would allow for some aesthetic exploration of Teutonic paganism, which writers

---

[56] Alfred Tennyson, *Becket and Other Plays*, Eversley Edition, vol. 9 of *The Works of Alfred Lord Tennyson*, ed. Hallam Tennyson (London: Macmillan, 1908), 62.
[57] Turner, *History* (Tennyson's copy), 2:437.
[58] Ibid., 2:439–440.

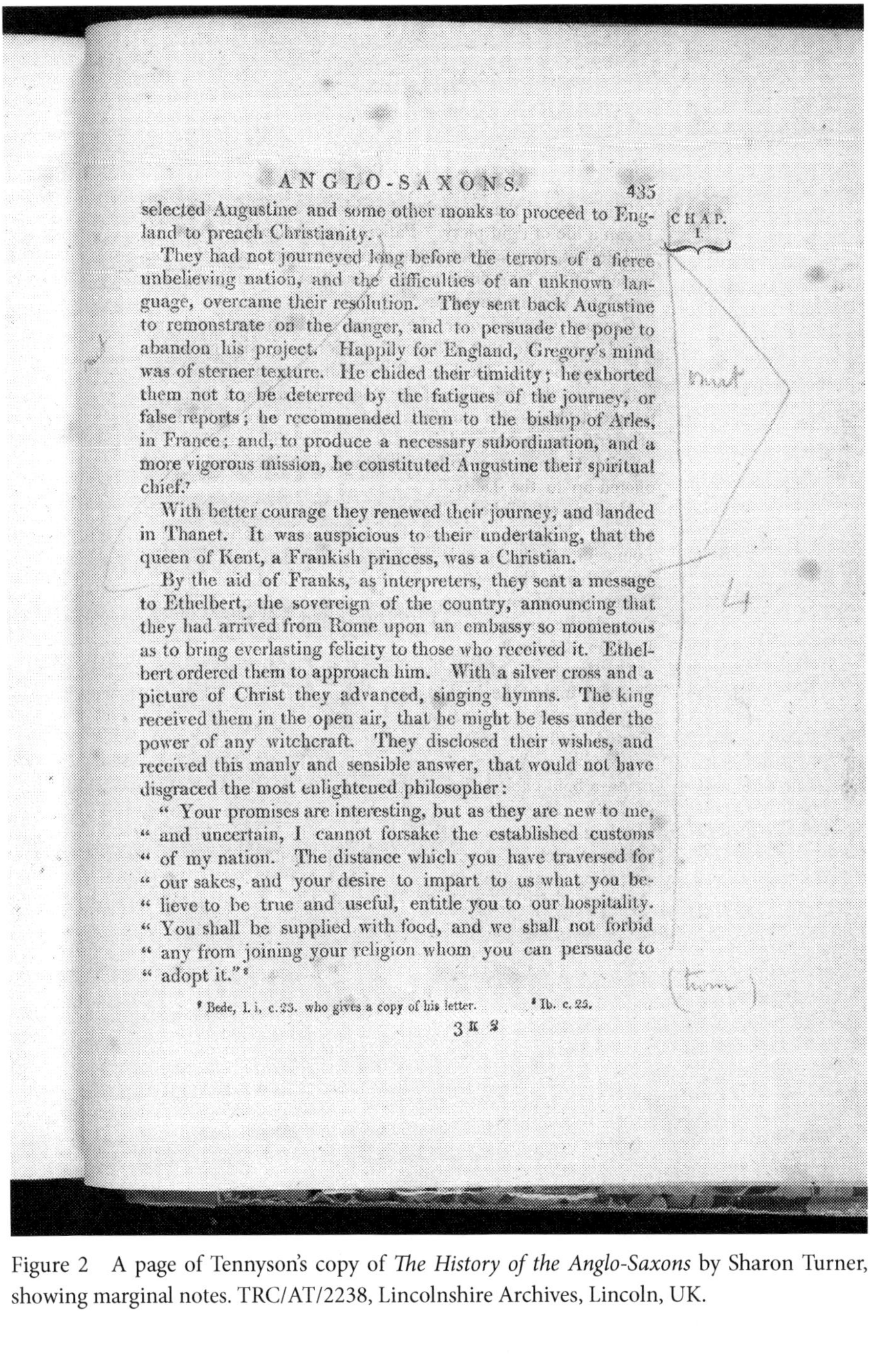

ANGLO-SAXONS. 435

selected Augustine and some other monks to proceed to England to preach Christianity.

They had not journeyed long before the terrors of a fierce unbelieving nation, and the difficulties of an unknown language, overcame their resolution. They sent back Augustine to remonstrate on the danger, and to persuade the pope to abandon his project. Happily for England, Gregory's mind was of sterner texture. He chided their timidity; he exhorted them not to be deterred by the fatigues of the journey, or false reports; he recommended them to the bishop of Arles, in France; and, to produce a necessary subordination, and a more vigorous mission, he constituted Augustine their spiritual chief.[7]

With better courage they renewed their journey, and landed in Thanet. It was auspicious to their undertaking, that the queen of Kent, a Frankish princess, was a Christian.

By the aid of Franks, as interpreters, they sent a message to Ethelbert, the sovereign of the country, announcing that they had arrived from Rome upon an embassy so momentous as to bring everlasting felicity to those who received it. Ethelbert ordered them to approach him. With a silver cross and a picture of Christ they advanced, singing hymns. The king received them in the open air, that he might be less under the power of any witchcraft. They disclosed their wishes, and received this manly and sensible answer, that would not have disgraced the most enlightened philosopher:

" Your promises are interesting, but as they are new to me,
" and uncertain, I cannot forsake the established customs
" of my nation. The distance which you have traversed for
" our sakes, and your desire to impart to us what you be-
" lieve to be true and useful, entitle you to our hospitality.
" You shall be supplied with food, and we shall not forbid
" any from joining your religion whom you can persuade to
" adopt it."[8]

[7] Bede, l. i, c. 23. who gives a copy of his letter. [8] Ib. c. 25.

3 K 2

Figure 2   A page of Tennyson's copy of *The History of the Anglo-Saxons* by Sharon Turner, showing marginal notes. TRC/AT/2238, Lincolnshire Archives, Lincoln, UK.

often found attractive. Primitivism, indeed, was a common theme in depictions of the Anglo-Saxons, even as historians traced a multitude of modern practices back to them.

Primitivism and Cultural Continuity

Nineteenth-century British Anglo-Saxonism thrived on the belief that certain qualities of ancient English culture were still working in and on a Victorian population. In the preface to his history, Turner explains that his first volume offers a general history of the period, and the second volume treats:

> the manners, landed property, government, laws, poetry, literature, religion, and language of the Anglo-Saxons. So much of our present state in all these interesting subjects has originated from our Anglo-Saxon ancestors, that it was necessary to be minute and faithful in the inquiry concerning them.[59]

This summary makes explicit the basic assumption of Turner's work, and that of his successors: the Anglo-Saxons are the origin of much of "our present state." This premise had been the basis of medievalist study in certain subjects since the days of Elizabeth I, but in the nineteenth century, researchers found persistent Anglo-Saxon practices within many more aspects of English society.

The organization of civic society, for example, was commonly understood as having early medieval roots. Kemble's *The Saxons in England* – published at the midpoint of the century – reads at times more like a treatise on political theory than a history, hypothesizing about the early stages of communal society with supporting evidence from charters and the etymologies of place names. He takes great care to establish how much land was granted to each freeman, how much land was available for common use, the rights and responsibilities of leaders, the origin of aristocracy, and similar matters. He was delighted to hear from readers who reported that in some places the division of farmland was nearly unchanged, further supporting the idea that the Anglo-Saxons still influenced daily life in his own time. From examining legal documents, Kemble concluded that the English had long had the innate ability to govern – a trait he credited to the Teutonic element of their heritage – though he was annoyed that the records showed them inclined to cede power to kings. Echoing the nativist Norman Yoke theory of history, he wrote to Grimm in a moment of frustration in 1839 that "The admixture of Norman feudalism early destroyed the integrity of our own law." However, his continued study of "our own law" belied that momentary pessimism, and three years later he exclaimed, "It is astonishing how much of [Anglo-Saxon law] still subsists unchanged among us!"[60]

Tennyson similarly idealized the political past in "Hail Briton!" (written between 1831 and 1833, but not published). Though now Britain's "steps are swift and rash," he writes:

---

[59] Sharon Turner, *The History of the Anglo-Saxons*, 2nd ed., vol. 1 (London: Longman, Hurst, Rees, and Orme, 1807), iii.

[60] Kemble, *Correspondence*, 273, 276, 181, 230.

> A stiller time thy fathers saw
> When each man by his hearth could sit,
> And lightly round his will were knit
> The cords of order and of law.   (22–28)

Like Kemble and Turner and many others before him, Tennyson associates the Anglo-Saxons with early British law and a sound societal organization. That stability was disturbed when power "festered in the hands of few" (32), a phrase that accords with Kemble's annoyance that history showed a tendency to grant increasing amounts of power to royalty. The same poem calls the English "men of Saxon pith of nerve," using *Saxon* as a metonym for all masculine values. In a similar vein, the "Ode on the Death of the Duke of Wellington" (1852) compares its subject to the great Anglo-Saxon king: "Truth-teller was our England's Alfred named; / Truth-lover was our English Duke" (188–189). Here the hero of the Napoleonic wars echoes the monarch who defended the nascent English nation against foreign invasion.

The impetus for investigating Anglo-Saxon history, then, was the belief that "we have a share in the past, and the past yet works in us." However, this enthusiasm for the past was complicated by the fact that, as much as nineteenth-century writers referred to "our forefathers," they did not credit them with many virtues except common sense and courage. Kemble was the most passionate of Anglo-Saxonists, but he also saw the subjects of his study as quite unsophisticated. He dedicated *The Saxons in England* to Queen Victoria, calling it a "history of the principles which have given her empire its pre-eminence among the nations of Europe … It is the history of the childhood of our own age – the explanation of its manhood."[61] This depiction of "childhood" epitomizes the combination of primitivism and reverence for origins that constituted nineteenth-century Anglo-Saxonism. In his introduction to *Beowulf*, Kemble exhorts his readers "to judge this poem, not by the measure of our times and creeds, but those of the times which it describes" – an apologetic argument for his material that was quite common by this time. He demonstrates his ambivalence about that period by describing it as "an age, wanting indeed in scientific knowledge, in mechanical expertness, even in refinement, but brave, generous and right-principled."[62] The description is typical in its contradictions.

When Jacob Grimm asked Kemble for any English references to the fable of Reynard the fox, the Englishman replied, "It is foreign to the genius of Anglo-Saxon morality. They were an extremely dull, calm, sober, common-sense people, and as for satire, God help them! they had not an atom." A few months later, he reiterated, "I do not think the story was known at all to the Saxons, its whole character was quite out of their way; they were a plain, hard headed and excellent people, full of common-sense, but for any thing beyond, quite dull."[63] More publicly, Kemble concluded an article on Anglo-Saxon runes with a discussion of riddles, noting, "[I]t may not be uninteresting to give the explanation of what our simple-minded forefathers may have exercised their wits upon, ten centuries ago."[64] He expressed

---

[61] Kemble, *The Saxons in England*, 1:viii, v.
[62] Kemble, *Beowulf*, 1:xxxi–xxxii.
[63] Kemble, *Correspondence*, 39, 57.
[64] John Mitchell Kemble, *Anglo-Saxon Runes* (Pinner: Anglo-Saxon Books, 1991), 62.

the paradox of Victorian Anglo-Saxonism best in the self-aware reflection, "There is a sanctity about the darkness in which the early history of nations is buried." It is a statement that acknowledges that the history of national origins is especially appealing when partly obscured. Yet, without completely drawing the veil of imagination, a historian could still peer at the "dim and shadowy giants which keep watch within the temple of ancient worlds."[65]

Primitivist fascination, combined with pride in an imagined social continuity, only increased as the century wore on; late in his career, Tennyson treated the subject in his most sustained portrayal of the Anglo-Saxons, the play *Harold*. He had first turned to the stage in 1874, twenty-four years into his term as poet laureate and having just finished writing the last of the *Idylls of the King*. His plays were self-consciously shaped in the tradition of Shakespeare's history plays, his first effort being *Queen Mary*. *Harold*, published two years later, told the story of the brief reign of the last Anglo-Saxon king. Tennyson's dedication cites his research sources as "old-world records – such as the Bayeux tapestry and the Roman de Rou"[66] (he had seen the Bayeux Tapestry on a trip in 1864),[67] followed by Edward Freeman's *History of the Norman Conquest* (1867–1876) and Edward Bulwer-Lytton's novel *Harold, the Last of the Saxon Kings* (1848).[68]

In his play, Tennyson emphasized the need for the people of Britain to unite. For example, Harold fails tactically because William the Conqueror is able to land while the Anglo-Saxon king is in the north, fighting off an invasion spurred by a dispute between Northumbrians and their former earl. The Northumbrians shout that they "are Danes, / Who conquer'd what we walk on, our own field." Harold replies with the analogy of a bundle of sticks being harder to break than a single twig and urges that they "snap not the faggot-band" of the nation, whatever their origins. Even William's final speech explicitly calls for unity:

> Of one self-stock at first,
> [I will] Make them again one people – Norman, English;
> And English, Norman; we should have a hand
> To grasp the world with, and a foot to stamp it…
> Flat.

Although Harold's common moniker, "the last English king of England," privileges the Saxon heritage, Tennyson depicts England as a land that transforms immigrants into its own citizens. In *Harold*, "the free wind from off our Saxon downs" seems to affect all those who make the land their home. After a military victory, Harold assures his soldiers that their deeds will shine as brightly as those of past kings, including "English Ironside / Who fought with Knut, or Knut who coming Dane / Died English." When William stands victor after a difficult battle in the closing

---

[65] Kemble, "Lajamon," 4.
[66] Alfred Tennyson, "Harold," in *Queen Mary and Harold*, Eversley Edition, vol. 8 of *The Works of Alfred Lord Tennyson*, ed. Hallam Tennyson (London: Macmillan, 1908), 109.
[67] Hallam Tennyson, *Alfred Lord Tennyson: A Memoir*, vol. 2 (London: Macmillan, 1897), 5.
[68] Tennyson, "Harold," 109.

lines of the play, he announces, "I am king of England ... And I will rule according to their laws."[69] There is no reason to make this resolution, having derided English custom earlier in the play, except that William is already becoming English, like Knut before him.

Tennyson also suggests a solution to the old problem of absorbing the Conquest into the noble history of Britain, pointing out that the Normans were originally seafarers from the same region as the Anglo-Saxons. As quoted earlier, William resolves to take people "Of one self-stock at first, / [and] Make them *again* one people" (my emphasis). The *Times* reviewer, whose words are included as an appendix in the Eversley Edition, makes the connection explicit by attributing William's ferocity as an opponent to "the spirit of the sea-wolves":

> If the old Norse speech hardly survived..., if the old Norse freedom had vanished from the settlement on the Seine, if the children of the pirates had become feudal nobles, yet at least there was one man [William] in whom the spirit of the sea-wolves lived on.[70]

Here, then, is an interpretation in which the Norman Conquest was really a rejoining of two Germanic branches, one of which – the Anglo-Saxons – had better preserved the "old Norse freedom." Tennyson does not appear to have delved deeply into Norse history, but he was at least somewhat familiar with it. He owned an edition of *Grettis Saga* as translated from Icelandic by Eirikr Magnusson and William Morris (1869), as well as *The Story of Burnt Njal* "from the Icelandic of the Njals Saga" (1861). Hallam Tennyson also recorded a conversation with his father in which the poet "touched on the old religions and the 'old god of war'; 'the Norse mythology,' he said, 'is finer than the Greek with its human gods, though the Greek has more beauty.'"[71] In *Harold*, Tennyson develops a narrative that runs counter to the nativist Norman Yoke interpretation of history. In this understanding, it was the very amalgamation of nationalities that made the Victorian British population strong. Tennyson, for example, positioned his play as one of a trilogy that "portray[s] the making of England," noting: "In *Harold* we have the great conflict between Danes, Saxons, and Normans for supremacy ... and the forecast of the greatness of our composite race."[72]

Shortly after *Harold* was published, Tennyson replied to a letter from the American poet Henry Wadsworth Longfellow and wrote, "You ask 'What old ancestor spoke through you?' I fear none of mine fought for England on the Hill of Senlac, for, as far as I know, I am part Dane, part Norman."[73] This remark makes clear that the collective Anglo-Saxon ancestry was understood to be at least partly an imaginative construct. The Anglo-Saxons were ancestors of the Victorians more by virtue of their language, laws, institutions, superstitions, sayings, and place names than by biology. Tennyson's genes were Danish and Norman, to the best of his knowledge,

---

[69] Ibid., 284–285, 327, 312, 379, 263, 327. Ellipses are Tennyson's.
[70] Ibid., 363–364.
[71] Hallam Tennyson, *Memoir*, 1:256.
[72] Tennyson, "Queen Mary," 331.
[73] Tennyson, *Letters*, 1982, 3:141.

yet he was unquestionably an inheritor of Anglo-Saxon society. He, too, could "love [his] land, with love far-brought / From out the storied Past, and used / Within the Present" ("Love thou thy land" 1–3).

For nineteenth-century historians, an especially intriguing connection between the "storied Past" and the present was the lingering paganism that they found hidden within modern life. In fact, Wright declared in 1846 that mythology and superstitions reveal the "inner texture of the national character, more deeply than any other circumstances, even in language itself."[74] Wright's former mentor Kemble may not have gone so far as to rank any other cultural touchstone above language, but his writings express a typical fascination with the pagan component of Anglo-Saxon culture. Though the Anglo-Saxons were Christianized centuries before the Norman Conquest, they had brought with them to Britain a pantheon related to Norse mythology, and Kemble wrote that an echo of these pagan beliefs "yet subsists among us in many of our most cherished superstitions," having been retained by the pre-Reformation church. They might even "yet lurk in the habits and belief of many Protestants." Further, he claimed that although Christian missionaries had suppressed Teutonic national deities, yet old household gods "inform the daily life of a people who are still unconsciously acted upon by ancient national feelings."[75]

Wright certainly imbibed this belief from his teacher; he likewise argued that although Christianity eliminated the worship of Woden/Odin, belief in lesser supernatural entities endured:

> The common ceremonies of life at every minute bore allusions to them; things so difficult to eradicate, that now, after so many centuries ... in our salutations, in our eating and drinking, even in our children's games, we are perpetually, though unwittingly, doing the same things which our forefathers did to honour or in fear of the elves and nymphs of the heathen creed.[76]

A generation before, Thomas Warton had hypothesized in his *History of English Poetry* (1871) that those who converted to Christianity were "rarely free" from the impressions that paganism had made on their minds in infancy, for such impressions "always maintain ground in the recesses of the mind." As a result, "many must have retained a lurking conviction of the truth of their former belief," and the old and new faiths blended together over time.[77]

In *Harold*, Tennyson depicts pagan beliefs as being fresh in the collective memory of the Anglo-Saxons. As Harold chafes under the idea that the Norman saints on whose bones he swore might aid William's cause, he cries:

> better, Woden, all
> Our cancell'd warrior-gods, our grim Walhalla,
> Eternal war, than that the Saints at peace

---

[74] Wright, *Essays*, 1:237.
[75] Kemble, *The Saxons in England*, 1:328–329, 332.
[76] Wright, *Essays*, 1:240.
[77] Thomas Warton, *History of English Poetry from the Twelfth to the Close of the Sixteenth Century*, ed. W. Carew Hazlitt, vol. 1 (Reeves and Turner, 1871), 38–39.

> The Holiest of our Holiest one should be
> This William's fellow-tricksters[.]

Harold is clearly not a pagan; on the contrary, he sees the belief system to which Woden belonged as a barbaric one. He uses it as a rhetorical comparison to condemn the idea of saints participating in trickery. Nonetheless, the reference also reinforces an affinity with those old beliefs – they are "ours," and despite being "cancelled," they have a place in cultural memory. Woden receives another reference in the penultimate scene, as Archbishop Stigand describes the climactic battle in real time:

> how their lances snap and shiver
> Against the shifting blaze of Harold's axe!
> War-woodman of old Woden, how he fells
> The mortal copse of faces!

Kemble had suggested that the old northern gods still lurked within daily life in superstitions, place names, and expressions – as indeed the memory of alliterative verse lurks in these lines. Certainly, in this play, Tennyson presents characters who are barely removed from a religious system that is tied to their character. After a military victory, one thane describes the fight as:

> a war-crash, and so hard,
> So loud, that, by St Dunstan, old St Thor –
> By God, we thought him dead – but our old Thor
> Heard his own Thunder again, and woke and came
> Among us again, and mark'd the sons of those
> Who made this Britain England, break the North.[78]

St. Dunstan, an Anglo-Saxon Christian bishop, is soon superseded by the nonexistent, impossible "St Thor" – the Germanic god, not dead after all but awoken and walking among the English in their moment of glorious battle.

In his poetry, Tennyson rarely referred to ancient religion, but he considered doing so at different times throughout his career. Thor appeared in an unadopted stanza of "The New Timon, and the Poets," for example:

> And mobs no doubt will often make
> The judgment private taste abhors;
> We shall not wonder if they take
> Your penny-hammer, Sir, for Thor's.[79]

The pagan god had a more substantial presence in "What Thor Said to the Bard Before Dinner," a poem that Hallam Tennyson printed in his memoir. In this work, the elder Tennyson used the dynamic imagery of Thor's hammering to react against a negative review. Transforming the poet's instrument into a *rhymehammer*, Thor

---

[78] Tennyson, "Harold," 278, 319, 298.
[79] Tennyson, *The Poems of Tennyson*, 1987, 2:180.

urges him to make truth ring out against any and all offenders. The first stanza gives a flavor of this remarkable poem:

> Wherever evil customs thicken
> Break through with the hammer of iron rhyme,
> Till priestcraft and kingcraft sicken
> But papmeatpamper not the time
> With the race of the thunderstricken.
> If the world call out, lay harder upon her
> Till she clapperclaw no longer,
> Bang thy stithy stronger and stronger,
> Thy rhymehammer shall have honour.   (1–9)

Appropriately, the subtitle was "The sledge-hammer song." Its rhythm is conspicuous and cannot be described satisfactorily by classically derived metrical terms.

Derek Attridge remarks that "From the start of his career as a poet Tennyson enjoyed varying both the numbers of beats in the line and the number of syllables between the beats."[80] Such rhythmic variety no doubt owed something to ballad tradition and other forms of popular song; a notebook from his university days contains nearly twenty pages of collected nursery rhymes, indicating an interest in their rhythm and effect.[81] Tennyson's accentual freedom may also originate in the dolnik pattern Attridge identifies as unconsciously structuring so much of English poetry. "What Thor Said" is a good candidate for inclusion as dolnik, alternating (after the first two lines) between lines of four and three realized beats. Yet it also strains the qualities of dolnik with deviations such as when the second stanza collapses into a two-beat pair in which the reader can easily stumble when determining where to place stresses: "This way and that, nail / Tagrag and bobtail" (16–17). Tennyson's sense of freedom – particularly in poems involving Thor – surely also derived from Old English prosody, which is based on alliteration and is free to vary the number of syllables in a line. "What Thor Said" is also full of faux-archaic compounds (priestcraft, kingcraft, papmeatpamper, clapperclaw, thunderstricken, rhymehammer) that imitate Old English both linguistically and poetically.

Tennyson's only published poem to portray northern European heathendom revives stylistic traits that had gone into "What Thor Said" thirty-five years earlier. "The Victim" (1868) describes how a priest seeks to relieve a land ravaged by plague and famine through the sacrifice of the person dearest to the king. The king's son having been selected, the queen intervenes and demands her right to die in the place of her child. When the monarch's face betrays that his wife is, in fact, dearest to him, she is killed accordingly. Taking the story from Charlotte M. Yonge's *Book of Golden Deeds*, which attributes "neither time nor place" to it, Tennyson "made it Scandinavian" (his term) by naming Thor and Odin as the gods to whom the priest prays.[82]

---

[80] Derek Attridge, "Beat," in *The Oxford Handbook of Victorian Poetry*, ed. Matthew Bevis, Oxford Handbooks of Literature (Oxford: Oxford University Press, 2013), 41.
[81] Tennyson, *Notebooks 1–4*, 1:171–190.
[82] Tennyson, *Poems II*, 375.

Tennyson composed his tale of human sacrifice with an overabundance of matching sounds and pounding rhythm, accentuating the traits he associated with primitive verse. From its opening lines, the poem molds its style to match its subject matter:

> A plague upon the people fell,
> A famine after laid them low,
> Then thorpe and byre arose in fire,
> For on them brake the sudden foe; (1–4)

The first line alliterates with *p*'s on three of its four stresses; then *fell* and *famine* bridge the line break with more alliteration before the second line provides another pair with "laid them low;" the third line chimes with an internal rhyme (byre/fire); and the fourth echoes the preceding line with *brake* hearkening back to *byre* and *foe* to *fire*. If "language in its spontaneous period is sensuous," as Kemble admonished, then Tennyson applies the sensuality of his sound effects generously to replicate the linguistic experience of a barbaric period.[83]

The bulk of each stanza consists of four-stress lines, generally in iambic tetrameter, but the end of each stanza falls into two-stress lines in which accents float more freely, as with the priest's appeal to the gods:

> Help us from famine
> And plague and strife!
> What would you have of us?
> Human life?
> Were it our nearest,
> Were it our dearest,
> (Answer, O answer)
> We give you his life. (9–16)

There is a trace of Old English prosody (discussed in more detail later in this chapter) in the alliteration between "What would you have of us? / Human life?" and "Were it our nearest, / Were it our dearest." In addition, Tennyson has subjoined a great deal of additional sonic patterning, including rhymes (strife/life/life, nearest/dearest) and repetition ("Answer, O answer").

Ultimately, however much it appealed to Kemble and his contemporaries, they found it much more difficult to reveal an unbroken tradition in pagan religion than in law – though he argued that the practice of concluding an auction with a gavel strike derived from Thor's hammer. A generation before, historian Turner had written of the Anglo-Saxons "in their pagan state" that "our curiosity must submit to disappointment on this subject," because their beliefs were not written down and so must be pieced together.[84] The same frustration faced scholars decades later. Even establishing which beliefs had been specific to the Anglo-Saxons was challenging. Because so little mythology survives in Old English as compared to Old Norse literature, most had to be reconstructed from broader Teutonic mythology and oblique references within English texts. Indeed, Kemble wrote to Grimm in 1834 that he

---

[83] Brookfield, *The Cambridge "Apostles,"* 178.
[84] Turner, *History of the Anglo-Saxons*, 1807, 2:1.

was disappointed that "my late researches which have been very much among the dirty records of Anglo-Saxon superstition, spells & witchcraft, have hitherto added little, or nothing to our knowledge of their heathen condition." Most of the spells he found related to saints; thus, "in short the *Abracadabra* of our forefathers had very little meaning indeed."[85]

Those of a literary bent made up for the dearth of evidence by blending their impressions of Norse, Celtic, and Anglo-Saxon cultures. "The rise of primitivism," writes Inga Bryden, also "allowed the ancient Celts to be viewed with patriotic pride." Specifically, in order to reconcile King Arthur as a national but non-Saxon hero, writers "promote[d] the idea of racial unity and harmony between Celts and Saxons."[86] Tennyson, ever in tune with the trends of his time, owned multiple books on Welsh and was interested in Celtic topics, including religion. In an 1855 letter, for example, he replied to a query from friend Charles Richard Weld: "I was grieved that I had no books to refer to here whereby I might have enlightened you as to Teutates," a Celtic deity.[87]

Tennyson also owned and annotated a copy of *Notes on Ancient Britain and the Britons* (1858) by William Barnes, whose dialect poems he admired. Where Barnes notes that "the laws of the Isle of Man were formerly promulgated at Midsummer from a mound," Tennyson inserted a caret after *formerly* and wrote in the margin, "and still are." He also drew a line alongside a passage describing how Druids lit fires on barrows on holy days, which suggests he was especially interested in that section. Where Barnes states that "Welsh is spoken by about five millions of people," Tennyson responded in the margin, "not *Welsh*. The Celtic dialects taken together may be – Welsh is spoken by 1–1 ½ million." And on the back of the last page, he jotted a brief index with page references for "Scots," "A Picture" (a description of the landscape), and "the Bard" – sections that depict important elements of primitive British society.[88]

Tennyson's interest long pre-dates these notes, however. Several poems from 1827's *Poems by Two Brothers* explore early British society with a primitivist bent, derived from Celtic inspiration but also sharing themes with Old English poetry. "The Exile's Harp," for example, is written in the voice of an exile literally hanging up his harp as he departs his home. Although the speaker is not explicitly identified as an Anglo-Saxon, lines 25–28 call up elegiac images often associated with them:

> Oh! Harp of my fathers!
> No more in the hall,
> The souls of the chieftains
> Thy strains shall enthral.

Exile was a common theme for lamentation in the poetry of the Anglo-Saxons, whose society relied heavily on kinship bonds. The sense that glorious days have passed away is also typical.

---

[85] Kemble, *Correspondence*, 104, 55, 109.

[86] Inga Bryden, *Reinventing King Arthur: The Arthurian Legends in Victorian Culture*, Nineteenth Century (Aldershot: Ashgate, 2005), 35.

[87] Tennyson, *Letters*, 1982, 2:134.

[88] William Barnes, *Notes on Ancient Britain and the Britons* (Tennyson's copy) (London: John Russell Smith, 1858), TRC/AT/494, Lincolnshire Archives, Lincoln, UK. 94, 113.

"The Old Chieftain" likewise strays into other supposedly primitive cultures. The word *chieftain* indicates that the setting is archaic, an impression reinforced by remembered battle songs that were accompanied by harp, and armies arrayed with lances, swords, and shields. John Lovelace shows this composition to be inspired by one of James Macpherson's Ossianic poems and therefore categorizes its speaker as an aged Celtic warrior. In particular, he convincingly identifies the "song of the hundred shells" as a Celtic drinking song. "Tennyson's poem," he continues, "with its abundance of aspirates and forceful consonant sounds, approximates in its meter a rousing, rowdy mead-hall chorus" – despite the fact that the mead-hall was a Germanic rather than a Celtic institution.[89] Lovelace's casual conflation of Celtic and Anglo-Saxon societies is informative, for the same confusion was common in the popular imagination of the nineteenth century.

The primitivist perception of the Anglo-Saxons also extended to their literature. For example, Wright (who placed so much importance on mythology) found that "The Saxon bards seem to have possessed most of inspiration while their countrymen retained their paganism."[90] His remark exemplifies an ongoing critical tradition of elevating whatever seems rude, pagan, or nature-oriented in Germanic literature in order to satisfy a desire for origins.[91] As a result, the language of the Anglo-Saxons occupied a conflicted position; texts such as *Beowulf* were simultaneously native and foreign, a supposed source of "essential Englishness" written in an unfamiliar tongue with alien orthography.[92] That paradox of otherness and inheritance played out in the meandering evolution of typesetting practices for Old English text.

Typesetting and Typifying Old English

Old English exemplified the debate over whether language – and therefore mankind – had improved or deteriorated over time. Kemble remarked that English lost inflections as it became "what is somewhat questionably called improved and polished."[93] For him, English had lost much, although *the* English had only improved. He offered a solution to this apparent contradiction when he wrote that in "the early times of a nation … Nature is felt, not reasoned upon. Everything is symbolic, everything brings a visual image with it, a part or the whole of an object. The very language which men speak announces this to us as a fact."[94] Kemble shared with other Victorian philologists a belief that older, more inflected languages were more vivid, more concrete, and expressed relations between objects more clearly. In this passage, he offers Old English as evidence that its speakers possessed minds that thought more in pictures than those of later generations. They could not think as abstractly as their descendants were to do, because their language was too vividly

---

[89] John Timothy Lovelace, *The Artistry and Tradition of Tennyson's Battle Poetry* (New York: Routledge, 2003), 38.
[90] Wright, *Essays*, 1:14.
[91] Stanley, *Imagining the Anglo-Saxon Past*, 3.
[92] Christie, "'An Unfollowable World': Beowulf, English Poetry, and the Phenomenalism of Language," 519.
[93] Kemble, *Anglo-Saxon Runes*, 54.
[94] John Mitchell Kemble, *Anglo-Saxon Dialogues of Salomon and Saturnus* (Printed for the Aelfric Society, 1848), 4.

associated with real objects. Even Anglo-Saxon poetry was sparse in simile, favoring metaphor instead – proof of their pictorial thinking. In this way, Kemble makes a brilliant move to resolve two competing interpretations of human history, one of decay and one of progress. His interpretation of inflections preserves respect for the greater perfection of Old English's grammatical abilities, but it reads that precision as necessary for simpler minds, thereby allowing a progressive view of English culture – and maintaining the primitivist appeal of those rude ancestors.[95]

A similar tension was at work in the matter of how to interpret and therefore represent Anglo-Saxon writing in contemporary publishing. Over the course of the nineteenth century, texts that had remained in manuscript form or been issued in small editions – often foreign and/or expensive ones – became more widely available in print, foregrounding an ongoing dilemma of how to visually present Old English writing. Was it a language peculiar to its age that should be distinguished by imitating the handwritten manuscript, or was it an intrinsic core of modern English speech, making plainer typography more fitting? The Victorian urge to classify, particularly in the growing field of historical linguistics, conflicted with a broader cultural project to identify Anglo-Saxon society as the foundation of English society. Those who published medieval texts had to decide to what extent they should maintain a visual reference to the source material.

Early publications had taken for granted that medieval writing should be replicated faithfully, which required specialized (and therefore expensive) type. William Somner's 1659 Anglo-Saxon dictionary, for example, had featured an imitative typeface, which Oxford University purchased and leased out.[96] The Elstob siblings, at the beginning of the eighteenth century, ran out of money to continue printing their work in part because the type they had paid to have cut was lost in a fire.[97] As discussed in the Introduction, they had opted not only to print runic letters that had since disappeared from the alphabet but also to use medievalist versions of letters that still exist in Modern English.

In the first decades of the nineteenth century, the scarcity of full-length Anglo-Saxon publications meant that readers usually interacted with Old English in fragmentary form – in dictionaries, excerpts in history books, and quotations. These collections reinforced the perception of Anglo-Saxon writing as a different kind of text, collected as specimens. However, an important shift began to occur in the early nineteenth century. Michael Murphy identifies it in terms of Anglo-Saxonists changing "from antiquary to academic," meaning that they became increasingly interested in the language and the content of their materials, rather than emphasizing the quaintness of the manuscripts as objects.[98] As Richard C. Payne puts it, "for the first time, a distinctly literary interest became the driving force behind Anglo-Saxon scholarship in England, replacing English nationalism, the study of law, and ecclesiastical controversy, which had motivated students of the discipline since its

---

[95] Elsewhere, Kemble remarked, "Declension is not arbitrary but a necessary consequence of our own reasoning power: it expresses relations which man's nature required to be expressed." Kemble, "History of the English Language," 8.
[96] Jones, *Fossil Poetry*, 242.
[97] Simmons, *Reversing the Conquest*, 22.
[98] Murphy, "Antiquary to Academic."

beginnings in the English Reformation."[99] Literary interest hardly replaced English nationalism; on the contrary, each reinforced the other. But as the literature came to be appreciated for its content, scholars became more motivated to make it legible to their readers, quite literally.

This change in attitude was evidently starting to take place by the time Conybeare's *Illustrations of Anglo-Saxon Poetry* came out in 1826. The publishers retained some archaic flair by using a Gothic typeface on section title pages, but the work as a whole domesticates the appearance of the Old English in its excerpts of "Cædmon's Hymn" and *Beowulf*. Conybeare employs yogh for his *g*'s and uses thorn and ash for *th* sounds, but resemblance to a manuscript is otherwise minimal. He was not terribly impressed with "Cædmon's Hymn" as a poem,[100] but nonetheless the book's existence in itself indicates a relatively new interest in early vernacular literature *as* literature.

The advocates of new philology who came after Conybeare wholeheartedly embraced using simpler fonts. In Benjamin Thorpe's translation of Rasmus Rask's Anglo-Saxon grammar (1830) – a book Tennyson owned – thorn, eth, and ash are the only traces of medieval orthography in most of the book. Thorpe was a friend of Kemble's, and one of the few contemporaries of whom the latter scholar approved. Between them, they produced an impressive number of editions of Anglo-Saxon documents, and they founded the English Historical Society to encourage publication of even more. Thorpe's *Analecta Anglo-Saxonica* (1834) continued his practice of employing a modernized font. The one exception was the book's printing of John's Gospel, one chapter of which Thorpe typeset to replicate medieval script. His reasoning was as follows: "One chapter is given in the Saxon character, that the student may have no difficulty when he meets with any work in that character, either printed or manuscript."[101] Clearly, then, it was still possible that readers might encounter texts "in that [older] character," and indeed, by then a standardized imitative font had been established. However, Thorpe assumes that his reader is interested in Old English material and may not be familiar with that style of writing.

Kemble, like Thorpe, also used simpler typesetting, to the point that Grimm questioned how far he went. When Grimm expressed doubts in 1837 about his friend's use of *w* instead of wynn, Kemble wrote back:

> [D]o you object to it palaeographically, or do you deny that the A.S. wên had the same sound of our w? ... That the A.S. *w* had the sound of our *w* is certain, and on that account I use it ... nor do I see any reason for keeping ... the particular letter by which an A.S. scribe denoted any other sound. The only two letters I keep are ð and þ, and after all *dh* and *th* (the earliest form in use among the A.S. themselves was *th* not þ) would answer the purpose nearly as well: only if I left the two signs out no Englishman would believe that what he read was Anglo-Saxon.[102]

---

[99] Richard C. Payne, "The Rediscovery of Old English Poetry in the English Literary Tradition," in *Anglo-Saxon Scholarship: The First Three Centuries*, ed. Carl T. Berkhout and Milton McC. Gatch (Boston: G.K. Hall, 1982), 149.

[100] John Josias Conybeare, *Illustrations of Anglo-Saxon Poetry*, ed. William Daniel Conybeare (London: Harding and Lepard, 1826), 5.

[101] Benjamin Thorpe, ed., *Analecta Anglo-Saxonica: A Selection, in Prose and Verse, from Anglo-Saxon Authors of Various Ages* (London: John and Arthur Arch, 1834), iv.

[102] Kemble, *Correspondence*, 147–148.

Kemble's last remark points to lingering aesthetic conceptions of Old English text among his countrymen. In fact, he was not entirely honest about his own practice, since he also included ash (æ) and the Tironian symbol for *that*. Generally, though, Kemble was in favor of any measure that made information more accessible to more people. Writing to Grimm in 1849, he defended the value of translations, though they are always imperfect copies of their original material:

> It is one of my principles, [that] knowledge ought not to be made the property only of a learned class ... it is highly pleasant to be able to read our old chroniclers as we would read a newspaper or a novel: but it is delightful to know that translations of those very chroniclers are read with avidity by thousands who would otherwise have never been able to master their contents.[103]

On this same principle, Kemble preferred to present even original text in an alphabet closely resembling the standard roman type.

The shift to simpler Old English typography was both philosophical and practical. Simplifying the typesetting made publications more readable but also more financially accessible – an important change if Anglo-Saxon texts were to be of interest to more than a small coterie of Oxbridge academics and gentleman scholars. Kemble and Grimm bemoaned in their early correspondence that contemporary editions of Old English texts forfeited the possibility of wider distribution by clinging to expensive distinctions. They objected that paleographic types both obscured content and made publications too expensive for wide circulation. In 1832, for example, Grimm wrote to Kemble that he was annoyed by the Roxburghe Club in England, because their lavish productions (printed at the author's expense) meant that only a few copies could be distributed: "I hate these bibliomaniacs who degrade science to an easily satisfied and tedious hobby."[104] Despite these disadvantages, Kemble snidely predicted in 1834 that "it will be some time before the bibliomaniacal foppery of using these types ceases,"[105] and he was right. Twenty-five years later, the Philological Society grumbled about the difficulty of accessing works that would be helpful for its dictionary project (the eventual *OED*), saying, "Many poems and other pieces ... still lie hid in [manuscript]. Others have been brought out by printing clubs of exclusive constitution ... and might, for all that the public in general is the better for them, just as well have remained in [manuscript]."[106]

As these complaints suggest, the price of Anglo-Saxonist publications was a major obstacle to making medieval content available to the literate public. In September of 1832, Kemble reported with regret that his publisher would not let him include "a very complete verbal and glossarial index" he had prepared for his *Beowulf* edition, because it would cost too much, especially given the intended modest print run of 100 copies. Eight months later, he had happier news: he was delighted to report that Cambridge University Press had agreed to cover "all expense of printing, paper, &c" of an edition of the Anglo-Saxon Gospels, so that he and Thorpe could "hope to

---

[103] Ibid., 293.
[104] Ibid., 22.
[105] Kemble, "Review of Analecta," 393.
[106] Philological Society, *Proposal*, 7.

give the learned, a very handsome book at no exorbitant price."[107] That particular project never came to fruition, but evidently cost was a consideration, even with the minimally specialized font that both Kemble and Thorpe preferred. Table 3 shows the cost of books of Anglo-Saxonist scholarship from the first few decades of the nineteenth century. As the Introduction discussed, five to seven shillings was a significant but not impossible purchase for a middle-class reader. For this price, an enthusiast could acquire one of several available grammars, a copy of a text such as King Alfred's will or Apollonius of Tyre, or a history of the Anglo-Saxons. Generally, the more thorough or lengthy a work, the greater its price; Kemble's volumes of *Beowulf* cost fifteen shillings despite his obvious desire to bring Old English literature to a Victorian readership.

Table 3   Grammars and editions of Anglo-Saxon texts listed in Bosworth's 1838 dictionary, in order of publication date. When possible, information that Bosworth did not provide has been added in square brackets.[108]

Editor	Title	Year	Format	Pages	Price
Grímur Jónsson Thorkelin	*De Danorum Rebus Gestis Secul. III et IV* (Copenhagen)	1815	4to		14s.
J.L. Sisson	*The Elements of Anglo-Saxon Grammar*	1819	12mo	84	5s.
Thomas Silver	*A Lecture on the Study of Anglo-Saxon*	1822	8vo		3s.
Jacob Grimm	*Deutsche Grammatik* (3 vols.) 2nd ed.	1822 1826 1831	8vo		[3*l*. 3s. in 1834][109]
James Ingram	*The Saxon Chronicle: With an English Translation, and Notes, Critical and Explanatory*	1823	4to	463	3*l*. 13s.
Joseph Bosworth	*Elements of Anglo-Saxon Grammar*	1823	8vo	330	16s.
Joseph Bosworth	*Compendious Grammar of Primitive English or Anglo-Saxon*	1826	8vo	84	5s.
John Josias Conybeare	*Illustrations of Anglo-Saxon Poetry*	1826	8vo	286	18s.
Owen Manning (original), J.S. Cardale (1828)	*Ælfred's Will, in Anglo-Saxon, with a literal and also a free English translation, a Latin version, and notes*	[1788] 1828	[royal 4to] 8vo	51 32	7s. 5s.

[107] Kemble, *Correspondence*, 27, 33.
[108] Bosworth, *A Dictionary of the Anglo-Saxon Language*, xviii–xxi.
[109] "Works Published by Bach & Co. Foreign Booksellers to Her Majesty, 21, Soho Square, London," in *Tutti Frutti*, vol. 2 (London: Bach and Co., 1834), 247.

J.S. Cardale	*King Alfred's Anglo-Saxon version of Boethius, de Consolatione Philosophiæ*	1829	8vo	425	1*l*. 5s.
Joseph Gwilt	*Rudiments of a Grammar of the Anglo-Saxon Language*	1829	8vo	56	6s.
Samuel Fox	*Menologium, seu Calendarium Poeticum, ex Hickesiano Thesauro: or, The Poetical Calendar of the Anglo-Saxons, with an English translation and notes*	1830	8vo	64	6s.
Rasmus Rask (trans. Benjamin Thorpe)	*A Grammar of the Anglo-Saxon Tongue* (Copenhagen)	1830	8vo	[224]	15s. 6d.
Franz Joseph Mone	*Quellen und Forschungen zur Geschichte der Teutschen Lit. und Sprache* (Leipzig)	1830	8vo		10s.
Francis Palgrave	*History of the Anglo-Saxons*	1831	16mo	391	5s.
Benjamin Thorpe	*Cædmon's Metrical Paraphrase of Parts of the Holy Scriptures*	1832	8vo	341	1*l*. 1s.
John Mitchell Kemble	*The Anglo-Saxon Poems of Beowulf; the Traveller's Song, and the Battle of Finnes-burh* [2nd ed.]	1833	Small 8vo	259	13s. [15s.]
George William Collen	*Britannia Saxonica: A Map of Britain during the Saxon Octarchy*	1833	4to	[55]	12s.
Sharon Turner	*History of the Anglo-Saxons* 5th ed.	1834	8vo	3 vols	2*l*. 5s.
Benjamin Thorpe	*Analecta Anglo-Saxonica*	1834	8vo	266	20s.
Benjamin Thorpe	*The Anglo-Saxon version of the story of Apollonius of Tyre*	1834	12mo	92	6s.
Benjamin Thorpe	*Libri Psalmorum versio antiqua Latina*	1835	8vo	[446]	[£1][110]
Samuel Fox	*King Alfred's Anglo-Saxon version of the Metres of Boethius*	1835	8vo	144	12s.
John Mitchell Kemble	*Beowulf, an English Translation, with a copious Glossary*	[1837]	[Foolscap 8vo]		[15s.][111]

[110] "Supplement for 1835," *Bent's Monthly Literary Advertiser, and Register of Engravings, Works on the Fine Arts, Etc.*, January 1836, 156.

[111] "William Pickering's Publications, 177, Piccadilly, London," in *Bibliotheca Piscatoria: A Catalogue of Books Upon Angling* (London: Pickering, 1836).

Despite its financial benefits, the change of typesetting standards was by no means a linear process; books continued to be printed with the older font. Indeed, sometimes a type became more elaborate than in earlier printings of the same publication. For instance, the chapters on Anglo-Saxon poetry in the first edition of Turner's history mostly provided translations and paraphrases, Turner not being interested in the literary merit of the poems he discussed. In a footnote offering the original text of "Cædmon's Hymn," only ash deviates from the early nineteenth-century printing alphabet for Modern English, and it would have already been in the printer's box for producing Latin.[112] However, by the time of the 1852 edition – nearly fifty years later – the same poem had been moved into the main body of text, parallel to its Modern English translation, and in highly stylized typography, having reverted to decorative font for common letters. Perhaps because "Cædmon's Hymn" was now considered literature, the text had evidently become worthy of being foregrounded. Why this poem should be typeset archaically in the middle of the century as compared to its beginning is more difficult to explain, but the different typographical practices taking place reflect the contradictory ways in which the Victorians viewed their cultural forebears. The idea of an overarching cultural Teutonism was highly attractive in constructing English national character, but the Anglo-Saxons were also considered picturesquely primitive. The dual impulses of the antiquary and the academic, in other words, both remained active.

Archaic typesetting was still at work, for example, as late as the three-volume book *Leechdoms, Wortcunning, and Starcraft of Early England* by Oswald Cockayne (1864–1866). With facing-page translations of medicinal recommendations and herbal recipes, this book employed the by-then-standardized archaic typeface, complete with thorns, eths, Tironian "and" symbols, yoghs, wynns, and descending *s*'s.[113] Its author shared much in common with other Anglo-Saxonists of his time. Educated at Cambridge (St. John's College) around the same time as Kemble and Tennyson,[114] Cockayne taught school in London for nearly thirty years, where he counted among his pupils the future philologists Walter Skeat and Henry Sweet. Alongside those duties, he found time to be "an early and active member of the London Philological Society" and publish on Old English as well as classical texts. Like other contemporaries, his talent was overshadowed by (in the words of the *Oxford Dictionary of National Biography*) "his pugnacious personality and abrasive *ad hominem* attacks on influential critics [which] closed the doors to higher academic positions."[115] Anglo-Saxonism seems to have been a field that attracted fiercely opinionated and undiplomatic men – a fact that contributed to the intensity of their academic debates.

---

[112] Sharon Turner, *The History of the Manners, Landed Property, Government, Laws, Poetry, Literature, Religion, and Language, of the Anglo-Saxons* (Longman, 1805), 379.

[113] Oswald Cockayne, *Leechdoms, Wortcunning, and Starcraft of Early England*, vol. 2, 2 vols. (London: Longman, Green, Longman, Roberts, and Green, 1865).

[114] Cockayne was a student at Cambridge 1824–1828, Kemble 1824–1829, Tennyson 1827–1831.

[115] Daniel F. Kenneally, "Cockayne, Thomas Oswald," in *Oxford Dictionary of National Biography*, September 23, 2004.

Alongside those debates, the fluctuating printing practices for Old English embodied the paradox of categorization that the language presented to the Victorians. Over the course of the nineteenth century, the effort to reclaim an Anglo-Saxon heritage led to a gradual move away from distinctive, categorizing types toward a transparency that suggested continuity in English society. When Kemble argued for the value of being able to "read our old chroniclers" (either in the original or in translation), he was making the case for the importance of reconnecting the contemporary population with the society that had supposedly formed the basis of their nation and by extension the British Empire.[116] Yet the estranging symbols remained attractive, mirroring uncertainty as to Old English's place in the history of English culture. The next chapter shows how Tennyson participated in both schools of thought. In his early years, he meticulously replicated medieval script in his notebooks and valued archaisms for their "singularity" (as one reviewer put it). As he matured as a poet, his medievalist use of language became more subtle – but it remained at the core of his style. His specifically Anglo-Saxonist interest also spanned his career. Two direct translations from Old English testify to this ongoing interest, and they also illustrate how he understood the Anglo-Saxons.

Tennyson as Translator

At the beginning of the nineteenth century, Turner's landmark history of the Anglo-Saxons was blunt in his assessment of poetry during the period, saying "it existed in a rude and barbaric state. It could, indeed, have been scarcely more uncultivated." English poetry, he concluded, "has attained to its perfection by slow degrees;" during this early period, "little else seems to have been done than the formation of a style of composition different from prose. If we call this style poetry, it is rather by complaisance than truth." Since "True poetry is the offspring of cultivated mind," Turner is clear that the Anglo-Saxons as a society had neither. He does admit that vernacular poetic style required effort, even suggesting that "the genuine ballad" emerged as a consequence "from men who could not bend language into that difficult and artificial strain which the genius of the Anglo-Saxon bard was educated to use."[117] In other words, the style of the *scop* was so difficult that common men came up with an easier form – the ballad familiar to later generations.

This attitude dominated the field when Tennyson came up to Cambridge in 1827. Anglo-Saxon literature was not yet appreciated as having literary merit of its own; at best, it helped illustrate arguments about the Anglo-Saxons generally, and sometimes their language. Tennyson, however, seriously engaged in study of the language, probably encouraged by his friends and teachers at Trinity. For example, in a handmade glossary of Old and Middle English words (discussed in the next chapter), one entry is *uhtfloga*,[118] which Chris Jones points out is only recorded in *Beowulf*. This begs the question of where Tennyson found his source material; at the time of this notebook (it is watermarked 1828), the original text of *Beowulf* was not

---

[116] Kemble, *Correspondence*, 293.
[117] Turner, *History of the Anglo-Saxons*, 1807, 2:277, 282, 286, 293.
[118] Weaver, *Tennyson's Notebook Glossary and Rhyme Lists*, 34.

widely available. "Unless Tennyson had been reading Grimm's *Deutsche Grammatik* on his own (which is unlikely)," Jones writes, "then the only place he could reasonably have come across" the word was in Conybeare's *Illustrations of Anglo-Saxon Poetry*.[119] Conybeare's collection is certainly the most likely source, but two of the poet's college affiliates make it possible that he did read Grimm's work by the time he compiled his glossary.

The first potential source of access to Grimm was Julius Charles Hare, the Trinity College tutor to many of the Apostles. Hare was an avid proponent of German thought and collected a "comprehensive set of the Grimms' works"[120] – including the second edition of *Deutsche Grammatik*, which glosses *uhtfloga*. Given his intellectual influence on the group, it is easy to believe Hare might have shared his books with them. Within the Apostles themselves, Kemble's knowledge of Grimm is a given, but how early did he become acquainted with the latter's German grammar specifically? A tantalizing clue suggests Kemble may have known *Deutsche Grammatik* while he and Tennyson were still at Cambridge – and therefore possibly Tennyson did, as well.

In July 1830, Kemble was in London preparing to leave the country as part of the subgroup of Cambridge Apostles who hoped to support a democratic revolution in Spain.[121] Fellow Apostle R.J. Tennant wrote to him from Cambridge:

> From your mentioning A. Tennyson's arrival in town "the day before yesterday", I conclude [that] your note, which is without date, is rather aged: however I have executed your commission as soon as I could get your Grimm, & this note will go along with your linen tonight.[122]

Kemble, then, was reading Grimm no later than the summer of 1830; "your Grimm" indicates that Kemble already owned a copy that Tennant had to retrieve from somewhere at Cambridge – perhaps from his rooms, or from someone to whom he had loaned it. In any case, Kemble clearly wished to take his Grimm along on his adventure. The mention of Tennyson being in town with Kemble earlier in the summer is probably coincidental, though it is tempting to speculate that something in their conversation sparked the latter's interest in having "his Grimm" sent to him. Whatever the source of Tennyson's *uhtfloga*, this context underlines the fact that the budding poet was surrounded by men discussing Anglo-Saxon literature that, at the time, was obscure to the vast majority of the population.

---

[119] Jones, *Fossil Poetry*, 243.

[120] Roger Paulin, "Julius Hare's German Books in Trinity College Library, Cambridge," *Transactions of the Cambridge Bibliographical Society* 9, no. 2 (1987): 184.

[121] The details of the "Spanish Adventure" are available in the various histories of the Cambridge Apostles and in the journal that Kemble kept during the experience. Peter Allen, *The Cambridge Apostles: The Early Years* (Cambridge: Cambridge University Press, 1978); Brookfield, *The Cambridge "Apostles"*; Richard Deacon, *The Cambridge Apostles: A History of Cambridge University's Élite Intellectual Secret Society* (London: Royce, 1985); W.C. Lubenow, *The Cambridge Apostles*; Eric W. Nye, ed., *John Kemble's Gibraltar Journal: The Spanish Expedition of the Cambridge Apostles, 1830–1831* (Basingstokw: Palgrave Macmillan, 2015).

[122] Nye, *Gibraltar Journal*, 267.

Beowulf

Tennyson's notebook testifies to his dedication to studying Old English, not least because it contains a brief translation of several lines from *Beowulf*. The circumstances surrounding this translation are opaque, but its existence is extraordinary. In the late 1820s and early 1830s (the notebook is watermarked 1828), it was a rare young man who would have been aware of the Old English text of *Beowulf* and equipped to translate it. The only printed version of the poem's full original text was an 1815 book published in Copenhagen by the Danish scholar Grímur Jónsson Thorkelin, which offered Old English text alongside a Latin translation. Thorkelin's edition prompted English Anglo-Saxonists to examine the manuscript and include excerpts in their own publications, but it is unlikely that Tennyson had access to it. Moreover, Thorkelin "went repeatedly and wildly astray in the accuracy of his text."[123] His transcription is so faulty that we can discount it as a resource for Tennyson, even had the poet seen a copy. For example, for the passage in question, instead of "Him se yldesta," Thorkelin has "Him scyld esta," a misreading that could not be translated as Tennyson has done in his notebook.[124]

Discounting Thorkelin, then, the most widely available resources for excerpts of Old English texts at this time were Turner's *History of the Anglo-Saxons* and Conybeare's *Illustrations*, both of which contained the original text of this passage and a translation. Turner supplies them in separate contexts: His chapter on vernacular poetry offers lengthy excerpts translated into Modern English, including the lines that appear in Tennyson's notebook. In his subsequent chapter on versification (which consists largely of the historian admitting that no one understands Anglo-Saxon versification principles), he transcribes the original text for the section that Tennyson handled.[125] Adding to the evidence, we know that Tennyson owned and read Turner's volumes. There is no firm evidence that he consulted Conybeare's compilation, but several scholars see reason to identify it as a source.[126] For example, his translation shares certain words in common with Conybeare's Modern English rendering, such as *Goths* for *Geats*.

Tennyson may have also had the benefit of Rasmus Rask's *Grammar of the Anglo-Saxon Tongue*, as translated by Kemble's friend and colleague Benjamin Thorpe in 1830.[127] Thorpe's English-language translation of Rask's grammar (originally written in Danish) came out roughly contemporaneously with Tennyson's notebook translation and provided part of the original text of this section (beginning "We synt gumcynnes"), along with a translation, in a discussion of meter.[128] Given Kemble's

---

[123] J.R. Hall, "The First Two Editions of Beowulf: Thorkelin's (1815) and Kemble's (1833)," in *The Editing of Old English: Papers from the 1990 Manchester Conference*, ed. D.G. Scragg and Paul E. Szarmach (Cambridge: D.S. Brewer, 1994), 246, 244.

[124] Grímur Jónsson Thorkelin, *De Danorum Rebus Gestis Secul. III. & IV. Poëma Danicum Dialecto Anglosaxonica* (Copenhagen: Rangel, 1815), 22.

[125] Turner, *History of the Anglo-Saxons*, 1807, 2:300, 330.

[126] Jones, *Fossil Poetry*, 243.

[127] Nancie Campbell, *Tennyson in Lincoln: A Catalogue of the Collections in the Research Centre*, vol. 1 (Lincoln: Tennyson Society, 1971), 86.

[128] Erasmus Rask, *A Grammar of the Anglo-Saxon Tongue*, trans. Benjamin Thorpe (Copenhagen: S.L. Møller, 1830), 156.

friendship with Thorpe and obsession with Anglo-Saxon manuscripts, it is possible that Tennyson consulted the book. He later owned a copy, which he received as a gift a decade and a half after his notebook translation. That copy shows undeniable evidence of use – strong proof of his ongoing interest in the subject. Most prominently, in the midst of a passage "From King Alfred's Boethius" (the Old English translation of "On the Consolation of Philosophy"), a flame has burned through the corner of about 20 pages.[129] Tennyson was myopic,[130] and it seems he held this book too close to the light; clearly he was still interested in the language years later.

Although it is far from a finished product, Tennyson's working translation shows that he charted his own course through his material, hewing closely to the Anglo-Saxon original in word order and word choice. Comparing his draft with other early translations throws his decisions into relief; Table 4 gives the original lines of Old English (258–263 in modern editions of *Beowulf*) as given by Turner, alongside Turner's and Tennyson's translations.

Table 4   Early versions of lines 259–263 of *Beowulf*.

Old English (Turner)	Turner (1807)	Tennyson
Him se yldesta answarode	Him answered	Him the eldest
Weordes wisa	the eldest of the host.	Answerèd.
Worde hord onleac	He unlocked his treasure	The army's leader
Wey synt gum cynnes	of wise words.	His wordhoard unlocked.
Geata leode	"We are of the race	We are by race
And Higelaces hearth	Of the Jute people,	Gothic people
geneatas	and Higelac's	And Higelac's
Wæs min fæder	hæarth-geneat	Hearth ministers
Folcum gecythed[131]	was my father,	My father was
	to the world known:[132]	To folk known[133]

Conybeare's 1826 rendition reads:

> Him answering straight, the chieftain freely oped
> The treasury of his speech: "Our race and blood
> Is of the Goth, and Higelac our lord:
> My sire was known of no ignoble line[134]

Thorpe's edition of Rask's grammar only provided a translation of the end of this excerpt: "We are of the race of the Gothic people and Higelac's retainers: my father

---

[129] Erasmus Rask, *A Grammar of the Anglo-Saxon Tongue* (Tennyson's copy), trans. Benjamin Thorpe (S.L. Møller, 1830), TRC/AT/1854, Lincolnshire Archives, Lincoln, UK, 181.
[130] Martin, *Tennyson*, 53.
[131] Turner, *History of the Anglo-Saxons*, 1807, 2:330.
[132] Ibid., 2:300.
[133] Tennyson, *Notebooks 1–4*, 1:284.
[134] Conybeare, *Illustrations*, 40.

was known to the nations."[135] Like Conybeare and Tennyson, Thorpe uses *Goth(ic)* for *Geats*.

Kemble's translation of the same lines, published roughly seven years after Tennyson's private effort, ran, "Him the loftiest answered; the leader of the band unlocked the treasure of words: 'We are *as far as concerns our* race, people of the Geáts, and household retainers of Higelác. My father was well known to nations'" (italics are Kemble's). Emphasizing the new-philological principle that past stages of languages represent their speakers, Kemble claimed that he had stayed close to his source material. He explained that he had opted for a literal translation, "because had the Saxon poet thought as we think, and expressed his thoughts as we express our thoughts, I might have spared myself the trouble of editing or translating his poem."[136] It was the same idea that Tennyson expressed in "The constant spirit of the world exults" from this same timeframe (1830): "some high-thoughted moods and moulds of mind / Can never be remodelled or expressed / Again by any later century" (9–11). Perhaps with this premise in mind, Tennyson was dutifully faithful in bringing the Old English forward into Modern English, retaining phonemes whenever possible – more so, in fact, than Kemble was to do. Others, indeed, found Kemble's translation quite removed from its source material. Anglo-Saxonist J.S. Cardale wrote to Bosworth: "Where plain and simple English words would naturally present themselves he frequently prefers unusual, bombastic, and sometimes nonsensical and un-english expressions."[137]

Tennyson writes *eldest* for *yldesta*, which could mean eldest or leader. In this, he may have been guided not only by Turner's translation but by the historian's observation that "the Saxon societies, in their early stages, were governed by the aged," as proved by the fact that "the words of their language which denote authority, also express age." Turner specifically cites *yldest*, which "is used as synonymous to greatest," and *ealdorman* for other leaders.[138] Conybeare used *chieftain* to represent the same word; Kemble chose *loftiest*. Tennyson's translation also marks the last syllable of *answerèd* for *andswarode*; keeps *wordhord* intact (with updated spelling), which none of the other translations do; retains *hearth* within the compound word used for Higelac's retainers; and preserves word order even at the expense of modern syntax – for example, "The army's leader / His wordhoard unlocked" and "My father was / To folk known." He is also the only one to use *folk*, the modern descendent word of *folcum* (of which *um* is merely a case ending). The other translations offer "the world" (Turner), "of no ignoble line" (Conybeare), and "nations" (Thorpe and Kemble).

Tennyson's draft translation, in short, shows attention to fidelity of vocabulary, at least at this first stage. The rest of his notebook makes it obvious that he was educating himself in earlier forms of English to a degree that made this hyper-accurate translation possible. Jones has reconstructed the range of Anglo-Saxon texts from which Tennyson may have gleaned his glossary entries, showing that his notes

---

[135] Rask, *A Grammar of the Anglo-Saxon Tongue*, 156.

[136] John Mitchell Kemble, *A Translation of the Anglo-Saxon Poem of Beowulf*, vol. 2 (London: Pickering, 1837), 11–12, l.

[137] Bruce Dickins, *Two Kembles, John and Henry* (Cambridge: The author, 1974), 18.

[138] Turner, *History of the Anglo-Saxons*, 1807, 2:8.

reveal "the young Tennyson as applying himself quite studiously to the task of learning Anglo-Saxon vocabulary, grammar, and … 'letters' (in the literal sense)."[139] These lines show Tennyson working closely with Old English as a young man, finding the phonemic echoes of his linguistic ancestors within his own stock of words. Nevertheless, it is still a draft. For an example of how the Victorian poet presented a translation of Old English verse for public consumption, we must look to a work he produced more than forty-five years later.

"The Battle of Brunanburh"

Tennyson's other translation from Anglo-Saxon poetry was considerably more involved. He wrote his interpretation of "The Battle of Brunanburh" around 1877 and published it in 1880's *Ballads and Other Poems*. It less precisely follows the phonetic contours of its source, but it shows the same preference for words that sonically echo their parent terms. As a polished poetic production, it also exhibits an attention to rhythm and alliteration that he had not applied to his working notes. In producing this work, Tennyson had the benefit of more published versions from which to potentially draw, not to mention a readership with more widespread appreciation of Anglo-Saxonist productions.

It is challenging to disentangle which elements the laureate took from his available sources, for there were several that we know he used and a good number more that he could have consulted. By his own attestation, we know he worked from a prose translation made by his son, published in the *Contemporary Review* the previous year.[140] This is noteworthy in itself, as it indicates that study of Old English was encouraged in the household. Jones has examined the drafts of the elder Tennyson's poem, showing how he produced it "in collaboration with Hallam [Tennyson] and at least one other" in "a socialized compositional process driving towards denser alliterative patterning, slightly more archaically Saxonist diction, and greater accuracy with respect to the meaning of the original."[141] The sociality of that process included a multitude of available Modern English adaptations of the poem, for "Brunanburh" garnered early and frequent attention in Anglo-Saxon scholarship; Conybeare noted that it had been "repeatedly translated" even before he handled it in 1826 (at which point Tennyson had not yet started university).[142] In addition, scholars agree that both Tennysons worked directly with an Old English text, but there was more than one at their disposal. Before assessing the poet's choices, therefore, it is worth reviewing the published versions that were available to him and Hallam by 1877, if the pair chose to employ them.

The earliest translations of "Brunanburh" were Henry of Huntingdon's Latin rendition in his *Historia Anglorum* (circa 1123–1154), which focused on literal translation but also incorporated alliteration and rhyme in its new rendering,[143] and the

---

[139] Jones, *Fossil Poetry*, 243, 246.
[140] Hallam Tennyson, "The Song of Brunanburh," *The Contemporary Review*, November 1876.
[141] Jones, *Fossil Poetry*, 253.
[142] Conybeare, *Illustrations*, lxxx–lxxxi.
[143] Kenneth Tiller, "Anglo-Norman Historiography and Henry of Huntingdon's Translation of 'The Battle of Brunanburh,'" *Studies in Philology* 109, no. 3 (2012): 175.

seventeenth-century editions of the Anglo-Saxon Chronicle by Abraham Wheloc (1643) and Edmund Gibson (1692). Both of the latter works printed Old English and Latin in parallel columns.[144] However, there is no reason to believe that Tennyson had access to these rare books, nor to Anna Gurney's privately printed 1819 translation, taken from the Old English of other printed sources.[145] His source poem was available, though, in multiple publications from his own century, some of which we know he used.

Proceeding in chronological order, the 1801 edition of George Ellis's *Specimens of the Early English Poets* provided the Old English text (with modern-day orthography, an unusual choice at the time) paired with a facing-page "literal" translation, followed by a more creative one written in imitative fourteenth-century poetic style.[146] Tennyson was certainly familiar with Ellis's collection; he read it extensively when constructing his notebook glossary as a young man in the late 1820s.[147] By the time he was translating "Brunanburh," he owned both a 1790 (original) edition and the 1801 edition, which included the poem in question. He had acquired both versions midcentury, according to their inscriptions. Moreover, Jones points out that Tennyson's stanza breaks – a feature not present in the original – match Ellis's exactly up to the seventh one.[148] Ellis is therefore a good candidate for being one of Tennyson's sources. However, his Old English text contains some transcription errors that would have made it very difficult for Tennyson to translate as he did if this had been his only primary source. For example, his reading of "Ha mera" (rather than *hamora*) leads Ellis far astray: he takes *mera* – which is not, in fact, in the original – to mean *marches*, consequently offering the strange translation "The marches (*borders*) they leave" instead of referring hammered swords. We must therefore continue seeking Tennyson's other possible sources. A few years after this edition of Ellis's book, the second edition of Turner's Anglo-Saxon history offered a translation of "The Song on Ethelstan's Victory at Brunanburh," but not the original words.

Two publications came forth in 1823 that may or may not have helped the Tennysons half a century later. Bosworth's *The Elements of Anglo-Saxon Grammar* gives the poem in parallel columns of Old and Modern English.[149] It is impossible to say whether Tennyson consulted this book, but he owned Bosworth's Anglo-Saxon dictionary, and Kemble had railed against his perceived enemy loudly enough, so it is plausible that the poet remembered or sought out this scholar's other work. The same year, "Brunanburh" appeared in James Ingram's edition of the Anglo-Saxon

---

[144] Bede, *Historiae Ecclesiasticae Gentis Anglorum: Libri V.*, ed. Abraham Wheloc (Cambridge: Roger Daniel, 1643), 555–557; Edmund Gibson, *Chronicon Saxonicum* (Oxford: E Theatro Sheldoniano, 1692), 112.

[145] Anna Gurney, *A Literal Translation of the Saxon Chronicle* (Norwich: Stevenson, Matchett, and Stevenson, 1819).

[146] George Ellis, ed., *Specimens of the Early English Poets*, vol. 1 (London: W. Bulmer, 1801), 14–17.

[147] Weaver, *Tennyson's Notebook Glossary and Rhyme Lists*, 43.

[148] Jones, *Fossil Poetry*, 254.

[149] Joseph Bosworth, *The Elements of Anglo-Saxon Grammar* (Harding, Mavor, and Lepard, 1823), 323.

Chronicle, in parallel columns of original and translated English;[150] however, apart from Kemble occasionally mentioning Ingram's work in his own, there is no evidence of a Tennysonian relationship. It has also been suggested that father and/or son made use of the Old English and the translation that Edwin Guest included in *A History of English Rhythms* (1838),[151] though Jones finds the evidence to be inconclusive.[152]

An 1848 printing of the Chronicle was produced by command of the Queen, which gave both the Old English (still in archaic typeface) and a modern translation, but there is no way of knowing whether Tennyson or his son read it or even knew of it.[153] A volume with a more likely connection appeared in 1862, when Benjamin Thorpe published a remarkable pair of volumes. The first tome printed all the different manuscript texts of the Chronicle – six of them for the year of the battle of Brunanburh (937) – side by side in narrow columns.[154] The second volume comprises Thorpe's translation.[155] Kemble was dead by this time, but he had praised Thorpe's work enthusiastically during his lifetime, and Tennyson had read at least part of Thorpe's edition of Rask's grammar. Could the memory of Thorpe's earlier work have brought Tennyson to his version of "Brunanburh"?

Approaching yet closer to the date of composition, Tennyson owned a copy of Thomas Warton's *History of English Poetry*. First published in the late eighteenth century, the book had gone through two subsequent editions in the first half of the nineteenth that changed the poetic selections and added notes by a pantheon of experts on early literature – first in 1824, then in 1840. In fact, Kemble and his supposed rival Madden both worked on the latter edition.[156] Thirty years later, a complete overhaul was undertaken, incorporating the latest knowledge of historical English. This final version, from 1871, was in Tennyson's library.

This book, with layers of prefaces and footnotes from its various revisions, comprehends within one volume the progression of Anglo-Saxon studies in England. As the newest editor wrote, "bibliography and philology had not, in [Warton's] day, attained the scientific elevation, which is now accorded to them." Warton felt, and his first subsequent editor Richard Price concurred, that:

> the poetry of a rude and earlier age, with very few exceptions, can only command a share of later attention in proportion as it has exercised an influence over the times producing it, or conveys a picture of the institutions, modes of thinking, or general habits of the society for which it was written.

---

[150] James Ingram, ed., *The Saxon Chronicle, with an English Translation, and Notes, Critical and Explanatory* (London: Longman, Hurst, Rees, Orme, and Brown, 1823), 141–145.

[151] Edwin Guest, *A History of English Rhythms*, ed. Walter W. Skeat, vol. 2 (London: William Pickering, 1838), 60–69.

[152] Jones, *Fossil Poetry*, 249.

[153] Henry Petrie and John Sharpe, *Monumenta Historica Britannica, or Materials for the History of Britain, from the Earliest Period*, vol. 1 (London: George E. Eyre & William Spottiswoode, 1848), 383–386.

[154] Benjamin Thorpe, ed., *The Anglo-Saxon Chronicle According to the Several Original Authorities*, vol. 1 (London: Longman, Green, Longman, and Roberts, 1861), 200–208.

[155] Benjamin Thorpe, ed., *The Anglo-Saxon Chronicle According to the Several Original Authorities*, vol. 2 (London: Longman, Green, Longman, and Roberts, 1861), 86–88.

[156] Ackerman, "J.M. Kemble and Sir Frederic Madden," 170.

Writing when the ideas of new philology had barely reached Britain, much less been widely accepted, Price was confident that it was obvious to "everyone else who has duly canvassed the subject" that early poetry was valuable only insofar as it gave depth to present-day life. In contrast, the heavily revised edition that Tennyson had on hand, published just six years before he began his translation, contained a new appendix on Anglo-Saxon literature. It cites Kemble, who had become an Anglo-Saxonist authority by then. The Old English text of "Brunanburh" in this edition was a nineteenth-century contribution from Henry Sweet.[157] Sweet was a member of the generation of linguists who came up behind Kemble, Madden, and their cohort; he was born in the middle of the nineteenth century and died in 1912, so that he grew into his scholarship within the no-longer-very-new new philology. He imbibed its principles so well, in fact, that his Anglo-Saxon primer is still in print.[158] In their accuracy, Sweet's text or Thorpe's are the most likely candidates for being Tennyson's reference source (with the possible addition of Ellis), with Sweet having the advantage of having been in the poet's library.

Whatever combination of publications he drew upon for the Anglo-Saxon text, Tennyson also made use of multiple academic resources. For his lexical and grammatical needs, he owned Thorpe's English translation of Rask's grammar, as well as Bosworth's dictionary. Kemble had been unimpressed with the latter work when it first began being printed, declaring, "It will be a pitiful performance, for the man is as devoid of philology, as an ox of milk; yet it will be better than nothing."[159] Kemble had intentions of producing a dictionary of his own, but he never did so; thus, Bosworth's remained the best available. In addition, in Tennyson's notebook glossary (created in the late 1820s and/or early 1830s), he had cited two dictionaries of Old English. The first, which he called "Benson's Anglo-Saxon Glossary," was a 1701 abridged student edition of William Somner's 1659 dictionary. The other was Edward Lye's massive 1772 production, of which Kemble was typically disparaging a few years after the period of Tennyson's notebook,[160] but which remained the standard until Bosworth's. Having used these reference books for his medievalist self-education as a young man, Tennyson might well have turned to them again.

Armed with an array of potential resources, Tennyson was well equipped to understand "The Battle of Brunanburh" in its original form and then choose how to reflect its qualities in his own version. In this later and lengthier translation effort, he prioritized creating echoes of Old English verse through what he understood to be sonic similarity at the scale of rhythm and alliteration, rather than word-by-word precision. He emphasized the cadence of Anglo-Saxon poetry, which he imagined "was chanted to a slow, swinging recitative."[161] Michael Alexander, Edward B. Irving, Jr., and Chris Jones have each discussed Tennyson's handling of the poem, with varying degrees of skepticism and appreciation. Alexander writes that Tennyson attempted to create a similar aural effect rather than a mimetic copy of

[157] Warton, *History of English Poetry*, 1:ix, 8, 68, xii.
[158] Tennyson owned a copy of Sweet's "The Elementary sounds of English: a paper read before the Spelling Reform Association on 22 November, 1881."
[159] Kemble, *Correspondence*, 57.
[160] Kemble, "Review of Analecta," 392.
[161] Tennyson, "Harold," 360.

"Brunanburh," concluding that as a result "Tennyson has sacrificed much to music." As a medievalist, Alexander admits initially being put off by the laureate's "excessive musicality and Technicolour diction."[162]

This latter assessment is somewhat unfair; Tennyson's lexical choices are explored below, but they generally prove to be viable selections, especially given the translations that preceded him. Alexander is correct, however, that Tennyson's rhythm does have a far more propelling momentum than its Old English source. Irving similarly objects to the Victorian poet's "boisterous and rollicking rhythms." He writes that "Tennyson doubtless had a good idea of what Anglo-Saxon sounded like, and his translation is clearly imitative of some of the basic rhythms of the original." Yet he is too consistent for Irving's taste; Irving counts between eighty-five and ninety percent of the poem in the same Sievers Type,[163] lending it a "monotonous hammering effect which is not at all in fact the sound of Old English verse."[164]

Regarding Tennyson's particular metrical choice for "Brunanburh," he explained in his own headnote: "In rendering this Old English war-song into modern language and alliterative rhythm I have made free use of the dactylic beat."[165] Guest (whose *History of English Rhythms* Tennyson may or may not have consulted) had called the poem "The Brunanburgh War-Song," and his book describes the effect of dactylic meter thus:

> When a verse or section opens with an accent, followed by two unaccented syllables, the rapid utterance, immediately preceded by muscular exertion, produces in some cases a very striking effect … and such a flow of rhythm will frequently raise the idea, not merely of power, but of power in energetic action.

Guest goes on to qualify his statement by saying that this particular rhythm is most effective as a contrast in the midst of what he calls "the common measure" (that is, iambs). However: "The peculiar nature of Anglo-Saxon poetry allowed great scope for the recurrence of the same rhythm, and the ear of the Anglo-Saxon poet seems to have been most sensitively alive to its beauty."[166] If Tennyson did read Guest, such reasoning would have lent force to his decision to use repeated dactylic rhythms. Hallam Tennyson recalled, "My father … liked the rush of the alliterative verse" in his translation "as giving something of the old English war-song."[167] In "sacrific[ing]

---

[162] Michael Alexander, "Tennyson's 'The Battle of Brunanburh,'" *Tennyson Research Bulletin*, 1985, 158–159.

[163] Sievers Types, first published in 1893, have been used to describe the most common patterns of stress in Old English poetry. For further details, see Bruce Mitchell and Fred C. Robinson, *A Guide to Old English*, 6th ed. (Oxford: Blackwell, 2001), 163–166.

[164] Edward B. Irving, Jr, "The charge of the Saxon brigade: Tennyson's *Battle of Brunanburh*," in *Literary Appropriations of the Anglo-Saxons from the Thirteenth to the Twentieth Century*, ed. Donald Scragg and Carole Weinberg, Cambridge Studies in Anglo-Saxon England 29 (Cambridge: Cambridge University Press, 2006), 187.

[165] Tennyson, "Harold," 359–360.

[166] Edwin Guest, *A History of English Rhythms*, ed. Walter W. Skeat, vol. 1 (London: William Pickering, 1838), 172.

[167] Hallam Tennyson, *Memoir*, 2:255.

much to music," then, Tennyson followed a nineteenth-century interpretation of "what Anglo-Saxon [poetry] sounded like."

Visually, Tennyson's poem consists predominantly of short lines, a reflection of nineteenth-century printing standards for Anglo-Saxon poetry. Old English verse has no lineation in manuscript, but patterns of alliteration and stress have been identified that dictate how modern editions present the text. The current standard is to print it as two half-lines separated by a caesura of white space. At the simplest organizational level, each half-line contains two stressed syllables and a varying number of unstressed ones. Alliteration is placed on the stressed syllables and spans the half-lines; the alliterative sound appears in either one or both of the stressed syllables in the first half-line, plus the first stressed syllable of the latter half-line. All stressed initial vowels are considered to alliterate with each other.[168] For a visual depiction of this pattern, see Table 5.

Table 5   Alliteration placement on the stressed syllables in a long line of Old English poetry.

1		2	caesura	3	4
(✓)	and/or	(✓)		✓	

Nineteenth-century scholars had noticed these general patterns, but they tended to print Anglo-Saxon poetry by short line – that is, the half-line as now interpreted. Kemble's 1833 *Beowulf* edition, for example, prints the text in lines that break at the caesura, as Turner and Conybeare had done before him. When Jacob Grimm suggested the longer line format, Kemble rejected it, replying in 1840: "I am not the least converted to your *long lines*, nor do I admit your grounds as valid: in the first place, the MSS themselves mark a point at the end of each half-line as you call it" – besides which, he added, alliterative Middle English verses "*always* have *three* alliterative words … two invariably in the first, one invariably in the last: now this accuracy is intelligible in couplets but hardly in single lines." Recognizing that lineation was not of primary importance, Grimm declined to argue the point further, saying, "The disposition of AS verse into half or whole lines is rather a side issue over which we do not want to dispute. Your reasons in my eyes do no injury to mine."[169]

Kemble maintained his position and continued to print short lines in subsequent publications of Anglo-Saxon poetry, a rare example of him agreeing with his fellow British Anglo-Saxonists. Grimm was in the minority on this point, and it remained standard in Tennyson's lifetime to print by short line. For example, Rask (whose grammar Tennyson owned in translation) explicitly rejected the practice of "some recent Scholars" of "combining two lines as one." Among his numerous objections, he judged it "hig[h]ly absurd" to create a dead weight of unstressed syllables and/or a caesura in the middle of what he considered an artificially lengthy line.[170] Tennyson, in both his notebook translation of lines from *Beowulf* and in his adaptation of

---

[168] Mitchell and Robinson, *A Guide to Old English*, 161–162.
[169] Kemble, *Correspondence*, 200–01, 206. Emphasis is Kemble's.
[170] Rask, *A Grammar of the Anglo-Saxon Tongue*, 149–152.

"Brunanburh," followed contemporary practice in using short lines. Moreover, his use of dactyls front-loaded the emphasis in his lines, avoiding the dreaded caesura.

Tennyson's meter for each short line of "Brunanburh" often consists of a dactyl and a trochee. When the ear expects another dactyl, the missing last syllable pulls us up short, creating a strong caesura across the line break. His metrical pattern does vary, however. Sometimes an extra unstressed syllable makes for two full dactyls or a leading initial syllable. He also occasionally breaks into long lines, which Jones shows to have been allowed by Victorian authorities.[171] The extent to which Anglo-Saxon meter was structured by fixed rules was under debate for most of the nineteenth century, until Sievers Types emerged as an agreed-upon standard.[172] In fact, the extent of the *scop*'s metrical restrictions is a topic that has continued to challenge researcher into the twenty-first century.[173] As far as Tennyson knew, Anglo-Saxon meter was determined solely by the stresses of alliterating words, and it is difficult to reproduce the effect within a meter that has a more rigid pattern of stresses. Because of his additional filigrees, which complicate the web of connecting sounds in this poem, it is tempting to accuse Tennyson of having only a caricatured sense of Anglo-Saxon prosody. However, he built upon a solid foundation, generally observing the fundamentals of Old English poetry though usually distributing his triplets of alliteration toward the end of a line or phrase. Indeed, it is more surprising when the pattern of linking alliteration fails, whether or not the reader recognizes what she had been expecting. This failure takes the form of orphaned lines that have no partner linked by alliteration.

Tennyson's translational choices at the lexical level appear most clearly by comparing the original text and the translations to which he had access. Below, the first stanza of his "Brunanburh" is set beside Sweet's version of the Old English, followed by the translations of Ellis, Turner, Guest, Sweet, and Hallam Tennyson. For ease of comparison, spacing has been adjusted to align original and translation.

Sweet's transcription (1871)	**Tennyson (1880)**
Æthelstan cyning,	Athelstan King,
earla drihten,	Lord among Earls,
beorna beáh-gyfa,	Bracelet-bestower and
	Baron of Barons,
and his brother eac,	He and his brother,
Eadmund ætheling,	Edmund Atheling,
ealdor langne-tir;	Gaining a lifelong

[171] Jones, *Fossil Poetry*, 256–257.
[172] Joseph Phelan, *The Music of Verse: Metrical Experiment in Nineteenth-Century Poetry* (Basingstoke: Palgrave Macmillan, 2012), 89.
[173] For example, A.J. Bliss, *The Metre of Beowulf* (Oxford: Basil Blackwell, 1967); Robert Payson Creed, *Reconstructing the Rhythm of Beowulf* (Columbia: University of Missouri Press, 1990); Thomas Cable, "Kaluza's Law and the Progress of Old English Metrics," in *Development in Prosodic Systems*, ed. Johanna Paula Monique Fikkert and Haike Jacobs, Studies in Generative Grammar 58 (Berlin: Mouton de Gruyter, 2003), 145–158.

geslogon æt secce, / Glory in battle,
sweorda ecgum, / Slew with the sword-edge
ymbe Brunanburh. / There by Brunanburh,
Bord-weal clufon, / Brake the shield-wall,
heowon hetho-linda, / Hewed the lindenwood,
/ Hacked the battle-shield,
hamora lafum. / Sons of Edward with hammered brands.
eáforan Eadweardes.[174] / (1–14)

Ellis (1801)

Here Athelstan King,
Of Earls the Lord,
Of Barons the bold chief,
And his brother eke,
Edmund Atheling,
Elders a long train,
Slew in the shock (*of war*)
With the edges of swords
Round Brunangburh. [*sic*]
They cloven the hard walls,
They hew the lofty ones,
The marches (*borders*) they leave,
As aforen in Edward's days.[175]

Turner (1807)

Here Athelstan king,
of earls the lord,
the giver of the bracelets of the nobles,
and his brother also,
Edmund the ætheling,
the Elder! a lasting glory
won by slaughter in battle
with the edges of swords
at Brunan burh. [*sic*]
The wall of shields they cleaved,
they hewed the noble banners:
the survivors of the family,
the children of Edward.[176]

Guest (1838)

Now
Æthelstan king, of earls the Lord,

Of barons the beigh-giver, and his brother eke,

Edmund the etheling, elders a long tire,

Sweet (1871) (original brackets)

Æthelstan (the king),
lord of [men]

bracelet-giver of [chieftains],
and his brother eke,

Eadmund (the) prince,
[A life-long glory they won

---

[174] Warton, *History of English Poetry*, 1:150–151.
[175] Ellis, *Specimens of the Early English Poets*, 1:15–17.
[176] Turner, *History of the Anglo-Saxons*, 1807, 2:289.

Slew in battle, with sword-edges,	by striking at the battle, with edges of swords,
Round Brunanburgh. [sic]	near Brunanburh.
Shield-wall they clave,	(They) clove the board-wall,
They hew'd battle-lindens, with hammer-glaives,	hewed the [war] lindens, with relics of hammers (i.e. swords),
The sons of Edward!	(the [offspring] of Edward.[177]

Hallam Tennyson (1876)

Athelstan King, lord of earls, giver of costly gifts among barons, and his brother Edmund Atheling – life-long glory they gain'd in the strife by Brunanburh with the edges of their swords. They clove the wall of shields; they hew'd the battle-shields of linden-wood; with hammer'd brands they hew'd them – these sons of Edward.[178]

Alfred Tennyson tends to ignore the workings of case endings, a crime for which Kemble called some of his fellow philologists worthy of "a sound flogging."[179] This was not a result of ignorance on Tennyson's part, however; in addition to his earlier studies of Old English, he knew Latin, Greek, and German and thus was quite familiar with the importance of cases. Moreover, Sweet took pains to identify them. "For the benefit of the Anglo-Saxon student," he wrote, "a close attention has been paid in rendering the grammatical inflections of the text, a practice almost wholly disused since the days of Hickes [1705]; but which cannot be too strongly recommended to every future translator from this language."[180] Tennyson's deviations are therefore best considered as purposeful choices. In this context, it emerges that he cared more about his rhythm, his alliteration, and each word's relationship to its Modern English equivalent rather than its specific grammatical use in the sentence before him.

In this first stanza, his handling of *eorla* and *beorna* illustrates how he weighed the competing priorities that confront every translator, especially when creating a poetic result. Sweet specifically gives permission for liberal interpretation of these words in a footnote, saying, "The terms eorl and beorn – man and [chief] – are used with great latitude of meaning in Anglo-Saxon poetry," though they were generally applied to "persons of eminent rank or exalted courage."[181] Sweet was the only authority to state that *eorl* was simply a generic term for man. Tennyson, like the other translators whose work he had at his disposal, opted for *earls* as the Modern English equivalent. It is an appropriate choice as a translation of *nobleman*, especially because it is the descendent of the word in the original poem. However, *eorla* is a genitive plural, making Athelstan (strictly speaking) a lord *of* earls, not *among* them – a fact that all the other translations preserved. Tennyson's deviation seems to be a concession to meter, creating a dactylic phrase ("Lord among Earls") that

---

[177] Warton, *History of English Poetry*, 1:150–151.
[178] Hallam Tennyson, "Brunanburh," 920.
[179] Kemble, "Oxford Professors of Anglo-Saxon," 603.
[180] Warton, *History of English Poetry*, 1:150.
[181] Ibid., 1:150. Brackets are Sweet's.

replicates that pattern established naturally by the faithfully copied first line, "Athelstan King."

In the original poem, Athelstan is a bracelet-bestower (*beag-giefa*) to men (*beorna*). Tennyson expands the single word *beorna* into a new title for the king: "Baron of Barons." In terms of his word choice, he was in good company. Although his dictionaries told Tennyson that *beorn* could mean simply *man* as well as some kind of nobility, Ellis, Guest, and his son Hallam had given *barons* for *beorna*; Turner used *nobles*, Sweet *chieftains*. Given the translations Tennyson was reading, then, *barons* seemed a fair choice and had the benefit of sonic similarity to what it translated. All the translations except that of his son presented *beorna* as a genitive ("of barons"), an idea that the phrase "Baron of Barons" echoes. It wreaks some havoc on what Kemble had called the "couplets" of Anglo-Saxon meter, however. "Baron of Barons" amplifies the *b*-alliteration from the previous line ("bracelet-bestower"), but it forces "he and his brother" to stand alone as an extraneous alliterative short line without a partner save the following line "Edmund Atheling," which shares no sounds in common.

In the last lines of the stanza, Tennyson's various stylistic commitments demand careful navigation. All his predecessors brought *clufan* forward into a modern form as *cloven*, *cleaved*, *clave*, or *clove*. However, by translating *bordweal* as *shield-wall* (an accurate substitute compound), Tennyson was in danger of losing the *b*-alliteration of his "couplet" (Brunanburh/bordweal). To regain that alliteration, he chose *brake* for the destructive act described by *clufon*. He does adhere to the genealogy of *heowan* by using its descendant word *hew'd*, just as the earlier translators did. He then faces a choice of what to do with *heaþolind*. The first part of the compound lacks a Modern English phonetic echo for the idea of battle, but scholars had long recognized *lind* as an Anglo-Saxon metonym for *shield*. Rask's preface had done so early in the century,[182] and Sweet offers a footnote that occupies most of a page proving that "'lind' ... evidently means shield," providing multiple quotations to show that "in this interpretation of 'lind' all our vocabularies agree."[183] Ellis and Turner had gone astray in their translations, but the three most recent to Tennyson's work had given *battle-lindens* (Guest), "[war] lindens" (Sweet), and "battle-shields of linden-wood" (Hallam). Tennyson chooses *lindenwood*; it is a compound that contains a piece of the source text and replicates its metonymy for shield. This solution is a good one, but it removes the alliteration of "heowan heaþolind." To remedy this shortfall, the Victorian poet added an entirely new line: "Hacked the battle-shield." It is an unnecessary addition, for "hammered brands" in the next line would have created an alliterative "couplet;" but it does allow him, like his son, to clarify that battle-shields are the things being broken.

The next section continues:

---

[182] Rask, *A Grammar of the Anglo-Saxon Tongue*, xliii.
[183] Warton, *History of English Poetry*, 1:151.

Swa him geæthele wæs	Theirs was a greatness
from cneo-mægum,	Got from their Grandsires –
thæt híe æt campe oft,	Theirs that so often in
with lathra gehwæne,	Strife with their enemies
land ealgodon,	Struck for their hoards and their hearths and their
hord and hámas	homes.

In this stanza, Tennyson takes more liberties with the Anglo-Saxon meaning and style. A more literal translation might be:

> It was natural for them
> as received from their ancestors,
> that they at battle often
> against each of the hostile ones
> defended land,
> hoard and homes.

Tennyson adds alliteration, preferring (as he does throughout this translation) to form groups of three alliterating words, even if the original has only a pair. For example, he replaces *land* with *hearths* in order to join it with *hoards* and *homes*.

It is not unusual for Anglo-Saxon poetry to have three alliterating words in one long line (or one "couplet," as the Victorians would have it), but in that context, two must appear in the first half and one in the second. In this stanza, Tennyson strains the rules of Anglo-Saxon prosody. The pair "Theirs was a greatness / Got from their grand-sires" loads the alliteration in the second half. In addition, his alliteration proliferates beyond what is necessary to fulfill the requirements of the original's style. Anglo-Saxon alliteration only applies to words that share the entire cluster of initial consonants. In this stanza, for example, Tennyson pairs *strife* with *struck*, faithfully matching their initial consonant sounds. This rule means that "greatness" and "grandsires" alliterate, but "got" is superfluous. Alexander states that Tennyson's alliteration "is ornamental and optional where the original alliteration is instrumental and compulsory, pointing out the stress pattern." This fact is nearly inevitable once Tennyson chose to write in a metrical pattern other than Anglo-Saxon prosody. It is important to observe, however, that Tennyson made an effort to maintain alliteration in his own fashion.

These techniques continue in the rest of the translation. Thus, there is some justice to Alexander's assessment that the poem's alliteration as "ornamental and optional," though it would be more accurate to say that ornamental alliteration interacts with a strong echo of Anglo-Saxon structure. Whereas "the original alliteration is instrumental and compulsory, pointing out the stress pattern," Tennyson works within a pre-set stress pattern. He therefore tends to place alliterative words at the beginning of lines so that the pseudo-dactylic meter will make them coincide with accented syllables, as with "Glode over earth till the glorious creature / Sank to his setting" (29–30). The longer lines that often end stanzas still roughly conform to Anglo-Saxon alliterative rules, with occasional stand-alone lines that lack a partner with which to alliterate.

Ultimately, as Irving aptly puts it, "all this is only to say that Tennyson's translation distorts the original. All translations do that." The point of interest for Tennyson scholars is "not what Tennyson did for Anglo-Saxon, but what Anglo-Saxon did for Tennyson." Irving sees the "Brunanburh" translation as a return to interest in Old English after a gap of more than forty years, prompted by a renewed interest in English history. He then sees its influence on Tennyson's late poems, which "show much interesting experimentation in meter, the use of dialect and general register."[184] I argue, however, that Tennyson's early exposure to this verse helped shape his style throughout his life, including experimentation with meter, fondness for dialect, and a keen sensitivity to register. The following section, for example, looks at how Tennyson incorporated alliteration patterns and apposition into his work.

Anglo-Saxonist Thomas Wright wrote in an 1846 essay that "To feel [Old English] poetry, it is necessary that we should understand well the language, and that we should also be acquainted with the character of the people; we can know nothing of it by *literal* translations into our form of the language ... or by the translation of poetical words into the most prosaic that we can find to answer to them."[185] By these measures, Tennyson was well equipped to "feel" Anglo-Saxon poetry – even when writing his own.

Anglo-Saxon Stylistic Echoes

Tennyson's translational decisions were intended to create the effect of listening to "echoes from the deserted temples of the past" rhythmically and phonetically.[186] While the few lines of *Beowulf* and the later "Battle of Brunanburh" are his only known direct translations from Old English, his original compositions also reverberate with memories of Anglo-Saxon prosody. Its influence is subtle and therefore difficult to tease out, but it was not, for that, less important. In the introduction to his 2002 translation of *Beowulf*, poet Seamus Heaney explains that after studying Old English poems as an undergraduate, he "developed ... a feel for the language." Years later, he realized that "without any conscious intent on my part certain lines in the first poem in my first book conformed to the requirements of Anglo-Saxon metrics ... Part of me, in other words, had been writing Anglo-Saxon from the start."[187] Heaney's experience testifies to the effect that familiarity with a distinctive poetic style can have.

Turner's history from the beginning of the nineteenth century describes the style of Anglo-Saxon poetry written in the vernacular as follows:

> [I]t consists chiefly of periphrasis, and metaphors expressed in a metrical but simple arrangement of words, with some alliteration. The usual particles are most frequently omitted; and the intended meaning is conveyed in short and contracted phrase, multiplied by the periphrasis and metaphor. The position of the words is

---

[184] Irving, Jr, "The Charge of the Saxon Brigade," 178, 187.
[185] Wright, *Essays*, 1:13–14.
[186] Kemble, *Beowulf*, 1:xxxii.
[187] Seamus Heaney, "Translator's Introduction," in *Beowulf: A Verse Translation*, Norton Critical Edition (New York: W.W. Norton, 2002), xxxii–xxxiii.

forced out of their natural arrangement by a wilful [sic] inversion, and the regular course of the subject is frequently interrupted by violent and abrupt transitions.[188]

Despite its disapproving tone, this passage successfully sketches the main features of Old English verse. Nearly fifty years later, Wright summarized the characteristics of Anglo-Saxon style as "loftiness of expression, exuberance of metaphor, intricacy of construction, and a diction differing entirely from that of prose." Like his former tutor Kemble, Wright noted that similes were rare; he counts only five in the whole of *Beowulf*, "and those are of the simplest description."[189] These general traits find an echo in Tennyson's verse. For example, "Aylmer's Field" (1864) decries hypocritical Christians who cherish wealth and comfort, sacrificing nothing for God:

> not a hair
> Ruffled upon the scarfskin, even while
> The deathless ruler of thy dying house
> Is wounded to the death that cannot die.   (659–662)

In addition to the unhyphenated compound *scarfskin*, these lines offer a Victorian version of another kind of Anglo-Saxon metaphor, called a kenning – that is, a compound phrase that describes something by means of one of its attributes. The Eversley Edition glosses "deathless ruler" as meaning "the soul." Later in the same line, "dying house" is another kenning, this one directly echoing Old English poetry that calls the body the lifehouse. *In Memoriam*'s use of "the narrow house" (xxxv.2), which Tennyson glossed as "the grave,"[190] is a similar Anglo-Saxon stylistic revival.

More commonly, in looking for echoes of Anglo-Saxon style, two characteristics stand out: apposition and alliteration. Old English poetry delights in apposition – that is, "syntactically parallel words or word-groups which share a common referent and which occur within a single clause."[191] This feature constitutes one of the greatest challenges for translators; as Alexander admits of his own translation process for "Brunanburh," "the juggling of near-synonyms in dense apposition is hard to translate with any elegance into verse."[192] The opening lines of Tennyson's rendition – "Athelstan King, / Lord among Earls, / Bracelet-bestower" – form typical Anglo-Saxon apposition, as do "He and his brother ... sons of Edward." So, too, does the sequence of verbs for the brothers' actions: "Slew ... brake ... hewed ... hacked."

In more recent compositions, the technique allows for extended emphasis and nuance of meaning. Fred C. Robinson writes that "the distinguishing feature of apposition (or variation) is its parataxis – its lack of an expressed logical connection between the apposed elements." The parallel grammatical structure leaves gaps full

---

[188] Turner, *History of the Anglo-Saxons*, 1807, 2:278.
[189] Wright, *Essays*, 1:13–14.
[190] Tennyson, *Enoch Arden and In Memoriam*, 233.
[191] Fred C. Robinson, "Two Aspects of Variation in Old English Poetry," in *Old English Poetry: Essays on Style*, ed. Daniel Gillmore Calder, vol. 10, Contributions of the UCLA Center for Medieval and Renaissance Studies (Berkeley: University of California Press, 1979), 129.
[192] Alexander, "Tennyson's 'The Battle of Brunanburh,'" 158.

of implications.[193] Variation, in other words, is not simply a matter of rotating vocabulary. Thus, there is an important insight into Tennyson's Ulysses when he cries, "How dull it is to pause, to make an end, / To rust unburnish'd, not to shine in use!" (22–23). That Ulysses thinks pausing is the same as ending and rusting indicates his restless urge for action. Variation's lists can create emphasis, but they are also a device that responds to linguistic imprecision. By accumulating "near-synonyms," the writer may be able to better approximate the reality of what he describes. If a word can never (or no longer) describe one thing exactly, then we can at least learn the shape of its idea by looking at it from many angles. *In Memoriam* performs a similar task when, as William A. Wilson puts it, "without the apt word to fit his dead friend, Tennyson gives him to us in a wealth of similitudes."[194] Old English variation describes its objects by mentioning their origins, their different functions, their relations to people and institutions, and so forth. By the same token, it is informative which aspects a writer brings together for the reader's consideration.

We may see Tennyson employing the technique in a forceful unpublished sonnet, written in a notebook among poems that were published in the 1832 volume:

> Woe to the double-tongued, the land's disease,
> Lords of the hustings, whose mob-rhetoric rends
> The ears of Truth! How shall they make amends,
> Those that would shatter England's ancient ease
> Built on broad bases and the solid peace   (5)
> Wherein she prospered? – Woe to those false friends
> That mouth great things and for their own vile ends
> Make swarm with brazen clang the humming bees;
> Those that would turn the ploughshares into swords,
> Those that inflame themselves with idle words   (10)
> In every market-place. Their doom is signed,
> Though they shall cause confusion and the storms
> Of civil blood – moths, cankers, palmer-worms
> That gnaw the bud, blind leaders of the blind.

The poem's outrage makes its apposition appropriate; Tennyson amasses insults, using variation to condemn his subjects thoroughly. The first lines exhibit the practice clearly: we read of "the double tongued, the land's disease, / Lords of the hustings." This apposition is especially damning as *land's disease* equates with *lords*, who should – by virtue of that position – be protectors of the land. Later, there are "false friends ... those that would turn ploughshares into swords, / Those that inflame themselves," with an elaboration of *they* as "moths, cankers, palmer-worms ... blind leaders."

As in this sonnet, Tennyson's apposition commonly appears when his tone is emphatic or urgent, particularly in his nationalistic poems. One such poem – published

---

[193] Fred C. Robinson, *Beowulf and the Appositive Style*, The Hodges Lectures (Knoxville: University of Tennessee Press, 1985), 3–4.

[194] William A. Wilson, "Victorian Philology and the Anxiety of Language in Tennyson's *In Memoriam*," *Texas Studies in Literature and Language* 30, no. 1 (1988): 31.

in the 1842 volume – opens with the imperative, "Love thou thy land, with love far-brought / From out the storied Past, and used / Within the Present" (1–3), an exhortation that might have come from Kemble or any number of other Anglo-Saxonists. Tennyson writes that such love will not endure "sordid ends" for "English natures, freemen, friends, / Thy brothers and immortal souls" (7–8). Yet the next stanza warns against pandering to "the herd, wild hearts and feeble wings" (11). Other lines give the impression of apposition through interruption: "neither hide the ray / From those, not blind, who wait for day" (14–15); "Make knowledge circle with the winds; / But let her herald, Reverence, fly / Before her" (17–19); "let the change which comes be free … And work, a joint of state" (45, 47). The lines "If New and Old, disastrous feud, / Must ever shock" (77–78) form a strange apposition, because the units are not in truth syntactically parallel. One of the most tangled passages offers hope for the future:

> A slow-developed strength awaits
> Completion in a painful school;
> Phantoms of other forms of rule,
> New Majesties of mighty States –
> The warders of the growing hour,
> But vague in vapour, hard to mark   (57–62)

Here the grammar is so fragmented that many parallels seem possible, and it takes some concentration to parse the sentence. Indeed, so much of the poem is punctuated by semicolons, colons, commas, and dashes that it presents the reader with raw materials and multiple potentialities for combining them. It leaves the reader with an impression of "phantoms" that are "vague in vapour, hard to mark." Yet its emphatic tone instills a confidence, born of the speaker's assertiveness, that something good ("a slow-developed strength") will come to the land.

Despite these instances, Tennyson generally preferred a flow of continuous syntax. The attribute that reading Old English poetry most encouraged in his writing was alliteration. Joseph Phelan and Meredith Martin have each discussed how nineteenth-century scholars grappled with the idea of Anglo-Saxon meter, often recruiting it for nationalistic purposes or struggling to adapt it to nineteenth-century compositions.[195] Phelan's book on *The Music of Verse* provides good insight into the theories that various writers and thinkers formulated in dialogue with traditions both classical and English. His third chapter in particular explores their efforts to describe the system behind the "native tradition" of alliterative verse, from Conybeare's "essentially relaxed and unsystematic" approach to the schema laid out by Thorpe's translation of Rask's grammar. Yet surprisingly, Tennyson appears exactly once in Phelan's book – as an example of logaoedic verse – and nowhere in the Anglo-Saxon chapter.[196] Tennyson was a poet immersed in the very same debates and experiments Phelan describes, as is evident from his friendships, his personal library, and his sensitivity to criticism about his meter.

---

[195] Martin, *Rise and Fall of Meter*, 111.
[196] Phelan, *The Music of Verse*, 92, 147–148.

Tennyson's interaction with Old English literature spanned most of his poetic career and, as we shall see, affected his sonic patterning. For example, the early poem "Buonaparte" (published and probably written in 1832) imitates some elements of Old English poetics, an appropriate choice for a nationalistic, anti-French sonnet:

> He thought to quell the stubborn hearts of oak,
> Madman! to chain with chains, and bind with bands
> That island queen who sways the floods and lands
> From Ind to Ind, but in fair daylight woke,
> When from her wooden walls, – lit by sure hands, –   (5)
> With thunders, and with lightnings, and with smoke, –
> Peal after peal, the British battle broke,
> Lulling the brine against the Coptic sands.
> We taught him lowlier moods, when Elsinore
> Heard the war moan along the distant sea,   (10)
> Rocking with shattered spars, with sudden fires
> Flamed over: at Trafalgar yet once more
> We taught him: late he learned humility
> Perforce, like those whom Gideon schooled with briars.

The opening lines lend an archaic flavor, for it is typical of both Old English and Latin poetry to describe actions redundantly, as in "to chain with chains, and bind with bands." The first two lines also feature interwoven apposition: "He … Madman!" and "to quell … to chain." Rhythmically or grammatically, most lines can be divided into half-lines similar to Old English. Sometimes Tennyson achieves this explicitly through commas or other punctuation, but other times the end of a grammatical unit suggests a dividing point. Roughly half the lines begin with a dactyl and then resolve into trochees, with the important alliterative words usually falling within the trochees. They thus take the form of Anglo-Saxon lines with an added initial dactyl.

"Buonaparte" also contains a remarkable amount of alliteration, and indeed critics commented that Tennyson's verse in general was (as he reported them saying) "studiedly alliterative." He denied that the effect was studied; in fact, he described composing so alliteratively that he often had to reduce the effect later.[197] This aspect of Anglo-Saxon style, therefore, suited Tennyson's taste. His earliest extant letter comments on Milton's *Samson Agonistes*: "In line 147th 'the gates of Azza' this probably … was to avoid too great an alliteration which the 'Gates of Gaza' would have caused, though (in my opinion) it would have rendered it more beautiful."[198] The alliteration in "Buonaparte" is generally constrained to half-lines (for example, "late he learned"), though the occasional link imitates Old English poetics, as in line 4, which bridges across the comma's pause with stressed words beginning with *i*: "From **I**nd to **I**nd, but *i*n fair daylight woke." Line 7 decisively splits itself with heavy-handed alliteration: "peal after peal, the British battle broke." This line ignores all the rules of Anglo-Saxon poetry, but it achieves a unity of sound and meaning that Tennyson enjoyed and therefore would have taken priority: the bilabial plosives

---

[197] Hallam Tennyson, *Memoir*, 2:15.
[198] Tennyson, *Letters*, 1982, 1:2.

(*p*'s and *b*'s) imitate the hammering sounds of battle; the dactylic first half suggests endless repetition of peals, after which the trochaic "British battle broke" reflects the pounding of the warfare.

An additional, alternative pattern of Old English poetry was available to the poet in the form of longer chains of alliteration, which Kemble recognized. As he explained to Grimm in 1840:

> It is of this kind, where, in the second part of the line (or the 2d line) the word that does not alliterate with the first line, leads to the alliteration of the next couplet ... This occurs, as it appears to me, about once in every twenty lines ... sometimes it binds six or eight lines together in the same continuous way.[199]

"Buonaparte" echoes this technique by bridging alliteration across lines. The alliteration of line 4 lies in its vowels (Ind/Ind/in); the *w* of *woke* then sets up the alliteration of the beginning of line 5: "When from her wooden walls." Line 11's primary alliteration is *s*, but *fires* leads to the following line, which contains "Flamed over: at Trafalgar." (Though "flamed" is not stressed, the alliteration is impossible to ignore as it follows *fires* immediately.) Across lines 6 and 7, the main alliteration of "British battle broke" recurs in the "brine." Again, the "distant sea" of line 10 prefigures the *s*-alliteration of "shattered spars" and "sudden fires."

"Buonaparte" provides an early example of the Anglo-Saxon stylistic echoes in Tennyson's poetry, but they were not limited to his unpublished or obscure efforts. "Mariana," for example, was one of his first critical successes. Reviews of the 1830 volume *Poems, Chiefly Lyrical* singled it out for praise; the *Westminster Review* named it the best poem in the book.[200] It was reprinted in anthologies, and it was often cited as a token of Tennyson's talent – for example, in commenting on what could be expected of "the author of 'Mariana.'"[201] J.F.A. Pyre argued that "Mariana" is one of the most successful early poems precisely because Tennyson adheres to a regular meter;[202] within that regularity, though, the poem arranges alliteration in a fashion similar to the structure of Old English poetry.

In "Mariana," the iambic tetrameter lines reproduce a four-stress unit. Within these, Tennyson employs what I will call a balanced line – that is, one that distributes alliteration in both halves. The following examples adhere strictly to the distribution pattern of Anglo-Saxon meter:

Either at morn or **e**ventide (16)	Stresses 1 & 3
She drew her **c**asement-**c**urtain by (19)	Stresses 2 & 3
And **gl**anced athwart the **gl**ooming flats (20)	Stresses 1 & 3
Which to the **w**ooing **w**ind aloof (75)	Stresses 1, 2, & 3

The following samples, strictly speaking, violate Old English meter by including the fourth stressed syllable. However, they are balanced and thus make a similar impact:

---

[199] Kemble, *Correspondence*, 201.
[200] John D. Jump, ed., *Tennyson: The Critical Heritage*, Critical Heritage Series (London: Routledge & Kegan Paul, 1986), 28.
[201] Shannon, *Tennyson and the Reviewers*, 4, 20, 29, 31, 63, 66.
[202] Pyre, *The Formation of Tennyson's Style*, 26.

The rusted **n**ails fell from the **kn**ots (3)	Stresses 2 & 4
A **sl**uice with blackened waters **sl**ept (38)	Stresses 1 & 4
Upon her **b**ed, across her **b**row (56)	Stresses 2 & 4
Old **f**ootsteps trod the upper **f**loors (67)	Stresses 1 & 4

Further enhancing the effect of these lines, alliterative sound bleeds into surrounding lines in several places. If Tennyson had been trying to imitate Old English directly, the sound should always appear *before* the alliterative line as a kind of sonic foreshadowing, as in the lines "And o'er it **m**any, round and small, / The clustered **m**arish-**m**osses crept" (39–40); or again, "The **s**parrow's chirrup on the roof, / The **s**low clock ticking, and the **s**ound (73–74). But the poet lets the links drift in both directions, creating longer sonically linked sections such as:

> I would that I were **d**ead!
> All **d**ay within the **d**reamy house,
> The **d**oors upon their hinges creaked;   (60–62)

and:

> Old **f**aces glimmered through the doors,
> Old **f**ootsteps trod the upper **f**loors,
> Old voices called her **f**rom without.   (66–68)

In these two passages, the alliterative sound both anticipates and recalls the line in which it dominates.

There are also, of course, several instances of "unbalanced" alliterative lines; repeated initial consonants can happen without conscious effort, and Tennyson was especially fond of the effect, even without an Anglo-Saxonizing agenda. For example, "**W**eeded and **w**orn the ancient thatch" front-loads the *w* sound with nothing in the latter half of the line that links to it (7). Lines 28 ("**F**rom the dark **f**en the oxen's low") and line 30 ("In **s**leep she **s**eemed to walk forlorn") do the same. These three are the only such lines, however. The majority of lines that contain alliterating stressed syllables do so within a pattern loosely imitative of Anglo-Saxon verse, far more often than we would expect from a random sample.

The understated presence of Old English traits in Tennyson's poetry often leads to their being overlooked or, alternatively, being considered the result of a lazy understanding of the Anglo-Saxons. Both Alexander and Irving, for example, underestimate the depth of Tennyson's knowledge of the language. Irving writes that the poet, when he settled down to translate "The Battle of Brunanburh," was partly aware of the sound of Anglo-Saxon from "whatever faint memories he may have had of Kemble's conversations,"[203] but he objects that the Cambridge Apostles showed no sign of taking Kemble's obsession seriously. However, club alumnus Henry Sidgwick (who came up to Cambridge in 1855) described the society as:

---

[203] Irving, Jr, "The Charge of the Saxon Brigade," 186, 177–178.

a group of intimate friends, who were perfectly frank with each other and indulged in any amount of humorous sarcasm and playful banter, and yet each respects the other, and when he discourses tries to learn from him and see what he sees ... The gravest subjects were continually debated, but gravity of treatment ... was not imposed.[204]

If this was the case for serious matters of philosophy and spirituality, we should be wary of reading light-hearted banter between Apostles as a sign of Tennyson's inattention to, or dismissal of, Kemble's passion for philology – not to mention the group's larger interest in linguistics. As this chapter has shown, the poet remained interested in Old English literature throughout his life, continuing to acquire and study reference books on the language, for example. Although there is no reason to believe that Tennyson programmatically tried to revive Anglo-Saxon prosody in his original compositions, stylistic elements from Old English poetry did infuse his writing, just as Old English itself lay within the structure of Victorian speech.

Conclusion

Tennyson's Anglo-Saxonism is partly that of the academic Anglo-Saxonists he knew and read, and partly it is an imaginative touchstone. Just as, for Müller, linguistic roots stood as "barriers between the chaos and the cosmos" of speech, the Anglo-Saxons acted as cultural roots.[205] They stood between the chaos of unknowable early humanity and the cosmos of English national character (whatever one's genealogical descent). The marks of Tennyson's ongoing interest are spread throughout his corpus, but this very distribution also confirms that Britain's pre-Conquest heritage remained active in his imagination.

Tennyson brought together his familiarity with Old English style and his ideas about history and heritage in the sonnet "Show-Day at Battle Abbey, 1876," which prefaced his play *Harold*. The poem contemplates the simultaneous realities of past and present at the location of the fateful battle that changed the course of English history and the history of the English language:

> A garden here – May breath and bloom of spring –
> The cuckoo yonder from an English elm
> Crying "with my false egg I overwhelm
> The native nest:" and fancy hears the ring
> Of harness, and that deathful arrow sing,   (5)
> And Saxon battleaxe clang on Norman helm.
> Here rose the dragon-banner of our realm:
> Here fought, here fell, our Norman-slander'd king.
> O Garden blossoming out of English blood!
> O strange hate-healer Time! We stroll and stare   (10)
> Where might made right eight hundred years ago;

---

[204] Arthur Sidgwick and Eleanor Mildred Sidgwick, *Henry Sidgwick: A Memoir* (London: Macmillan, 1906), 34.

[205] Müller, *Lectures*, 5th ed., ix.

> Might, right? ay good, so all things make for good –
> But he and he, if soul be soul, are where
> Each stands full face with all he did below.

The speaker's imagination hears echoes of the battle beneath the quiet of a spring day, and the poem itself is likewise dense with compounds and alliteration, the latter mostly decorative except for lines 9 (blossoming … blood) and 10 (strange … stroll and stare). *Norman-slandered* is also worthy of note as it employs an obsolete definition of *slandered*. In terms of losing the battle, Harold is slandered in the sense "To bring into discredit, disgrace, or disrepute." The play makes much of Harold being tricked out of his characteristic honesty into swearing falsely, and in this sense the Normans slander him as "In or after Biblical use: … to cause to lapse spiritually or morally." Both definitions are obsolete, with the *OED*'s most recent quotations dating no later than 1603 and 1563 respectively. Thus in these fourteen lines we find samples of the philological techniques that this book maps in the larger Tennysonian canon, which the next chapter explores further.

The poem is also a succinct summary of Tennyson's attitude toward the impact that the Battle of Hastings had on English society. There is a modest lament for the Anglo-Saxons (the cuckoo ventriloquizes the Norman invasion, overwhelming the "native nest" in the "English elm"), but there is also pride in the nation that was forged in the aftermath ("ay good, so all things make for good"). Moreover, the introductory sonnet and the play taken together suggest that the battle is always happening in some ghostly world. Importantly, its presence is aural: people hear echoes of the battle both just before and centuries after its occurrence. The arrow that the Bayeux Tapestry shows killing Harold "sings" in the imagination. And just as the speaker of the sonnet hears "the ring / Of harness, and that deathful arrow sing, / And Saxon battleaxe clang on Norman helm," so in the play the conflict is heard ahead of its occurrence. As Harold's predecessor King Edward lies on his deathbed, Archbishop Aldred reports that someone passing by Senlac hill heard:

> A ghostly horn
> Blowing continually, and faint battle-hymns,
> And cries, and clashes, and the groans of men;
> And dreadful shadows strove upon the hill,
> And dreadful lights crept up from out the marsh –
> Corpse-candles gliding over nameless graves – [206]

It is a battle that defines England and so is always taking place at Senlac, just as its aftermath is reverberating through the English language.

In the play itself, Tennyson's sensitivity to the origins of English words is apparent, somewhat to its detriment. The words are generally monosyllabic and Germanic, which is something of a challenge to Tennyson's usual music. Although he tended to prefer words of Germanic origin in general (as shown in Chapter 4), the self-conscious effort to write plain, pre-Conquest English adds an awkward artificiality to the dialogue. This choice to only use Anglo-Saxon-derived words

---

[206] Tennyson, "Harold," 275.

made sense for a play focused on Anglo-Saxons before the Norman Conquest brought a flood of Romance-language vocabulary into English. Tennyson's skills, however, lay in revealing language history in its full richness, as the next chapter explores. His Anglo-Saxonism was an appreciation for that period, not a rejection of what followed.

Both Tennyson and Kemble found in language an unbroken connection to the past. It was linguistic research that most engaged Kemble, providing the basis for his opinions on other aspects of Anglo-Saxon culture. His philological focus is evident in the syllabus for his Cambridge 1834 lecture series on "History of the English Language, First, or Anglo-Saxon Period," particularly in the circular reasoning that he offers for the course. The introduction outlines a plan in which poems will prepare students "to understand the nature and character of the people, whose language we are to examine."[207] Yet his students would undoubtedly have had difficulty tackling poems without a grounding in Old English, and he made it abundantly clear in his other writings that a firm grasp of Anglo-Saxon grammar was necessary before attempting translation (in fact, although eighty people signed up for his lectures, attendance soon dropped off, and it is unclear whether he delivered the full course).[208] Language was the beginning and the end for Kemble; it was both the means to understand medieval documents and a subject about which those documents could provide insight. For him and a growing number of other Victorians, the Anglo-Saxons were "the people whose tongue we speak, and under whose laws we live."[209] Tennyson, too, was drawn to the idea that nineteenth-century Britons were still speaking their language. Their language was the most direct manner in which that history lived on in the present day – a more literal version of hearing the echoes of the Battle of Hastings. Tennyson was intrigued by the ways in which speech can return on itself through rhyme and repetition, and the traces of Old English within Modern English are a kind of continual return.

Jason Camlot reads nineteenth-century Anglo-Saxonism, or "Teutomania," as one of two traditions of Victorian rhetoric. In contrast to the cosmopolitan approach that was tolerant of eclecticism, a stance articulated most clearly by Walter Pater near the end of the century, Camlot describes "the Saxonist theory of style" as calling for "the reversal of foreign influence upon the English language so that the common racial characteristics and national identity held in common by the English might be restored."[210] There were, of course, voices who promoted this simplistic view. Turner the historian, for one, thought that "Saxon terms might be substituted for almost all the words not marked as Saxon" in a set of passages he quoted from famous writers.[211] Dialect poet William Barnes was one of the most prominent devotees of returning to purely Germanic language; he was so committed to constructing his writing with "native" components that he employed starkly literal compounds in

---

[207] Kemble, "History of the English Language," 3.
[208] Kemble, *Correspondence*, 49.
[209] Kemble, "Review of Cædmon," 329.
[210] Jason Camlot, *Style and the Nineteenth-Century British Critic: Sincere Mannerisms*, Nineteenth Century (Aldershot: Ashgate, 2008), 115.
[211] Turner, *History of the Anglo-Saxons*, 1807, 2:471.

his prose such as *word-building, word-wear, book-speech, upbuilding, out-working, speech-craft*, and *rede-craft* (logic).

Barnes's program is evident in his book *An Outline of Rede-Craft (Logic): With English Wording* (1880). The table of contents – or "Heads of Matter" – reveals the contortions he has had to go through to make "native" English vocabulary express classical concepts – such as "fore-begged (hypothetical) thought-puttings" and "in-lurking rede-ship (enthymeme)." Despite the supposed clarity of his word-stock, he quite rightly felt it necessary to offer the original terms in parentheses.[212] Of Barnes's project to replace Romance-originated words with Saxon equivalents, Gerard Manley Hopkins wrote a few years later (1882), "He does not see the utter hopelessness of the thing ... He calls degrees of comparison pitches of suchness: we *ought* to call them so, but alas!" Referring to Barnes's *An Outline of English Speech-Craft* (1878), Hopkins describes the book's language as "an unknown tongue, a sort of modern Anglosaxon."[213]

For the more philologically minded, though, the aim was to reconnect with the past, not return to it. The Anglo-Saxonism of Tennyson's circle did not lead to a conviction that style should be exclusively "native." Kemble was among the most passionate advocates for the study of Anglo-Saxon language and traditions, but even he was measured in his goals for reacquainting the English with their cultural forebears. "Without wishing [my countrymen] to turn back the stream of the world's great flow," he wrote to Grimm, "without calling upon them to become once more Anglo-Saxons, a patriot may wish them to look backward a little upon the great and good of olden time, and to emulate the virtues of their forefathers, without losing the wisdom of our own times."[214] As a result, Kemble was "little fond of modern Anglosaxon [sic] verses" (or for that matter, "modern Latin hexameters or modern Greek iambics"), because it was pointless to write contemporary material in an idiom that had expressed a different way of thinking.[215]

Tennyson's use of Old English likewise reflected his sense of that heritage as central to nineteenth-century life yet not always detectable. He did not wish "to turn back the stream of the world's great flow" any more than Kemble did, but he did appreciate where his words had come from. "Love thou thy land," published in 1842 but written with a number of other political poems around 1833–1834, confirms (like its companions) Tennyson's preference for slow, steady, considered change in politics, acknowledging: "Meet is it changes should control / Our being, lest we rust in ease. / We all are changed by still degrees" (41–43). The same poem describes the forces of history working in the dark, obscurely detectable – similar, we might say, to the way that language evolves incrementally within each speech act, adapting "by small degrees" to the needs of its speakers.

Tennyson employed the echoes of Old English most successfully when they live in "sonic patterns of recurrence," in Seamus Perry's words. Returns, repetitions, and

---

[212] William Barnes, *An Outline of Rede-Craft (Logic): With English Wording* (London: C. Kegan Paul & Company, 1880), ix.
[213] Gerard Manley Hopkins, *The Collected Works of Gerard Manley Hopkins*, ed. R.K.R. Thornton and Catherine Phillips, vol. 2 (Oxford: Oxford University Press, 2013), 551.
[214] Kemble, *Correspondence*, 35.
[215] Kemble, *The Saxons in England*, 1:viii, 366.

echoes are distinguishing features of Tennyson's poetry,[216] and there are many ways to attempt a return to the idea of Anglo-Saxon heritage. Echoes have been the dominant metaphor of this chapter, suggesting as they do a weaker, distorted recurrence of utterance – a fitting description of both Tennyson's perspective on Old English language and the memories of its literature that appear in his own work. When talking about the Anglo-Saxons, or translating their literature, he leveraged the nineteenth-century impression of their verse as hammering, energetic, and primitive, with Thor and Odin still in the back of society's mind. Yet the subject did not seem to suit him for overt use in his own compositions, despite his evident interest in it. It was in language that Tennyson found that the past most undeniably "yet works in us." If, as *Harold* suggested, the old gods are lurking in the landscape, transforming invaders into native Englishmen, then I suggest that the language and literature of the Anglo-Saxons are haunting Tennyson's ear. To adapt one of his patriotic poems, he was keenly aware that his words were "far-brought / From out the storied Past, and used / Within the Present." The next chapter explores the methods by which he brought the past and present of his words into resonance with each other.

---

[216] Perry, *Alfred Tennyson*, 23, 29.

3
Removing the Veil of Custom and Familiarity

WHILE FORMS OF government, land division, and superstition supposedly still lurked in the unconscious habits of the English people, language inextricably connected them to past generations. More powerfully than ethnic origin, the Anglo-Saxon linguistic heritage defined English culture for Tennyson and his friends. It lived on the very breath of modern speakers. John Kemble was fond of describing the past as a temple, and he took the metaphor further by asserting that language was the key to that temple.[1] And yet – to stretch the metaphor yet further – the temple was something of a pantheon. Victorian linguists knew that Old English was but one element of their etymological inheritance. Furthermore, the "new philology" imported from the continent emphasized that words were sociological artifacts with complex histories. For Tennyson's circle, taking account of the entire history of English added depth and richness to its possibilities.

Just as Tennyson's Anglo-Saxonism is thrown into relief through the work of Kemble (and his friends and enemies), the poet's affinity for lexical artifacts can be helpfully illuminated through the writings of another Cambridge Apostle, Richard Chenevix Trench. Trench became one of the century's most persuasive and popular authors on the significance of philology, and his writings bring into focus Tennyson's interest in gathering curious words "from out the storied past" and using them in the present ("Love thou thy land" 2). Trench wrote that it was important even for non-scholars to "remove the veil which custom and familiarity have thrown over" the words of everyday speech. Tennyson's style performs this task; in addition to using the strangeness of archaic vocabulary and pronunciation to artistic effect, it shows a dedication to removing the veil of familiarity from the more familiar words in his poems. He achieved this by using archaic meanings for a term or alluding to its literal etymological metaphor. Trench also argued that "the old and the familiar will often become new in [a poet's] hands."[2] Tennyson was indeed innovative with his usage, both experimenting with compounds – an Anglo-Saxon inheritance and a way to explore word-as-metaphor – and using words in new senses. This chapter distinguishes the methods that constitute his philological medievalist poetic language, which draws attention to itself *as* language and reverberates with historical echoes.

---

[1] Kemble, "Lajamon," 4.
[2] Trench, *On the Study of Words*, 27, 116–117.

Both Tennyson and Trench were good friends with Kemble, who invited Tennyson to a dinner of Apostolic alumni by including the enticement, "I am not sure that ... Trench will not be with us." Shortly after he left Cambridge, Tennyson remarked, "It is impossible to look upon Trench and not love him, though he be ... always strung to the highest pitch."[3] The caveat speaks to a difference in personality between the two men, which was to play out in their respective engagements with philology. According to biographer Robert Bernard Martin, the poet did not enjoy an especially warm friendship with Trench, but that was an effect of different temperaments rather than incompatible worldviews. Arthur Hallam acknowledged to Trench, "Perhaps you [two] could never become very intimate, for certainly your bents of mind are not the same."[4] The difference in their personalities is evident from a report that "Trench ... maintained that mimicry was a weapon to be feared and not a toy to be played with," for all that he was "forced into merriment" after an especially amusing performance.[5] In contrast to Trench's disapproval, Tennyson was a gifted mimic and would occasionally demonstrate his talents to small gatherings.[6]

Their disparate characters are reflected in what they produced in reaction to their exposure to philology, each man exploring in his own way their joint fascination with the historical strata of words. In writing about philology, Trench stressed the lessons to be learned by unpacking the histories of how people's minds had taken form in words and then had altered those same "exponents of thought."[7] Tennyson worked ossifying terms into his verse for the vivid imagery they provided. He was less strictly moralistic than his college comrade, but his poetic techniques were grounded in the same philological ideas that Trench articulated so successfully. They also both had an abiding affection for the Cambridge Apostles as the forum in which they had broadened their minds, and they maintained contact through mutual reading and mutual friends into old age, sending each other editions of their latest books.[8]

Trench's books on philological subjects were published midcentury but drew upon ideas that were circulating at Trinity during his undergraduate days. They consist of *On the Study of Words* (1851), *English, Past and Present* (1855), *On Some Deficiencies in Our English Dictionaries* (1857), and *A Select Glossary of English Words Used Formerly in Senses Different from Their Present* (1859). The first two volumes were published versions of lectures that he had delivered to undergraduates; *Deficiencies* (of which Tennyson owned an inscribed copy) originated from two speeches that Trench gave to the Philological Society, which eventually prompted the project that became the *New English Dictionary*, the precursor to the *OED*. In addition to these explicitly language-focused works, Trench published two works of Scriptural close reading, *Notes on the Parables of Our Lord* (1841) and *Notes on the Miracles of Our Lord* (1846), as well as *Synonyms of the New Testament* (1854) and

---

[3] Tennyson, *Letters*, 1982, 1:98, 70–71.
[4] Martin, *Tennyson*, 112.
[5] Brookfield, *The Cambridge "Apostles,"* 32.
[6] Hallam Tennyson, *Memoir*, 1:184; Tennyson, *Letters*, 1982, 2:347.
[7] Trench, *On the Study of Words*, 9.
[8] Emily Tennyson, *Lady Tennyson's Journal*, 199.

On the Authorized Version of the New Testament (1858), all of which apply philological methods to theology. In all his books, he emphasized that words have social histories; that English is especially rich in linguistic sources and thereby connotations; and that poetry is a powerful method for both preserving older usage and creating new idioms.

When Trench wrote of the effect a poet can have on language, he could have been describing the work of his university friend. It bears quoting at length once more:

> the old and the familiar will often become new in his hands; ... he will give the stamp of allowance ... to words ... which hitherto have lived only on the lips of the multitude, or been confined to some single dialect and province; ... he will enrich his native tongue with words unknown and non-existent before.[9]

This is not to suggest that Tennyson took instruction from his friend. The poet's hunger for unusual, impactful words obviously came from within and from an early age. Nevertheless, Trench's framework helpfully outlines the practices that the linguistically attuned saw at work in the complementary fields of poetry and philology.

Tennyson's philologically informed linguistic flamboyance early caught the attention of critics, though it did not earn their praise. The *Athenaeum* review of the 1832 volume lamented that he too often strayed from the simplicity of style that brought out his best work:

> So strong, indeed, seems to be Mr. Tennyson's love of *singularity*, that either that which is antiquated, or that which is palpable innovation, (be it in thought, or expression, or orthography,) [*sic*] possesses an irresistible charm for him; and accordingly his poetry is marred ... not only by discarded phrase and obsolete pronunciation, but by words newly compounded after the German model.[10]

This chapter explores how Tennyson deployed discarded phrases, new compounds, and related techniques, and to what effect; Chapter 4 discusses his use of obsolete pronunciation. I argue that the reviewer in the *Athenaeum* was right: the poet was aiming for singularity – for language that made the reader take notice of it. And as the reviewer observed, he did this through both "antiquated" language and "palpable innovation."

"Mr. Tennyson's love of singularity": Strategic Strangeness

The *Athenaeum*'s 1832 reviewer noted that Tennyson was "imbued with an evident love of our own early writers" but therefore had "transplant[ed] into his own style the quaint conceits, the elaborate subtilties ... and but too many of the affectations" that were hard to forgive in those past writers, much less one composing in the nineteenth century.[11] It is true that some of the archaisms Tennyson used early in

---

[9] Trench, *On the Study of Words*, 116–117.
[10] "Poems, (Now First Published) By Alfred Tennyson. London: Moxon," *Athenaeum*, December 1, 1832, 770. Emphasis is original.
[11] Ibid., 770.

his career serve only to make his language sound old as a proxy for sounding literary – for example, such specimens as *I wis, he wist not, I wot, sooth, whilome,* and *thou* and its associated conjugations. These are a kind of performative medievalism at the lexical level, in the service of sounding poetic. His simplest method for producing old-fashioned flair was to add *y* or *ly* to a noun to form an adjective. Thus we have *mazy, arrowy, stilly, massy, loathly, billowy, beamy, nightly,* and *steepy*, as well as the adverbs *angerly* and *cheerly*, for the latter of which Tennyson cited Shakespeare.[12] He favored this technique in his early efforts, indicating that it served as an ornamental filigree appropriate for experiments that imitated eighteenth-century verse – see, for example, "The Devil and the Lady," in which several of these constructions appear. Just as in his childhood he "wrote hundreds and hundreds of lines in the regular Popeian metre," so he imitated outmoded adjectival constructions.[13]

Even as his style matured, however, Tennyson continued to use archaic words, an impulse that drew on both poetic tradition and his growing philological knowledge. In part, the attraction of such words derived from the antiquarian motivation behind language study and was itself a kind of medievalism. In Anglo-Saxonist circles, for example, the idea that typefaces must re-create the visual impression of manuscripts persisted into the middle of the century (as discussed in Chapter 2). Tennyson's markedly archaic vocabulary can stand out as much as a þ or an ð, and to similar effect. Critics tended not to like the effect, but it is abundantly evident that the poet did, for it continued to mark his verse despite their protests. J.F.A. Pyre wrote in 1921 of the poet's youthful approach to diction:

> Tennyson's method consisted partly in taking words that had always been sequestered to poetical uses, partly in adopting rare words from Shakspere [*sic*] and Milton, partly in appropriating words to special poetic use after the analogy of these, as, for example, by the use of Latinisms in a special or primitive sense. Partly, it consisted in the introduction of archaic and folk words after the fashion of preceding poets of the romantic school. There was no absolute novelty in this method; but few English poets seem to have been so enamored of words for their own sake, as was Tennyson at this period.[14]

Note that this description maps quite well onto Trench's list of how poets rework the language in which they write.

Pyre broadly summarizes the origins of Tennyson's poetic vocabulary, but he seems puzzled by the poet's habit of employing language "surpassingly rich and strange."[15] His own descriptor is key: the language is "strange." In similar fashion, section xcv of *In Memoriam* describes an epiphany of sorts, occasioned by reading Arthur Hallam's letters:

---

[12] *mazy* (trans. Horace II 27), *arrowy* (The Devil and the Lady I.i.3, Timbuctoo 141), *stilly* (The Devil and the Lady I.i.93, Arabian Nights 103), *massy* (Devil/Lady I.v.96), *loathly* (Coach of Death 154), *billowy* (God's Denunciations 16), *beamy* (Thou camest ... 7), *nightly* (King Charles 7), *steepy* (Lover's Tale II.73), *angerly* (Madeline 45), *shrilly* (Coach of Death 11), *cheerly* (Lady of Shalott 30).
[13] Hallam Tennyson, *Memoir*, 1:11.
[14] Pyre, *The Formation of Tennyson's Style*, 225.
[15] Ibid., 225.

> ... strangely on the silence broke
> The silent-speaking words, and strange
> Was love's dumb cry defying change
> To test his worth; and strangely spoke
>
> The faith, the vigour ... (25–28)

Critics such as Donald Hair have read this passage in the context of philosophies of language, the paradox of "silent-speaking words" embodying theories of the mutual influence of thought and speech on each other.[16] In addition, the repetition of *strange* reinforces the importance of language being unusual if it is to have an impact.

Victor Shklovsky, writing in the twentieth century, formalized into literary theory what had frequently been suggested in the philological discussions of the nineteenth century. He wrote that "art exists that one may recover the sensation of life" – that is, it is crafted so as to be unusual, the purpose being to trigger heightened awareness of the ordinary.[17] Reading Victorian philologists as anticipating Russian Formalism in their aims for language is a useful way to consider the poetry of those who were steeped in philological concerns. For example, Trinity tutor Julius Charles Hare positioned his fragmentary book *Guesses at Truth* as an antidote to what he called "mechanical reading" because it continually forces the reader to construct opinions from the raw material of evocative statements.[18] Among Hare's statements was the assertion that using commonplaces – describing objects with stock words and phrases – was worthless in poetry.[19] If he shared that idea with his students, then Tennyson took the lesson to heart. In Shklovsky's words, "A work is created 'artistically' so that its perception is impeded and the greatest possible effect is produced through the slowness of the perception ... Thus 'poetic language' gives satisfaction." He cites Aristotle – whose work classically educated men such as Tennyson knew – and agrees that "poetic language must appear strange and wonderful." Philology took the same stance with regard to all language. Trench's eloquent arguments for the importance of "remov[ing] the veil which custom and familiarity have thrown over" the words of everyday speech anticipate Shklovsky's concept of defamiliarization in literary language.[20]

We might at first anticipate some difficulty in applying these maxims to Tennyson's poetry. Even in his own time, it had a reputation for lulling readers with its sound, leading some to suspect there might not be any substance to uncover. Yet his penchant for strikingly outmoded terms was recognized during his lifetime, to the point that critics found the practice a distraction. The *Spectator*, for example, complained of "a great fondness for old words" in the 1830 collection.[21] At the end of a lengthy, otherwise positive assessment of the same book, the *Westminster Review*

---

[16] Hair, *Tennyson's Language*.
[17] Victor Shklovsky, "Art as Technique," in *Russian Formalist Criticism: Four Essays*, trans. Lee T. Lemon and Marion J. Reis, Regents Critics Series (Lincoln, NE: University of Nebraska Press, 1965), 12.
[18] Quoted in Distad, *Guessing at Truth*, 72.
[19] Hare, *Guesses at Truth, by Two Brothers: Two Series in One Volume*, 41.
[20] Trench, *On the Study of Words*, 27.
[21] Shannon, *Tennyson and the Reviewers*, 4.

quibbled, "We must protest against ... the use of antiquated words ... in which our author indulges so freely ... Nor certainly is anything gained by a song's being studded with words which to most readers may require a glossary."[22] Two years later, the *Athenaeum* (quoted earlier) noted Tennyson's "love of *singularity*," which often took the form of "discarded phrase."[23]

Tennyson, however, clearly felt there *was* something to be gained by strewing his verse with unfamiliar words. In section cxxviii of *In Memoriam*, we read that one of the effects of time is "To change the bearing of a word," a reminder that Tennyson saw etymological shifts as the aesthetic equivalent of "mak[ing] old bareness picturesque" and "tuft[ing] with grass a feudal tower" (16, 19–20). The medievalist image is especially appropriate, for he drew upon medieval and early modern texts in building for himself a lexical collection. He was, in fact, a connoisseur of verbal arcana. Hallam Tennyson remembered his father "reviv[ing] many fine old words which had fallen into disuse" and being disappointed that he had never managed to use the word *yarely*,[24] an Old English word meaning *quickly*. In point of fact, Hallam was only partially correct; his father's unpublished teenage play "The Devil and the Lady" includes among its characters a sailor who shouts, "Yare! yare!" – an exclamation meaning "Quick! esp. in nautical use." The OED cites only two uses after Shakespeare. Still, Tennyson had hoped to fit *yarely* into a published poem; indeed, while at university, he had jotted *yarely* into a list of rhyming words in a notebook, keeping it as a possible partner for *barely, rarely*, or *fairly*.[25]

It is well documented that, as his grandson Charles put it, "Tennyson often stored observations and similes for long periods before finally working them into his poems."[26] In a similar fashion, he stored up antiquated words for later use. When the poet "his wordhoard unlocked" for composition, he had a well-stocked verbal storehouse at his disposal. His "studied poetic vocabulary," to use Pyre's phrase, was the product of an active effort at collecting, to which his friends contributed.[27] Shortly after they had left Cambridge, for example, Arthur Hallam was "culling for Alfred poetic words," according to the memoir written by the poet's son.[28]

We can see the process in action in a letter from Hallam to Tennyson in February of 1832. Hallam had just been admitted to the Inner Temple to study law, an educational decision forced upon him by his father. Though he did not intend to practice law, he set about the usual course of self-instruction by reading the standard textbooks.[29] Among these was Sir William Blackstone's *Commentaries on the Laws of England*, "the most celebrated, widely circulated, and influential law book ever published in the English language," according to the *Oxford Dictionary of National*

[22] Jump, *Tennyson*, 32.
[23] "Poems (Now First Published)," 770. Emphasis is original.
[24] Hallam Tennyson, *Memoir*, 2:133.
[25] Alfred Tennyson, *The Harvard Manuscripts: Notebooks 5–15* (MS Eng 952), ed. Christopher Ricks and Aidan Day, vol. 2, Tennyson Archive (New York: Garland, 1987), 185.
[26] Quoted in Christopher Ricks, *Tennyson's Methods of Composition*, Chatterton Lecture on an English Poet (London: Oxford University Press, 1966), 214.
[27] Pyre, *The Formation of Tennyson's Style*, 224.
[28] Hallam Tennyson, *Memoir*, 1:82.
[29] Martin Blocksidge, *"A Life Lived Quickly": Tennyson's Friend Arthur Hallam and His Legend* (Brighton: Sussex Academic Press, 2011), 181.

124   *Tennyson's Philological Medievalism*

Biography.[30] Hallam reported to Tennyson, "I read Blackstone and rather enjoy the old fellow. Even you would like some things in him – for instance such a word as 'forestal,' a legal adjective from forest."[31] Although Hallam seems to have misread this particular word, he thought his friend would be interested in adding it to his poetic lexis, and Tennyson was certainly collecting unusual words at the time.

In a notebook from his days at Trinity, the budding poet wrote out some lines from Leigh Hunt's poem *The Story of Rimini* (1816), underlining certain words: <u>a clipsome waist</u>, the jerk'd feather <u>swaling</u> in the bonnet, a <u>pin-drop</u> silence.[32] Although Tennyson did not use these specific phrases in his poetry, it is further evidence of his practice of noting down interesting expressions. These particular excerpts from Hunt were definitely out of the ordinary: none of Tennyson's dictionaries through the end of the decade contain *clipsome* or *pin-drop*. For both these terms, Hunt's poem is the first example in the current *OED*. In the case of *clipsome*, Hunt's use is one of only two quotations, the other being an excerpt from *Blackwood's Edinburgh Magazine* six years later that is an obvious allusion to his line: "It may be said of them, 'with their clipsome waists', that they belong to the Cockney school." Tennyson's dictionaries defined *swale* as either an Anglo-Saxon verb for *burn* or the past tense of *swell*; to this day, the *OED* gives the first example of Hunt's meaning, "to move or sway up and down or from side to side," as an 1820 article from *Blackwood's Edinburgh Magazine*, which in fact is a later and slightly altered quotation from his poem: "Here's a jerked feather that swales in a bonnet."

Later in the same notebook, between an anthology of nursery rhymes and some notes on astronomy and Italian, Tennyson devoted more than ninety pages to creating his own repository of literary words. There he gathered exemplary expressions from across the history of the English language. The glossary contains words out of sources ranging from Anglo-Saxon texts to Chapman's Homer, taken from his wide-ranging reading and mostly organized into alphabetically headed pages. At one level, this glossary operated as a practical support to Tennyson's reading, and as such it offers insight into what he was reading during his years at university. One page, for example, neatly corresponds to progress through Chaucer's "Knight's Tale," while another is headed "Hamlet" and – together with the subsequent two pages – serves as a reference for Shakespearean vocabulary such as *crants* and *strewments*. Likewise, its large number of Old English words may well have aided the literary exploration that produced his short translation from *Beowulf*, discussed in the previous chapter.[33]

In addition to its practical use, the glossary reveals an antiquarian impulse in the its representation of Old English text. Tennyson's handwriting for entries taken from Anglo-Saxon differs from his normal hand; it is precise and visually distinct, imitating insular minuscule script. As Chapter 2 describes, he would have seen such

---

[30] Wilfrid Prest, "Blackstone, Sir William," in *Oxford Dictionary of National Biography* (Oxford University Press, September 17, 2015).

[31] Hallam, *Letters*, 522.

[32] Tennyson, *Notebooks 1–4*, 1:162; Leigh Hunt, *The Story of Rimini: A Poem* (London: J. Murray, 1816), 10, 15, 17.

[33] For a full transcription of the notebook glossary and a list of Tennyson's sources, see Weaver, *Tennyson's Notebook Glossary and Rhyme Lists*.

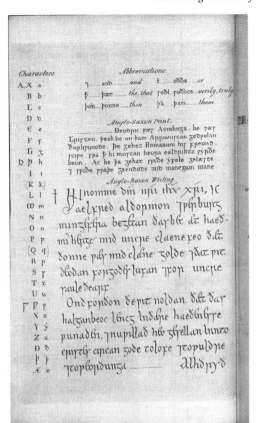

Figure 3 Frontispiece of Rasmus Rask's *Grammar of the Anglo-Saxon Tongue*, edited by Benjamin Thorpe. Photographer: Amélie Deblauwe / Reproduced by kind permission of the Syndics of Cambridge University Library.

script in any number of reference books he consulted, such as Benjamin Thorpe's translation of Rasmus Rask's *Grammar of the Anglo-Saxon Tongue* (1830). Thorpe's frontispiece offers an alphabet and a sample text, the mid-ninth-century inscription written on the Canterbury "Codex Aurelius."[34] (See Figure 3). Tennyson uses this paleography for every letter of his Anglo-Saxon words, even characters that Old and Modern English share (see Figure 4). The interplay of visual and linguistic history on display here symbolizes how Tennyson's poetry brings together words from across the centuries of English speakers.

In addition to working with reference books on Old English, Tennyson took many of his entries from collections of medieval and Renaissance literature. Chaucer is a major presence, often drawn from the fourteen-volume set in his father's library. From the 1801 edition of George Ellis's *Specimens of the Early English Poets*, Tennyson copied such words as *poyntil* from *Piers Plowman* and *vecke* from John Gower's "Tale of Florent." Additionally, two books of early modern plays proved fertile ground for collecting unusual terminology. From *The Old English Drama* (1830), the sixteenth-century plays *Ralph Royster Doyster* and *Gammer Gurton's*

[34] Rask, *A Grammar of the Anglo-Saxon Tongue*.

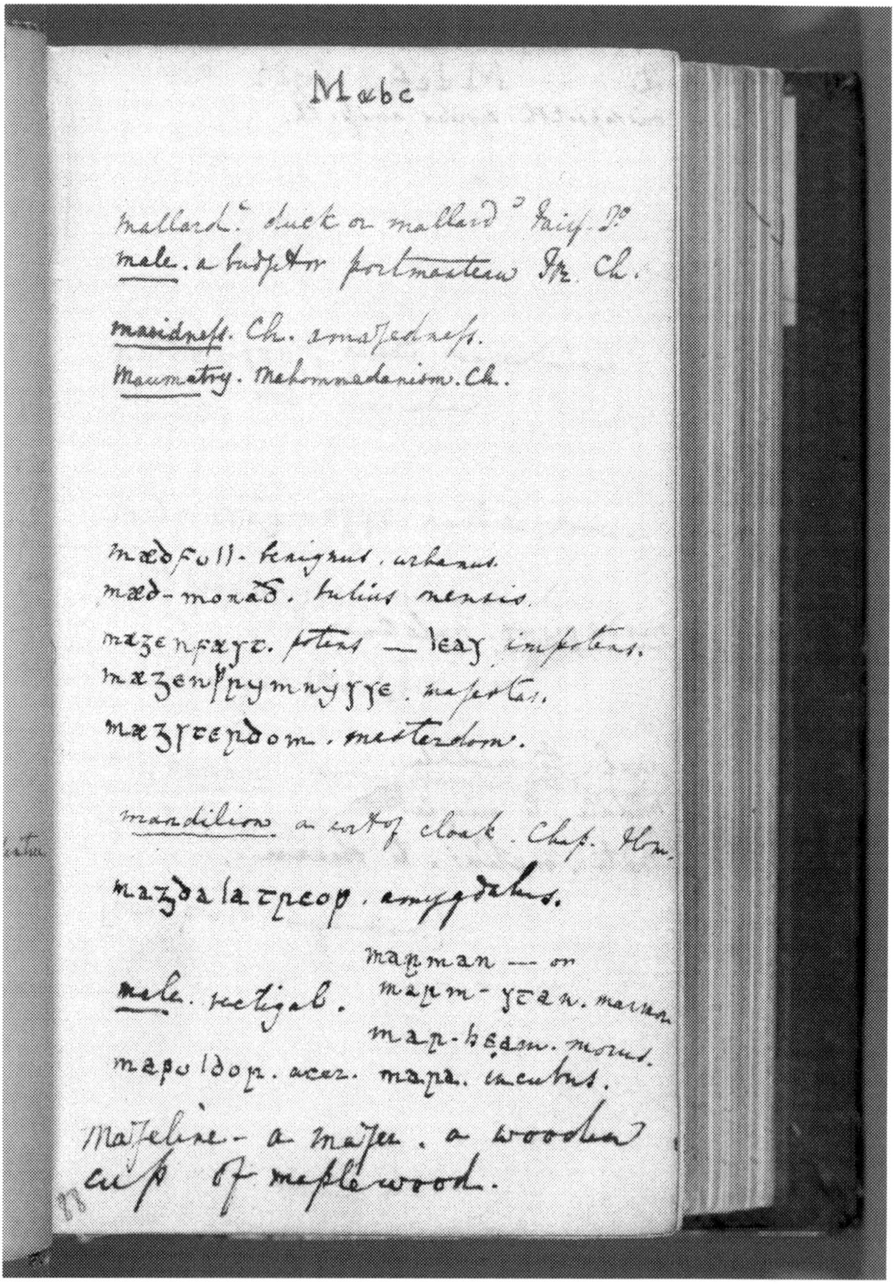

Figure 4 A page of Tennyson's notebook glossary. MS Eng 952 (Notebook 4), Houghton Library, Harvard University.

Needle provided many curious terms, whether recording that a *balk* was "The crossbeam in kitchens to hang bacon on" or that *hoddypeke* was a term of abuse. Another source of early English drama seems to have been *A Select Collection of Old Plays in Twelve Volumes* (1825), edited by Isaac Reed and, later, by Robert Dodsley. Equally fruitful were George R. Kinloch's collection of Scottish ballads (1827) and Joseph Ritson's collection of "Poems, Songs, and Ballads" about Robin Hood (1820).[35]

The evidence for these sources is to be found in Tennyson's direct citations or in quotations only found in certain volumes or editions.[36] But although Tennyson copied many definitions directly from the footnotes in these literary collections, or from a dictionary or glossary, he did not accept the authority of his sources blindly. For the word *vecke*, he writes: "'old woman', says Ellis most likely generalizing this sense from the context." He drew on Ellis's *Specimens of the Early English Poets*, but he did so critically: Tennyson thinks that Ellis is guessing the meaning from context. We read, too, that *rhethor* is "a nasty Latinism of Chaucer" meaning *orator*;[37] even the poet whom Spenser had called the "well of English undefiled" did not escape critique.

In a skeptical remark on the words *tombestere* and *timbestere*, Tennyson comments, "[lexicographer Edward] Lye supposes [they are] the same words without giving sufficient reason." He cites the glossary in the Tyrwhitt edition of Chaucer that his father owned (1782), which says that *timbestere* "is supposed by Lye … to mean the same with *Tombestere*." In the similarity of their phrasing, it is clear that Tennyson adopts Tyrwhitt's skepticism of Lye's 1772 *Dictionarium Saxonico et Gothico-Latinum*, though it stood as the major Anglo-Saxonist dictionary for many years. He likewise copies down Tyrwhitt's proposed etymology of *timbestere* as a woman who threw "basons" (sticks) in the air. But he also goes further and writes that both words come from "Saxon tumban to dance," a definition he took from Thomas Benson's 1701 dictionary.[38] Similarly, the next entry – for *trow, trowin* – might well take its definition as "to believe" from Tyrwhitt's Chaucer glossary, the source of many other entries. However, Tennyson's full notebook definition is "to believe, trust, truwian" – with the last word written in his imitative insular script.[39] Lye and Rask/Thorpe could have informed him of this word's meaning, printed in medievalist type. These are but two examples of extensive notes that demonstrate an engagement of some academic rigor with the literary language of the past.

Beyond displaying his eclectic reading, Tennyson's lexical collection is also a valuable anthology of terms that appealed to him. For all its usefulness, many entries require little or no translation, such as *assistfull* and *witnesfully* (evidently). Having caught his attention once, words from this glossary recurred in Tennyson's poetry throughout his career. For example, he compiled the following list from *The Faerie Queene*:

---

[35] Weaver, *Tennyson's Notebook Glossary and Rhyme Lists*, 11, 23, 43–44.
[36] For more detail, see Ibid., 5–9.
[37] Ibid., 31.
[38] Thomas Benson, *Vocabularium Anglo-Saxonicum* (Oxford: Samuel Smith and Benjamin Walford, 1701).
[39] Weaver, *Tennyson's Notebook Glossary and Rhyme Lists*, 34. His likely source for "tumban" was Benson, *Vocabularium Anglo-Saxonicum*. His likely source for "truwian" was Rask, *A Grammar of the Anglo-Saxon Tongue*.

moiety, discounsel, fortilage, falsèd, dilate …⁴⁰ sappy, scruze, embay, abash, attemper, balefulness, threesquare (shield), shamefuller, purveyance, dispread, displode, surcease, bullion, spicory, forestall, fulmined, fulgid, coralline, stardust, downage.⁴¹

Within Tennyson's oeuvre, a character in "The Princess" "fulmined out her scorn" (II.117); the hothouse gardens described in "Amphion" are "neither green nor sappy" (90), unlike the "sappy field and wood" envisioned in "My life is full of weary days" (16); the admired figure in "Isabel" has "locks not wide-dispread" (5), while the portrait in "The Ante-Chamber" has a "large table of the breast dispread, / Between low shoulders" (5–6); *abashed* appears in *Enoch Arden* and several of the *Idylls*; and several other poems contain *dilate*.⁴²

Also drawing from the glossary, "Recollections of the Arabian Nights" (published 1830) makes use of *rosaries* as "places where roses grow"⁴³ to describe a garden consisting of:

> stately cedar, tamarisks,
> Thick rosaries of scented thorn,
> Tall orient shrubs, and obelisks
> Graven with the emblems of the time.   (105–108)

This usage was apparently so abnormal that Arthur Hallam singled it out for critique in his otherwise glowing 1831 review of *Poems, Chiefly Lyrical*, which he wrote to promote his friend's talents. Hallam wrote, "'*Rosaries* of scented thorn,' … is, we believe, an entirely unauthorized use of the word. Would our author translate '*biferque rosaria Paesti*' – 'And *rosaries* of Paestum, twice in bloom?'"⁴⁴ Unbeknownst to Hallam, Tennyson did have an authority for this use – a play by Lewis Machin. He had cited Machin in his notebook, where the Victorian poet did, in fact, equate *rosary* and *rosaria*.⁴⁵ "Arabian Nights" also describes "a brow of pearl / Tressèd with redolent ebony" (ln. 137–138). Hallam felt obliged to "hint to Mr. Tennyson that 'redolent' is no synonyme [*sic*] for 'fragrant,'" asserting that there was no authority for using *redolent* without *of* immediately following. Though Tennyson did not place *redolent* in his notebook, it appears twice – standing alone, without *of* – in a work that he cited for other items in his glossary.⁴⁶ He knew the usage had literary precedent.

---

⁴⁰ Here Tennyson quotes: "did broad dilate / Their clasping arms in wanton wreathings intricate"

⁴¹ Weaver, *Tennyson's Notebook Glossary and Rhyme Lists*, 38.

⁴² *abash'd*: Enoch Arden 287, Marriage of Geraint 765, Balin and Balan 69, Pelleas and Ettarre 74; *dilate*: Aylmer's Field 77, In Memoriam xxviii.10; *dilating*: The Princess II.155 *dilation*: The Princess VI.172.

⁴³ Weaver, *Tennyson's Notebook Glossary and Rhyme Lists*, 31.

⁴⁴ Arthur Hallam, *The Writings of Arthur Hallam*, ed. T.H. Vail Motter, Modern Language Association of America General Series 15 (New York: Modern Language Association of America, 1943), 193.

⁴⁵ Weaver, *Tennyson's Notebook Glossary and Rhyme Lists*, 31.

⁴⁶ Tasso, *Godfrey of Bulloigne; or, The Recovery of Jerusalem*, ed. Charles Knight, trans. Edward Fairfax, 5th ed. (Windsor: Knight, 1817), 16, 136.

Similarly, Tennyson took the plant *galingale* from a footnote glossing George Chapman's Homer and placed it (by way of his notebook) on the hillsides of the land of "The Lotos-Eaters" (ln. 23). Several political poems describe politicians "liming" (trapping) the people, as hinted in the notebook entry for *limerod*. "Supposed Confessions of a Second-Rate Sensitive Mind" (1830) is one of only two citations in the *OED* for the word *profulgent* (identified as obsolete, rare, and poetic), the other being Chaucer's "Nine Ladies Worthie," from which the Victorian poet gleaned it.[47]

The glossary makes clear that there is a strong element of intertextuality in Tennyson's archaisms, for he drew freely on the vocabulary of his literary forbears, especially in the earliest stages of his career. His juvenilia in particular rely on the borrowed literary sound of his predecessors, but the examples given above demonstrate that he drew upon his wordhoard until the end of his life. The phenomenon of poetic borrowing becomes starkly apparent in "Crossing the Bar" (1889), where we read that the tide may carry the speaker "from out our bourne of Time and Place." For Shakespeare, *bourne* meant *limit* or *boundary*; but owing to its appearance in Hamlet's "To be or not to be" soliloquy, it is often used as here to mean *region*. None of Tennyson's dictionaries gave this meaning until the *New English Dictionary* (*A–Boz* published 1884–1887), but the literary genealogy is clear.

Footnotes identifying poetic precedents abound in Ricks's *Poems of Tennyson*, as in the following passage from "Recollections of the Arabian Nights":

> From the green rivage many a fall
> Of diamond rillets musical,
> Through little crystal arches low
> Down from the central fountain's flow
> Fallen silver-chiming, seemed to shake
> The sparkling flints beneath the prow.
> ...
> Above through many a bowery turn
> A walk with vary-coloured shells
> Wandered engrained.   (47–52, 56–58)

Ricks identifies *rivage* as "Spenserian" and finds that *rillets* reflects Keats's "Endymion," while *engrained* recalls Spenser's "Shepherd's Calendar."[48] When, a little over thirty lines later, the poem describes "the deep sphere overhead, / Distinct with vivid stars" (89–90), the sense of *distinct* as *decorated* or *adorned* derives from Spenser, Milton, Pope, and Shelley, with whom Tennyson's line shares space in the *OED* entry for this "Latinism, chiefly poetic." In other words, Tennyson's poetry purposely sounded old-fashioned from the day it was written. This strangeness at the word level is a key component of his artistic language.

As described by Linda Dowling, the Coleridgean view of language relied upon writing as a source of communal identity. In this schema, the "common inheritance of Poets" was "a vital and enabling inheritance," which "Coleridge knew

---

[47] Weaver, *Tennyson's Notebook Glossary and Rhyme Lists*, 21, 25, 30.
[48] Alfred Tennyson, *The Poems of Tennyson*, ed. Christopher B. Ricks, 2nd ed., vol. 1, Longman Annotated English Poets (London: Longman, 1987), 227.

was essential, not only for new poets, but for any idea of English culture worthy of the name."[49] Coleridge's *lingua communis* drew from the well of the King James Bible, Shakespeare, and Milton, sources that Tennyson – whose Trinity friends were Coleridgians – likewise saw as sources of beautiful language. His notebooks and Eversley Edition citations demonstrate his thorough knowledge of Shakespeare and Milton, and he personally remarked, "The Bible ought to be read, were it only for the sake of the grand English in which it is written, an education in itself."[50] The words he harvested and reused function as antiquarian artifacts, wrought by poets of the past; because they are alien from common speech to varying degrees, they stand as aesthetic objects themselves.

Moreover, if and when Tennyson were to be challenged about a non-idiomatic item of his lexicon, he could defend himself by pointing out that, for example, Milton had also used *vans* to mean *wings* ("Love and Death" 8). Indeed, he cited Milton in an Eversley Edition note to *In Memoriam* to defend the phrase "arrive at last the blessed goal" (lxxxiv.41), which lacks the second *at* that modern usage would demand ("arrive at last at the blessed goal").[51] The Eversley Edition of "Œnone" (originally published 1832) provides the source for *o'erthwarted*, saying it is "[f]ounded on the Chaucerian word 'overthwart,' across" and citing the exact line from *Troilus and Criseyde*.[52] In "Aylmer's Field" (written 1863), a bucolic hut is described as being "parcel-bearded with the traveller's-joy / In Autumn, parcel ivy-clad" (153–154). The Eversley note defines *parcel-bearded* as "partly bearded" and compares it to *parcel-gilt* from Shakespeare.[53] The *OED*'s entries suggest that this construction had been out of use for 200 years, except by Walter Scott, whose writing had a strongly historical bent of its own.

Tennyson employed archaic words throughout his career, but some early examples will show the practice at work. The speaker of "A Dirge" (1830) addresses the buried body of a loved one, saying they are beyond worldly worries: "Thee nor carketh care nor slander" (8). The sentence combines a medieval grammatical construction with the conspicuously archaic word *carketh*; the *OED* gives Tennyson's line as the only example after 1400. His Eversley annotation defines the word *carketh* as *vexeth*, and his son further explains its origin: "From late Latin *carcare*, to load, whence *charge*."[54] At the time of the poem's composition, neither of Tennyson's dictionaries defined the word in a way that matches his use. Johnson's dictionary (which gave a Saxon etymology) explicitly said the verb *cark* was "now very little used" as of 1755.[55] However, William Langland's medieval poem *Piers Plowman*, which Tennyson cited frequently in his notebook, used "over cark" in a similar way. Tennyson

---

[49] Dowling, *Decadence*, 18.
[50] Hallam Tennyson, *Memoir*, 1:308.
[51] Tennyson, *Enoch Arden and In Memoriam*, 247.
[52] Tennyson, *Poems I*, 362.
[53] Tennyson, *Poems II*, 358.
[54] Tennyson, *Poems I*, 346.
[55] N. Bailey, *An Universal Etymological Dictionary* (London: E. Bell, J. Darby, A Bettesworth, F. Fayram, J. Pemberton, J. Hooke, C. Rivington, F. Clay, J. Batley, and E. Symon, 1721). Because Bailey's dictionary does not have page numbers, future citations will be omitted if the source is clear. Samuel Johnson, *A Dictionary of the English Language*, vol. 1, 2 vols. (London: Knapton, Longman, Hitch, Hawes, Millar, and Dodsley, 1755).

must have mentally noted the word from Langland or similar historic reading. His son Hallam's etymology comes from W.W. Skeat's much later dictionary (1882).[56]

"Will Waterproof's Lyrical Monologue," a poem from the 1842 collection, similarly employs a word that was a poetic memory by the time Tennyson's readers would have encountered it. Offering reassurance that good things exist alongside the bad in the world, the speaker declares, "Let raffs be rife in prose and rhyme, / We lack not rhymes and reasons" (61–62). Tennyson defined *raffs* as *scraps* in the Eversley Edition, and his son added a supporting quotation from George Gascoigne's sixteenth-century poem "The Green Knight's Farewell to Fansie."[57] (As we have already seen, Hallam's additional notes typically gave historical evidence for his father's unusual words.) The *OED* sees Will Waterproof's expression as a very late example of the meaning of *raff* as "verse, esp. alliterative verse, of a crude kind, or in which sound is more prominent than sense; an instance of such verse." It cites Tennyson's use of this obsolete sense two-and-a-half centuries after its previous quotation. Whether Tennyson picked it up from Gascoigne, Chaucer, or elsewhere, the effect is undoubtedly archaic, with a medieval poetic pedigree. He also subtly alluded to its meaning through the alliteration of the lines: raff, rife, rhyme, rhymes, reasons.

Even a partial word could add antique flavor. For example, the prefix *dis-* seems to have been a favorite mechanism for creating antiquarian impact. Tennyson's corpus employs the following less-common words that begin with it, the following number of times: disarmed (3), disarray/'d (2), disband (used literally for "Geraint and Enid"), discaged, discourtesy (4, only in the *Idylls*), disedge (2, both in *Idylls*), disentwined, half-disfame, dishallow (*Idylls*), dishelm'd ("The Princess"), dishorsed (2, both in *Idylls*), disjoint(ed) (2), dislink'd (2, "The Princess" and *Idylls*), dispraise (2), disprinced, disproof, disquiet, disrelish, disrobed, (half-)disrooted (2, both in "The Princess"), and disyoke.[58] Even many of the more common *dis-*prefixed words only appear in the *Idylls* or "The Princess," such as *dishonour, dismount, disobey,* and *disorderly*. Given the poems in which these expressions appear, Tennyson evidently felt that *dis-* lent his vocabulary a medieval aesthetic.

"Will Waterproof" describes the title character's brain as "unsubject to confusion," which earns another *OED* quotation (86). Adding *un-* to a stem is a transparent and distinctly Anglo-Saxon way to construct a negative adjective. The Tennyson concordance catalogues numerous such combinations, revealing the poet's attraction to them, particularly in *In Memoriam* or poems with medievalist content, such as "The Princess" and the *Idylls of the King*. Leaving aside words that have remained in common use (*unkind, unknown, unlawful*, etc.), they include: unkinglike, unlaborious, unloverlike, unmanacled, unmeet, unmoulded, unmown, unnetted, unpaining, unpeopled, unpiloted, unprogressive, unprophetic, unriddled, unshadowable, unshatter'd, unsummer'd, unsunn'd, untuneful, unvenerable, and unvext. The *Idylls of the King* use *un-* to negate medievalist descriptors, amplifying the archaic flare

---

[56] Walter William Skeat, *An Etymological Dictionary of the English Language* (Oxford: Clarendon, 1882), 791.
[57] Tennyson, *Poems II*, 349.
[58] Arthur E. Baker, *A Concordance to the Poetical and Dramatic Works of Alfred, Lord Tennyson* (London: Kegan Paul, Trench, Trübner, 1914), 151–152.

132 Tennyson's Philological Medievalism

of the prefix in terms such as unknightlike, unknightly (used three times), unlamed, unled, unmannerly, unmelodious, unmockingly, unmortised, unsleek, unsolder, unsunny (the first OED quotation), and unswear. *In Memoriam* is hardly medievalist, but it still features *unlikeness, unpalsied, unquiet,* and *unsweet*.[59]

Despite the older nature of the construction, *un-* words make up nearly a quarter of the OED list of words for which Tennyson is the first quotation. Archaic yet sometimes also innovative, these terms produce an estranging effect – but only a gentle one, for it is always clear what they mean if the reader knows the core word. Furthermore, forming verbs and adjectives by prefixing *un-* allowed Tennyson to conjure an echo of Anglo-Saxon within his nineteenth-century language. In addition to poetic tradition, a major resource for finding medieval language alive within the modern world – and finding vivid expressions – was the speech of those who lived in rural regions of the country. Tennyson had a great interest in dialect for its own sake, and philological medievalism gave him yet more reason to find it fascinating. The following section explores this component of his style.

Provincialisms and Dialect

Trench listed one of a poet's effects on language as "giv[ing] the stamp of allowance … to words … which hitherto have … been confined to some single dialect and province."[60] As a child in rural Lincolnshire, Tennyson spent time among the local laborers, and he had "a sympathetic and retentive ear" for their speech; he could still reproduce it more than half a century later.[61] Indeed, he remained interested in provincial forms of speech all his life. As an adult, he became a member of the English Dialect Society, founded by his friend, the philologist F.J. Furnivall.[62] He also owned several books on dialect, such as William Barnes's popular *Poems of Rural Life in the Dorset Dialect* (1844). Other titles included *The Rural Fete; or Zeb. Gosling's Description of the Gala in Scrivelsby Park: A Lincolnshire Tale in the Dialect of the County* (1864); *An Etymological and Comparative Glossary of the Dialect and Provincialisms of East Anglia* (1866); *Sea Words and Phrases Along the Suffolk Coast: Extracted from the East Anglian Notes and Queries, January 1869*, a pamphlet bound together in Tennyson's library with *A Dictionary of the Sussex Dialect and Collection of Provincialisms in Use in the County of Sussex* (1875); and *A Dictionary of the Isle of Wight Dialect, and the Provincialisms Used in the Island* (1886), which lists Hallam Tennyson as a subscriber.[63]

The pamphlet on sea words was compiled by Tennyson's friend from Trinity days, Edward FitzGerald, who wrote additional annotations in it before sending

---

[59] Ibid., 253–256.
[60] Trench, *On the Study of Words*, 116–117.
[61] Campion, *Tennyson Dialect Glossary*, v.
[62] Michael P. Kuczynski, "Translation and Adaptation in Tennyson's *Battle of Brunanburh*," *Philological Quarterly* 86, no. 4 (Fall 2007): 422.
[63] William Henry Long, *A Dictionary of the Isle of Wight Dialect, and of Provincialisms Used in the Island* (London: Reeves and Turner, 1886), iv.

it to the laureate.[64] The slender dictionary calls the verb to *bark* "A poetical word, such as those whose business is with the sea are apt to use." FitzGerald also added to the definition of another entry, as follows: "A ship or boat begins to *complain* [^ or 'call out,'] when her nails, seams, or timbers, begin to give way." Elsewhere, his printed text cites a dialect scholar for a sense of *hefty* meaning rough weather or sea, but he has written by hand: "I have since heard of 'A hefty little fellow – quick tempered, irascible.'"[65] Tennyson does not seem to have reused any of his friend's curiosities, but like Arthur Hallam thirty-eight years before, FitzGerald was culling poetic words and sent them to his poetic friend.[66] Those words, as Tennyson had long known, could come from peasants as well as poets.

W.E.H. Lecky recalled that Tennyson "had a strong sense of the force and rhythm of words, and his knowledge of old English and of vivid provincial expressions was very great. 'How infinitely superior,' he said, 'is the provincial word *flitter-mouse* to the orthodox *bat!*'"[67] This was no hypothetical example; the sailors in "The Voyage of Maeldune" (1880) encounter an enchanted Silent Isle where "Our voices were thinner and fainter than any flittermouse-shriek" (22). Tennyson's son wrote that the poet "intended to represent, in his own original way, the Celtic genius" in this poem. He may have felt that provincial English, even if it was from England, could better reflect his sense of "the peculiar exuberance of the Irish genius."[68]

It is no coincidence that Lecky mentions "old English" and "provincial expressions" as two sides of the same coin. Dialect words had the same effect as several of the other philological techniques outlined in this book. They were unusual (un-"orthodox") outside their district of origin, providing vocabular texture to capture the reader's notice – and satisfying Tennyson's love of "singularity." In addition, dialect words could consist of vivid metaphorical compounds, such as *flitter-mouse*. Even a noncompound could be more obviously connected to its root idea than the standard term. For example, the dialect poem "The Northern Cobbler" (1880) uses *minded* instead of *remembered* (45). This dialect word obviously derives from the concept of mind, without the reader needing to etymologize. It is also the Anglo-Saxon word for the idea.

It was a common refrain among Victorian scholars that rural regions often preserved many aspects of medieval life, including vocabulary. Whereas the fashionable segments of the population followed fashion into all sorts of linguistic

---

[64] The contents of the notes make it clear that FitzGerald wrote them. One entry quotes "a sailor," but he has underlined "a sailor" and written in the margin, "my Captain here" (1). Another entry describes how local boats have started acquiring names derived from classical learning, including one named "Meum and Tuum." He underlined the name of the ship and wrote in the margin note: *"our* lugger;" FitzGerald had paid for the Meum and Tuum to be built for his friend, a herring-boat captain (mentioned in the earlier note) (6).

[65] Edward FitzGerald, *Sea Words and Phrases Along the Suffolk Coast: Extracted from the East Anglian Notes and Queries, January 1869* (Lowestoft: Samuel Tymms, 1869), 1, 3, 5.

[66] It would be an interesting exercise to check which words from his various dialect dictionaries appear in Tennyson's corpus, but it has not been practical to do so for this publication.

[67] Hallam Tennyson, *Memoir*, 2:203.

[68] Alfred Tennyson, *Ballads and Other Poems*, Eversley Edition, vol. 6 of *The Works of Alfred Lord Tennyson*, ed. Hallam Tennyson (London: Macmillan, 1910), 387.

corruptions, the argument went, the people of the countryside did not drift so far from their roots. Habits and language that had been preserved in remote districts tied the Anglo-Saxons to the present day in an unbroken chain, proving that some aspects of medieval culture were still alive. For example, in his 1838 Old English dictionary, Joseph Bosworth took pains to show "that what is generally termed 'vulgar language,' deserves some notice, and claims our respect from its direct descent from our high-spirited Anglo-Saxon ancestors." No provincial dialect "can boast that they retain the language of their early forefathers unimpaired," he wrote, "but all may prove that they possess strong traces of it."[69] As a result, philology developed hand-in-hand with the nineteenth-century interest in folklore, as the work of the brothers Grimm most famously attests. Tennyson's homemade anthology of nursery rhymes (in a notebook watermarked 1828) arguably sprang from the same complementary interests in the expressions of the common people and the people of the past; it immediately precedes his glossary of early English words.

Kemble, primarily an Anglo-Saxonist, was pleased to discover that his children's governess told stories with ancient precedents and used words that were obsolete in metropolitan society. He even contributed a list of Surrey provincialisms to the *Transactions of the Philological Society*.[70] Sadly, he wrote to Grimm in 1842, the Old English expressions still used by his elderly gardener "are fast going out under the influence of schoolmasters and railroads." Six years later, he repeated his complaint, this time about other remnants of medieval culture: "the railroads and the schoolmaster are sweeping away customs and superstitions which would fill a chapter of the *Deutsche Mythologie*."[71] The mobility that trains afforded threatened to eliminate the isolation of these rustic pockets, which had maintained traditions uninterrupted since the Middle Ages. Meanwhile, education was forcibly pushing medieval words into obsolescence in the name of standardization.

Kemble clearly disliked projects that were severing the English from their native national language, and he was not alone. Anglo-Saxonist Thomas Wright, whom he had mentored, bemoaned around the same time (1846):

> The distinguishing characteristics of a people are most prominently visible among its uncultivated peasantry – in their superstitions and their prejudices, their legends and their proverbs ... In our country, how speedily are the legends and superstitions of the peasantry passing away before the rod of the schoolmaster.[72]

Twenty-five years later, an essay "On English Dialects" by a John Earle rehearsed the by-then typical observation that "in many ... parts the old Dialects are growing faint, finding the coalition of the schoolmaster and the railroad too strong for them."[73] Soon after (1875), the dictionary of Sussex dialect that Tennyson owned

---

[69] Bosworth, *A Dictionary of the Anglo-Saxon Language*, xxvii.
[70] John Mitchell Kemble, "Surrey Provincialisms," *Transactions of the Philological Society*, no. 3 (February 24, 1854): 83–84.
[71] Kemble, *Correspondence*, 243, 268.
[72] Wright, *Essays*, 1:124.
[73] John Earle, "On the English Dialects," in *Rhymes and Reasons* (London: Joseph Masters, 1871), 1.

declared, "The march of education must sooner or later trample down and stamp out anything like distinctive provincial dialect in England; but when this result shall have been effected, much that is really valuable will be lost to our language."[74]

It was in this milieu that William Barnes wrote *Poems of Rural Life in the Dorset Dialect* (1844) and, like his neighbor Thomas Hardy, campaigned for preservation of Anglo-Saxon vocabulary. Dennis Taylor's book on Hardy shows that poet recording dialect even as it faded away around him.[75] Barnes was especially devoted to preserving Dorset dialect. In his book *TIW* (1862), he states that "the provincial dialects are not jargons but true and good forms of Teutonic speech, with words which, if the speech had grown into full strength in every stem, ought to be or to have been somewhere in the speech of Teutonic tribes." Barnes, like Kemble, was disgusted by "corrections" to historically sound, regional terms, lamenting, "Many are the cases in which names of places, of good meaning in British or Saxon-English, are corrected from the tongues of the common folk into nonsense."[76]

Although Barnes wrote treatises on language, he was most famous as a poet who not only recorded local idioms but adjusted his spelling to reflect Dorset pronunciation. When he sent his poems to Tennyson in 1861, the laureate wrote to thank him, saying, "I have for many years known and admired this volume of your Poems."[77] Barnes visited Farringford in 1863 and 1865, and the Tennysons found him "very good and simple and interesting," although uncomfortable with his host's speculative theological conversation.[78] A couple of years later (in 1867), William Allingham recorded in his diary that he and Tennyson, while in Dorchester, stopped by to visit Barnes, "whose Poems in the Dorset dialect T. knows and likes."[79] When Barnes died, Tennyson wrote to the deceased's daughter, "Your Father seems to me one of the men most to be honoured and revered in our day." Though their personal acquaintance was "slight," he clearly respected Barnes's literary-linguistic projects.[80]

Tennyson himself tried his hand at writing in the dialect of his childhood county in seven poems, beginning in 1861.[81] These compositions, like Barnes's, attempt to re-create the voice of their characters through semi-phonetic orthography, as in the opening line of "Northern Farmer, Old Style": "Wheer 'asta beän saw long and meä liggin' 'ere aloän?" Representing speech in this way creates potential obstacles for readers, which Tennyson recognized and limited to some extent. Writing about the word *sights* in "Northern Cobbler," he says, "it might be better if the text were written more phonetically … But I prefer being easily readable to using a more correct

---

[74] William Douglas Parish, *A Dictionary of the Sussex Dialect and Collection of Provincialisms in Use in the County of Sussex* (Lewes: Farncombe & Company, 1875), i.
[75] Taylor, *Hardy's Literary Language and Victorian Philology*, 117–123.
[76] Barnes, *TIW*, xvii–xviii, xxi.
[77] Tennyson, *Letters*, 1982, 2:271–272.
[78] Emily Tennyson, *The Letters of Emily Lady Tennyson*, ed. James O. Hoge (University Park: Pennsylvania State University Press, 1974), 196; Hallam Tennyson, *Memoir*, 1:514.
[79] Tennyson, *Letters*, 1982, 2:465.
[80] Tennyson, *Letters*, 1982, 3:349–350.
[81] They are: "Northern Farmer, Old Style"; "Northern Farmer, New Style"; "The Northern Cobbler"; "The Village Wife; or, the Entail"; "The Spinster's Sweet-Arts"; "Owd Roä"; and "The Churchwarden and the Curate."

phonetic."[82] Even when representing regional speech, then, Tennyson preferred to make his poems accessible – and unlike Barnes, his poetry as a whole is stylistically occupied with employing the full breadth of English language history. He therefore used dialect in his main corpus alongside the other techniques that this chapter describes to create a literary language just unusual enough to serve his artistry.

Tennyson's provincialisms are most often names for living things in nature. Bird enthusiast John Crompton, for example, has identified several of "Tennyson's delightful dialect words" for birds, such as *mavis, merle, ouzel, throstle, glimmergowk*, and *dor-hawk*. The Eversley Edition note on *yaffingale* in "The Last Tournament" (1871) calls it an "Old word, and still provincial for the green wood-pecker (so-called from its laughter). In Sussex 'yaffel.'" An "old word" makes sense in an Arthurian idyll. In fact, many of Tennyson's special names for birds appear in the *Idylls of the King*.[83] Tennyson later owned a dictionary of Sussex dialect (1875) that included *yaffle* (note the different spelling) as a word for woodpecker. This particular dictionary was published four years after Tennyson's idyll, but based on the "List of Authorities" it provides, Tennyson may have drawn on an earlier glossary of Sussex provincialisms by William Durrant Cooper, either its 1836 or 1853 edition.[84] It is the only reference source that spells *yaffel* as Tennyson does, though it says nothing about the color of the woodpecker.[85] Whatever his source, Tennyson's note makes a connection between his "old word" and modern-day speakers who still use it in dialect.

"The Brook" (1855) describes one character as chattering all day, "like the dry / High-elbowed grigs that leap in summer grass" (53–54). The Eversley Edition translates *grigs* as *crickets*; this passage serves as one of only three examples in the *OED* for this presumed dialectical use that was supposedly extracted from the common expression "merry as a grig." The poem "A Dirge" (1830) uses the unusual form *birk* for a birch tree (5), a form Ricks notes as being northern.[86] In a notebook collection of rhyming words, Tennyson entered "hulver (holly)" as a possible pairing for *culver*, though he did not end up using it in his work.[87] Two dialect dictionaries catalogue *hulver* as a word from eastern England, including East Anglia; might Tennyson have heard it during his time at Cambridge?[88]

The title character of "The Princess" (as published in 1847) reproaches a student for singing a song full of regret. Ida tells her, "'Let the past be past; let be / Their

---

[82] Campion, *Tennyson Dialect Glossary*, 19.
[83] John Crompton, "Haunts of Coot and Tern: Tennyson's Birds," *Tennyson Research Bulletin* 8, no. 2 (2003): 108.
[84] Parish, *A Dictionary of the Sussex Dialect and Collection of Provincialisms in Use in the County of Sussex*, 131, iii.
[85] William Durrant Cooper, *A Glossary of the Provincialisms in Use in the County of Sussex*, 2nd ed. (London: John Russell Smith, 1853), 87.
[86] Tennyson, *The Poems of Tennyson*, 1987, 1:255.
[87] Weaver, *Tennyson's Notebook Glossary and Rhyme Lists*, 66.
[88] John Greaves Nall, *An Etymological and Comparative Glossary of the Dialect and Provincialisms of East Anglia* (London: Longmans, Green, Reader & Dyer, 1866), 583; James Orchard Halliwell, *A Dictionary of Archaic and Provincial Words, Obsolete Phrases, Proverbs and Ancient Customs, from the Fourteenth Century*, vol. 1 (London: John Russell Smith, 1852), 466.

cancelled Babels: though the rough kex break / The starred mosaic ... and the wild figtree split / Their monstrous idols'" (IV.59–62). Several dialect glossaries of the period have an entry for *kex*, indicating it was in use in several counties. It is also worth noting that this regional word breaks up a (presumably Roman) mosaic floor, symbolizing on a small scale, Ida's overall argument: that we should look forward to better things promised, not be sad about what has passed by. The *scrawl* in "The Sailor Boy" (written by 1849) Tennyson defines as "the young of the dog-crab,"[89] a use the OED only recognizes in this instance and in the 1847 book *A Dictionary of Archaic and Provincial Words, Obsolete Phrases, Proverbs and Ancient Customs from the Fourteenth Century*, compiled by J.O. Halliwell. Ricks concludes therefore that Tennyson's use is "apparently quoting from" that dictionary.[90] It is certainly possible; Tennyson owned several other dialect dictionaries, and it is easy to believe that he consulted Halliwell's, as well. However, Halliwell's entry for *scrawl* cites the dog-crab meaning as being dialect from Lincolnshire; if that is correct, Tennyson may well have known it first-hand from his youth.[91]

Tennyson was curious and studious about dialect, as with other aspects of language. His annotations show that he generally knew which regions his dialect words came from and used them to reflect the settings of his poems. For example, he glossed *pike* in the 1820 poem "Ode to Memory" ("the high field on the bushless Pike") as a "Cumberland word for Peak."[92] In "Locksley Hall" (written 1837–1838), the line "the many-wintered crow ... leads the clanging rookery home" apparently conflates two different bird species (68). Tennyson's choice to use dialect in this case must have earned him some criticism as late as 1892, because he defended himself with some annoyance in a letter to Walter Theodore Watts by citing his personal knowledge of Lincolnshire speech: "In my county and I believe all through the North Rooks are called 'Crows'. I am not such a ninny as not to know a crow from a rook ... Accuse me if you like of provincialism not of ignorance in this matter."[93] He made the point again – and more publicly – in the Eversley Edition, which informs readers that "Rooks are called crows in the Northern Counties." The imaginary hall is located in just such a northern county, making the "provincialism" especially appropriate in this poem. Tennyson evidently felt the value of this terminology long after he first used it poetically. More than fifty years after composing "Locksley Hall," he again used the two words as synonyms in "The Ring" (written 1887): "I heard the sober rook / And carrion crow cry 'Mortgage'" (149–150).

In between these occurrences, Tennyson employed his home dialect for *In Memoriam*. This was an appropriate choice given how the poem follows the contours of his real-life journey through grief, including Christmases at his childhood home and moving away from it for good. The Eversley notes help translate *tangle* as "oar-weed" and *wold* as upland. Dialect dictionaries give *tangle* as being "North"

---

[89] Tennyson, *Poems II*, 374.
[90] Tennyson, *The Poems of Tennyson*, 1987, 2:300.
[91] James Orchard Halliwell, *A Dictionary of Archaic and Provincial Words, Obsolete Phrases, Proverbs and Ancient Customs, from the Fourteenth Century*, vol. 2 (John Russel Smith, 1847), 714.
[92] Tennyson, *Poems I*, 343.
[93] Tennyson, *Letters*, 1982, 3:439.

as well as East Anglian. And as Chapter 1 discussed, Tennyson used the word *bees* to refer to flies. In *Enoch Arden* (1864), a provincial turn of phrase appears in the penultimate stanza: "There came so loud a calling of the sea / That all the houses in the haven rang" (904–905). Tennyson explained "the calling of the sea" in his Eversley annotation thus: "a term used, I believe, chiefly in the western parts of England, to signify a groundswell."[94] The expression was obscure enough that an illustrated edition of the poem in the late 1880s depicted stormy waves crashing into the port. Tennyson complained about the error in a letter, explaining, "The 'calling of the sea' is an expression for the sound of a ground swell, not of a storm. The timber of old houses would never have rung to such a sound except upon a still night when the calling of the sea is often heard for miles inland."[95] Contemporary articles explaining the natural phenomenon of "the calling of the sea" describe it as occurring in Cornwall, where Tennyson took multiple holidays.[96]

These examples give a sense of Tennyson's extensive use of dialect words. In fact, he deployed them often enough that he himself became a resource for dictionaries. For example, the second edition of Hensleigh Wedgwood's *A Dictionary of English Etymology* (1872) quotes *buzzard-clock* from "Northern Farmer, Old Style" (18) in a discussion of insects named for the sounds they make.[97] As discussed in Chapter 1, Tennyson proved a prolific source of quotations for the *OED*, and there were several reasons for that. First, his status as an already canonical poet naturally positioned him to serve as an authority on words. He also tended to use them in a context that made their meanings clear, which allowed his quotations to illustrate various meanings. And he used them in ways that ranged across the spectrum of conventionality. He might employ a given word in its common (metropolitan, middle- and upper-class) Victorian usage, in a sense that had gone out of use, or in a way that literally gave it new meaning. By interacting with all the layers of its history, he demonstrated the richness of the English language – and even of a single word.

"The history of a word ... in all its completeness": Historical Meanings

In addition to using words that were unfamiliar in themselves, Tennyson re-activated less-common meanings in known vocabulary, thereby making "the old and the familiar ... new" (to quote Trench yet again). Engaging older definitions is a manifestation of the same philological investment that led to the early poems being littered with terms that had no contemporary usage. However, this practice produces a different effect: re-estrangement. Whereas already obsolete terms stand out as curiosities, this method forces a re-evaluation of words that seem common at first glance. Antiquarian medievalism valued the preserved artifacts of the past

---

[94] Tennyson, *Enoch Arden and In Memoriam*, 228, 193.

[95] Alfred Tennyson, *The Complete Poetical Works of Tennyson*, ed. W.J. Rolfe, Cambridge Edition (Boston: Houghton Mifflin, 1898), 840.

[96] R. Edmunds, "Appendix: 'The Calling of the Sea,'" in *A Guide to Penzance and Its Neighbourhood, Including the Islands of Scilly*, by J.S. Courtney (Penzance: E. Rowe, 1845), 53–55; "Hydrography," *The Edinburgh New Philosophical Journal* 37, no. 74 (1844): 403–404.

[97] Hensleigh Wedgwood, *A Dictionary of English Etymology*, 2nd ed. (London: Trübner & Company, 1872), xix.

(whether physical or lexical) that had brought their historical form unchanged into the present. Philological medievalism found value in every stage of change. Max Müller, for example, wrote that the source of a word's definition was not to be found in its etymology; rather, it was embedded within all of its past usages. In short, "the history of a word, if only we could get at it in all its completeness, is always its best definition."[98] Tennyson embraced his own version of this idea by exploring the histories of his words.

As early as "The Fall of Jerusalem" from 1827's *Poems by Two Brothers*, Tennyson recalled the sense of *waft* meaning "to convey safely by water," as back-formed from the word *wafter*, or convoy vessel. The poem eulogizes:

> those rich and happy times
> When the ships from Tarshish bore
> Incense, and from Ophir's land,
> With silken sail and cedar oar,
> Wafting to Judea's strand
> All the wealth of foreign climes.   (15–20)

Likewise, *In Memoriam* asks the "fair ship" that carries Arthur Hallam's remains to "spread thy full wings, and waft him o'er" (ix.1–4). The *OED* uses this line to illustrate this meaning; but it also uses Tennyson to demonstrate two other meanings for *waft*. Several poems written around 1833–1834 show Tennyson exploring the possible senses of the word. "The Captain" concludes, "And the lonely seabird crosses / With one waft of the wing" (71–72). Here he employs *waft* as "an act of waving (the wings or something held in the hand)." He used the same meaning again decades later in "In the Children's Hospital" (1880), where flowers "freshen and sweeten the wards like the waft of an Angel's wing" (38). The poem that begins "You ask me, why, though ill at ease" (written around 1833) utilizes a sense specific to the wind propelling a person or ship safely: "Yet waft me from the harbour-mouth, / Wild wind!" (25). To illustrate the idea of carrying through the air generally, the *OED* quotes "the woodbine spices are wafted abroad" from "Maud" (written 1854). Tennyson even broke new ground by coining a new meaning. In the poem "Youth" (1833), the speaker is "dizzy on the track, / A light wind wafts me from my feet" (99–100). This meaning of *waft* – to move, drive, or carry away by producing a current of air – has only two examples in the *OED*, from several years later. Tennyson was on the cutting edge of this meaning as it was developing.

As the "Maud" example above demonstrates, he continued the practice of sampling historical senses well beyond his youthful compositions. Elsewhere in the same poem, the speaker is "plagued with a flitting to and fro, / A disease, a hard mechanic ghost / That ... moves with the moving eye" (II.82–85). In describing a visual effect in the eye, he uses *mechanic* in an obsolete sense: "Characterized by an apparently automatic or involuntary reaction or response." Importantly, Tennyson usually places his philological words in a context that helps the reader to infer the older definition. Section cv of *In Memoriam* reflects on how celebrating Christmas

---

[98] Taylor, *Hardy's Literary Language and Victorian Philology*, 228, 233.

away from Somersby allows the family to break from old habits, stating, "No more shall wayward grief abuse / The genial hour" (9–10). Hallam Tennyson's Eversley Edition note tells us that *abuse* is to be understood "in the old sense – wrong."[99] Its context suggests this, however, even without the annotation.

In the early manuscript poem "The constant spirit of the world exults," the speaker says that later centuries cannot express certain "high-thoughted moods and moulds of mind" from former ages. The origin of the word *mood* is Old English *mōd*, a word that is notoriously difficult to translate because of its many possible meanings, including *mind, thought, spirit, courage,* or *heart*.[100] In fact, the Anglo-Saxon historian Sharon Turner (whom Tennyson read) had cited *mōd* as one example of how ideas proliferate from an original noun.[101] Thus "high-thoughted moods" is a nineteenth-century self-defining translation of the complex idea of *mōd*. "The Palace of Art" (1832) revisited this cluster of ideas when it described the palace as having every kind of room, "fit for every mood / And change of my still soul" (59–60). It likewise has "every landscape fair, / As fit for every mood of mind" (89–90).

In similar fashion, "The Lover's Tale" (1832) describes a "pleasure-boat that rocked … Upon the dappled dimplings of the wave, / That blanched upon its side" (I.41, 43–44). Although none of Tennyson's dictionaries offer a definition of *blanch* that fits the action of water against a boat, he is evidently reviving an obsolete verb derived from *blandish* in the sense "to act upon with caressing action," as the *OED* has it. The poem "Tithonus" (likewise written in the 1830s) probes the histories of its apparently ordinary words with a deft touch. The immortal, ever-aging speaker wonders:

> Why should a man desire in any way
> To vary from the kindly race of men,
> Or pass beyond the goal of ordinance
> Where all should pause, as is most meet for all?   (28–31)

In this context, *goal* can only mean a boundary or limit, and indeed the Eversley Edition glosses "goal of ordinance" as "appointed limit."[102] This is a definition for which the *OED* cites only two examples, from around 1350 and 1647. *In Memoriam* revisits this meaning when it tells the "disastrous day" to "Climb thy thick noon, … / Touch thy goal of joyless gray, / And hide thy shame beneath the ground" (lxxii.26–28). Hallam's Eversley Edition note confirms that "goal of joyless gray" refers to "the dull sunset."[103] Given that these lines sketch the sun's journey through the sky, the more modern meaning of *goal* as an endpoint of a journey could apply here, but the goal itself has a color and is something the sun can touch. The older sense better fits with the overall imagery, with the horizon as a boundary beyond which the day is hidden.

---

[99] Tennyson, *Enoch Arden and In Memoriam*, 256.
[100] Mitchell and Robinson, *A Guide to Old English*, 361.
[101] Turner, *History of the Anglo-Saxons*, 1807, 2:457.
[102] Tennyson, *Poems II*, 340.
[103] Tennyson, *Enoch Arden and In Memoriam*, 244.

Removing the Veil of Custom and Familiarity 141

In the same passage from "Tithonus" quoted above, "kindly race of men" makes most sense with the knowledge that the adjective comes from the same root as *kin* and is being used here to mean "of the same species," an etymology that Johnson's dictionary recognized.[104] Tithonus does not mourn the pleasant, friendly race of men but rather regrets having become a different kind of being than man. In fact, an earlier draft of the poem ("Tithon") had: "Why should a man desire in any shape / To vary from his kind" (20–21). In addition, Ellis's *Specimens of the Early English Poets*, a turn-of-the-century source for much of Tennyson's notebook glossary, had glossed *kind* in an excerpt from *Piers Plowman* as meaning *nature*.[105] By becoming an immortal creature between man and god, Tithonus has strayed from natural laws. This is the source of his grief: being unable either to die or to enjoy immortality.

When *kindly* describes the mourner of *In Memoriam*, the potentialities of meaning create uncertainty within an apparently straightforward statement. The speaker explains his sometimes-cheerful appearance by saying, "The shade by which my life was crost … Has made me kindly with my kind, / And like to him whose sight is lost" (lxvi.5, 7–8). The proximity of *kindly* and *kind* calls attention to their similarity of form and therefore hints at their possible similarity of meaning, as does the parallelism of the following line, "and like to him." However, the excusatory tone of the stanza also supports an interpretation of this phrase using the common sense of *kindly*. In this reading, these lines would say that the speaker is sometimes "gay among the gay" because he has become good-spirited toward mankind. The next chapter looks more deeply into how *In Memoriam* leverages the ambiguity inherent in a word's multiple possible meanings, but this example demonstrates how Tennyson exposed verbal histories through context.

James Knowles recalled that Tennyson "often said … that 'there were many glancing meanings in everything he wrote.'"[106] He said this with regard to allegory, but Tennyson was also deeply knowledgeable about the "many glancing meanings" in his words. Through the prism of historical usage, he could make those meanings play off one another. Take, for example, the famous section of "Maud" in which the speaker implores his love to come into the garden. As dawn approaches, he says:

> … a breeze of morning moves,
> And the planet of Love is on high
> Beginning to faint in the light that she loves
> On a bed of daffodil sky,
> To faint in the light of the sun she loves,
> To faint in his light, and to die.   (I.856–861)

In this stanza, Tennyson makes a pun that combines old and contemporary definitions of the word *faint*. Venus is growing dimmer in the light of sunrise; the triple repetition of "faint in the [or his] light" makes this meaning clear, especially the line "faint in the light of the sun." This etymological sense, "to lose color or brightness,"

---

[104] Samuel Johnson, *A Dictionary of the English Language*, vol. 2, 2 vols. (London: Thomas Tegg, 1832).
[105] Ellis, *Specimens of the Early English Poets*, 1:157.
[106] Tennyson, *Idylls of the King*, 1908, 490.

derived from the adjective *faint*, was already chiefly poetic by the time Tennyson used it. At the same time, the stanza constructs a romance between the fading planet and the sun, retaining the more common reading of *faint* as swooning.

Complementing this exploration of the significations a given word might have held, Tennyson also showed off the metaphors of original meanings insofar as etymology could identify them. New philologists had shifted the focus of linguistic study away from the earlier obsession with origins, but they remained fascinated by the process of building metaphors out of root ideas. It was equally intriguing to Tennyson, for as a poet, his craft was the exploration of how words can combine existing ideas to form new ones.

"Alike a word and an Iliad": Revealing Etymology

The most common response to the seeming chaos of linguistic imprecision has always been to place faith in the inbuilt metaphor of each word. Large portions of Plato's *Cratylus* are devoted to showing the correctness of specific "names" based on their metaphorical description of what they signify. More than two millennia later, Trench contended that mental clarity and precise speaking could be greatly enhanced by knowing the histories of the words we use. Yet because everyday words are so familiar, he said, we do not recognize their depth. In such ignorance, wrote Trench:

> we walk up and down in the midst of intellectual and moral marvels with a vacant eye and a careless mind, even as some traveller passes unmoved over fields of fame, or through cities of ancient renown ... We, like him ... miss ... that manifold teaching and instruction which ever lie about our path, and nowhere more largely than in our daily words.[107]

Trench was certainly not the first to note that familiarity may dampen the impact of a word. To cite only the most influential example for him, Trinity tutor Julius Charles Hare had written in 1827's widely read *Guesses at Truth* that "many expressions once apt and emphatic have been so rubbed and worn away by usage, that they retain as little substance as the skeletons of wheels which have made a tour on the continent."[108] It was to resist this inevitable wearing-out, argues Richard Marggraf Turley, that Tennyson selected archaic and "emphatically 'meaningful' words" for his poetry, as described in the previous sections of this chapter.[109] In addition to employing old words themselves, etymological study could restore the vitality of the imagery encased in a word.

Trench neatly summarized the effect of familiarity in *Notes on the Parables of Our Lord* (1841), remarking that:

---

[107] Trench, *On the Study of Words*, 2.
[108] Julius Charles Hare, *Guesses at Truth, by Two Brothers*, vol. 1 (London: John Taylor, 1827), 302.
[109] Richard Marggraf Turley, "'Knowledge of Their Own Supremacy': 'Œnone' and the Standardization of Tennyson's Diction," *Victorian Poetry* 37, no. 3 (October 1, 1999): 300.

while all language is, and of necessity must be figurative, yet long familiar use is continually wearing out the freshness and sharpness of the stamp – (who, for example, that speaks of *insulting*, retains the lively image of a leaping on the prostrate body of a foe?)[110]

As it happens, Tennyson did allude to the originally physical nature of an insult in "The Marriage of Geraint" (completed by 1857). Guinevere sends her maiden to ask the name of a haughty prince, whose servant then "struck at [the maiden] with his whip" (201). Geraint wishes to "avenge this insult, noble Queen, / Done in your maiden's person to yourself," an idea he reiterates several times in the poem (215–216). Neither Trench nor Tennyson was primarily interested in finding the "real meaning" of a word – the language of Adam and Eve – but they were not entirely immune from the appeal of the idea of inherent meaning. Trench certainly did not care for the idea that language was only conventional. In discussing part of the marriage vows, "with my body I thee worship," he explains that to *worship* formerly meant no more than to *honour* someone. He admits that it would be useful to alter the phrasing of the service to avoid misunderstanding, "but," he writes, the vows "did not mean at the first, and therefore do not now really mean any more than, 'with my body I thee *honour*.'"[111]

From Trench's standpoint that words are "not merely arbitrary signs, but living powers" (a Coleridgean idea and turn of phrase), a word still retains some of its original signification, even if contemporary speakers are not aware of it. And while conceding that some expressions almost completely become "only forms ... as in our 'good-by' or 'adieu' we can hardly be said now to commit our friend to Divine protection; yet still they were not such at the first, nor would they have held their ground, if ever they had become such altogether." Etymological study, in short, can reveal what people are really saying at some level whenever they speak. Through his popular works, Trench helped to spread the appealing notion that "men are continually uttering deeper things than they know." The premise is especially relevant to poetry, where conscious effort attends the arrangement of words and their connotations. By revealing the metaphors that had formed all but the simplest of words, etymology demonstrated that:

> poetry, which is passion and imagination embodying themselves in words, does not necessarily demand combined words for this; of this passion and imagination a single word may be the vehicle. As the sun can image itself alike in a tiny dewdrop or in the mighty ocean ... so the spirit of poetry can dwell in and glorify alike a word and an Iliad ... On every side we are beset with poetry.[112]

If a single word may be unpacked to become a poem, then poets have available an additional level of metaphor, allowing further suggestiveness, precision, or indeed contradiction or ambiguity.

---

[110] Trench, *Parables*, 24.
[111] Trench, *English, Past and Present*, 168–169.
[112] Trench, *On the Study of Words*, 27, 62, 10, 7.

It is also the poet's privilege – and possibly duty – to reveal those metaphors. Tennyson was adept at making the "dewdrop" of a word mirror the "mighty ocean" of the poem in which he placed it, as with the sonnet analyzed in the first chapter, "The constant spirit of the world exults." In "The Palace of Art" (1832), the speaker's soul is "plagued … with sore despair" and "[d]eep dread and loathing of her solitude" (224, 229). She begins to see gruesome visions in her palace:

> … in dark corners of her palace stood
> Uncertain shapes; and unawares
> On white-eyed phantasms weeping tears of blood,
> And horrible nightmares,
> And hollow shades enclosing hearts of flame,
> And, with dim fretted foreheads all,
> On corpses three-months-old at noon she came,
> That stood against the wall. (237–244)

In the Eversley Edition, Tennyson clarified the sense of *fretted* in these lines. He refers to the presumably common expression "moth-fretted garments" and explains that the foreheads of the corpses are "[n]ot wrinkled, but worm-fretted (Old English *fretan*, to eat)."[113] In other words, the corpses have been eaten by worms. At the time Tennyson composed this poem, the etymology of *fret* was somewhat uncertain, but the sense of eating or devouring and the Old English root *fretan* appears in the dictionaries of Benson, Bailey (as "gnaw or corrode"), Lye, and Johnson. Whether he came across it in one of these sources or through his study of Anglo-Saxon literature, Tennyson employed the root meaning to describe the horrifying visions.

In like manner, the second stanza of "Maud" begins, "For there in the ghastly pit long since a body was found" (I.4). *Ghastly* shares a root with *ghost*, which dictionaries had pointed out from Bailey onward. Later in the same poem, the speaker describes Maud's brother leaving to indulge his gluttony in town:

> This lump of earth has left his estate
> The lighter by the loss of his weight;
> And so that he find what he went to seek,
> And fulsome Pleasure clog him, and drown
> His heart in the gross mud-honey of town,
> He may stay for a year who has gone for a week. (I.537–542)

The passage emphasizes the brother's obesity, beginning with *lump* and *weight*. Richardson's dictionary mentions the possibility of *fulsome* being a compound of *full* and *some*, alongside the etymology given by earlier authorities of *foul* plus *some*. Tennyson's lines bring together connotations of fullness to highlight that metaphor:

---

[113] Tennyson, *Poems I*, 370. Note the unusual use of the phrase "Old English" instead of Anglo-Saxon.

the brother will be clogged and drowned. *Gross*, derived from the French word for large size, carries the same combination of meanings and reinforces them.[114]

Patrick Greig Scott has pointed out that "sometimes Tennyson's use of etymology is not so much additional as essential to the understanding of his imagery." Bringing an etymological sensitivity to the text, Scott rightly argues, can help explain particular lexical choices and, more broadly, shows that "[Tennyson's] use of etymology often relies on extended networks of etymological allusion, and these sustain the impact of the single word." Looking through this lens, we find, for example, that the *heart-affluence*, which *In Memoriam* attributes to Arthur Hallam, is in fact part of "a consistently developed water-image."[115] In fact, another watery etymological pun had already appeared in "The Lotos-Eaters." The section reads:

> How sweet it were, hearing the downward stream,
> …
> To watch the crisping ripples on the beach,
> And tender curving lines of creamy spray;
> To lend our hearts and spirits wholly
> To the influence of mild-minded melancholy.   (99, 106–109)

Imagery of stream, beach, and waves suggests an obsolete meaning of *influence*: "a flowing in/into," as Bailey and Richardson put it, both providing the Latin that makes this meaning obvious to those with classical education.[116] In these lines, Tennyson very consciously hinted at the physical origin of the word's metaphor.

As with *influence*, Tennyson seems to have been especially drawn to dissecting Latinate words into fragmentary literal meanings in his early poems, probably because it was easy for a classically educated Victorian to identify their components. When the etymology is relatively transparent, the philological re-estrangement is noticeably at work, as when the early notebook poem "O Bosky Brook" describes a mountain lake that "blackly lay / Beneath the sunny living noon, / Most like an insulated part of night" (24–26). As taken from the Latin *insula*, the verb to *insulate* means "to make into an island"; thus, in a clever inversion, water itself becomes an island. Similarly, Tennyson's notebook glossary entry for *implied* (spelled *implide*) quotes Chapman's Homer ("his head with curls implied").[117] *In Memoriam* follows the etymological sense that Chapman exemplifies – "to infold" (Bailey), "to intangle" (Johnson) – when it refers to "that vague fear implied in death" (xli.14). The metaphor emerges from the root, but this was a sense that Johnson had already said was "not in use" decades before.[118]

Likewise, *involve* may be divided into its Latin roots *in-* and *volvere* (to roll) and thus create the sense "to roll into or upon, to wrap up, envelop, surround, entangle."

---

[114] Charles Richardson, *A New Dictionary of the English Language*, vol. 1 (London: Pickering, 1836), 863, 940.
[115] Scott, "Flowering in a Lonely Word," 377–379.
[116] Richardson, *A New Dictionary of the English Language*, 1836, 1:1107.
[117] Tennyson, *Notebooks 1–4*, 1:224.
[118] Samuel Johnson, *A Dictionary of the English Language*, vol. 1 (London: Thomas Tegg, 1832), 949.

146   *Tennyson's Philological Medievalism*

In "The Devil and the Lady," the titular evil spirit offers to serve his master by fetching a tooth of "that mighty snake whose folds / Far stretching through the unconfinèd space / Involve seven worlds" (55–57), while "Timbuctoo" describes "a maze of piercing, trackless, thrilling thoughts, / Involving and embracing each with each" (113–114). The thoughts being in a *maze*, combined with *embracing*, helps evoke the etymological metaphor of *involve*, as does the following line, which says the thoughts are "inextricably linked." As with his historical uses, Tennyson often placed his etymological meanings – which are, of course, also historical – within poetic settings that help define them. The poem "The Sleeping Beauty" says of the maiden, "Her constant beauty doth inform / Stillness with love, and day with light" (15–16). First, there is a faint echo of *constant*'s literal meaning (standing still) suggested by the maiden's stillness. More prominently, these lines help define the etymological sense of *inform* so well that the *OED* uses these lines to illustrate the sense "to imbue or impregnate with a specific quality." Two decades later, "Maud" contains the line, "Courage, poor heart of stone" (II.132); *courage* literally means heart, as Chaucer uses it in the Prologue to the *Canterbury Tales*.

"Timbuctoo," the poem that won Tennyson the Chancellor's Gold Medal at Cambridge, is especially dense with philological unveiling. Its creator was later embarrassed by it, presumably because he had "patched up an old poem" to form it, without the careful crafting he put into so much of his verse.[119] Yet unpolished as it may be, his skill at etymological exhibition is already apparent in this work. In an epic simile, we read that "thrilling thoughts" ran through the speaker's mind:

> Expanding momently with every sight
> And sound which struck the palpitating sense,
> The issue of strong impulse, hurried through
> The riven rapt brain; as when in some large lake
> From pressure of descendant crags, which lapse
> Disjointed, crumbling from their parent slope
> At slender interval, the level calm
> Is ridged with restless and increasing spheres
> Which break upon each other, each the effect
> Of separate impulse, but more fleet and strong
> Than its precursor, till the eye in vain
> Amid the wild unrest of swimming shade
> Dappled with hollow and alternate rise
> Of interpenetrated arc, would scan
> Definite round.   (116–130)

Through a combination of etymology and redundancy, Tennyson emphasizes the physicality of the literal Latin meanings for many of his words in this passage. *Descendant* (literally, down-climbing) crags *lapse* (glide, slip, stumble, fall, hence "fall away by slow degrees"). The Latin meaning of *impulse* as "a push against" emerges twice in these fifteen lines, first as the noun for sensations that "struck the

---

[119] Hallam Tennyson, *Memoir*, 1:45–46.

palpitating sense" (with *palpitating* further reinforcing this physicality), then as a description of rocks striking a lake.

Another term stands out from the grammatical and visual confusion of the dazzling spectacle when we read that "the eye in vain … would scan / Definite round." The grammatical role of *definite* is difficult to assign, but as the speaker's eye *scans* (literally, *climbs*, the same root that forms *descend* and *ascend*) among the "hollow and alternate rise" of ripples, it seeks to bring the chaos within limits – or as *definite*'s origin would suggest, bring it to an end. Twenty-seven lines later, the speaker's thoughts gain strength to take wing like butterflies and "bear them upward through the trackless fields / Of undefined existence far and free." The context easily presents *undefined* as meaning unlimited or unending, in accordance with its etymons. In these passages, thoughts – the most intangible of things – are likened to physical objects through extended similes, and those very similes are further solidified by a lexicon of expressions that lay bare their inbuilt metaphors.

This passage from "Timbuctoo" shows that already during his university years Tennyson was learning to arrange context to illuminate etymological definitions, a skill that only strengthened with time. For example, the dictionaries of Bailey, Johnson, Richardson, and Skeat give the origin of the word *goal* as French *gaule* or "a Pole, which being set in the Ground, was the Place to run to" (as Bailey has it). While the *OED* now asserts that "there is no evidence … that English *goal* ever meant 'pole,'" Tennyson used it as such in the poem "Tiresias" (written in stages between the early 1830s and 1883). The eponymous life-weary prophet looks forward to an afterlife where his "eyes will find / The men I knew, and watch the chariot whirl / About the goal again" (167–169). Ancient chariot races, as these lines suggest, took place around two turning-posts that were "whirl[ed] about," and thus the word *goal* regains its supposed etymological meaning.

The fact that Bailey, Johnson, Richardson, Skeat, and therefore Tennyson assigned the wrong origin to *goal* makes little difference to the serious poetic-philological work that these lines accomplish. As Steven Connor writes, speakers invest in, or invent, origins for their words in order to locate the meanings of those words within a rational act of observation once performed by some linguistic ancestor.[120] New philology offered more reliable sources for the origins of words, but they still served to "stand … between the chaos and the cosmos of human speech" (in Müller's expression).[121] Whether or not twenty-first century scholars agree with the origins that Victorian writers believed in – whether or not the *OED* now discredits an etymology – those supposed roots undeniably affected how Tennyson wrote. This book is not concerned with the accuracy of his philology but rather with his techniques for employing its revelations as he understood them.

Tennyson was not the first to utilize the literal senses of his words, of course. J.F.A. Pyre (quoted earlier in this chapter) diagnosed this poet's diction as partly consisting of "appropriating words to special poetic use after the analogy of [Shakespeare and Milton], as, for example, by the use of Latinisms in a special or primitive

---

[120] Steven Connor, *Beyond Words: Sobs, Hums, Stutters and Other Vocalizations* (London: Reaktion Books, 2014), 15–16.
[121] Müller, *Lectures*, 5th ed., ix.

sense."¹²² W. David Shaw recognized that, like Milton, "Tennyson also enlivens faded metaphors."¹²³ And indeed Christopher Ricks identifies a key component of "Milton's grand style" to be literal usages through which "the metaphor [of a word] is enlivened."¹²⁴ Tennyson himself recognized the practice in his predecessor, which can only have reinforced the value of this practice. His first extant letter, from 1821, consists of a commentary on *Samson Agonistes* in which he cites a Milton chorus, "See how he lies at random carelessly diffused." Tennyson tells his aunt, "If you look into Bishop Newton's notes, you will find that … 'this beautiful application of the word "diffused," is borrowed from the Latin.'"¹²⁵

The nineteenth-century poet was also aware that even Milton's consciously strange lexis could be assimilated and lose "the freshness and sharpness of the stamp" (to borrow Trench's phrase). Many years later, he remarked to his son, "Our English language alters quickly. This great line would be almost commonplace now: 'The dismal situation waste and wild.'"¹²⁶ Etymological metaphors, in other words, needed to be continually refreshed; Tennyson's philological acumen equipped him to do just that, and his peers noticed the similarity between his style and that of his literary forebear. Writing of the Arthurian *Idylls*, William Gladstone said of Tennyson's style in 1859 that "Milton has contributed to its formation, and occasionally there is a striking resemblance in turn and diction." Tennyson, however, brought a broader range of philological understanding. As a result, he was not limited to dissecting Latinisms, and Gladstone found that "Mr. Tennyson is the more idiomatic of the two."¹²⁷

In an essay defending "Maud" (1856), the noted scientific popularizer Robert James Mann argued that it was hard for the general populace to appreciate Tennyson's poetry because "The people does not [sic] yet comprehend the precision of language. Nine-tenths of the words it employs, it actually does not know the *precise* meaning of, the condensed and finished meanings."¹²⁸ Mann concluded that Tennyson's audience was bound to grow as the population had more time to absorb the poet's precise, condensed, finished (philologically informed) meanings. Without much broader research into Tennyson's reception, it is difficult to judge to what extent his readers detected his moments of philological revelation, though the Introduction to this book lays out the evidence for an overlap in his readership and those familiar with philological ideas. Many etymologies, no doubt, passed unnoticed, especially if his usage remained close to a standard one. However, there are numerous cases in which a sentence can only make sense if a word takes on an older sense. Sometimes that older sense was one excavated from another stratum of linguistic history; sometimes it was the imagery of its "primitive" metaphor. Tennyson also reversed the process, forging new terms by joining two existing words – a

---

[122] Pyre, *The Formation of Tennyson's Style*, 225.
[123] Shaw, *Tennyson's Style*, 30.
[124] Christopher Ricks, *Milton's Grand Style* (Oxford: Clarendon Press, 2001), 59.
[125] Tennyson, *Letters*, 1982, 1:2.
[126] Hallam Tennyson, *Memoir*, 2:518.
[127] Jump, *Tennyson*, 263.
[128] Robert James Mann, *Tennyson's "Maud" Vindicated: An Explanatory Essay* (London: Jarrold & Sons, 1856), 37.

practice that harkened back to the earliest poetics of word formation and, more recently, Anglo-Saxon style.

Compounds as "Vigorous" Metaphors

If words were all once metaphors, then compound words re-create that formative process, welding together two ideas to form a new one that has not yet lost "the freshness and sharpness of the stamp." In this way, newly created compounds recall the "sensuousness" of "language in its spontaneous period" (as Kemble put it).[129] They remind us that words are "vitally metaphorical" (to use Shelley's phrase)[130] and illustrate how "many a single word ... is itself a concentrated poem" (to use Trench's).[131] First, such a word is often alien to modern speakers; it has not been "rubbed and worn away by usage," because it has never been used. Second, its component pieces belong to contemporary English, so the metaphor stands out clearly. For a philologically informed writer, therefore, the vigor of compound words was another way to revitalize one's language through artistic strangeness. Among Tennyson's contemporaries, for example, both Thomas Hardy and Gerard Manley Hopkins found compounds stimulating for their verse.

Dennis Taylor writes of Hardy's compounds that they "are variously archaic and coined, and sometimes coined out of archaisms." Hardy's compounding, writes Taylor, in combination with "his wide-ranging use of prefixes in old and new ways[,] reflects the confused history" of English.[132] Hardy and his neighbor William Barnes also appreciated how their local dialect had preserved Germanic language, which no doubt inspired their use of compounds. In response to Barnes's efforts to create new compounds to replace Latinate verbiage, Hopkins wrote to his friend Robert Bridges, "It makes one weep to think what English might have been; for in spite of all that Shakespeare and Milton have done with the compound I cannot doubt that no beauty in language can make up for want of purity."[133]

As Hopkins's remark suggests, compounds were associated with the Anglo-Saxon branch of English, earning them additional favor. Already in 1826, Anglo-Saxonist Joseph Bosworth had remarked in the preface to his dictionary of Old English:

> The facility and simplicity of combining several short indigenous words to express any complex idea, practiced by the Anglo-Saxons and other Gothic nations, is now too seldom used. Instead of adopting technical terms from other languages, or forming them from the Greek or Latin, as is the present English custom, our Anglo-Saxon forefathers formed words equally expressive by composing them from their own radical [i.e., new and original] terms.[134]

---

[129] Brookfield, *The Cambridge "Apostles,"* 178–179.
[130] Shelley, "A Defence of Poetry," 512.
[131] Trench, *On the Study of Words*, 5.
[132] Taylor, *Hardy's Literary Language and Victorian Philology*, 356.
[133] Hopkins, *Letters*, 162–163.
[134] Bosworth, *A Dictionary of the Anglo-Saxon Language*, xxxiii–xxxiv.

In addition to being poetic by virtue of their metaphorical nature, compounds feature prominently in Old English poetry itself. Kemble noted that the poetry of the Anglo-Saxons featured far more metaphor than simile, taking that to be a sign of their literal-mindedness. Whether we accept the latter conclusion or not, it is true that metaphorical compounds are a hallmark of Old English poetry. As Donald Scragg explains, the practice of variation (describing the same thing in several ways within a short space) "makes great demands on the poet's vocabulary." Combined with the demands of meter, variation "encouraged the use of compound words." Indeed, one-third of *Beowulf*'s lexicon consists of compound expressions.[135] Historian Sharon Turner, who otherwise did not think much of Anglo-Saxon vernacular poetry, nevertheless considered Old English language itself to have been recorded "in a very cultivated shape," as shown by "its copiousness – by its numerous synonimes [*sic*] ... but also by its immense number of compound words applying to every shade of meaning."[136]

Trench also valued compounds – especially Germanic ones that had gone out of use. In *English, Past and Present* (1855), he mentions that among those items lost from English, "A number of vigorous compounds we have dropped and let go." He then provides a list of examples: *dearworth* for beloved; *ear-sports* for "entertainments of song or music;" *hotspur* for "young men of hasty fiery valour;" *witwanton*; *grimsirs* or *grimsires* for grouchy old men; *rootfast*; *book-hunger*; *word-warriors*. He continues:

> Those who would gladly have seen the Anglo-Saxon to have predominated over the Latin element in our language, even more than it actually has done, must note with regret that in a great many instances a word of the former stock has been dropped, and a Latin coined to supply its place; or where the two once existed side by side, the Saxon has died, and the Latin lived on.

The examples he gives of this lost vocabulary are almost all compounds: *soothsaw* (proverb), *sourdough* (leaven), *afterthink* (repent), *medeful* (meritorious), *foreword* (promise), *freshman* (proselyte), *mooned* (lunatic), *foretalk* (preface), *sunstead* (solstice), *star-conner* (astrologer), to *eyebite* (fascinate), *waterfright* (hydrophobia), *wanhope* (despair), *middler* (mediator). Words compounded of a verb and its object, such as *scarecrow*, he found to be inelegant but still vigorous.[137]

Although Trench was more moderate than other voices of the nativist linguistic camp, it is typical of its nostalgic bent to call lost compounds "energetic" and "vigorous." Others used the same descriptors for Old English in general, and a large part of this sense of its vitality came from its tendency to form compact metaphors. Indeed, the impression is common even in the present time. When translating *Beowulf* at the turn of the twenty-first century, poet Seamus Heaney found like many before him that "Old English abounds in vigorous, evocative and specifically poetic words,"

---

[135] Donald Scragg, "The Nature of Old English Verse," in *The Cambridge Companion to Old English Literature*, ed. Malcolm Godden and Michael Lapidge (Cambridge: Cambridge University Press, 1991), 65.

[136] Turner, *History of the Anglo-Saxons*, 1807, 2:461.

[137] Trench, *English, Past and Present*, 103–104, 126.

especially compounds for battle-related items.[138] Heaney's observation loosely echoes Rask's 1830 grammar, which observed (in Thorpe's translation): "The Anglo-Saxon, like the other Gothic languages, abounds in compound words, as well philosophical as poetical."[139] Turner had essentially agreed, though with some disdain. He thought that "the violence of metaphor" characteristic of Old English poetry "naturally arises [in primitive societies] from not having immediately new terms to express the new, or more intellectual ideas … till new words are devised" (284–285).

The idea that compounds – along with other medieval words – are robust and inherently metaphorical (and therefore densely poetic) made them appealing to the young Tennyson. His poems reveal an especially strong affinity for compounds in his early years, when he was in close contact with the Cambridge Apostles. He and his Trinity acquaintances seem to have shared a curiosity about what elements made for a cohesive union when creating composite terms. For example, all of them were ambivalent about hyphens, and Tennyson likewise eschewed them early on. Reviews noticed this experimentation and disapproved. The *Athenaeum*'s review of the 1832 volume complained that the poetry was "marred, and its beauty disfigured, and sometimes absolutely concealed" both by archaisms and "by words newly compounded after the German model; and which the eye is some time before it has learned to read."[140] The *Christian Remembrancer*'s reviewer of the 1842 collection was "glad to see" Tennyson's previous "mannerisms [have] nearly all disappeared, (especially one which we once feared was destined to grow upon him – a passion for compound words)[.]"[141]

Trench later commented that when forming a new word, "much more is wanted … than merely to unite two or more words to one another by a hyphen; this is not to make a new word: they must really coalesce and grow together."[142] In this opinion, he was echoing his old mentor Julius Hare, who decried philosophers who coined new terms instead of using common words for new ideas. Hare cited Bentham as an unfortunate example, saying that, "unable to understand organic unity and growth … [he] looked upon a hyphen as the only bond of union."[143] Nor was compounding only a matter of literary theory among the Apostles; Arthur Hallam employed unhyphenated compounds in correspondence, as in an 1832 letter to his fiancée Emily Tennyson in which he refers to his "longimprisoned senses," asks Emily to be of good cheer rather than "quarrel with the summerskies," and recalls sitting in the Somersby "diningroom."[144] The following year, he reported that Alfred Tennyson had attended and enjoyed a recent "supperparty."[145]

In a draft of an unpublished philological work, Kemble similarly uses the words *publicspirited*, *selfsatisfaction*, and *surfacesmooth* in his preface.[146] However, in his

---

[138] Heaney, "Translator's Introduction," xxxviii.
[139] Rask, *A Grammar of the Anglo-Saxon Tongue*, 113.
[140] "Poems (Now First Published)," 770.
[141] "Book Review," *Christian Remembrancer*, July 1842, 46.
[142] Trench, *English, Past and Present*, 67.
[143] Hare, *Guesses at Truth, by Two Brothers*, 1827, 1:121.
[144] Hallam, *Letters*, 582–583.
[145] Tennyson, *Letters*, 1982, 1:91.
[146] Kemble, "Lajamon," 1–6.

publications of Old English, he opted to use hyphens generously to visually mark the component parts of his compounds. Jacob Grimm wrote to his friend in 1836 about his printing of the original *Beowulf* text: "For my sake you must omit in your future books the connecting dash in the middle of compounds. The ear can not hear it, and it has no benefit at all for the eye." Kemble replied the following year (1837) that he had printed the compounds that way simply to aid readers in using the glossary and assured his friend, "You will not be troubled with any more hyphens in any thing I publish."[147] However, his *Beowulf* translation of the same year also hyphenates Modern-English equivalents. The first two pages alone offer an abundance of compounds, several of them invented as such by Kemble: Gar-Danes, mead-thrones, out-cast [*feasceaft*, not a compound], dwelling-places [*geardum*, not a compound], evil-need [*fyrrenðearfe*], war-prince [*geong guma*, young man], ring-prowed [*hringedstefna*], battle-weapons [*hildewæpnum*], and war-weeds [*heaðowædum*].[148]

The potential conflict between eye and ear that Grimm flagged had implications for the use of compounds in nineteenth-century poetry, as well; recall the reviewer who wrote that "the eye is some time before it has learned to read" Tennyson's closed compounds. Among other considerations, their written form impacts whether they are perceived as one word or two, and thus how their accents are to be read. Richard Marggraf Turley has discussed Tennyson's early "penchant for unusual compounds and idiosyncratic hyphenation," which often led his editors to make unsolicited changes.[149] In later life, the poet recalled, "I had an idiotic hatred of hyphens in those [early] days, but though I printed such words as 'glénríver,' 'téndríltwine' I always gave them in reading their full two accents. Coleridge thought because of these hyphened [*sic*] words that I could not scan."[150] This remark acknowledges a potentially problematic effect of compounds on rhythm, a possibility also present in the work of other Victorian poets, including Browning, Hopkins, and Hardy. In rebutting Coleridge, Tennyson has had to mark his stresses, as Hopkins famously did in his verse.[151] Yet Tennyson was more concerned than Hopkins with being the people's poet; he therefore gradually stopped printing adjoined compounds, though he remained fond of combining two words to perform the Shelleyan task of arranging ideas into new relations with one another.

Most of Tennyson's compounds are nouns and adjectives. A handful of his verbs also take compound form, usually created by joining two nouns and then using the new phrase as a verb. They include: to *ribroast*, to *clapperclaw*, *lilyflowering* (a present participle), and to *papmeatpamper*; it is no coincidence that several of these verbs appear in "What Thor Said to the Bard after Dinner." To examine how he preferred to form other parts of speech, it is useful to employ a categorization scheme from Bruce Mitchell and Fred C. Robinson's *Guide to Old English*. Anglo-Saxon nouns could be created by combining: noun and noun (e.g., night-watch); adjective

---

[147] Kemble, *Correspondence*, 126, 148.
[148] Kemble, *Translation*, 2:1–2.
[149] Turley, "Knowledge of Their Own Supremacy," 291.
[150] Tennyson, *Poems I*, 359.
[151] It must also be noted that the problem was that they were *not* hyphenated.

and noun (e.g., all-ruler); or adverb and noun (e.g., in-travelling for expedition).[152] The lists of Tennyson's closed compounds below are not exhaustive, but they reveal his favored way of combining words. He had an overwhelming preference for constructing nouns out of two other nouns, as we see in the following inventory:

Noun-noun

> altarthrone, blossomtufts, bobtail, brookbank, cedarshade, chestnutboughs, chestnutbuds, daybeams, deathmote, deathsong, eastwind, figtree, firehill, flagflower, foambow, foamfountains, fossilbones, fruittree, glenriver, groundflame, harpwire, heartburning, hillbrow, ivyleaves, joybeams, kingcraft, ladylove, landwind, lightningstroke, lilyflower, lilygarlands, lotoseaters, lotusflute, lovetale, lutestring, marriageday, Maydews, millbridge, millpool, mountainthrone, mountainstreams, palacehall, pearlgarland, priestcraft, rhymehammer, rivereddy, roselips, sandfield, scarfskin, seasmell, seawind, selfgood, showerdrops, sleetwinds, starcraft, steppingstones, stormblast, summerflowers, summerhours, summernoon, summerplain, summerpride, summertide, summervault, summerwind, summerwoods, swingebuckler, tagrag, tendriltwine, tennisballs, thistledown, thunderfires, thunderfit, thundersong, wildweed-flower, wintertide

Adjective-Noun

> backcurrent, evilwilledness, hoarhead, northwind, squarecap, twinsisters, westwind, wildbird

Adverb-Noun

> crossbuttock, midforest, midnoon, oftentime, overwatchings, understream

Old English compound adjectives could be shaped through fusion of: noun and adjective (for example, honor-worthy); adjective and adjective (for example, wide[ly]-known); adverb and adjective (for example, very-good); and adjective and noun (for example, kind-mind[ed]).[153] Tennyson's favorite adjectival construction, as shown below, seems to have been the combination of two other adjectives, with the second usually formed from a noun – *ringed, winged, circled, gated, walled, towered, columned, sandaled,* and so on. Like his nouns, he frequently formed his adjectives with colors and to describe nature. Some examples follow:

Noun-Adjective

> beaconlike, blastborne, bloodred, bloombright, blosmwhite, blossomstarrèd, browhigh, cedardark, cedarshadowy, cloudwhite, dawncrimson, diamondeyed, eddylike, falconhearted, fathomdeep, featherfooted, flowergirt, foamwhite, fountainpregnant, globefilled, godbuilt, goldbright, grassgreen, heartdeep, honeysweet, hornfooted, icelike, ivorylike, ivymatted, laughterloving, leafthick, lightningbright,

---

[152] Mitchell and Robinson, *A Guide to Old English*, 56.
[153] Mitchell and Robinson, 56.

154   *Tennyson's Philological Medievalism*

lightwreathed, lilybraided, lilywreathèd, lionsouled, lutetoned, marblecold, marblewhite, meadowlevel, milkwhite, muskscented, nutbrown, raylike, realmdraining, rockhewn, rosehued, roselipt, rubylike, selfpoised, silverclad, silverfleckèd, snowwhite, sunchanged, sunpierced, sunsmitten, sunwhite, thundercloven, thundershaken, vinelike, violetwoven, warworn, windtost, winedark

Adjective-Adjective

baseborn, blackgreen, brightblack, broadbased, broadleaved, broadmaned, brownringed, darkblue, darklatticed, darklustrous, darkspired, deepeyed, deephearted, dewyswarded, firstmovèd, fourfacèd, fulleyèd, fullfaced, glassyfair, goldencored, goldenkernelled, goldenlockèd, goldensandalled, greengulphed, greensheathèd, hardfeatured, heavywallèd, highnecked, hollowhearted, largebrowed, lightblue, lightgreen, longdrawn, lowburied, lowhung, manycircled, manyfacèd, manyfolded, manygated, manytowered, muskybreathèd, newstarrèd, palecold, purpledelled, purplefringèd, quickwinged, raggedrimmèd, redcombed, rosywhite, scarletwinged, sharpshadowed, singlegrown, snowycolumned, subtlefangèd, thickribbèd, thickstarrèd, thickstemmed, twinfold, violeteyed, warmbreathèd, whitebreasted, whitehooved, whitehorned, whiterobèd, yellowleavèd

Adverb-Adjective

deepfurrowed, deepshadowed, deeptrenched, deepwounded, downdropt, downringing, everchanging, everduring, everwhirling, farfamed, farsheening, freshcarved, freshflushing, fullflowing, newmown, overquick, overwandering, overwise, thickstudded, wellnigh, wellwon, wellremembered

Interestingly, given the Apostles' fondness for compounds, one of Arthur Hallam's few quibbles with "Recollections of the Arabian Nights" was this: "we doubt the propriety of using the bold compound 'black-green,' at least in such close vicinity to 'gold green.'"[154] It is unclear what Hallam objected to in this formation, but it is a useful reminder that compounds were not universally liked, even among those who had plenty of philological reason to approve of them.

By the time he was an old man, Tennyson was embarrassed that he had had "an absurd antipathy to hyphens, and put two words together as one word."[155] Yet the change of practice was not entirely a matter of chronology. For example, in "The Hesperides" (published 1832), conjoined and hyphenated compounds exist side by side: "As the snowfield on the mountain-peaks, / As the sandfield at the mountain-foot" (19–20). Later we read of "Keen-eyed Sisters" (38) and the "sunset-ripened" apple that is "goldenkernelled, goldencored" (102–103). The poet later ceded to convention and broke his compounds into hyphenated pairs or separate words, but he still liked to qualify or modify one word with another to form a new concept. Though the poems that contain these compounds pre-date Trench's philological works (published midcentury), the two men evidently agreed on the merits of the

---

[154] Hallam, *Writings*, 193.
[155] Hallam Tennyson, *Memoir*, 1:50.

practice. *English, Past and Present* remarks on the language's capacity to form compounds, offering several from Milton and other writers as proof: "Many of [Milton's] compound epithets, as 'golden-tressed', 'tinsel-slippered', 'coral-paven', 'flowry-kirtled', 'violet-embroidered', 'vermeil-tinctured', are themselves poems in miniature," he writes.[156] Notably, Trench's examples match Tennyson's preferred style of double adjective, especially if one of the components is a color.

The complexity of the influences in Tennyson's use of compounds is emblematic of the difficulties that arise when seeking to document his relationship with Anglo-Saxonism and philology more broadly. It is likewise complicated to probe into his linguistic innovations, for they grew out of his deep knowledge of his mother tongue's history and the examples of poets who came before him. Thus he could make new words that either drew attention to themselves or blended in so naturally that it is surprising to find them as the first example in an *OED* entry.

"Words unknown": Linguistic Innovation

Tennyson's fondness for the old went beyond a mere preservation of dying forms. In addition to reviving authentically archaic words and usages, he took older terms as a template for creating new words or senses. Whereas Milton "is concerned mainly to lead us back," in the words of Ricks, Tennyson moves forward, adding a new layer of meaning to existing terms or indeed creating entirely new ones.[157] He places an apparently known word in an unexpected setting and thereby creates a new combination of associations for it as the reader attempts to apply its historical meanings and then must accept a new one layered atop them, but not obliterating their connotations entirely.

One early example appears near the beginning of "Timbuctoo." The speaker muses on lost mythical lands, wondering, "Where are your moonlight halls, your cedarn glooms, / The blossoming abysses of your hills?" (42–43). Although *abyss* originally meant a bottomless pit, Richardson's dictionary (1836–1837) allows the expanded sense of something "unfathomable, endless, unbounded, unlimited," suggesting that the vanished hills once extended beyond view.[158] Yet the overwhelmingly negative connotations of *abyss* as it is usually employed remind us that the blossoming hills have been destroyed. Later, as part of the speaker's vision, he sees mystical pyramids:

> Each aloft
> Upon his narrowed Eminence bore globes
> Of wheeling Suns, or Stars, or semblances
> Of either, showering circular abyss
> Of radiance. (166–170)

Here *abyss* represents the opposite of its definition: it describes light rather than the darkness implied by bottomless pits or primal chaos, and while it seems intended

---

[156] Trench, *English, Past and Present*, 68.
[157] Ricks, *Milton's Grand Style*, 58.
[158] Richardson, *A New Dictionary of the English Language*, 1836, 1:10.

to suggest immensity of radiance, the fact that it is "circular" curtails the extent to which these abysses can be considered unbounded or unlimited.

Tennyson again plays with linguistic contradiction near the end of the "The Vision of Sin" (published 1842), when there appears a group of "men and horses pierced with worms, / And slowly quickening into lower forms" (209–210). The use of the word *quickening* here is productively baffling. First there is the initial impression of a paradox created by the juxtaposition of *slowly* and *quickening*. As Trench described in *English, Past and Present*, most readers would have encountered the older meaning of *quickening* – "To come or bring to life" – only through reciting the creed in church ("He shall come to judge the quick and the dead"). This archaic use at first seems to fit the line; the poem's title and allegorical structure suggest that the scene is the resurrection of bodies on Judgment Day. If this were the case, it would be an example of poetic diction borrowed from "the solemn and thus stereotyped language of Scripture."[159] However, the men and horses are becoming "lower forms," not being restored to the fullness of health. Tennyson uses *quickening* here to mean *enlivening*, in that the bodies are giving life to the worms eating them. In fact, a draft of the poem had "quickening into worms." Tennyson employed the same imagery many years later in his play *Queen Mary* (1875), where a character describes how victims of torture, once dead, are "Cast on the dunghill naked, and become / Hideously alive again from head to heel."[160]

Philology fed Tennyson's creative use of seeming archaisms, which becomes evident if we compare his contributions to the 1827 collection *Poems by Two Brothers* and his first single-author publication, 1830's *Poems, Chiefly Lyrical*. Tennyson's verses in the former volume are more conventional in their language than his later efforts. Working from traditional poetic patterns, they read as the exercises of a poet in training; Hallam Tennyson confirmed that "The book is ... full of the boyish imitation of other poets."[161] They also contain relatively few obsolete words or uncommon usages. In contrast, the more innovative book from 1830 features at least double the occurrence of notably philological diction.

Poems by Two Brothers was published before Tennyson came up to Cambridge; he had been exposed to some ideas about language through the books in his father's library, but he had not yet encountered the "Platonico-Wordsworthian-Coleridgean-anti-Utilitarians" at Trinity.[162] After he did, he became more of a Platonic crafter of words. Some twenty-five years later, Kemble wrote to Jacob Grimm:

> I could wish that in [English] we had retained a little more of the sound Anglo-Saxon element. But I cannot regret those changes which formed the tongue in which Shakespeare & Milton wrote, and which Alfred Tennyson writes [sic][163]

There is a suggestive ambiguity in Kemble's statement. Perhaps he has omitted a word and meant to write "the language ... *in* which Alfred Tennyson writes." However, the

---

[159] Trench, *English, Past and Present*, 147–148.
[160] Tennyson, "Queen Mary," 159.
[161] Hallam Tennyson, *Memoir*, 1:22.
[162] Trench, *Letters and Memorials*, 1:10.
[163] Kemble, *Correspondence*, 310–311.

philologically inclined Trinity set believed that part of the poet's role was to create language – and, conversely, that word coiners were themselves poets of a sort. The third effect Trench cites a poet as having on language recalls the task of Plato's poetic name-makers: "enrich[ing] his native tongue" with new expressions.[164] It is not out of place, therefore, for Kemble to describe Tennyson as writing English – that is, creating it as much as he used its pre-existing forms.

In fact, the current online edition of the *OED* cites his poetry as the first example of eighty-seven words, and the first evidence of a particular meaning for a staggering 631 more. Thus, the speaker of "Supposed Confessions of a Second-Rate Sensitive Mind" (1830) agonizes over his lack of faith, likening himself to "a full-sailed skiff, / Unpiloted i' the echoing dance / Of reboant whirlwinds" (95–97). Taken from classical Latin, *reboant* tells us that the whirlwinds are literally re-bellowing – which is to say, they are resounding, reverberating, or echoing loudly. This is the first example cited by the *OED*, and Tennyson helps define his neologism with "echoing dance" in the preceding line. Nor is it surprising that *In Memoriam* coins words such as *intervital*, *orb* used as a verb, and *plumelets*.[165]

Tennyson's practice of coining or redefining is also present in lines of "Inscription by a Brook," written in John Heath's commonplace book and dated 1833, which speaks of "Full fields of barley shifting tearful lights / On growing spears" (8–9). The *OED*'s only definitions for *tearful* are "Full of tears; weeping; lachrymose" and "Causing tears; mournful, melancholy," the latter with only one citation and therefore of uncertain definition. Neither makes much sense as "tearful lights." Searching among the definitions of *tear*, we find "a drop of any liquid" or "anything resembling tears," but this is not much more help. Nevertheless, we receive some sense of liquid light, constructed from the known definitions for *tear* and *tearful*. This innovative use is easy enough to take in, because the new poetic usage shares an affinity with pre-existing forms. Indeed, Tennyson often adapted existing words to new purposes. The adjective *dully* appears in "The Palace of Art" (1832) and is the only example listed in the *OED*, but it echoes *mazy*, *arrowy*, *stilly*, *massy*, and similar archaic constructions that he used elsewhere; thus, it is both imitative and innovative. It is also familiar as an adverb; it is its use as an adjective that is new.

Tennyson similarly adapted a familiar word in "The Goose," written in 1833 and published in 1842. The poor old woman in the story grows rich from the goose's golden eggs "Until the grave churchwarden doffed, / The parson smirked and nodded" (19–20). The churchwarden acknowledges her newfound respectability by *doffing*, a word that the *OED* records only as transitive – that is, taking a direct object – unless used with the word *with*. Presumably, the churchwarden doffs his hat, but the object is not named, and the verb appears in parallel with the intransitive ones *smirked* and *nodded*. Bailey's and Johnson's dictionaries only recorded transitive uses for the word. Tennyson's intransitive application of *doff*, therefore, was and remains unattested. Adding to the complexity of this instance, Johnson had proclaimed, "This word is in all its senses obsolete, and scarcely used except

---

[164] Trench, *On the Study of Words*, 116–117.
[165] Sinfield, *The Language of Tennyson's In Memoriam*, 45.

by rusticks [sic]; yet it is a pure and commodious word."¹⁶⁶ The poet, then, took an obsolete word that had become provincial and adapted it to a new use. Thus the churchwarden's *doffing* represents the larger story of Tennyson's philological medievalism.

Tennyson continued to innovate later in his career, too, as some examples from "Maud" demonstrate. When the speaker fears that the object of his love will be deceived into thinking "a wanton dissolute boy" is a paragon of manly virtues, he wishes for a heroic man "Like some of the simple great ones gone / For ever and ever by, / One still strong man in a blatant land" (I.392). It is unclear what *blatant* means in this context, and for once Tennyson does not help his reader interpret it. None of the *OED* definitions seem to fit – noisy or obtrusive to the eye, or in the specific phrase "blatant beast," which is where Spenser coined it. Tennyson had saved the word in his early notebook, but without any definition.¹⁶⁷ Similarly, the following passage provoked consternation when it first appeared:

> When the happy Yes
> Falters from her lips,
> Pass and blush the news
> O'er the blowing ships;
> Over blowing seas,
> Over seas at rest,
> Pass the happy news,
> Blush it through the West   (I.579–586)

At least two reviewers criticized this use of the word *blowing* in relation to ships. One of them – writing for the *Press* – called it "unpardonable." The other, in the *Morning Post*, was baffled: "what is the meaning of a 'blowing ship'?" Tennyson later changed the line to "glowing ships,"¹⁶⁸ but originally he may have been reusing a sense he had coined twenty years earlier: he is the first two *OED* quotations for the verb *blow* in the sense "To be driven or carried by the wind; to move before the wind." Those quotations are from the 1842 volume, from "The Goose" and "The Day-Dream."

The number of linguistic innovations in Tennyson's work makes it impossible to examine them all here. The examples above give some sense of his techniques, however, and we may explore some with further context by taking samples from "Sea Dreams," written in the late 1850s and published in 1860. This poem centers on a city clerk and his wife, made poor after being swindled into a bad investment. For their daughter's health, they go to "a coast, / All sand and cliff and deep-inrunning cave" (16–17). The meaning of *inrunning* is easy to infer, but the *OED* doesn't observe the word appearing until 1861 (one of only two examples that it cites). As a descriptor of sea caves, this word also carries an echo of Tennyson's use of *influence* and related words to do with flowing, discussed above. The next day, husband and

---

[166] Johnson, *Dictionary*, 1832, 1:562.
[167] Weaver, *Tennyson's Notebook Glossary and Rhyme Lists*, 40.
[168] Edgar Finley Shannon, "The Critical Reception of Tennyson's 'Maud,'" *PMLA* 68, no. 3 (June 1953): 408.

wife go to chapel, being "pious variers from the [Anglican] church" (19). This line is the only quotation in the *OED* for *varier* as "One who varies or dissents from something." After service, the couple so accustomed to city living walks by the sea and can hardly believe they are really seeing it because "The sootflake of so many a summer still / Clung to their fancies" (35–36). Like *inrunning*, *sootflake* is an easy compound to parse, but it has only one *OED* quotation, from shortly before the composition of this poem.

When the pair return to their dwelling, the wife urges her husband to forgive the swindler, prompted by her faith; she "kept a tender Christian hope, / Haunting a holy text, and still to that / Returning" (41–43). The sense of *haunting* is intuitive from context, but it does not easily fit any *OED* definition. Its closest match is an obsolete usage: "To use or employ habitually or frequently." Overnight, a full tide with groundswell breaks upon the rocks and "upjetted in spirts of wild sea-smoke" (52), *upjet* being another archaic-sounding construction for directional action. As the storm rages, the clerk dreams of entering a sea cave and seeing an embodiment of the mine in which he had invested: "a giant woman ... All over earthy, like a piece of earth, / A pickaxe in her hand" (97–98). This line's repetition-definition ("earthy, like a piece of earth") might seem unnecessary, but if the sense of *earthy* is "covered in or full of earth," then it was only about fifty years old at the time of composition.

Upon waking, the clerk discusses with his wife his anger at the man who deceived them. He recites a satirical poem about a con man who "Made [God] his catspaw and the Cross his tool" (186). Richardson's dictionary defines a "cat's-paw" as "the tool, the instrument" and notes that the term is "common in vulgar speech, but not in writing."[169] It turns out that the man who caused their ruin has died, and the wife received the news while her husband was "running down the sands, and made / The dimpled flounce of the sea-furbelow flap" to amuse their daughter (256–258). Tennyson defined *sea-furbelow* as a specific kind of seaweed (and was cited in the *OED* as such), but he acknowledged that "the name 'sea-furbelow' is not generally known."[170] The poet, then, chose to use a dialect word, as he often did when referring to plants and animals.

"Sea Dreams" shows Tennyson at work to renew his words, a task to which he brought his considerable knowledge of past usage, provincial speech, and etymological roots. That he succeeded in making his literary language draw attention to itself is clear from the critical reactions it elicited. A review of the 1832 volume, for example, objected to the "picturesque coinages" that interfered with his meaning.[171] Indeed, much of the poet's philological wordsmithing provoked displeasure among reviewers, who felt that its strangeness made the poems sound artificial – a major offense for Victorian poetry.

---

[169] Richardson, *A New Dictionary of the English Language*, 1836, 1:275.
[170] Tennyson, *Poems II*, 362.
[171] Marion Sherwood, "'Mr. Tennyson's Singular Genius': The Reception of 'Poems' (1832)," *Tennyson Research Bulletin* 8, no. 4 (November 2005): 256.

Accusations of Affectation

The various reviews quoted thus far prove that old words, old meanings of current words, and new compounds stood out to Tennyson's readers – vigorous, strange, singular, uncomfortable. Critics did not approve. They remarked on the poet's archaizing tendencies, and even positive reviews pointed them out as flaws. When the *Westminster Review* protested against "the use of antiquated words and obsolete pronunciation" in the 1830 collection, it stated that such traits exposed Tennyson to charges of "indolence and affectation."[172] Indeed, Turley notes that because of a "wide critical dislike of affected archaisms," critics were wary of Tennyson's early output.[173] Affectation was also the main complaint in reviews of the 1832 volume.[174] Where the poet might use a rare or obsolete term to enhance his text, the reader might detect artifice, and the application of this highly subjective criterion earned Tennyson some censure. His simultaneous experimentation with meter and form probably amplified the perceived strangeness of these expressions.

In reviewing the 1842 volume, the *Spectator* reiterated the flaws it saw in Tennyson's style, saying:

> [T]he worst point in Tennyson's poetry is that this peculiarity is not always his own. The most obvious defect in this way ... is his diction; which ... is piebald with the spots of various times – an obsolete word here, a cant phrase there, and anon a vulgarism by way of being natural.

This critique summarizes rather well the variety of techniques this chapter has outlined. His diction being "piebald with the spots of various times" is an amusing way of expressing my main thesis: that Tennyson's deep and widespread knowledge of the English language enabled and encouraged him to select words from across its history and its homeland. Critics regularly objected to the resultant style – his inclination toward "affected choice of phraseology" got in the way of his natural genius, according to this review – but this is one area in which Tennyson was not swayed by the opinions of others.[175]

Jason Camlot describes "Victorian critic[s] as naturalizing agent[s]," charging themselves with the duty of forging a good national character by shaping an indigenous style and a unified language.[176] Camlot, Turley, and Meredith Martin[177] describe a prescriptive theoretical milieu in critical practice in the nineteenth century, and Camlot interprets that prescriptiveness as "a solution to the disturbing ... spectre of language raised by philology."[178] Since Tennyson incorporated philological ideas into his poetry, it is unsurprising that reviewers disliked the peculiarities of his style. He discomfited them because he responded to philology not by restricting

---

[172] Jump, *Tennyson*, 32.
[173] Turley, "Knowledge of Their Own Supremacy," 299.
[174] Sherwood, "'Mr. Tennyson's Singular Genius,'" 256.
[175] "Tennyson's Collected Poems," *The Spectator*, June 4, 1842, 544.
[176] Camlot, *Sincere Mannerisms*, 111.
[177] Martin, *Rise and Fall of Meter*, 6–9.
[178] Camlot, *Sincere Mannerisms*, 110.

his language but by doing the opposite: pulling specimens from across the entire history of English, both ennobled and "vulgar."

The very strangeness that I have argued was central to Tennyson's use of archaic language proved to be a common point of objection. The reviewer of the 1830 volume for the *Westminster Review* concluded: "Nor certainly is anything gained by a song's being studded with words which to most readers may require a glossary."[179] It's true that at their most extreme, archaisms can become equivalent to the cleverly coined nonsense nonce words in Lewis Carroll's "The Jabberwocky," a text that has become indispensable in discussions of linguistics. Alice demonstrates the potential difficulty of unrecognized lexis when she says in response: "'It seems very pretty ... but it's *rather* hard to understand! ... Somehow it seems to fill my head with ideas – only I don't exactly know what they are!'"[180] When "The Jabberwocky" first appeared in a family magazine-scrapbook, it was labeled a "Stanza of Anglo-Saxon Poetry," demonstrating the blurry boundaries between old, alien, and invented language.[181] Likewise, William Morris's renderings of Old Norse and Old English contain examples of antiquarianism so extreme that they sacrifice understanding on the altar of phonetic similarity to the words they translate. In rendering *Beowulf*, for example, Morris writes that Grendel is *bale-heedy*. This term sounds nearly identical to the Old English *bealohydig* for which it stands, but the reader must work hard to discover that the monster is *evil-thinking*.[182] Simply to drop obsolete expressions into a text is not to revive them. Tennyson seems to have intuited this and worked to give his readers context enough to do without a dictionary. In his first published efforts, however, critics saw only obstacles as troublesome as Carroll's slithy toves. It is a thin line – perhaps an invisible one – between artistry and artifice.

With his style often accused of affectation, it is useful to view Tennyson in relation to literary Decadence, a movement that came to Britain from French writing in the 1880s and 1890s. Authors who have regularly been identified with its traits include Oscar Wilde, Arthur Symons, and William Butler Yeats; those traits include "eroticism, nihilism, and the predominance of 'foreign' verse forms (largely French)."[183] Stylistically, Linda Dowling identifies the underlying principle of Decadent literature as a specific nihilism that saw words as empty signifiers. She describes the movement as "a cult of artifice in art and literature ... a counterpoetics of disruption and parody and stylistic derangement" that critiques the very notion of a Wordsworthian description of simple natural pleasures.[184]

Tennyson, numerous scholars have indicated, was well informed of the causes for concern with regard to language: its imprecision, its operation and evolution

---

[179] Jump, *Tennyson*, 32.

[180] Lewis Carroll, *Alice's Adventures in Wonderland and Through the Looking-Glass and What Alice Found There*, ed. Roger Lancelyn Green (London: Oxford University Press, 1971), 136.

[181] Chris Jones, "Anglo-Saxonism in Nineteenth-Century Poetry," *Literature Compass* 7, no. 5 (May 1, 2010): 364.

[182] William Morris, *Three Northern Love Stories; The Tale of Beowulf*, vol. 10 of *The Collected Works of William Morris*, ed. May Morris (New York: Longmans Green, 1911), 200.

[183] Alex Murray, "Decadent Histories," in *Decadence: A Literary History* (Cambridge: Cambridge University Press, 2020), 1, 6.

[184] Dowling, *Decadence*, ix–x.

outside human control, and its potential arbitrariness. Accordingly, these scholars have found an unresolved anxiety in his many poems that treat the question of communication. Although the problems of language unquestionably preoccupied him, I argue that he was far too creative with his words to have believed they were empty signifiers. Tennyson's poetry does share certain qualities with that of Decadent writers, such as an obsession with craftsmanship that many have read as artifice; Decadence is partly defined by its "mannered literary style."[185] However, his work is far from "parody and stylistic derangement." Instead, he works on his surface impressions in order to engage the "recesses of [his] words," to borrow William Empson's phrase.[186]

Tennyson's alleged failure to address linguistic anxiety satisfactorily is a conclusion resulting from the same academic retrospection that assumes Trench and Müller must have known themselves to be fighting a losing battle with their encouraging interpretations of philology's discoveries. If, however, we view the writings of these philologists and Tennyson from a nineteenth-century perspective, we find them picking their way through the philosophical hazards of Victorian philology to insist that (adapting Kemble's phrase) the past yet works in Modern English. When, a century and a half later, poet Seamus Heaney worked on his translation of *Beowulf*, he was thrilled to discover the vocabulary of his elderly relatives in the mouths of eighth-century heroes, the connection suddenly locating them within a long progression of linguistic and migratory movements. "It was as if ... I had undergone something like illumination by philology," he writes.[187] Such an effect is one purpose of using archaic forms of English as Tennyson did.

Turley argues that "in response to bleak projections ... Tennyson resolved to shore up meaning in language by using old, and presumably less fatigued words in his poetry, accumulating unusual, archaic, and emphatically 'meaningful' words to deploy against historical erosion."[188] In a similar vein, Aubrey de Vere thought the practice derived from a common desire in the first decades of the century to be precise. He recalled his impression of the 1830 volume many years later: "The diction ... was elaborate in accordance with a certain artificiality belonging to the time, that is, whenever strange combinations of words were needed in order to produce a corresponding exactitude of significance."[189] However, a greater array of mechanisms is at work in the poetry than Turley or de Vere acknowledge. Of the three tasks Trench assigned to poets, one is explicitly generative, one values colloquial speech (if selectively), and the one that addresses decay emphasizes throwing latent metaphors into relief rather than despairing of the strength of modern words. The Cambridge Apostles were ambitious to save the world from dullness of thought through well-crafted language, and therefore it is more fitting to look for an optimistic program in Tennyson's philological practices. He and his friends worked by a less polemical, more artistic program than the critics: showing off words and their histories like a building composed of many generations of architecture.

[185] Murray, "Decadent Histories," 1.
[186] Empson, *Seven Types of Ambiguity*, 199.
[187] Heaney, "Translator's Introduction," xxxv.
[188] Turley, "Knowledge of Their Own Supremacy," 300.
[189] Hallam Tennyson, *Memoir*, 1:502.

Nevertheless, Tennyson's style did shift away from stark antiquarianism. De Vere reported that "the youthful poet very soon ... discarded that elaborateness," which had characterized the 1830 poems, though this is not quite correct.[190] Philology had moved away from an antiquarian predilection for historical curiosities toward an appreciation of the social histories of words. Tennyson made an equivalent move, becoming flexible in his application of philological principles. From placing uncommon terms into his text for striking effect, he increasingly integrated them into his lines or revealed historical meanings of familiar terms. This move toward subtler explorations of linguistic layers may have been prompted by the remarks of critics who did not appreciate encountering "fine old words" in abundance.

Tennyson's innovations are a reminder that he engaged with the ideas of philology as part of a dynamic creative process. He was scornful of those who claimed to locate his influences, and it is worth bearing in mind that detecting a source of Tennyson's knowledge is only the beginning of understanding his style. For example, Trench was a published poet himself. In addition to translating Calderón from Spanish and editing a book of medieval sacred Latin poetry that Tennyson admired,[191] Trench published books of his own compositions. Wordsworth complimented Trench on his efforts, and the Apostles encouraged him with praise while at Trinity.[192] Indeed, Marion Shaw states that at Cambridge, the Apostles considered Trench and a few others of the group just as likely as Tennyson to become successful poets.[193] However, his verse is markedly different from that of his friend. It is much more linguistically conventional; no one accused Trench of affectation. And although he employed some of the same techniques that this chapter has described, there is no confusing their styles. Where Tennyson excelled was in being able to call upon his great knowledge of past literature, as well as linguistic history, and then use that expertise to do new things with his language.

Conclusion

Insofar as Tennyson regularly and deliberately used his words unusually, "affectation" is present in his work – is, in fact, central to his diction. Ricks writes that "one of [Tennyson's] major claims is simply that of craftsmanship";[194] to expand the metaphor, the craftsman had to hand a variety of tools – some for decorative purposes (aesthetic archaisms), some for the anthropological task of amplifying the echoes of former usages, some for exposing the structure of a word (revealing etymology), and some for the Platonic-Shelleyan work of forming a new meaning out of familiar materials. And although the categories delineated in this chapter help describe his

---

[190] Ibid., 1:502.
[191] Tennyson, *Letters*, 1982, 3:130–131.
[192] J. Bromley, *The Man of Ten Talents: A Portrait of Richard Chenevix Trench, 1807–86, Philologist, Poet, Theologian, Archbishop* (London: S.P.C.K., 1959), 73.
[193] Marion Shaw, "Friendship, Poetry, and Insurrection: The Kemble Letters," in *Tennyson Among the Poets: Bicentenary Essays*, ed. Robert Douglas-Fairhurst and Seamus Perry (Oxford: Oxford University Press, 2009), 217.
[194] Ricks, *Methods*, 211.

methods, Tennyson used all his tools in combination to create poetry that participates in the history of its own language.

As an example, the early poem "The Dying Swan" (published 1830) contains a lexical moment that enacts all these themes. The bird's death song floods the landscape, including "the wavy swell of the soughing reeds" (38). Tennyson later provided his own note for the word *soughing*: "Anglo-Saxon *sweg*, a sound. Modified into an onomatopoeic word for the soft sound or the deep sighing of the wind."[195] (The same poem has "the wind did sigh" [15].) Tyrwhitt's glossary to Chaucer, which Tennyson used extensively during his university years, has an entry for *Swough*, defined as "Sax[on] sound, noise."[196] Here Tennyson simultaneously draws on the Old English wordhoard and uses a term in a new way, while also troubling the distinction between speech and onomatopoeia. He kept the word in mind for future use, as well; a notebook fragment from 1834 includes the line, "The Southwind soughs in gusty fits"[197] (note, too, the unhyphenated compound *Southwind*).

To take another case, Ricks observes that "'circumstance' was an important word to Tennyson in that it suggested an earlier usage as 'the totality of surrounding things', hence 'the heavens.'"[198] That earlier usage was a literal concept taken from the Latin roots *circum* (around) and *stāre* (stand). "The Palace of Art" uses the word as such in the following lines:

> A star that with the choral starry dance
> Joined not, but stood, and standing saw
> The hollow orb of moving Circumstance
> Rolled round by one fixed law.   (255–256)

Tennyson's note on these lines informs us, "Some old writer calls the Heavens 'the Circumstance' … Here it is more or less a play on the word."[199] In this case, the etymological meaning was already obsolete, its previous *OED* quotation being from the mid-sixteenth century. Thus *circumstance*, despite seeming familiar, proves to be quite different from what a reader might expect. Tennyson helps his reader understand its etymological meaning at two levels. The stanza overall describes a fixed star and a hollow orb rolling around, which allows the reader to infer that *circumstance* means the heavens. In addition, the poem offers English translations of the Latin etymons in these lines: *stood, standing, round*.

Tennyson's diction bears the marks of multiple philological and medievalist inclinations: reverence for earlier poets, a feeling of connection to the Anglo-Saxons as the center of English language and culture, a sense of his position in a process of continual linguistic evolution, and his role as a shaper of words. Trench said that words have an atmosphere about them "which we insensibly inhale;"[200] Tennyson clearly

---

[195] Tennyson, *Poems I*, 345.
[196] Geoffrey Chaucer, *Poetical Works of Geoffrey Chaucer in Fourteen Volumes*, ed. Thomas Tyrwhitt, vol. 14, Bell's Edition, *The Poets of Great Britain Complete from Chaucer to Churchill* (Edinburg [sic]: Apollo Press, 1782), 203.
[197] Tennyson, *The Poems of Tennyson*, 1987, 2:31.
[198] Tennyson, *The Poems of Tennyson*, 1987, 1:273–274.
[199] Tennyson, *Poems I*, 370.
[200] Trench, *On the Study of Words*, 55.

familiarized himself with the history of many English words and was interested in how to arrange their valences of connotation and historical usage. As Seamus Perry writes, "when readers find unadmitted meanings lurking in the depths of the poetry, they are ... on to an important part of the Tennysonian effect";[201] much of this effect is owing to his use of philological meanings.

As with Milton, it can be difficult to locate the "invisible line that separates the vivified metaphor from word-play."[202] In line 10 of "The Exile's Harp" (1827), when the speaker laments, "Thy chords shall decay," it literally refers to the harp's strings – a meaning evident in line 22, in which "roses are twining / Thy chords"; however, the subsequent lines suggest a pun: "One by one with the strings / Shall thy notes fade away." With the combination of strings and notes that these lines encourage, the "chords" that decay are equally the physical strings and the musical harmonies they once produced. A "Miss Rundle," who spent the day with Tennyson when he visited her uncle in 1848, recalled that the poet "spoke of Milton's Latinisms and delicate play with words, and Shakespeare's play upon words."[203] His friend Mrs. Montagu Butler noted that the poet was aware of the registers attendant upon Latinate and Germanic roots, explaining that "a baby crying in the night" would have sounded "ridiculous," while "an infant crying in the night" did not.[204] The next chapter analyzes his use of etymological origins and their corresponding registers for literary effect, but as a number of critics have recognized, the etymological sense of *infant* as "unable to speak" is also fitting to the moment in which *In Memoriam*'s mourner calls himself "An infant crying for the light: / And with no language but a cry" (liv.19–20).

Whether or not readers noticed Tennyson's etymologically based wordplay – though it seems likely that a good many of them would have been equipped to do so – reviewers evidently observed his eclectic word choices, generally judging them negatively. This disapproval then influenced him to interpret for his readers the strange fossils that he brought before them. The 1832 version of "The Miller's Daughter" opens with a stanza that describes "The wealthy miller's mealy face, / Like the moon in an ivytod."[205] The *OED* lists *ivytod* – which Tennyson used again in "Balin and Balan" (written 1872–1874) – as archaic, but the poet thought the word was clear enough to use without explanation. When T.H. Rawnsley queried him about it, Tennyson wrote back, "You never heard the word 'ivy-tod'; but you have heard of 'tods of wool', and I take it they are the same words originally, a certain weight or mass of something."[206] Between the first publication of "The Miller's Daughter" and Tennyson's letter to Rawnsley, Richardson's dictionary had defined *tod* as "a certain measure of wool ... a bush, a thicket" and quoted Spenser's "yvie todde," whence the Victorian poet may have taken it.[207] Nevertheless, the 1842 volume omitted this stanza altogether.

---

[201] Perry, *Alfred Tennyson*, 14.
[202] Ricks, *Milton's Grand Style*, 66.
[203] Hallam Tennyson, *Memoir*, 1:277.
[204] Hallam Tennyson, ed., *Tennyson and His Friends* (London: Macmillan, 1912), 218.
[205] Tennyson, *The Poems of Tennyson*, 1987, 1:407.
[206] Tennyson, *Letters*, 1982, 1:191.
[207] Charles Richardson, *A New Dictionary of the English Language*, vol. 2 (London: Pickering, 1837), 1,942.

"Few English poets," J.F.A. Pyre observed, "seem to have been so enamored of words for their own sake" as Tennyson was in his developing years as a poet. Pyre's assessment is both accurate and misleading. Words were not appealing to Tennyson only for their aesthetic properties, though they certainly served that purpose, as well. Instead, he sought to peel away the surface of well-worn phrases in order to give back to language some of its "vitally metaphorical" quality.[208] Although the words of his early efforts rang with the echoes of the great poets from whom he took them, he soon took command of the English language with an understanding of its history and a poet's role in its progress. Though growing out of literary tradition, and drawing on vocabulary gleaned from Chaucer, Langland, Spenser, Milton, Chapman, Scott, and others, his achievement is linguistic and literary innovation that utilizes as its material the remains of the past. When *In Memoriam* describes how Arthur Hallam's conversation delighted "men of rathe and riper years," the first adjective is immediately recognizable to a student of Old English as a descendent of *hraðe* (quickly), but it had come to mean "earlier" (cx.2). Pairing it with *riper* indicates that it should stand in contrast to it – meaning less ripe (younger). Yet *rathe* is not cited in the *OED* as meaning *young*, which it does here by implication. Tennyson has taken a very old item from the English language and made it new, while still attending to its history. Not long afterward, Trench suggested that *rathest* worth reviving.[209] Tennyson returned to the word in "Lancelot and Elaine" (1859) but used it differently again: The Eversley Edition glossed *rathe* in that poem as "early (thence 'rather')."[210]

As a product of the age of philology, Tennyson's output is a hybrid of potential reactions to a general anxiety about both spoken and literary language. Aware of concerns about language wearing out, he addressed them with a generative methodology paradoxically drawn from roots and archaism. Anticipating Decadence by decades yet ultimately having faith in language to remain inventive, he combined an antiquarian affection for the aesthetics of the archaic, a philologist-poet's investigative urge to unpack the dormant content of his words, and a craftsman's ingenuity in (as Plato said of name-makers) "discover[ing] the instrument naturally fitted for each purpose."[211] Both Trench and Tennyson ultimately favored a broad view of philology in which lexical revitalization might be achieved by revealing the construction of words.

Fellow Cambridge Apostle William Bodham Donne wrote to Trench in 1829, "I see but faint hopes of … regeneration [in writing] in the present age, since our writers seem to have little confidence in their own native energies, and pride themselves upon imitation of the 'Early English Writers.'"[212] Tennyson, true to Donne's wishes (though not necessarily driven by them), soon moved away from imitation to employ his "own native energies" through language that announces itself to be aware of its own history. Turley astutely writes that Tennyson's idiosyncratic practices, which included "neologisms, factitious usages, neo-archaisms, unfamiliar

---

[208] Shelley, "A Defence of Poetry," 512.
[209] Trench, *English, Past and Present*, 123.
[210] Tennyson, *Idylls of the King*, 1908, 483.
[211] Plato, "Cratylus," 27.
[212] Trench, *Letters and Memorials*, 1:22.

orthography, and innovative diction," were "suggestive of processive views of language."[213] He argues that they were thus "supremely unnerving" for the self-appointed guardians of culture. Tennyson was never interested in a culture or a language that was static. Rather, he believed in the benefits of gradual, persistent change, and he repeatedly speculated that humanity was developing toward a higher type of species and/or a greater good. The early sonnet "The constant spirit of the world" expressed a delight in "old principles still working new results," and this was the governing principle of his relationship with philology, which dovetailed with his sense of the past working in the present. The following chapter compares two very different expressions of how old words might work in new poems.

---

[213] Turley, "Knowledge of Their Own Supremacy," 304.

4
"All that men have been doing and thinking and feeling": Evoking and Invoking the Past

THUS FAR, I have drawn examples from a varied selection of Tennyson's poems, many from the first few decades of his professional career. The early works – especially those from notebooks – witness the poet experimenting with style, from unhyphenated compounds to complex rhyme schemes to archaic vocabulary. This experimentation is an informative point of entry for examining the philological-medievalist features of Tennyson's style, which are manifest throughout his corpus. As the previous chapters demonstrate, a philological interest in one's words – to say nothing of a medievalist one – is an interest in the relationship between the past and the life of a modern speaker. This chapter looks at major examples of the different ways in which Tennyson explored that relationship between past and present. It first considers techniques that make the reader confront the distance of pronunciation change. It then outlines the evidence of Tennyson's sensitivity to connotations that inhere to etymological origins, and tests his claim that he gave preference to Germanic vocabulary. The chapter concludes by analyzing the range of philological techniques at work in two book-length efforts, *Idylls of the King* and *In Memoriam*, which exhibit very different dynamics between the past and present.

The Arthurian *Idylls*, I argue, mostly form a recognizable instance of performative medievalism, their archaisms reinforcing the atmosphere of their imagined past, though they also employ subtler effects. *In Memoriam*, in contrast, demonstrates how the past can reverberate through modern experience, at both small and large scale. Tennyson brings to bear his impressive knowledge of verbal history, sometimes finding the right word in an archaism and sometimes purposefully blurring his metaphysical claims through the ambiguity of multilayered meanings. The difference might be understood as the distinction between *evoking* the history that shaped the English language and *invoking* it. Both strategies call upon the past (see the Latin root *vocare*), but *evoking* is a calling forth into existence, whereas to *invoke* is to entreat for aid or summon by incantation. *Idylls of the King* evokes a mythical Middle Ages, using its archaisms to drag a whole world out of the mists of time and construct it around the reader. *In Memoriam* invokes the history of key words by calling them in (*in-vocare*) to the mourner's nineteenth-century experience.

"The enlivening spirit ... is found in the vowels": Conjugation, Rhyme, and Pronunciation

The preceding chapters have shown that the archaic words that populate Tennyson's lines are the result of his fascination with the ways in which earlier generations – especially poets – had expressed themselves. As described in Chapter 1, the foundation of new philology was the concept that a language at any given moment expressed the mindset of those who spoke it. Thus "fine old words" both aesthetically draw attention to themselves and – ideally – revive a way of seeing the world. For some Victorians, they also held the allure of cultural purity, if they dated to before the Norman Conquest or other events that supposedly damaged the English language.

Those who took an interest in Old English, such as Tennyson's friend John Mitchell Kemble, even "without wishing ... to turn back the stream of the world's great flow,"[1] often found that nineteenth-century English bore the marks of "conquest, commerce, and international communication" – and worse, misguided attempts to fix it.[2] As described by language historians Albert C. Baugh and Thomas Cable:

> In its effort to set up a standard of correctness in language the rationalistic spirit of the eighteenth century showed itself in the attempt to settle disputed points logically, that is, by simply reasoning about them, often arriving at entirely false conclusions. The respect for authoritative example, especially for classical example, [took] the form of appeals to the analogy of Latin.[3]

It is due to such efforts, for example, that English lost the emphatic double- or triple-negative, since logical reasoning and Latin dictated that two negatives must make a positive. Such regularization stemmed from the perception of English as a chaotic mess.

In short, the eighteenth century had moved toward regulating English by rigid, artificial grammatical laws, without recognizing the laws already at work. Kemble found such efforts infuriating. They were based on a poor understanding of how the language functioned, and they disrupted its natural evolution, severing modern speakers from their linguistic ancestors. Anglo-Saxonist Joseph Bosworth likewise wrote in 1838 that "the chaos of tongues ... begins, when grammarians, ignorant of the operations of the mind, and its exertions to express its thoughts, obtrude their arbitrary rules." Fortunately, he wrote, "language, ruled by an indomitable inward principle, triumphs in some degree over the folly of grammarians."[4]

Especially irksome to new philologists was the effort to standardize verb conjugations. In an unpublished review of Jacob Grimm's *Deutsche Grammatik* (intended for the press in 1833), Kemble included a scathing passage on the purposeful

---

[1] Kemble, *Correspondence*, 35.
[2] Kemble, "History of the English Language," 4.
[3] Albert C. Baugh and Thomas Cable, *A History of the English Language*, 5th ed. (London: Routledge, 2002), 256.
[4] Bosworth, *A Dictionary of the Anglo-Saxon Language*, xxxviii–xxxvix.

elimination of strong verbs during the previous century – that is, verbs that form the past tense by changing their root vowel. In the new system, a simple *-ed* ending would serve for all verbs. He excoriated the ignorant grammarians who had imposed the change:

> These truly original and groundforms of the language having been called *irregular*, a logical fallacy suggested to the purists that what was irregular must be wrong, and language was inundated with new weak preterites and participles ... the wind blew, and the cock crew no longer, – they now *blowed* and *crowed*. In short, these masters and doctors, though grammarians and lexicographers, *knowed* a thing or two less than they ought.

This was a particularly upsetting project to Kemble because strong verbs were the hallmark of Germanic languages, in which vowels were the life of words. As he put it, "There is perhaps nothing more important than the part played by the vowels in every Teutonic language; the consonants indeed form the bone and sinew, as it were, of the word, but its finer distinctions, the enlivening spirit that modifies and moulds it, is found in the vowels they contain."[5] This was an easy idea to embrace because vowels are literally sustained on the breath. The idea that vowels were the spirit of words was shared by scholars of other languages, but it was especially appealing in the context of Germanic languages, in which strong verbs were easily identifiable as a native phenomenon.[6]

Richard Chenevix Trench described the grammatical shift in *English, Past and Present* (1855), noting with approval that the terms *strong* and *weak* had supplanted "the wholly misleading terms, 'irregular' and 'regular.'" His explanation of the phrase "strong præterite" is telling: he says it is so called because "there is enough of vigour and indwelling energy in the word to form its past tense from its own resources, and with no calling in of help from without;" here again is the idea of energy and vigor residing in earlier forms of language. Citing Jacob Grimm, a major figure of continental philology, Trench further points out that strong verbs (in addition to their "vital energy") "contribute much to the variety and charm of a language." However, unlike Kemble, he did not blame grammarians as the reason for the shift from strong to weak verbs. Instead, he positioned it as part of the natural evolution of a language, which over time "simplifies itself" such that "where it has two or three ways of conducting a single operation, [it] lets all of them go but one; and in these ways becomes no doubt easier to be mastered, more handy, more manageable; but at the same time is in danger of forfeiting elements of strength, variety and beauty, which it once possessed."[7]

Though Trench's lecture was not intended as a poetic treatise, his comments shed light on the value that philologically informed archaism had to offer a poet. For Tennyson, a man who claimed to know the quantity of every English word but one, it was useful to be able to reach back to vowels he found most harmonious for a given composition. From his reading of both old literature and new philology, he was

---

[5] Kemble, *Review of Deutsche Grammatik*, 38, 9.
[6] Hair, "Soul and Spirit in 'In Memoriam,'" 186.
[7] Trench, *English, Past and Present*, 127–128.

familiar with strong-verb conjugations, and he did not shy away from using them. For example, his early notebook glossary of words that interested him includes the entry *quoke* with the comment, "now 'quaked.'" It also contains an entry for *dung*, for which the poet wonders, "Is this the past particip[le] of ding?"[8] Yet recovering strong versions of verbs was a matter of adding possibilities, not rejecting newer varieties; Tennyson's journal of a trip to Cornwall in 1848 records that he "Clomb over Isle," but also "dived into a cavern."[9]

In Tennyson's corpus, the Germanic preterits often (though not always) found a home in his medievalist works. To wit: one of the examples that Trench gave his students of a verb that had become weak was *glide*, for which the past tense (historically) was *glode*. Tennyson used *glode* in his "Battle of Brunanburh" translation (1877): "when first the great / Sun-star of morningtide ... / Glode over earth" (25–29). It is an appropriate echo of the original's *glad*, and it is a purposeful revision; in an earlier draft, Tennyson employed *glided*.[10] He used *clave* as the past tense for *cleave* on four occasions, all of them in the *Idylls*. Furthermore, Trench had also made the point that English sometimes had multiple versions of strong preterits, which were in the process of being reduced to only one (at most). Tennyson was aware of the variety available to him. He used *brake* instead of *broke* some forty-five times, all but five of them in medievalist poems – namely, the *Idylls*, "The Princess," and "The Battle of Brunanburh." Two more uses are from "The Victim," a tale of human sacrifice that Tennyson "made Scandinavian." The remaining examples are from "Œnone" ("the crocus brake like fire," 94), *In Memoriam* ("No spirit ever brake the band," xciii.2), and "Maud" ("The fires of Hell brake out of thy rising sun," II.9). He used *broke* more commonly, but he kept all his options available, especially when he needed some archaic flavor. Similarly, the Tennyson concordance identifies seven uses of *clomb* – four from the *Idylls* and one from the pseudo-medievalist "The Princess." It also offers twenty-five occurrences of *climbed* (many of which were also in the *Idylls*);[11] clearly, Tennyson was not dedicated to using only old verb conjugations, but he found them appropriate in the right context.

Using strong preterits allowed Tennyson to tap into the "strength, variety and beauty" of historical English (per Trench) and to revive the so-called souls of his words. He explored the echoes of historical vowels yet more literally in the sometimes idiosyncratic pronunciation he used in his compositions. The enormous variety of accents has always been a difficulty for theories of language,[12] but Tennyson additionally forced his readers to confront how previous generations had spoken the words he used.[13] Several reviewers complained of Tennyson's inclination toward

---

[8] Weaver, *Tennyson's Notebook Glossary and Rhyme Lists*, 30, 17.
[9] Hallam Tennyson, *Memoir*, 1:275.
[10] Jones, *Fossil Poetry*, 251.
[11] Baker, *Concordance*, 101.
[12] It also provides the occasional scholarly challenge to an American analyzing the sounds in the work of a Victorian poet from rural Lincolnshire.
[13] For example, an Eversley Edition note on "Aylmer's Field" informs readers that *retinue* should be pronounced with the "accent on the penultimate. Shakespeare and Milton accented this word in the same way." Note the authority of the two most revered of English poets.

archaic enunciation, and they were not alone in noticing this tendency; friends recalled the same propensity. W.E.H. Lecky remembered:

> With his love for old English he combined some taste for old forms of pronunciation. He once rebuked me for pronouncing "knowledge" in the way which is now usual, maintaining that the full sound of "know" should be given. I defended myself ... but he only said he hoped I would never pronounce the word in this way in reading his poetry.[14]

Tennyson made the same point formally in notes to the Eversley Edition, insisting on long vowels for the words *knowledge, shone,* and *knoll*.[15]

Arthur E. Baker's concordance notes thirty-nine instances of the word *knowledge* in Tennyson's poetry, the sound of which must be reconsidered in this light. "Œnone," for example, contains an internal repetition of *o* in the line, "In knowledge of their own supremacy" (133). So, too, does the poem "To J.S." – "And me this knowledge bolder made" (5) – and *In Memoriam*: "Let knowledge grow from more to more" (Prologue 25).[16] The concordance records thirty-three uses of *shone*, including lines with assonance such as "Shone out their crowning snows" ("Dying Swan" 13); "The light that shone when Hope was born" (*In Memoriam* xxx.32); and "star / Which shone so close beside Thee" (Dedication to the *Idylls* 46). Tennyson used *knoll* more sparingly (some thirteen times if we count the past-tense verb *knoll'd*), but worthy of note are "The knolls once more" (*In Memoriam* xcv.50) and "Nor hoary knolls of ash and haw" (*In Memoriam* c.9).

This affinity for long *o* was evidently established as early as the 1830s, when Tennyson created for himself a large set of rhyme lists in a notebook.[17] In these lists, for example, *costly* forms part of a triumvirate with *ghostly* and *mostly*. The notebook also indicates that he considered *kraken* to have a long *a*, rhyming with *awaken, (mis/under)taken, forsaken, bacon,* and *shaken*.[18] We must therefore consider the line "The Kraken sleepeth: faintest sunlights flee" to have a recurrence of that vowel (*Kraken* and *faintest*) ("The Kraken" 4). This handmade rhyme collection helps identify Tennyson's unusual pronunciation preferences, as do his Eversley footnotes. The 1830 reviewers, however, had no such references and still recognized nonstandard vocality in the poems. It was through his rhymes that the poet most forcibly brought forth the echoes of past pronunciation. In rhyme, readers can be led into confronting unexpected patterns of speech through their faith in the sound that they anticipate is about to arrive. For example, "Will Waterproof's Lyrical Monologue" (written *circa* 1837) serves to illustrate *pewit* (a type of bird also known as a lapwing) in the *OED*, but the dictionary makes special note of the fact that Tennyson used it to rhyme with *cruet*, in contrast to a conventional pronunciation that sometimes leads to the spelling *peewit* (230–232).

[14] Hallam Tennyson, *Memoir*, 2:203.
[15] Tennyson, *Poems I*, 334.
[16] Baker, *Concordance*, 373.
[17] The notebook flyleaf is dated 1834.
[18] Weaver, *Tennyson's Notebook Glossary and Rhyme Lists*, 56.

The 1832 *Poems* (Tennyson's second independent collection) contained a specimen of light verse that lauded the comfort of the speaker's room at home, saying that nothing he had seen in his travels could compare. It begins:

> O darling room, my heart's delight,
> Dear room, the apple of my sight,
> With thy two couches soft and white,
> There is no room so exquisite,
> No little room so warm and bright,
> Wherein to read, wherein to write.   (1–6)

The word *exquisite*, placed in the center of lines with relentlessly matching end-rhymes, poses a dilemma for phonetic harmony. In his brutally mocking review of the volume, J.W. Croker seized upon this moment to land an extra blow, writing, "We have ourselves visited all these celebrated spots, and can testify ... that we did not see in any of them anything like *this little room so exquiSITE*."[19] In reviewing the same volume, the *Athenaeum* found that the beauty of Tennyson's poetry was "disfigured, and sometimes absolutely concealed" by "obsolete pronunciation," among other characteristics that Chapter 3 explored.[20] Responding to the poet's previous collection (1830's *Poems, Chiefly Lyrical*), the *Spectator* had likewise complained of "a love for old modes of pronunciation."[21] The *Westminster Review* had had mostly good things to say about the 1830 collection but quibbled, "We must protest against ... the use of antiquated words and obsolete pronunciation, in which our author indulges so freely."[22]

Despite the disconnect between writing and speech (an issue which itself preoccupied Tennyson), these reviewers were forced to "hear" these obsolete pronunciations by the rhyme scheme. Peter McDonald writes that Tennyson, along with Wordsworth and Keats, "established a potent tradition of self-awareness about sound and meaning, which the issue of rhyme brought to a point of focus." Poetry in the age of new philology certainly had a manifest "self-awareness about sound and meaning," especially for a writer steeped in medieval literature. If "notions of control, determinism, and determination have often been recognized in the formality of rhyme," part of that poetic awareness in the nineteenth century was the newly urgent concern over language operating beyond the bounds of human will. Rhyme, McDonald writes, both asserts authorial control and calls it into question by "sounding out the impersonality of language's relations."[23] Rhyme awakens a fear that the phonetic similarity between (for example) *fickle* and *sickle* is entirely arbitrary; but Grimm's Law and other historical patterns offered explanations of how each word came to sound as it does, placing rhymes within a system of predictable changes, if still problematically outside human decision-making. For a philologically

---

[19] Jump, *Tennyson*, 81.
[20] "Poems (Now First Published)," 770.
[21] Shannon, *Tennyson and the Reviewers*, 4.
[22] Jump, *Tennyson*, 32.
[23] Peter McDonald, *Sound Intentions: The Workings of Rhyme in Nineteenth-Century Poetry* (Oxford: Oxford University Press, 2012), 26, 37, 41.

informed writer, historical rhymes occupy the space between the accident of which words chime with each other, and authorial intention. Enforced archaic pronunciation, in turn, reminds readers of the previous incarnations words have had and the transformations they continually undergo.[24]

Tennyson's relationship with rhyme is epitomized by his copy of John Walker's *Rhyming Dictionary*, on the fly-leaf of which he wrote the poem "The Skipping-Rope." He later remarked that he had found rhyming dictionaries too artificial because "There was no natural congruity between the rhymes thus alphabetically grouped together."[25] Matthew Rowlinson proposes that he preferred rhymes to emerge from a poet's mind rather than cold, alphabetical organization – the arbitrariness McDonald flags. Yet despite its name, the bulk of Walker's *Rhyming Dictionary* is not overtly concerned with rhyming at all; rather, it is a list of words ordered alphabetically from their ends toward their beginnings and claiming to be a useful tool for recognizing the building blocks of words. The dictionary positions itself as a philological educational aid. A book that Rowlinson sees as an unnervingly mechanical production of words – highlighting the "chance" that determines which words rhyme with each other, as McDonald has it – in fact is a work that positions itself as displaying the linguistic logic behind those rhymes.

Walker's dictionary draws attention to the ever-changing relationship between sounds and the letters meant to represent them, a theme many scholars have observed in Tennyson's poetry. Both Walker in 1775 and, ninety years later, editor John Longmuir were aware of the potential confusion of an alphabetically organized "rhyming dictionary," given that orthography often reflects obsolete pronunciations. Walker remarks that he will differentiate eye-rhymes with notes to avoid the confusion of trying to rhyme (for example) *dove* and *prove*. Still, the Victorian editor ruefully admits that "words that are brought together on account of their spelling, such as *bread* and *lead*, refuse to rhyme with one another."[26] It seems to be lost on Longmuir that *lead* – taken as the metallic element rather than the verb for leadership – can, indeed, rhyme with *bread*, an oversight that itself throws into relief the historically generated gap that can exist between written and spoken English.

Walker's appendix classifies words into groups of "perfect, nearly perfect, and allowable rhymes," and it was from this index that Tennyson drew the rhyming units for "The Skipping-Rope." Importantly, poets are Walker's source of authority for what is "allowable":

> Whatever has been constantly practiced by our most harmonious poets, may be safely presumed to be agreeable to the genius of our poetry … The delicate ears of a Pope or an Addison, would scarcely have acquiesced in the usage of imperfect rhymes, and sanctioned them so often by their practice, if such rhymes had been really a blemish.

---

[24] For a discussion of Tennyson's historical rhymes as compared with those of William Morris, see Sarah Weaver, "'A love for old modes of pronunciation': Historical Rhyme in Tennyson and Morris," *Tennyson Research Bulletin* 11, no. 4 (November 2020): 305–324.

[25] Hallam Tennyson, *Memoir*, 2:496.

[26] John Walker, *A Rhyming Dictionary*, ed. J. Longmuir (London: William Tegg, 1865), v–vi.

He posits the idea that vowels of the same "family" are acceptable as rhyming pairs, and that "the different sounds of the vowels, *i, e, a, o, u,* slide into each other by an easy gradation, each of which is sufficiently related to the preceding and succeeding sound to form what is called an allowable rhyme." He further argues that it is "better to tolerate them, than cramp the imagination by the too narrow boundaries of exactly similar sounds."[27] Imperfect rhymes, in other words, produce a relieving variety from the incessant tinkling of sounds that match each other too closely – a point that Tennyson's father had also made to him.

Although Walker offers a strictly literary explanation for allowing imprecise rhymes, his resulting lists would have demonstrated the heritage of changing pronunciation for a poet such as Tennyson, who read not only Pope but also Chaucer and Langland. Mid-nineteenth-century critics were less happy with such stretching, however. Longmuir commented that if he had been producing a new volume rather than an edition of a work from the previous century, "all that refers to *allowable* rhymes would certainly have been cancelled, as no longer tolerable to a poetic ear."[28] Pronunciations that Walker had considered acceptable, though not perfect, ninety years earlier had become distractingly alien to the Victorian editor. As we have seen in the previous chapter, reviewers of the time were not very tolerant of what they considered aberrant language.

Walker's dictionary engages with the same questions about language that Tennyson and his friends discussed. He may not have used Walker's book much after "The Skipping Rope," but he was very interested in the sounds of his words' souls. Around the same time he was using Walker's book, he wrote out a considerable number of lists of rhyming words in a notebook (see Figure 5). In addition to Walker, the evidence suggests that he also consulted *Poetic Endings* by John Trusler.[29] Trusler's guide was originally published eight years after Walker's (1783), and it resembles his predecessor's index in format. With Walker and Trusler at hand, Tennyson set about organizing their rhymes in his own fashion, adding some new items along the way. He broke down his rhyming dictionaries' groups into a system with more "natural congruity," both at the level of individual lists and how he grouped those lists within pages. Tennyson's organizational scheme favors clusters of terms whose contours match closely. His individual lists are substantially smaller than those in his reference sources, and their rhymes are more feminine – that is, they match for more syllables. He then collected these short word lists into pages according to similar endings. For example, one pair of pages contains words terminating in *-ess* and *-ous*. This schema is more nuanced than a dictionary in which words are "alphabetically grouped together."

This effort testifies to Tennyson's early commitment to mastering the sounds of his words and how they related to each other and past versions of themselves. When he used archaic vowels, therefore, it was not out of ignorance or whimsy but deliberate choice. For this poet, older pronunciation – like older words – not only provided the extra variety of rhyming indicated by Walker, it was a way to speak oneself into

---

[27] Ibid., vi, 669–671.
[28] Ibid., vi.
[29] Weaver, *Tennyson's Notebook Glossary and Rhyme Lists*, 47.

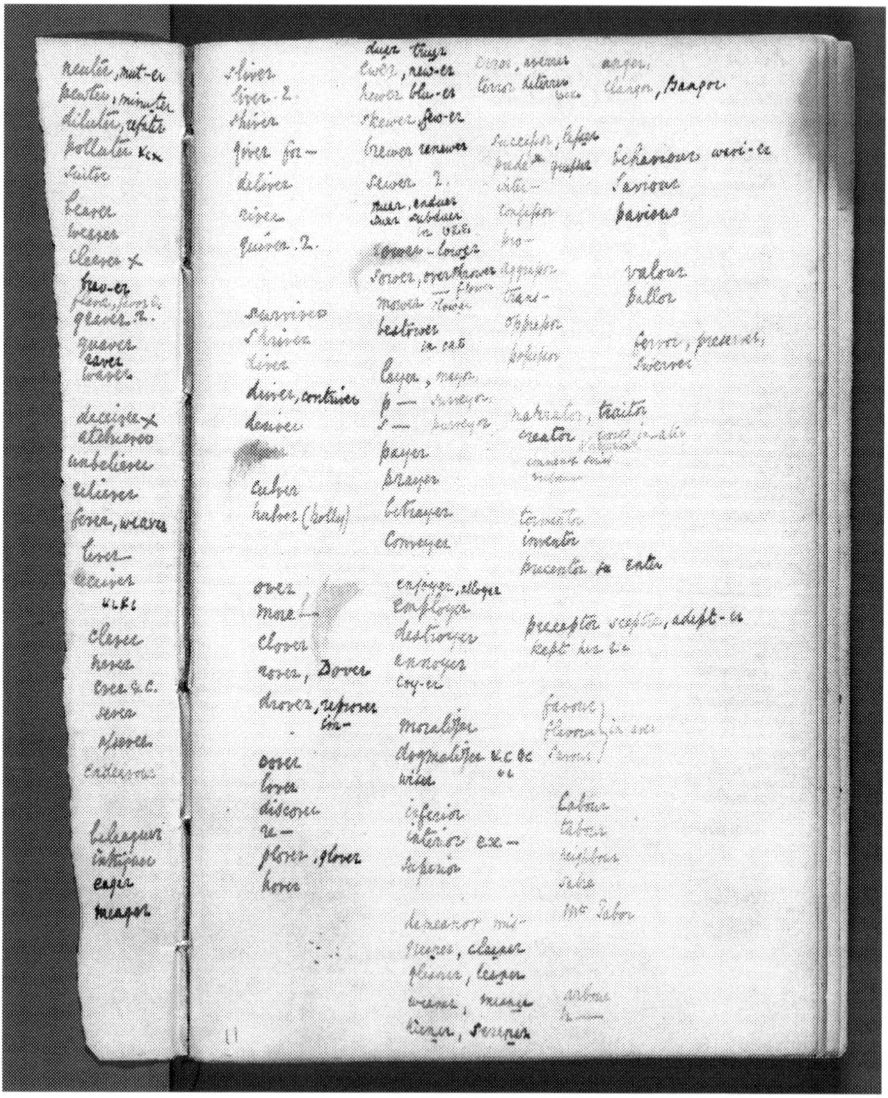

Figure 5 A page of Tennyson's notebook rhyme lists. MS Eng 95210, Houghton Library, Harvard University.

Evoking and Invoking the Past 177

the past. Drafts of *In Memoriam* and "The Gardener's Daughter," for example, show him giving two syllables to the word *four*, as in Old English *feower*.[30] There is something purposeful at work, then, when Tennyson employs eye-rhymes that no longer chime perfectly but once did. For example, we find the following stanza in "Maud" (written 1854):

> I said to the lily, "There is but one
> With whom she has heart to be gay.
> When will the dancers leave her alone?
> She is weary of dance and play."
> Now half to the setting moon are gone,
> And half to the rising day;
> Low on the sand and loud on the stone
> The last wheel echoes away.   (I.868–875)

This passage is especially troubled in rhyming *one*, *alone*, *gone*, and *stone*. Two stanzas later, *blood* is made part of a rhyming group with *stood* and *wood* (I.882–886). Rhyme scheme is made to invoke historical speech patterns, which draws attention to past pronunciation and thus to the fact that English is constantly changing.

If a rhyme-word both "casts itself forwards into the next lines of the poem" and is a way of "listening backwards within the poem," then historical rhymes extend the temporality of which they are markers. According to McDonald, nineteenth-century poetry recognized rhyme as a moment of memory;[31] historical rhyme is the ultimate exhibition of linguistic memory. Such rhymes expand the phonemic distance between paired words beyond what the reader expects. In the context of Tennyson's habitual devotion to repetition,[32] that unexpected distance, combined with the disjunction between written harmony and auditory discord, exerts pressure on the reader to reconcile imperfect pairs into a recurrence of phonemes. This is especially true if they are reading the poem aloud, which was a common Victorian practice. Such resolution is only possible by temporarily adopting medieval or early modern pronunciation. It is telling that when Tennyson observes that one of the effects of time is "to change the bearing of a word," he shows the very sound of *word* to have changed, because its position suggests that it ought to rhyme with *sword* from three lines before (*In Memoriam* cxxviii.13–16).

With this technique, Tennyson leveraged rhyme positions to encourage a sort of auditory time travel. The word *there* is not only an imperfect, echoing return of *sphere* in section lx of *In Memoriam*; it is also a return into the past of the English language, when *there* and *sphere* could rhyme. Much has been written on the structure of *In Memoriam*'s stanzas, in particular their embodiment of the poem's tendency to turn back on itself.[33] It is therefore noteworthy that the very first stanza fits this unvarying rhyme scheme only if the reader makes the leap to arcane pronunciation:

---

[30] Tennyson, *The Poems of Tennyson*, 1987, 2:341.
[31] McDonald, *Sound Intentions*, 12, 53.
[32] Perry, *Alfred Tennyson*, 22.
[33] Erik Gray, "Introduction," in *In Memoriam*, by Alfred Tennyson, ed. Erik Gray, 2nd ed., Norton Critical Edition (New York: W.W. Norton, 2004), xvi–xvii; McDonald, *Sound Intentions*, 172–173.

> Strong Son of God, immortal Love,
>   Whom we, that have not seen thy face,
>   By faith, and faith alone, embrace,
> Believing where we cannot prove;   (1–4)

The next stanza again disrupts the poem's purported regularity, with the interior couplet pairing *brute* and *foot*, and numerous other examples are to be found in the same poem.

As with the use of obsolete words, a rhyme may carry with it intertextual echoes that reinforce an archaic pronunciation. Victorian poets had available to them a range of rhymes made allowable by poetic convention rather than acoustic similarity, and those who were especially interested in the history of the English language employed a yet broader selection of rhymes whose resemblance on the page suggested an extinct alignment of vowels rather than a current one. This technique both troubles and contributes to our understanding of "a cultural climate that linked written poetry with orality, especially in terms of formal features including rhythm and rhyme," as Jennifer Esmail has put it.[34]

Tennyson's rhymes were tied to orality from different eras. For example, he partook of the flexibility of words containing *-ove*; in his notebook, he listed *over* and many if its companions together with *reprover*. He likewise drew a line connecting the lists "oval/removal/approval" and "hovel/shovel/novel/grovel." Similarly, *oven*, *cloven*, and *woven* supposedly match with *sloven*.[35] Because poetry frequently discusses love, words ending *-ove* had an especially strong legacy of being used together – so much so that Walker's 1775 preface mentions that he will use spelling to distinguish the vowels of *prove* and *dove* as *prove* and *duvv*. As a result of this history, the pair *love* and *prove* at the beginning of *In Memoriam* replicates the experience of reading a poem from an earlier century, recalling works such as Marlowe's "Passionate Shepherd to His Love." The authority of past poets could justify "imperfect" rhymes for Tennyson as it had for Walker.

Most commonly, many poets of Tennyson's day allowed the vowels *i* ("ee") and *ai* ("eye") to rhyme, as they had in Middle English. Thomas Smibert's *Rhyming Dictionary for the Use of Young Poets* (1852) confirmed:

> No rhymes are more uncertain … than those of words ending in *y* … In monosyllables and dissyllables so ending, as "try" and "rely," the termination always rhymes to *ie*, as in "vie" or "hie;" and it seems right to say that *y* should always so be rhymed. Nevertheless, it as often rhymes to an *e*, as in "be" and "she." The plural of nouns in *y*, again, having their termination in "ies," rhyme very uncertainly. They are sometimes placed to correspond with "lies," and sometimes with "lees." *There is no fixed rule on this subject.*[36]

---

[34] Jennifer Esmail, "'Perchance My Hand May Touch the Lyre': Orality and Textuality in Nineteenth-Century Deaf Poetry," *Victorian Poetry* 49, no. 4 (2011): 509.

[35] Weaver, *Tennyson's Notebook Glossary and Rhyme Lists*, 67, 55, 57.

[36] Thomas Smibert, *Rhyming Dictionary for the Use of Young Poets* (Edinburgh, 1852), 8. My emphasis.

Walker lists the words *by*, *cry*, *outvie*, and many others (including *belly* and *prophecy*) as sharing "perfect rhymes" with *high*, *nigh*, *sigh*, and *thigh*, and "allowable rhymes" with nearly two pages of words ending in *i* such as "bee, she, tea, sea ... pleurisy, chemistry, academy," and so on. The poetic pronunciation of words ending in the letter *y* was a matter of convenience, permitted to rhyme with both "ee" and "eye" sounds. Examples of this duality are overwhelming in their frequency, but a few from *In Memoriam* will suffice to show it in practice for Tennyson: die/sympathy (xxx.22–23), replies/mysteries (xxxvii.9–12), I/sympathy (lxiii.6–7), eyes/insufficiencies (cxii.2–3).

Generally, the historic pronunciations that Tennyson suggests by means of rhymes consist of a move toward long vowels. This is hardly surprising given that long vowels were understood to predominate in earlier forms of language, including English. For example, he evidently sometimes considered *wind* (the noun for the movement of air) to be uttered with a long *i*, rhyming it with *bind*, *blind*, *find*, *(be)hind*, *kind*, *mined*, *mind*, *rind*, and *(en)twined*. Tennyson's unpublished sonnet "To Poesy" (written 1828) spoke of "Mind," whose melody "May blow alarum loud to every wind;" the subsequent lines strongly suggest that "every wind" should also rhyme with "human kind" and "bind" (2, 4–5, 7). In the same way, "Ode to Memory" (1830) described memories as:

> Those peerless flowers which in the rudest wind
>   Never grow sere,
> When rooted in the garden of the mind (24–26)

In Memoriam muses how one "may find / A flower beat with rain and wind" (viii.14–15) and imagines that even if a ghost spoke of "days behind, / I might but say, I hear a wind" (xcii.6–7). Likewise "To J.S.":

> I will not say, "God's ordinance
> Of death is blown in every wind;"
> For that is not a common chance
> That takes away a noble mind. (45–48)

Rhyming dictionaries from the eighteenth and nineteenth centuries show some ambiguity on the word *wind*. John Rice's *An Introduction to the Art of Reading* from 1765 acknowledged that both pronunciations (short and long *i*) existed but stated that the vowel should be long when reading poetry: "the Syllable *wind*, whether pronounced short or long, in *polite Conversation*, is accounted long in the Measure of poetical Quantity."[37] Ten years later, Walker noted that although the verb to *wind* (as in winding around) rhymed with *mind*, the noun (for the movement of air) did not. Nevertheless, Tennyson used the noun in the older way. He used long *i* similarly for a rhyme in "The Two Voices" (written 1833):

---

[37] John Rice, *An Introduction to the Art of Reading 1765*, ed. R.C. Alston, English Linguistics, 1500–1800 161 (Menston, England: The Scolar Press, 1969), 53.

> If straight thy track, or if oblique,
> Thou knows't not. Shadows thou dost strike,
> Embracing cloud, Ixion-like   (193–195)

His explanation in the Eversley Edition, many years later, was: "Our grandfathers said 'obleege,' which is now *oblīge*; in the same way I pronounce 'oblique' *oblīque*."[38] In this case, Tennyson positions himself as following the trajectory of pronunciation change; it is a good reminder that he saw himself as participating in the history of the English language, not only mining its history.

Tennyson also shifted other vowels toward their long versions. For example, he evidently thought the pair of letters *-ar* leaned toward an open α ("ah") vowel. His notebook groups *warden* together with *pardon*, *garden*, and *harden*.[39] In verse, he placed *ward* as a match for *guard* ("Maud" [1855] I.247–249) and *evil-starred* ("Locksley Hall" [written 1837–1838] 155–156). He likewise used war/afar in "Riflemen, Form" ([1859] 1–3) and "Babylon" (21–22), and war/star in "Ode Sung at the Opening of the International Exhibition" ([1862] 25–28). War/are appeared in the "Ode on the Death of the Duke of Wellington" ([1852] 30–33). There are exceptions, of course – for example, ward/Lord ("In the Children's Hospital" [1880] 53–54) – but the balance of usage shows a preference for the open version of *a*.

Furthermore, Tennyson's fondness for long *o* extended beyond *knowledge*, *shone*, and *knoll*, mentioned above. For example, his preferred rhyme for *word* was *lord* (e.g., "The Fall of Jerusalem" [1827] 101–102, "Maud" [1855] I.560–561, the dialect poem "The Spinster's Sweet-Arts" [1885] 95–96), followed by *sword* ("The Poet" [1830] 53–55, *In Memoriam* cxxviii.13–16). His notebook also shows that he thought *melancholy* could rhyme with *lowly*, *wholly*, and the like. "The Lotos-Eaters" did just this: "How sweet it were ... To lend our hearts and spirits wholly / To the influence of mild-minded melancholy" (99–109). Yet the same notebook also allows *melancholy* to claim *folly*, *holly*, and *jolly* as companions,[40] as it did in "Maud":

> I tried today
> To beguile her melancholy;
> The Sultan ... perplext her
> With his worldly talk and folly   (I.788–793)

Tennyson was equally flexible with how he rhymed the word *come*, such as when he combined it with *home* several times in *In Memoriam* (vi.21–24, viii.1–4, xiv.9–12, xl.6–7). *Manipulus Vocabulorum*, a rhyming dictionary from 1570 by Peter Levins, had equated *come* and *home*,[41] but every such reference work afterward distinguished the words as belonging to different groups – UM for the former, OME for the latter. However, Walker left the door open to more flexible usage. His index indicated that *home* rhymed perfectly with, for example, *foam* (as in "Crossing the Bar" [1889]:

---

[38] Tennyson, *Poems I*, 354.
[39] Weaver, *Tennyson's Notebook Glossary and Rhyme Lists*, 56.
[40] Ibid., 75, 74.
[41] Peter Levins, *Manipulus Vocabulorum: A Rhyming Dictionary of the English Language, by Peter Levins (1570)*, ed. Henry B. Wheatley (London: Trübner, 1867), 161.

"Too full for sound and foam … Turns again home" [6–8]), but allowable rhymes included *come*.[42] Tennyson also placed *come* into relationship with *tomb* ("Antony to Cleopatra" [1827] 39–40), *womb* ("Day-Dream" [1842] I.6–8), and *gloom* ("Love thou thy land" [written early 1830s] 54–55). As with his use of strong verbs, Tennyson kept his options open.

Victorian critics certainly noticed the ghostly presence of Chaucerian rhymes. Yet poetic precedent was not enough to excuse historical rhymes in the eyes (or ears) of nineteenth-century judges. Even with that illustrious poet for exemplar, critics were less happy to read archaic rhymes than historically minded poets were to write them. One expert even blamed Spenser for (re)introducing them in the style of his predecessor. In his 1838 *History of English Rhythms*, Edwin Guest wrote that the rhymes in Chaucer's work are mostly correct, but:

> The writers who succeeded him seem to have been misled by the spirit of imitation. Many syllables, which rimed in the days of Chaucer and Gower, had no longer a sufficient correspondence, owing to change of pronunciation. Still, however, they were held to be legitimate rimes upon the authority of these poets. Hence arose a vast and increasing number of *conventional* rimes, which have since continued to disfigure our poetry.

Spenser, he goes on, "sinned grievously" in this respect: he "introduced a *vagueness* into our pronunciation, under which the language is still suffering."[43] The vagueness Guest identified was presumably the fluidity of pronunciation that certain nineteenth-century poets afforded their words. For Guest, even the example of canonical poets should not overpower the contemporary ear; Tennyson's reviewers held the same view. Indeed, as we have seen in the previous chapter, archaisms were generally subject to censure from literary authorities, suggesting that Tennyson was especially invested in drawing on medieval and early-modern language given that he did so in defiance of critical opinion, to which he was otherwise very sensitive.

The core practice of philology has always been to trace the changes that words undergo through subtle alterations in their sounds, and poetry often provides evidence for the philologist. Conversely, a poet may draw attention to such shifts by using historically rhyming words that have since drifted apart. Through would-be rhymes that depend on "old modes of pronunciation," Tennyson partially re-shapes readers' speech until they sound closer to their linguistic forebears. Or, if they persist in their native sound patterns, they are forced to acknowledge the echo of a lost similitude. As Chapter 3 discussed, however, Tennyson's medievalism did not focus exclusively on the past for its own sake. Rather, his poetry constantly explores its relationship with the world inhabited by English speakers of his own day. Sometimes that exploration took the form of bringing historical English – words or obsolete pronunciations – before his readers. More subtly, attention to linguistic history empowered him to work with the resonances of Modern English words based on their origins.

---

[42] Walker, *Rhyming Dictionary*, 704.
[43] Guest, *A History of English Rhythms*, 1838, 1:121.

"His use of English": Etymological Origins

The shortest possible philological summary of the Modern English is that it resulted from the Norman French of William the Conqueror and his people interacting with Old English, and the vocabulary of the new blended language was further supplemented with direct imports from Latin and occasionally Greek. The Cambridge Apostles were evidently discussing the matter with each other and with Trinity tutor Julius Charles Hare; in 1830, William Bodham Donne wrote to fellow Apostle Trench that he had deferred some other reading "until I had looked more to the right and left on English ... I am nearly convinced that the cry which Hare raises about *Saxon* English is a mistake, and that the real substratum of our language is *Norman*."[44] Donne was wrong, as scholars such as Rasmus Rask and Joseph Bosworth were already showing, and as Trench was to demonstrate to a broader audience in his books some twenty years later. Nonetheless, the Apostles were obviously aware of the amalgam of linguistic sources that constituted English, debating the effects of its various elements, as they did so many topics of the day, such as what constituted good literary style.

The previous year (1829), Donne had written to Trench:

> We have never written or thought like men, since we ceased to be English in idiom and in understanding; and we never shall write or think like men till we re-Anglicize ourselves. And I see but faint hopes of such regeneration in the present age, since our writers seem to have little confidence in their own native energies, and pride themselves upon imitation of the "Early English Writers," which expression is fast becoming one of the cant phrases of the day.[45]

This complaint, written while Tennyson was an undergraduate, represents the complex relationship with the past that the Apostles saw as appropriate in poetry. On one hand, Donne saw a need to "re-Anglicize" English writing. For example, in an 1829 letter to Kemble (another fellow Apostle), Donne commented on some poetic lines by Trench, which included the phrase "Skirling the desert," saying, "I could hug Trench for that noble English word 'skirling'" (to *skirl* is to make a shrill, wailing sound). Five months later, he told Kemble approvingly: "You are one of the few moderns ... who write pure English."[46]

As Marion Shaw has put it, "An English quality in poetry was a strong element in the Apostles' valuation: a desire to confirm links with a traditional past that seemed to be disappearing, and to provide a bulwark against an uncertain future."[47] Importantly, however, the solution was not to turn back time to some period of "pure English." Indeed, Donne's grievance is that writers of his own time "have little confidence in their own native energies, and pride themselves upon imitation of the 'Early English Writers.'" As the previous chapter discussed, critics accused Tennyson of this very sin: imitating early writers as a form of too-artificial artistry. I argue that

---

[44] Trench, *Letters and Memorials*, 1:43.
[45] Ibid., 1:22.
[46] Quoted in Shaw, "Kemble Letters," 216. Dates taken from Nye, *Gibraltar Journal*, 224, 230.
[47] Shaw, "Kemble Letters," 216.

he took a much broader view of his language, drawing upon its complex history strategically but without excluding any segment of it. With his philological knowledge, for example, he could consciously choose his words based on their origins.

It was and is a commonplace to note that within Modern English, words with Latinate etymology usually carry with them connotations of learning, aristocracy, and if used in overabundance, pomposity or affectation.[48] Novelist Walter Scott famously illustrated the idea in 1819's *Ivanhoe* with the example of *swine* in the field becoming *pork* on the table of the nobility.[49] Trench, too, would later observe (citing Scott) that Anglo-Saxon words became humbler in connotation after the Norman Conquest;[50] but by the same token, they remain the words of choice for dearer objects and for nature.[51] Surrounded by these discussions, Tennyson accounted for the effect of registers in his poetic calibrations. Though he was not interested in returning to solely "native" – that is, Germanic – word-stock, his poetry shows a commitment to weighting his vocabulary in favor of words of Anglo-Saxon heritage.

As quoted in the previous chapter, Trench wrote that "Those who would gladly have seen the Anglo-Saxon to have predominated over the Latin element in our language ... must note with regret that in a great many instances a word of the former stock has been dropped, and a Latin coined to supply its place."[52] Yet as Donne alluded in his letter quoted above, the Apostles' mentor Hare insisted that "In the English character, as in our language, the Teutonic or spiritual element has fortunately been predominant."[53] Kemble wrote to his friend and collaborator Grimm that he wished English had "retained a little more of the sound Anglo-Saxon element" but that he could not regret the language developing into the one written by Shakespeare, Milton, and Tennyson. Nevertheless, he noted, "I am myself careful to use an English word whenever I justly can, in preference to a French or Latin one."[54] His statement captures the essence of Tennyson's lexical leanings, as well: a preference for the Germanic paired with an appreciation for the richness afforded by additional sources.

In fact, Tennyson himself commented that what distinguished his style was the proportion of Anglo-Saxon words he used. According to his son, "If he differentiated his style from that of any other poet, he would remark on his use of English – in preference to words derived from French and Latin."[55] The *Christian Remembrancer*'s reviewer of the 1842 *Poems* recognized this quality, describing Tennyson's style as "on the whole such genuine and vigorous English."[56] Victorian writers on Anglo-Saxon topics often equated the early stage of English society with poetic force, as previous chapters have discussed. Bosworth the Anglo-Saxonist, for example,

---

[48] For my purposes, "Latinate" and "Romance" refer to classical Latin and all of its descendants, most pertinently French.
[49] Walter Scott, *Ivanhoe* (London: Penguin, 2000), 21.
[50] Trench, *English, Past and Present*, 38.
[51] Trench, *On the Study of Words*, 72.
[52] Trench, *English, Past and Present*, 104.
[53] Hare, *Guesses at Truth, by Two Brothers: Two Series in One Volume*, 62.
[54] Kemble, *Correspondence*, 311.
[55] Hallam Tennyson, *Memoir*, 2:133.
[56] Quoted in Shannon, *Tennyson and the Reviewers*, 66.

thought that the natural consequence was that poets were drawn back to the source of their language. Although foreign words are used for "scientific or abstract ideas," he wrote in his 1838 dictionary, such terms:

> do not suit the feelings of the poet; he involuntarily has recourse to the original stores of his native tongue – to the varied construction, and the energetic and picturesque diction of the Anglo-Saxon – a language formed by his valiant forefathers in their savage, that is, poetical state.[57]

A generation before, Sharon Turner (whose Anglo-Saxon history Tennyson owned and read) had seen the "copiousness and power" of Old English in the fact that "our own [Modern] English ... is principally Saxon." He found this earlier tongue to be "a very copious language, ... capable of expressing any subject of human thought. ... The Saxon abounds with synonimes. [sic]"[58] In other words, those of an Anglo-Saxonist bent contended that Latinate vocabulary is not necessary for expressive writing.

Turner illustrated his point by printing "some lines of our principal authors, and marking in *Italics* the Saxon words they contain." The excerpts are from Shakespeare (the first part of Hamlet's "to be or not to be" soliloquy), Milton (from Book IV of *Paradise Lost*), Abraham Cowley ("On the Shortness of Man's Life"), the King James Bible translation of Genesis 43:25–29 and John 11:32–36, James Thomson ("A Hymn"), Addison (from an essay in *The Spectator* describing a walk at sunset), Spenser (from Book IV of *The Faerie Queene*), an essay by Locke, Pope ("Eloisa to Abelard"), Edward Young ("The Complaint"), Swift (*A Tale of a Tub*), historian William Robertson (writing of Charles V, emperor of Germany), Hume (describing Mary, Queen of Scots), Gibbon (from *The History of the Decline and Fall of the Roman Empire*), and Johnson (*The Lives of the Poets*). The visual effect of all the italicized words makes his point quite effectively. Yet despite its centrality to Modern English, Turner writes that "much of our ancient language we have laid aside, and have suffered to become obsolete; because all our writers, from Chaucer to our own times have used words of foreign origin rather than our own."[59] The samples Turner provides are meant to demonstrate that "words of foreign origin" are not necessary for good writing. Indeed, he argues that the best authors rely on a predominantly Saxon vocabulary, from Shakespeare onward.

Tennyson evidently took to heart the idea that good literary language could and should comprise mostly words of Anglo-Saxon origin. It is impossible to say whether he imbibed the idea from Turner, Hare, the Apostles, or any of the other scholars who made similar arguments, or indeed from his own observation. Whatever the origin(s) of this etymological commitment, he identified using non-French, non-Latin English as a distinctive aspect of his own style. Applying a version of Turner's exercise to Tennyson allows us to test the latter's claim about his philological-medievalist style. It also helps identify where and how he chose to engage the echoes of Romance diction. Tennyson's claim to a wordhoard derived

---

[57] Bosworth, *A Dictionary of the Anglo-Saxon Language*, lxxvii.
[58] Turner, *History of the Anglo-Saxons*, 1807, 2:464.
[59] Turner, *History of the Anglo-Saxons*, 2:467–471.

primarily from Anglo-Saxon would seem to be contradicted by his mellifluous sound – the characteristics of syntax and phrasing that, when used in his less inspired verse, Gerard Manley Hopkins identified as the elements of Tennyson's particular brand of "Parnassian" writing.[60] However, analysis of sample poems reveals that Germanic vocabulary does indeed dominate his work. The Romance or Latinate portion of his vocabulary is simply placed deliberately, creating particular effects with those words.

Large-scale analysis of the etymological origins of the words in Tennyson's corpus could benefit from the kind of computational methods developed by scholars such as Ted Underwood, Jordan Sellers, and Natalie M. Houston. Such methods were unfortunately not available for the preparation of the present volume, but "The Lotos-Eaters" and "Maud" serve as useful case studies. On a practical level, their length gives enough scope for analysis while still being manageable for a human investigator. Furthermore, their dates of composition and revision span Tennyson's early career as he established himself as a widely read poet: 1830–1832 and 1842 for "The Lotos-Eaters," 1854–1855 and 1856 for "Maud." And their enduring fame gives them a good claim to our attention, whether that fame was the result of praise or criticism.

Tennyson began to compose "The Lotos-Eaters" in 1830, the year after Donne wrote about the need to be "English in idiom." First published in the 1832 volume, it was significantly revised for 1842. The following analysis is based on the 1842 version as the product most wrought by the poet's craftsmanship. The major change between versions was a rewriting of lines 150–173, which removed unhyphenated compounds such as *grassgreen*, *foamfountains*, and *Lotoseaters* and shifted the vocabulary slightly toward the Latinate. Even so, and especially given its classical origin in the *Odyssey*, a surprisingly high percentage of the poem is composed of words with Germanic or Scandinavian roots. Only 13 percent of the total word-stock is of French or Latin origin – or 14 percent once articles and pronouns are removed. For comparison, English as a whole is estimated to be composed of approximately 60 percent French or Latin vocabulary, though that includes technical and medical terms. In writing generally, the proportion generally averages out to half and half.[61] A study of Jane Austen's corpus found about 36 percent Latinate verbiage.[62]

To some extent, Tennyson's poetry was part of a trend over the course of the nineteenth century in literary language generally: Ted Underwood and Jordan Sellers have shown that poetry, drama, and fiction "began to rely much more heavily on the older part of the lexicon" over the course of the eighteenth and nineteenth centuries. Specifically, the proportion of older words – defined as entering the language before 1150 – increased beginning at the turn of the nineteenth century, especially in poetry. This shift, as Underwood and Sellers point out, "coincide[d] with a series of well-known debates about English diction" such as the literary theory behind the

---

[60] Gerard Manley Hopkins, *The Collected Works of Gerard Manley Hopkins*, ed. R.K.R. Thornton and Catherine Phillips, vol. 1 (Oxford: Oxford University Press, 2013), 68–69.
[61] Robert Burchfield, *The English Language* (Oxford: Oxford University Press, 2002), 111.
[62] Suzanne Romaine, "Corpus Linguistics and Sociolinguistics," in *Corpus Linguistics: An International Handbook*, ed. Anke Lüdeling and Merja Kytö, vol. 1, Handbooks of Linguistics and Communication Science, 29.1 (Berlin: Walter de Gruyter, 2009), 106.

Lyrical Ballads of Wordsworth and Coleridge. By analyzing the words that gained traction and those that declined in poetic use, they show a shift toward "elemental aspects of experience" and away from words related to sociality, but they suspect that "the etymological coloration of these lists is on the whole accidental."[63]

Tennyson's philological medievalist style, however, was not accidental, as we know from his own assertion about his "use of English." His scant 14 percent of Latinate vocabulary in "The Lotos-Eaters" is the result of a concerted effort "to use an English word whenever [he] justly [could]," to borrow Kemble's description of his own preference. A graph by Underwood and Sellers further helps position Tennyson in relation to his contemporaries. The graph shows the ratio of old words to newer ones, a proportion that tilted in favor of the archaic over the course of the nineteenth century. In the earlier decades they studied, there were on average 1.5 old words for every newer word; as the twentieth century approached, the ratio increased to 2.5:1 in poetry generally. "The Lotos-Eaters" has a ratio of 6.7 Germanic words per Latinate one. This is not an easy feat in Modern English if the resulting composition is not to sound awkward or simplistic, and "The Lotos-Eaters" on the contrary creates the impression of a lush natural world through its language.

The following passage demonstrates how Tennyson could maintain his sensual effects even with non-Latinate vocabulary:

> They sat them down upon the yellow sand,
> Between the sun and moon upon the shore;
> And sweet it was to dream of Fatherland,
> Of child, and wife, and slave; but evermore
> Most weary seemed the sea, weary the oar.   (37–41)

In these lines, every word is Germanic or Scandinavian except *slave*, which is attested in both Old French and older German. At this moment, the poem's narration relates simple fact and recalls unelaborated, home-related nouns. It is the last moment of clear-eyed perception just before the "choric song" takes over, shifting the poem's voice to that of the drugged men. Yet even then, Tennyson does not effect the impression of enervation by shifting to Romance vocabulary. In the following lines, for example, his intoxicated mariners complain that everything else in nature is allowed peaceful rest:

> Lo! in the middle of the wood,
> The folded leaf is wooed from out the bud
> With winds upon the branch, and there
> Grows green and broad, and takes no care,
> Sun-steeped at noon, and in the moon
> Nightly dew-fed; and turning yellow
> Falls, and floats adown the air.   (70–76)

Within these lines, only *branch* is non-Germanic. The poem overall averages one Latinate word per line for 173 lines, with up to five consecutive lines managing

---

[63] Ted Underwood and Jordan Sellers, "The Emergence of Literary Diction," *Journal of Digital Humanities* 1, no. 2, accessed February 15, 2023.

without any at all. It is not, then, through sheer volume of Latin- and French-origin words that Tennyson achieves his wrought style; his "studied poetic vocabulary" (in the words of scholar J.F.A. Pyre) remains grounded in Anglo-Saxon but somehow gives the impression of being more elevated than the mixture of its components would suggest.

In order to discover the effect these Latinate words have in "The Lotos-Eaters," we must examine them more closely. All of the unequivocally French- or Latin-derived words are listed below, grouped into rough categories. The first set comprises specifically classical references; they help to place the story and characters within Homer's *Odyssey*. A more sizeable list is the inventory of nature words. "The Lotos-Eaters" contains lengthy descriptions of the landscape, and despite Scott's (and later Trench's) general principle that words for nature tend to be Anglo-Saxon, some Romance-originated words would only be avoided with great effort. The result of trying to replace *mountain*, *branch*, or *flower* would likely be too awkward to merit the effort. Most of the words in this category are therefore more or less unavoidable – and more importantly, they have been so thoroughly absorbed into English that they are of equal register with their earthy Germanic neighbors. Some of the nature words, however, serve to create specificity; they are the names of particular species (galingale, acanthus) or types of rock (granite, emerald). Remember that *galingale* was a term Tennyson had collected from his reading of Chapman's translation of Homer and written in his notebook glossary,[64] and many of Tennyson's provincialisms are dialect names for natural objects.

The next category is composed of words whose Latin or French origins place them in a higher register, and whose foreign origins are often easy to recognize. Some of these, as appropriate to the history of English, are semi-legal terms: *perpetual*, *cease*, *inherit*, *strange*, *princes*, *reconcile*, *dues*. The next group consists of words that carry negative connotations in this poem. It is essentially an extension of the list of elevated words; except for *pain* and *monster*, they use their higher register to enhance the sense of a wearying, antagonistic world. The poem's many repetitions of *toil* have this effect, as do the cluster near the end of the poem that form part of an inventory of human suffering observed by the gods. The largest category, tellingly, are those words that reinforce the sensual nature of the land, which becomes the mariners' sole focus after eating the lotos. Hence we hear of *languid air*; the sunset is *charmed*, the lotos branches *enchanted*; and the mariners long for *balm*, *peace*, *rest*, *calm*, *pleasure*, and *melancholy*. In short, these words conform to the maxim that words of Latin or French derivation are less domestic than Germanic words. At an unconscious level, they reinforce that the mariners have become emotionally severed from "Fatherland, ... child, and wife." The words are here listed by category. The numbers in parentheses represent the line(s) where each term appears.

Classical references
lotos (27, 105, 145, 146, 149, 154), moly (133), nectar (156), Elysian (169), asphodel (170)

---

[64] Weaver, *Tennyson's Notebook Glossary and Rhyme Lists*, 21.

Nature

valley (7, 157, 169), river (14, 137), mountain (15, 19), pinnacle (16), copse (18), vale (22), faces (25, 26, 111), branches (28, 72), flower (29, 55, 81), fruit/fruitful (29, 83), voice (34), petals (46), pass (49), autumn (79), soil (83, 165), echoes (139), cave (140, 148), vine (140), fountain (152)

Specific nature

galingale (23), granite (49), poppy (56), myrrh (103), amaranth (133), emerald (141), acanthus (142)

Heightened Register

perpetual (62), cease (65, 97), crown (69), vaulted (85), influence (109), infancy (111), inherit (118), strange (118), princes (120), minstrel (121), substance (121), confusion (124, 128), remain (125), reconcile (126), divine (142), dues (167)

Negative

barren (42, 145), consumed (58), distress (58), toil (60, 69, 82, 166, 171), labour (87, 130, 172), suffer/suffered (116, 168, 169), trouble (119, 129), pain (129), monster (152), wasted (159), famine (160), plague (160), doleful (162), lamentation (163), enduring (166), perish (168), anguish (169)

Sensual

languid (5), air (5, 6, 134), pause (9), silent/silence (16, 79, 97), charmed (19), melancholy (27, 109), enchanted (28), receive (30), taste (31), rave (32), alien (33), music (36, 46, 50, 52, 162), gentlier (50), spirit (50, 67, 108), balm (66), calm (68), fades (82), pleasure (93), peace (94), ease (98), amber (102), tender (106), curving (107), creamy (107), muse (110), memory (110, 114), embrace (115), tone (147), spicy (149), reclined (154), secret (159), chanted (165)

Other

Courage (1), pointed (1), mounting (2), veil (11), roll/rolling/rolled (13, 151), aged (16, 130), bordered (22), pale (25, 26), return (43), joy (68, 119), juiced (78), urn (112), change (116), surely (117, 171), order (127), task (131), pilot (132), alley (148), action (150), motion (150), equal (153), clanging (161), praying (161), centred (162), ancient (163), used (165), race (165), storing (167), oil (167), mariners (173)

Considered individually, the Latinate words of "The Lotos-Eaters" are generally those that could not be avoided without awkwardness or obscurity; those that set the scene and tone (ancient myth, sensual experience); and those that simply help Tennyson's poem sound "poetic" through touches of higher register. Overall, the proportion of words from Germanic or Nordic stock suggests that Tennyson agreed with Kemble and Trench that while it was impossible – indeed undesirable – to exclude Latin-derived vocabulary entirely, one should choose Anglo-Saxon words when possible.[65] Tennyson selected his words and their attendant registers

---

[65] See, for example, Trench, *English, Past and Present*, 27.

thoughtfully, using Latin and French vocabulary sparingly – but effectively – to achieve calculated effects.

In practice, of course, Latinate words do not stand in isolation. Those of "The Lotos-Eaters" do not appear as they do in the lists above but interact with the Germanic body of the text. Precisely because they are distributed throughout the poem, we must also examine how they work with the rest of its vocabulary. The word *pause* is a good example. It is listed above among the Romance words that suggest the land's inertia, and the effect is even more apparent when viewed in context. Describing the landscape, the poem tells us: "the slender stream / Along the cliff to fall and pause and fall did seem" (8–9). *Fall* is an exemplary Germanic word (and indeed it is common to many Germanic languages): it is one syllable, a strong verb, and denotes motion. Tennyson sandwiches the inert *pause* between two iterations of *fall* – "fall and pause and fall" – to create an image of temporarily suspended motion. Notably, it is the single Latinate word that stills the action. In fact, of the Latinate words listed above, seventy-six are nouns as compared to only thirty-five adjectives, seventeen verbs, and two adverbs.

When the men imagine that the homes they left behind have been reshaped by others to function without them, the poem crashes together words from English's different sources:

> For surely now our household hearths are cold:
> And we should come like ghosts to trouble joy.
> Or else the island princes over-bold
> Have eat our substance, and the minstrel sings
> Before them of the ten years' war in Troy,
> And our great deeds, as half-forgotten things.   (117–123)

The first line is entirely composed of domestic words, except the metrical filler *surely*; French words come into play with *trouble joy*. *Princes* (an aristocratic, Latinate title) are *over-bold*, a very Anglo-Saxon adjective composition (compare the Old English *ofermod*, or over-spirited, usually used to describe excessive pride). *Have eat* is an archaic conjugation followed by *substance*, which has a much higher register. A *minstrel* is Latinate, but he *sings*. From here, the lines resolve into Germanic words again. Nonetheless, the passage is not as etymologically chaotic as it seems. As *ghosts*, the men would disturb the peace of their loved ones, who have settled into a state of Latinate-worded civil order. Interactions of this sort show Tennyson shrewdly matching not only his sound with his sense, but also the origins of his words with what they describe.

In short, Tennyson valued the Germanic portion of the English language and gave it precedence in contrast to centuries of rhetorical neglect; but the true evidence of his philological knowledge is how he wielded words from every origin. As Bosworth the Anglo-Saxonist observed:

> The fact is, that many thousand foreign words have been introduced when native terms already existed, and the English has, in this way, been endowed with the power of expressing the same idea by two different words – or, what is of still

greater value, of appropriating this new word to mark some modification in the meaning of the indigenous word.[66]

For Bosworth, "the great law of beauty and happiness" in language and everywhere else was "*variety in unity*."[67] Tennyson achieved this variety by leveraging the nuances of meaning made possible by a wordhoard stocked from multiple sources. When Kemble wrote to Grimm about the language of Shakespeare, Milton, and Tennyson, it was the richness made possible by hundreds of years of innovation that he appreciated as a gain for poets. Arthur Hallam, in his review of Tennyson's 1830 collection, wrote that the poet's language "with one or two rare exceptions, is thorough and sterling English." Where Tennyson strayed, it was because of his:

> generous enthusiasm for … that Saxon element, which constituted the intrinsic freedom and nervousness of our native tongue. We see no signs in what Mr. Tennyson has written of the Quixotic spirit which has led some persons to desire the reduction of English to a single form, by excluding nearly the whole of Latin and Roman derivatives. Ours is necessarily a compound language; as such alone it can flourish and increase[.]

According to Hallam's judgment, Tennyson's Anglo-Saxonism sometimes led him into stylistic errors, but it was right and good that he embraced "that fertility of expression and variety of harmony" that came from Latinate components, which had likewise enriched Shakespeare's work before him.[68] Another of Tennyson's friends (Agnata Butler) recalled that he "spoke of the great richness of the English language due to its double origin, the Norman and Saxon words," and he made use of that richness by bringing together words of varying origins.[69]

Sometimes Tennyson employed English's multiplicity in the form of synonymous near-redundancy. For example, the mariners of "The Lotos-Eaters" ask, "Why should we only toil, the roof and crown of things?" (69). *Roof* and *crown* are Anglo-Saxon and Latinate equivalents; phrases such as this duplicate the core meaning that the synonyms share while also comprehending within them the shades of sense that accompany each. In fact, this particular duplication proved useful for the revised edition of Bosworth's Anglo-Saxon dictionary, published posthumously in 1898 and known to this day as "Bosworth-Toller" after its two editors. This updated tome offered the following definition of *hróf*: "A roof, the top, summit, highest part [*cf.* Tennyson's 'Why should we only toil the *roof* and crown of things?']"[70] Tennyson, it seems, used *roof* in such an authentically Anglo-Saxon sense that he could serve as

---

[66] Bosworth, *A Dictionary of the Anglo-Saxon Language*, lxxvi–lxvii.
[67] Bosworth, *A Dictionary of the Anglo-Saxon Language*, xxxix. Original emphasis.
[68] Hallam, *Writings*, 198.
[69] Hallam Tennyson, *Tennyson and His Friends*, 218.
[70] Joseph Bosworth and T. Northcote Toller, *An Anglo-Saxon Dictionary: Based on the Manuscript Collections of the Late Joseph Bosworth* (Oxford: Clarendon Press, 1898), 562. Brackets in the original.

an illustration in a dictionary of Old English, and his double-barreled phrase helps define it, as well.[71]

Pairings such as these echo a practice common since the Norman Conquest of stating important items in Old English and French and/or Latin, to ensure complete understanding by all parties – hence, for example, the marriage vows to "love and cherish" one another. Tennyson's pairs often depict the same idea or object with two different registers, creating a modern version of variation that includes words with a Romance origin. A nineteenth-century reader would have understood each of his words alone, but because of the remaining nuances left by their histories, each one lends a different emphasis to the description. For example, the first line of "Tithonus" (1860) reads, "The woods decay, the woods decay and fall." *Decay* is simply Latin by way of French for "fall down" (*de cadere*).

Tennyson practiced this technique from a young age, though probably unconsciously at first. When his teenage play "The Devil and the Lady" refers to Satan's "fuscous and embrownèd cheek," the adjectives form a Latinate-Germanic pair in which each helps define the other (I.ii.9). *Fuscous* is almost unaltered from the Latin word for dark or dusky, used as such again in another teenage composition, "The Coach of Death": "To the ashy strand in an inky van / The mourning surges came, / In fuscous foam" (141–143). In "The Devil and the Lady," Tennyson helps his reader understand the word's meaning by pairing it with the more transparent English adjective *embrownèd*, for which the meaning of making dusky or dark was already "chiefly poetic" by the time it appeared in the *New English Dictionary* (predecessor of the *OED*).[72] That poetic usage was handed down through the "Pearl" poet, Milton, and Pope, and appeared again in Tennyson's "To the Reverend F.D. Maurice" (1855): "I watch the twilight falling brown" (14).

One of the nightmares of "Sea Dreams" (1860) involves waves of "luminous vapour" crashing against a cliff of "huge cathedral fronts," tearing down the statues; "Then from the gaps and chasms of ruin left / Came men and women" debating whether to repair the damage (202, 211, 218–219). *Gap* is of Norse origin, while *chasm* is Greek by way of Latin. Neither is so obscure that it needs translation, but the combination adds dimension to the description. In "The Lotos-Eaters," the waves seem to "mourn and rave" (32); one meaning of the Germanic *mourn* is "to utter lamentations," and the cluster of meanings for the French-derived *rave* share a sense of noise related to madness. After eating the lotos, the mariners wish to "muse and brood," a pair of equivalent French and Old English actions (110).

In addition, Tennyson clearly liked to combine words from different origins to amplify the effect of his description, even if they were not synonyms. Lines 159–160 of "The Lotos-Eaters" are replete with repetitions as the poem describes the gods carelessly observing:

---

[71] This new edition of the dictionary also cites Kemble more than eighty times, a sign of how much of an authority he had become forty years after his death.

[72] James A.H. Murray and Henry Bradley, *A New English Dictionary on Historical Principles: Founded Mainly on the Materials Collected by the Philological Society*, vol. 3 (Oxford: Clarendon Press, 1897), 116.

192   *Tennyson's Philological Medievalism*

> wasted lands,
> Blight and famine, plague and earthquake, roaring deeps and fiery sands,
> Clanging flights, and flaming towns, and sinking ships and praying hands.

Blight is of unknown origin but emerged into written English from farmers' speech and is therefore homespun enough to be the equivalent of Old English in its impact; its partner *famine* is French. *Plague* is a classical Latin equivalent to *blight*; it is followed by the compound *earthquake*. In the next lines, the gods smile, finding "music centred in a doleful song … a lamentation and an ancient tale of wrong" (161–162). *Song* and *tale* are Old English words decorated with French adjectives (doleful, ancient), while *lamentation* provides a French-origin equivalent of *song* and *tale*. Similarly, when the mariners ask why they are "utterly consumed with sharp distress," the phrase pairs an adjective from each branch (Latin-derived *consumed* and Germanic *sharp*) with words from the other (Germanic *utterly*, Latin *distress*) (58). When they wonder why humanity must "make perpetual moan," the adjective is French while the noun is of Germanic origin.

"The Lotos-Eaters" offers many examples of this technique, and it is one of many poems in which Tennyson exploited English's dual origins. To take another, "Maud" abounds with groups of words that elaborate a single concept. "Maud" has appeared in previous chapters, supplying examples of philologically informed style choices. It was also the poem that Tennyson most often recited aloud in company.[73] Among its mixed critical reception was a general approval of its focus on nineteenth-century concerns,[74] so it is a good example of Tennyson applying philology in his present moment as opposed to a historical setting. As early as the second stanza, we learn that the body of the speaker's father was found "Mangled, and flattened, and crushed, and dinted into the ground" (7). There is a hint here of Anglo-Saxon poetic variation, in which different facets of the same condition are offered in turn; in this particular poem, it also reflects the speaker's obsessive tendencies. In this line, we have *mangled* (Anglo-Norman), *flattened* (Old Norse/Germanic), *crushed* (Old French taken from German), and *dinted* (Middle English, with Scandinavian cognates). In combination, they convey many mutilations of the body.[75]

As for the poem's ratio of Germanic to Latinate verbiage, it further confirms Tennyson's "use of English – in preference to words derived from French and Latin." Overall, only 10.6 percent of its vocabulary falls into the latter category.[76] Multiple

---

[73] Philip Waller, *Writers, Readers, and Reputations: Literary Life in Britain 1870–1918* (Oxford: Oxford University Press, 2006), 368.

[74] Shannon, "Critical Reception," 400.

[75] Tennyson's dictionaries largely agree in the variety of origins, if not the exact etymologies: Bailey and Johnson offer roots of either Latin or Teutonic origin for *mangled*, apparently unable to decide. Johnson thinks *flatten* is French, but Richardson lists various cognates, starting with Dutch and German. Bailey and Johnson identify *crush* as French, while Richardson depicts it as French from the Gothic and gives an Anglo-Saxon cognate. Bailey and Johnson give *dint* Saxon origin.

[76] If a word was originally Latin but was in use in Old English, it is not included in the Latinate count because of having been "naturalized" for so long. For hyphenated terms – for example, *battle-bolt* – I count each half separately. If a closed compound is of divided

sequential lines can go without words of Latin origin, and passages such as the following use them sparingly (indicated in bold):

> But the broad light glares and beats,
> And the shadow flits and fleets
> And will not let me be;
> And I loathe the **squares** and streets,
> And the **faces** that one meets,
> Hearts with no love for me:
> Always I long to creep
> Into some still **cavern** deep,
> There to weep, and weep, and weep
> My whole soul out to thee. (II.229–238)

"The mad scene" that follows – Part II, section V – is starkly Anglo-Saxon in its vocabulary. Indeed, the relative density of vocabulary from each linguistic branch varies by stanza, and future research might probe more deeply into how that density maps onto the subject being discussed. For example, the opening stanzas, where the speaker wonders whether his father's death was intentional or accidental, are especially spare and almost entirely Germanic. In contrast, the section that introduces Maud (the speaker's love interest) is replete with Latinate vocabulary:

> a cold and **clear**-cut **face**, as I found when her **carriage past**,
> **Perfectly beautiful**: let it be **granted** her: where is the **fault**?
> All that I saw (for her eyes were downcast, not to be seen)
> **Faultily faultless**, icily **regular**, **splendidly null**,
> Dead **perfection**, no more; nothing more, if it had not been
> For a **chance** of **travel**, a **paleness**, an **hour's defect** of the rose
> Or an underlip, you may call it a little too ripe, too full,
> Or the least little **delicate aquiline curve** in a **sensitive** nose (I.78–86)

This lexical shift echoes the character's wealthy status and the speaker's disgust with her.

We might well ask at this point how common or unusual Tennyson's "use of English" was. The Cambridge Apostles, as quoted earlier, generally liked diction that favored a Germanic wordhoard. Several of them also wrote poetry, and their friends considered them just as likely to become successful in that arena as the future laureate.[77] Did they follow these same practices? Trench in particular published a good deal of poetry, and it was successful enough that his collections went through multiple editions. *The Story of Justin Martyr, and Other Poems* had at least six editions (between 1835 and 1862), while his *Poems* went through at least twelve (from 1841–1899). Trench's poem "The Story of Justin Martyr" dates to around the same time as Tennyson's "St Simeon Stylites" (written 1833) and has parallels with that work; it therefore offers an opportunity for comparing the etymological

---

origin – for example, *pickpocket* – I count the whole word as Latinate.

[77] Shaw, "Kemble Letters," 217.

balance of the vocabulary in the work of men with similar philological investment. Both are first-person poems in the voice of early Christian saints. Trench's tells how the speaker moved from despair to hope after his early ambitions had come to nothing. Tennyson's speaker raves in religious mania and imagines himself on the point of death after many years living atop a pillar. Trench's poem counts 12 percent non-Germanic words; Tennyson's comprises 11.6 percent. Tennyson's speaker is obsessed with salvation, revisiting the same ideas and Latinate words over and over – most commonly, *saint/saintdom* (fourteen times), *mercy* (seven times), *pain(ful)* (five times), *crown(s)(ed)* (five times), and *pillar, penance(s),* and *saved* (four times each). Trench employs a range of Romance-origin words, sometimes to elevate the register of his descriptions, sometimes to layer them alongside Germanic brethren.

Outside the Cambridge Apostles, William Morris is also a useful point of comparison. Morris's medievalism needs little introduction. In addition to his work at the Kelmscott Press and his decorative arts business, he translated a number of Old Norse sagas as well as *Beowulf*, believing that they belonged to a foundational Germanic culture. His style in these translations holds true to his nativist linguistic convictions: he selected the terms that most closely resembled the medieval ones they were supposedly translating. Morris was deeply committed to reviving the sound of English's linguistic ancestors and Germanic cousins, convinced that he was reconstructing a lost Teutonic ur-culture. Applying this nationalistic perspective to his work with early medieval sagas, Morris crafted translations that are often dense with obscure pseudo-descendent words. As described by Ian Felce, Morris's "literal rendering" can be seen as "an endeavour to bring the cultural authenticity of the progenitor-text at least part of the way to his readers, who [were] encumbered, as he deemed them, with a corrupted post-Norman Conquest, post-Renaissance industrialised idiom of English."[78]

Morris was best known in his lifetime as a poet of original material, which displayed the same propensities. His first success came in 1867 with *The Life and Death of Jason*, a book-length retelling of the classical myth. Reviews of *Jason* praised the work for its simplicity and "freshness." Swinburne called it "broad and sad and simple" and likened it to fresh March flowers. Henry James called it "remarkable among contemporary works for its simplicity and strength of diction." It was "a narrative poem on a Greek subject, written in a genuine English style," according to James, who further clarified that the style was "quaint, but not too quaint, more Anglo-Saxon than Latin, and decidedly laconic." As for the vocabulary: "in its abundance and studied simplicity, [it] leave[s] nothing to be desired."[79] James's review states explicitly what others seem to be suggesting: that Morris expressed the spirit of the Greek story using English of northern-European derivation. The numbers bear out this impression.

Several reviewers singled out Book 14 for particular praise. It features the ship *Argo* sailing past the Sirens and glimpsing the garden of the Hesperides. In addition to its positive critical reception, it is an excellent section to compare with Tennyson's

---

[78] Felce, *William Morris and the Icelandic Sagas*, 132–133.
[79] Peter Faulkner, ed., *William Morris: The Critical Heritage*, The Critical Heritage Series (London: Routledge and Kegan Paul, 1973), 65, 73, 76.

"Lotos-Eaters" for several reasons. First, both works explore classical content. Tennyson's mariners are drugged into lethargy when they eat the lotos-fruit; Morris presents a song-war in which the Sirens urge the delights of a drowsy existence beneath the waves, while Orpheus makes the case for the pleasures of earthly life. In addition, both poems were early critical successes for their respective poets, though appearing in print thirty-five years apart. If we discount the Greek names of people and places, then only 8.6 percent of Morris's lexis derives from Romance regions. This remarkable result speaks to how zealously he devoted himself to the Germanic component of his language – with far more ideological weight behind his efforts than Tennyson's style. A great many of Morris's Latinate words cluster around his description of the garden of the Hesperides, which lists specific species: cyprus, pomegranate, thyme, tiger, etc. Otherwise, his linguistic nativism is apparent. Nowhere in Book 14 does Morris use the word *people*, for example, always preferring *folk*. He also sprinkles his lines with Germanic compounds such as land-breeze, sea-witches, sea-fowl, earth-dwellers, over-bold, and flesh-meat.

Style, of course, is more than vocabulary percentages. For example, multiple reviewers compared the style of *The Life and Death of Jason* to Chaucer. Yet Chaucer's style is distinguished by how thoroughly he mixed his linguistic and literary sources: his poetic vocabulary is about half French.[80] And with similarly Germanic leanings, Morris's work was universally described as simple to the point of austerity, whereas Tennyson's land of the lotos-eaters is a sensory feast. The "simplicity" that so many cited in Morris's writing is partially owing to the repetition of words, whatever their origin. Indeed, he relies on stock phrases, which feature in both ancient Greek and Anglo-Saxon literature. A reviewer in the *Pall Mall Gazette* commented with some irritation: "A few … phrases, descriptive, or meant to be so, like 'the waters wan,' are repeated till we grow quite impatient of them."[81] Tennyson, on the other hand, creates the impression of a lush natural world through grammatical complexity.

Just as philological popularizer Max Müller and naturalist Charles Darwin used linguistic insights as evidence for opposing interpretations of history, Morris and Tennyson demonstrate how philological medievalism could appeal to poets with opposing politics and different literary styles. Morris explicitly wished to revert to an earlier way of life, whereas Tennyson found the past as it already existed within the present. Of course, his knowledge of historical English also proved useful when he wrote poems set in the Middle Ages. Edgar F. Shannon argues that Tennyson was "hurt and annoyed" by the reviews of "Maud" and "withdrew from the troublesome nineteenth century to his favorite era, the past, and diffidently began [working on] the *Idylls of the King*."[82] Leaving aside Tennyson's motivation of writing certain poems at certain times, it is a major claim of this book that he applied his knowledge of historical English to poems set in any century – but to different effect. The

---

[80] Steve Guthrie, "Chaucer's Language and Meter," *Chaucer's Troilus and Criseyde: A New Edition by Steve Guthrie, Agnes Scott College*. Based on Corpus Christi College, Cambridge Manuscript 61, 2014, https://agnesscott.edu/english/troilusandcriseyde/language.html.
[81] "Morris's 'Life and Death of Jason,'" *Pall Mall Gazette*, July 25, 1867.
[82] Shannon, "Critical Reception," 414.

remainder of this chapter highlights how he put his philological medievalism to work in *Idylls of the King* and *In Memoriam*.

Idylls of the King and Performative Medievalism

Thematically, the *Idylls of the King* are concerned with the strength – and weakness – of words. Donald S. Hair has explored this theme extensively, finding that the sequence as a whole tells a story about the rise and fall of vows: thoughtless talk ("babble") proves more destructive than intended malice, and lies unravel Camelot.[83] It should be no surprise, then, that in these poems, the idea of magic words becomes literal in the works of Merlin. The wizard explains to Vivien that the curse for which she yearns is written in a book in which every page encloses:

> A square of text that looks a little blot,
> The text no larger than the limbs of fleas;
> And every square of text an awful charm,
> Writ in a language that has long gone by.   (MV 669–672)

The mysterious text – in a language so old that "mountains have arisen" since it died out – is impossible for anyone to understand, and the densely packed marginal scholarship is legible only to Merlin (673). The curse that Vivien eventually extracts from him has come from the marginalia, implying a yet mightier tongue for the original material. Similarly, Merlin leaves behind at Camelot a chair (the Siege Perilous) carved with figures, around which "ran a scroll / Of letters in a tongue no man could read" (HG 170–171). The chair has the power to madden any who sit in it except (as it turns out) Galahad.

These scenes are emotionally successful exploitations of the ancient belief in language's power, but by making the magic explicit, they use this appealing notion in ways that make it purely fantastical. In "The Holy Grail," the grail appears in a vision: the roof cracks, and the knights hear "Thunder, and in the thunder was a cry" (185). As explored in Chapter 1, one of Tennyson's fixations was the near-language of noises in nature, but here the thunder is unequivocally a voice, and it is part of a miracle, together with "a beam of light seven times more clear than day" and the grail "all over cover'd with a luminous cloud" (187–189). Similarly, in "The Passing of Arthur," the king dreams of:

> the ghost of Gawain blown
> Along a wandering wind, and past his ear
> Went shrilling, "Hollow, hollow all delight!
> Hail, King! to-morrow thou shalt pass away.
> Farewell! there is an isle of rest for thee.
> And I am blown along a wandering wind,
> And hollow, hollow, hollow all delight."   (PA 31–37)

Section xcii of *In Memoriam* imagines that if Hallam's ghost appeared, the speaker might discount the visit as "a wind of memory," and even if the phantom gave

---

[83] Hair, *Tennyson's Language*, 139, 149.

prophecies that proved true, they might seem "spiritual presentiments" rather than otherworldly messages. In the elegy, the imaginary scene forms part of an ongoing rumination on the true meaning of the word *spirit*, discussed below. Here, the ghost is a straightforward harbinger, blown on the wind in accordance with classical tradition.

This moment is representative of the *Idylls* as a whole and their relationship with historical English. Language usage that, in another context, might encourage examination of Modern English, comes across as distinctly archaic because it is part of a cornucopia of explicit medievalism. *Idylls of the King* predominantly uses its historical words as aesthetic objects, maintaining their strangeness and purposely using terms that savor of the medieval in order to set the scene. The archaic words of this poem sequence are meant to establish the world of King Arthur, not to connect it to a Victorian reader's everyday speech or religious anxieties. Whereas Tennyson edited *In Memoriam*'s language to be simpler if possible, *Idylls of the King* makes the most of the decorative aspect of its archaisms. A handful of examples from "Gareth and Lynette" illustrates the principle well: a resentful knight suggests that Arthur repay an insulting suppliant with the "boon of gyve and gag" (362); Tennyson had recorded *gyve* (fetter) in one of his early notebook lists, and both it and *boon* connote medieval romances. Meat is roasted on a spit, and so it is Gareth's humble duty to "turn the broach" (476), a term Tennyson had pulled from the sixteenth-century play *Gammer Gurton's Needle* (as *broche*) when creating his glossary of archaic terms.[84] (He provided the definition in a note in the Eversley Edition.[85]) Evildoers are "caitiff-rogues" (799). These words do not speak to the ongoing vitality of the English language; this is pageantry.

Hopkins, though admiring much of Tennyson's skill, wrote to a friend in a letter of 1879, when all but one of the *Idylls* had been published:

> [Tennyson] sh[oul]d have called them *Charades from the Middle Ages* ... Each scene is a triumph of language and of bright picturesque ... just like a charade – where real lace and good silks and real jewelry are used ... but it is acting all the same and not only so but the make-up has less pretence of correct keeping than at Drury Lane.[86]

Hopkins objected that the *Idylls* were essentially performative, and although the costuming (that is, Tennyson's verbal skill) was luxurious, it did not even aspire to be as realistic as a theatrical production. Like Julia Margaret Cameron's photographic illustrations for them, the *Idylls* are poems playing dress-up. The wardrobe from which the costumes were taken included Malory's *Morte D'Arthur*, Layamon's *Brut*, the Middle English romance "Merlin," Geoffrey of Monmouth's history, and the other sources Tennyson consulted.

Defenders of the *Idylls* pointed to their moral, allegorical virtues – but allegory is itself a kind of dress-up. This is not necessarily a bad thing, but it leverages Tennyson's knowledge of historical language to only one kind of effect. His medievalist vocabulary remains part of the set design, as it were; it is the means by which he

---

[84] Weaver, *Tennyson's Notebook Glossary and Rhyme Lists*, 40, 13.
[85] Tennyson, *Idylls of the King*, 1908, 462.
[86] Jump, *Tennyson*, 334.

evokes the world of Camelot. Theatrical metaphors prove especially fitting when it comes to the objects that fill Tennyson's poems. In fact, many of the medieval words used in the *Idylls* are nouns for objects belonging to Arthurian romance, while others self-consciously evoke the speech of the late Middle Ages, as with *meseems*. His knights wear cuirasses and helms, and their damsels ride palfreys, while shields' designs are described using the terms of heraldry (with some terms helpfully defined in the Eversley Edition notes).[87] As for the characters, Arthur's court has seneschals and thralls, and the plot of "Gareth and Lynette" revolves around the former's pretense of being a mere *knave* (boy) rather than a knight.

As previous chapters have shown, Tennyson had a storehouse of appropriately aged words to employ in this project, some of them recorded in his handmade glossary of interesting archaisms. Indeed, many of the words that made it out of the glossary into his poetry did so in the *Idylls*. For example, Arthur's *tarriance* (LE 567) might have been remembered from Edward Fairfax's 1600 translation of Tasso. Tennyson retrieved *housel* (and its Old English root) from his notebook[88] to write that Guinevere "nor sought, / Wrapt in her grief, for housel or for shrift" (G 146–147) (the Eversley Edition notes inform readers that *housel* is from "Anglo-Saxon *husel*, the Eucharist").[89] *Shrift* may have come from his reading of *Hamlet* as an undergraduate, jotted down in a vocabulary list from that play. Drawing on Chaucer (via the notebook), Tennyson tells us that Guinevere plans to spend her days in a nunnery and repent through *almsdeed* (G 681).[90]

The difference of stylistic effect between the chivalry of the *Idylls* and the contemporary reflections of *In Memoriam* is exemplified by how *un-* adjectives strike the reader. The previous chapter discussed how this construction – slightly awkward for Modern English but entirely typical of older English – carries an archaic flavor. When Tennyson's Victorian mourner visits the "long unlovely street," the second adjective is embedded within otherwise ordinary language:

> Dark house, by which once more I stand
>   Here in the long unlovely street,
>   Doors, where my heart was used to beat
> So quickly, waiting for a hand   (vii.1–4)

In "Pelleas and Ettare," the same type of construction appears when Guinevere remarks to the surly Ettare:

> We marvel at thee much,
> O damsel, wearing this unsunny face
> To him who won thee glory!   (PE 172–174)

Placed among the royal *we*, the pronoun *thee* directed at a *damsel*, and the reference to a tournament victory, *unsunny* rings much more antiquated than *unlovely* does among a dark house, doors, and "my heart."

---

[87] Tennyson, *Idylls of the King*, 1908, 496.
[88] Weaver, *Tennyson's Notebook Glossary and Rhyme Lists*, 45–46, 33, 23.
[89] Tennyson, *Idylls of the King*, 1908, 506.
[90] Weaver, *Tennyson's Notebook Glossary and Rhyme Lists*, 40, 10.

Evoking and Invoking the Past 199

Unlike in other poems of Tennyson's oeuvre, historic usages remain archaic when they appear in the mythical medieval setting of the *Idylls*. As mentioned in Chapter 3, one of Trench's examples of how meanings shift over time was the portion of the Anglican marriage vows in which the bride and groom recite, "with my body I thee worship." Trench explains that to *worship* formerly meant no more than to *honor*.[91] Before Tennyson's Arthur enters his final battle, Bedivere promises that if "the dead have kings, / There also will I worship thee as King" (PA 148–149). The line undoubtedly re-introduces the original meaning of *worship* as *honor*, with assistance from its medieval context. Its modern sense is simultaneously present, coloring Bedivere's remark with a semi-blasphemous suggestion of Arthur's divinity. This ambiguity makes the moment interesting, but it is a closed loop: the archaic setting helps us see the old meaning, informing us of how people in the past formerly employed the word *worship*. In short, the poems' medievalism is a mutually reinforcing relationship between lexis and setting.

In "Gareth and Lynette," Gareth and his companions stare at the figures on the gate of Camelot until "it seem'd / The dragon-boughts and elvish emblemings / Began to move" (GL 229). Two word choices are noteworthy here. The first is *dragon-boughts*, which Tennyson explained with a lengthy note in the Eversley Edition, defining them as "bends (German *Beugen*), folds of the dragons' tails."[92] (Note the philological scholarship he calls in for support.) The poet then further supports his definition with quotations from Spenser's *Faerie Queene* and Milton's *L'Allegro*. The OED marks this meaning of *bought* as obsolete, with most quotations petering out in the seventeenth century. It further notes that the specific sense of "A coil, fold, or 'knot' formed by the body of a serpent, the tail of a horse, etc." is "Now poetic (revived by Tennyson)." The dictionary entry quotes "Gareth and Lynette" and the same excerpt of Spenser that Tennyson cited. As for Tennyson's dictionaries, Bailey (1721) had *bight* and *bought* as variant words for the bend of a horse's knees, and Johnson's dictionary (1831 edition) had offered the same passage of the *Faerie Queene* as well as some lines from Milton. Richardson (1836–1837) provided a much-expanded entry that gave an Anglo-Saxon root for bowing/bending and also was the first to specifically define "The *bought* of a serpent; the flexures, bends, curves, folds or involutions." He gave six quotations for this noun, including Spenser and Milton. Here, then, Tennyson is reviving a fine old word with an elite literary lineage in which it was already archaically poetic.

In addition to arcane vocabulary, the other techniques described in this book are present in the Arthurian sequence, but again the poems' pageantry influences how those techniques are perceived. For example, in the passage quoted above, *emblemings* is a noteworthy term. The OED has only one example of *embleming* as a noun, from Thomas Carlyle's "Heroes and Hero-Worship" (1841), where it is used (as the dictionary defines it) as the verb *to emblem* – that is, "To be the emblem of [something]." In Tennyson's poem, the emblemings are carved features – physical objects – that seem to move, an unattested sense (in Tennyson's dictionaries, as well). This is a rare example of linguistic innovation in the *Idylls*. But so strong is the medievalist context of the poem that even coinages or new usages have all the appearance of

[91] Trench, *English, Past and Present*, 168–169.
[92] Tennyson, *Idylls of the King*, 1908, 460.

archaisms, such as *misadvertence*, for which Tennyson is the first example provided in the *OED* (HG 175).

The *Idylls* also abound with strong-verb conjugations that enhance the archaizing work of their style: Arthur "drave the heathen hence" (GL 201); it is rare to read that characters spoke – usually they "spake;" after placing Arthur on the barge, Bedivere "clomb / Ev'n to the highest he could climb" (PA 462–463); and so forth. The principle behind these conjugations is no different from *In Memoriam*'s "dragons of the prime, / That tare [tore] each other" (lvi.22–23) or the happy times when "A guest, or happy sister, sung … A ballad to the brightening moon" (lxxxix.26, 28). Yet in the Arthurian tales, the antiquated conjugations form one part of a larger apparatus for locating the stories in the past, whereas *In Memoriam*'s strong verbs slightly raise the register of its reflections by being arcane.

The presence of these strong verbs demonstrates that Tennyson could write poems of romance and chivalry without relying heavily on Romance language to achieve his effects. Indeed, even in these chivalric works, the Germanic branch of English predominates.[93] In fact, contemporaries praised the relatively "pure" – that is, non-Latinate – origins of the words in these poems.[94] Matthew Reynolds sees the *Idylls* as using etymological origin to set up a contrast between Arthur's adamantly Anglo-Saxon vocabulary (and his adherence to vows), and his insidious Latinate enemies. Even as the kingdom falls apart, Tennyson's work "remains predominantly Anglo-Saxon in dictional character throughout," and Reynolds reads this continued "dictional character" as Tennyson's loyalty to the king's ideals.[95] Yet as we have seen, Tennyson and the Cambridge Apostles considered truth to be multifaceted. It would be more accurate to say that the poet's habitual preference for Anglo-Saxon word-choice becomes more prominent as the tragedy builds toward "The Passing of Arthur." This concluding poem constructed its tragedy with great benefit from Anglo-Saxon example.

"The Passing of Arthur"

Tennyson's great strength as a poet was the contemplation of character, states of nature, and states of mind. In poems that restrain themselves to such static subject matter, there is time and space in which to appreciate words used unusually. The *Idylls of the King* struggle somewhat with the need to progress through their plots, a problem that "The Princess" had also exhibited.[96] After mostly praising the *Idylls* in an 1859 review, Walter Bagehot concluded that Tennyson's imagination "seems to fix itself on a particular person in a particular situation" and explore that moment wonderfully, as in "Ulysses" – but "the power of writing a soliloquy is very different

---

[93] Matthew Reynolds, *The Realms of Verse 1830–1870: English Poetry in a Time of Nation-Building* (Oxford: Oxford University Press, 2001), 268–270.
[94] Hair, *Tennyson's Language*, 135–136.
[95] Reynolds, *Realms of Verse*, 269–270.
[96] "The Princess" announced its explicitly performative approach to medievalism by means of a frame narrative that premised the tale as a storytelling game among a group of young men contemplating a ruined abbey and an old statue.

from that of writing a conversation."[97] For these reasons, "The Passing of Arthur" is among the most successful of the idylls; it displays a more dynamic, philological, and ultimately effective, use of vocabulary than do the others. It also borrows from Anglo-Saxon poetic techniques, keeping its narrative connections minimal and juxtaposing blasts of sensation with simple grammar. Tennyson wrote in the Eversley Edition that "The form of the *Coming of Arthur* and of the *Passing* is purposely more archaic than that of the other Idylls," and examination bears out this claim.[98]

"The Passing of Arthur" grew around the core of "Morte d'Arthur," a poem that Tennyson composed in 1833–1834 under the influence of his grief for the passing of the real-life Arthur Hallam. He was also studying Old English literature at the time, and this "final" (but first-written) idyll blends its borrowed medieval vocabulary with touches from Anglo-Saxon tradition. Lexically, the Old English branch predominates. When Arthur is placed upon the barge, with "all his greaves and cuisses dash'd with drops / Of onset," the terminology is clearly that of chivalry (383–384), but it is more typical to read, in the lines immediately preceding, that Bedivere:

> called him by his name, complaining loud,
> And dropping bitter tears against a brow
> Striped with blood: for all his face was white
> And colourless, and like the withered moon
> Smote by the fresh beam of the springing east.   (378–382)

In this passage, only *complaining* and *colourless* derive from non-Germanic etymologies.

Throughout the poem, Tennyson solves the problem of plot by juxtaposing vignettes with very little connective tissue; in this, he took a page from Old English poetry, in which action often continues with a blunt *þa* ("then"), especially "then spoke." Consider the following first lines of sections in this idyll:

Then, ere that last weird battle in the west,	(29)
Then spake King Arthur to Sir Bedivere	(65, 136, 181, 234)
Then rose the King and moved his host by night	(80)
Then spake the bold Sir Bedivere	(147)
Then spake the King	(154)
And answer made the bold Sir Bedivere	(237, 283, 319)
Then went Sir Bedivere the second time	(250)
Then spoke King Arthur, breathing heavily	(281)
Then quickly rose Sir Bedivere, and ran,	(301)
Then spoke King Arthur	(316)
And answer made King Arthur, breathing hard	(330)
Then saw they how there hove a dusky barge	(362)
Then murmur'd Arthur	(373)
Then loudly cried the bold Sir Bedivere	(394)

---

[97] Jump, *Tennyson*, 230.
[98] Tennyson, *Idylls of the King*, 1908, 453.

> And slowly answer'd Arthur from the barge (407)
> Then from the dawn it seem'd there came (457)

The pattern employs simplicity and fracture rather than syntax that labors to create forward motion. Malory's version also begins sentences with *and* and *then*, but they are dispersed among more fluid sentences and therefore stand out less starkly.

Tennyson uses the same kind of disjointed transition in his masterful presentation of the final battle. In depicting the fight between the king's knights and Modred's army in the "deathwhite mist" (a late recurrence of unhyphenated compounding), he borrows heavily from Anglo-Saxon style. There is little narrative progression as such; rather, the battle takes place in a state of confusion comprised of bursts of sensory input, connected by "and":

> For friend and foe were shadows in the mist,
> And friend slew friend not knowing whom he slew;
> And some had visions out of golden youth,
> And some beheld the faces of old ghosts
> Look in upon the battle; and in the mist
> Was many a noble deed, many a base
> And chance and craft and strength in single fights. (100–107)

A disorderly concurrence of images bewilders judgment, so that the knights cannot tell whether they are fighting friend or foe, nor whether they are seeing the faces of real men or ghosts. The battle then becomes a series of sounds:

> Shocks, and the splintering spear, the hard mail hewn,
> Shield-breakings, and the clash of brands, the crash
> Of battleaxes on shatter'd helms, and shrieks
> After the Christ, of those who falling down
> Look'd up for heaven, and only saw the mist;
> And shouts of heathen and the traitor knights,
> Oaths, insult, filth and monstrous blasphemies,
> Sweat, writhings, anguish, labouring of the lungs
> In that close mist, and cryings for the light,
> Moans of the dying, and voices of the dead. (108–117)

Sight has completely disappeared, its only mention being the absence of vision for "those who falling down / Look'd up for heaven, and only saw the mist." We are left with the intriguingly impossible sound of "voices of the dead," the "cryings for the light" echoing *In Memoriam*'s "infant crying for the light."

Moreover, the sound of the words in the passage enhances the aurality of the battle. The alliteration of *splintering spear* is augmented by the partial alliteration of *shocks*, which is then echoed in the following line by *shield-breakings* – a Germanic compound that would be equally at home in a translation from Old English poetry. Line 108 creates a caesura after *spear* as the meter changes from dactyls to the alliterating iambs of "the hard mail hewn." Line 109 continues by linking *-breakings* with *brands*, as well as the onomatopoeic near-homonyms *clash* and *crash*. In the following line (110), the compound *battleaxes* recalls the earlier *b* sound, before *shatter'd* pairs with *shrieks*. The devastating contrast of line 112 is enhanced by the vowel alliteration when fallen men "look'd *u*p for heaven, and *o*nly saw the mist." The five lines that follow consist of an escalating catalogue of battlefield affliction. In addition to some further alliteration (labouring … lungs, close … cryings, dying … dead), Germanic and Latinate vocabulary multiply the range of suffering.[99]

Finally, silence falls. No voices are heard from either side, leaving "only the wan wave … rolling … The voice of days of old and days to be" (129, 134–135). From here, the action contracts to Arthur and Bedivere, Tennyson having excised Malory's additional knight. Roger Simpson[100] and J.M. Gray have offered illuminating readings of "how subtly Tennyson interwove Malory with elements from Homer, Virgil, and Milton to create and sustain an effect wholly his own."[101] Missing from this inventory is Old English, but intertwined with his other sources glint threads from Anglo-Saxon poetry. Arthur's passing, like Beowulf's, heralds political chaos that will soon overwhelm the land. Bedivere faces a bleak prospect:

> I, the last, go forth companionless,
> And the days darken round me, and the years,
> Among new men, strange faces, other minds.   (404–406)

Tennyson's description is a model of Anglo-Saxon woe – especially the horror at losing one's clan – conveyed with characteristic apposition. This is far different from Malory's text, which expresses a more open-ended lament: "'Ah my lord Arthur, what shall become of me, now ye go from me and leave me here alone among mine enemies?'"[102]

What makes "The Passing of Arthur" less performative than many of the idylls that precede it is not only the sincerity of its inspiration, though that may be the root cause of its stylistic success. This poem draws on Old English poetic characteristics to deliver its story with simplicity and universality, minimizing its reminders of the chivalric era in which it takes place. It shifts more toward invoking the past as compared to its companions, which evoke it. As the final idyll, it therefore proves effective in conveying that the medieval world of the Round Table is gone, that the performances of the knights in tournaments and deeds of honor have come to an end. Another poem with its genesis in Arthur Hallam's death is, of course, *In Memoriam*. It is much sparer than *Idylls of the King* in every regard, but it showcases the poet's philological prowess more than any other. The great elegy contains examples of all the techniques described in this book; the next section explores how Tennyson brought them all to bear to enhance the major concerns of his masterpiece.

---

[99] The non-Germanic words of this passage are: shocks, mail, battle, traitor, insult, monstrous, blasphemies, anguish, labourings, close, cryings, voices.

[100] Roger Simpson, *Camelot Regained: The Arthurian Revival and Tennyson, 1800–1849*, Arthurian Studies 21 (Cambridge: D.S. Brewer, 1990).

[101] J.M. Gray, *Thro' the Vision of the Night: A Study of Source, Evolution and Structure in Tennyson's "Idylls of the King"* (Edinburgh: Edinburgh University Press, 1980), 12.

[102] Thomas Malory, *Le Morte D'Arthur*, ed. Janet Cowen, vol. 2 (London: Penguin, 1969), 517.

"The spirit does but mean the breath": *In Memoriam*

Unsurprisingly, Tennyson's masterwork bears the marks of its author's philological curiosity. Donald S. Hair has discussed how *In Memoriam* engages with philosophy of language; close investigation reveals that these concerns are manifest on both large and small scales.[103] The poem wrestles simultaneously with the mysteries of death and language, each struggle informing the other. Thematically, *In Memoriam* is preoccupied with silence (Hallam's) and the limitations of words (Tennyson's). Section lxxxii, for example, succinctly states, "I wage not any feud with Death" except the severing of communication:

> For this alone on Death I wreak
>   The wrath that garners in my heart;
>   He put our lives so far apart
> We cannot hear each other speak.   (13–16)

As Elizabeth A. Hirsh notes, the silence is especially disconcerting because Hallam had been an eloquent speaker, suggesting that his death may be the death of meaningful speech altogether.[104] Left with only his own voice, the mourner is also frustrated by the inadequacy of words to describe experience. Peter M. Sacks argues that part of the psychological process of creating an elegy is "the elegist's reluctant submission to language itself," and this certainly holds true for Tennyson.[105] *In Memoriam* states the problem of language's limitations in section v – namely, that "words, like Nature, half reveal / And half conceal the Soul within" (3–4). The very process of creating the poem is untrue to the experience of grieving, for "My words are only words, and moved / Upon the topmost froth of thought" (lii.3–4). And again, "What practice howsoe'er expert / In fitting aptest words to things … Hath power to give thee as thou wert?" (lxxv.5–8).

Steven Connor observes that "seeing and hearing may be understood … as an active and interrogative scanning of the visual and auditory fields, in search of particular kinds of form." Human beings presented with a "confused set of sounds," he writes, seem "impelled to wonder at the outset if there is a voice to be made out of them." This is a useful perspective from which to view Tennyson's elegy, which is a poem in search of voice amidst a chaotic experience that seems to lack cohesion; the poem is an active scanning of every sensory field in hopes of discerning a pattern that will make sense of life and death. If we adopt Connor's distinction that "noise is accident, voice is intent" and therefore "noise has no importance, voice is full of portent," *In Memoriam*'s search for (Hallam's) voice is both literal and metaphorical.[106]

When in search of a firm foundation for nonarbitrary language, etymology is usually the first recourse. It is appealing because it seems to promise a real and/or original meaning, as well as offering a glimpse into a population's way of viewing the world at particular moments in its history. Yet, historical usage showed that the

---

[103] Hair, "Soul and Spirit in 'In Memoriam.'"
[104] Hirsh, "No Record of Reply," 133–134.
[105] Peter M. Sacks, *The English Elegy: Studies in the Genre from Spenser to Yeats* (Baltimore: Johns Hopkins University Press, 1985), 2.
[106] Connor, *Beyond Words*, 7.

same set of syllables could suggest wildly different or even contradictory ideas. The word *cleave* is a perfect example of how language can undo itself. It means – and has since at least the year 1100 – both to divide (as in "The Lotos-Eaters" 165) and to adhere (for example, in "Œnone" 160). Tennyson used the former sense eight times in his poetic corpus, the latter ten times.[107] For some, this linguistic imprecision was cause for alarm. Some philologists – whether they acknowledged it or not – were hunting for a lost language in which sound and sense were inseparable. However, both Trench and his college mentor Hare dismissed words that are mere one-to-one symbols – hence Trench's objection to including technical vocabulary in dictionaries, since they "are not for the most part ... words at all, but signs ... and, so to speak, the algebraic notation of some special art or science."[108] To wish for a language with one and only one meaning per word is to assume a certain literalism and rigidity to reality and human perception of it. Such a language would be precise, but it presumes that there is only one truth to tell.

In contrast, *In Memoriam* expresses ambivalence on every scale, and the uncertain meanings of important words help express the speaker's spiritual uncertainty. In Alan Sinfield's words, "*In Memoriam* is based upon the premise that statements about the truths which most vitally concern mankind cannot be definite."[109] Patrick Greig Scott finds that "in his earlier poems Tennyson uses the etymological root of a word forcefully and directly for his own meaning, while in his later poems such etymological 'meanings' seem rather to be possibilities, potential explications to be held in tension with the overlay of modern usage."[110] In his elegy, Tennyson moves toward the latter strategy, using his knowledge of multiple possible meanings to reflect the speaker's uncertainty about spiritual matters.

The philosophy of the Cambridge Apostles would have encouraged openness to unstable plurality in the search for truth. For Hare, parts did not need to reconcile into a consistent theoretical whole. What mattered was the honesty of each attempt to grasp at truth; as long as that was the case, contradictions were actually useful, because they prompted the reader to make sense of conflicting material. As one section of *Guesses at Truth* put it, "Contrast is a kind of relation." In describing Horace's writings, for example, Hare writes that although his statements might contradict one another, "Their very contradictions prove their truth."[111] In the case of *In Memoriam*, the multiple meanings available within Tennyson's words destabilize statements of faith, or more accurately allow possible truths to remain open.

William Empson makes a distinction between a word considered "poetically" and "prosaically" that is useful in examining this technique: "A poetical word," he says, "is a thing conceived in itself and includes all its meanings; a prosaic word is flat and useful and might have been used differently."[112] By this definition, new philologists such as Trench and Müller were interested in seeing the words of regular speech poetically. Tennyson wrote his poetry with the same inclusive attention: His

---

[107] Baker, *Concordance*, 100.
[108] Trench, *Deficiencies*, 57.
[109] Sinfield, *The Language of Tennyson's In Memoriam*, 68.
[110] Scott, "Flowering in a Lonely Word," 375–376.
[111] Hare, *Guesses at Truth, by Two Brothers: Two Series in One Volume*, 129, 2.
[112] Empson, *Seven Types of Ambiguity*, 252.

words are poetical not just because they appear in a poem but because he keeps active all of their meanings. As Sinfield puts it, "Traditional diction in [*In Memoriam*] encourages us to perceive ambiguities involving the operation of archaic meanings."[113] Although Empson was dismissive of Tennyson and nineteenth-century poetry in general, *In Memoriam* is rich in Empsonian ambiguity – particularly his third type, in which "two ideas, which are connected only by being both relevant in the context, can be given in one word simultaneously. This is often done by reference to derivations."[114] For example, when Tennyson describes Hallam "ere our fatal loss," the meaning of *fatal* hovers between the ordinary sense of Hallam's death and the etymological origin of the term as *fated* (xli.1). Similarly, the poem's obsession with the word *strange* reflects (in its etymological sense) Hallam having moved to the "undiscovered country" of whatever lies beyond death.

These moments consist of etymological puns, and as Matthew Bevis has discussed, "puns search out communities from within apparent solitude as a single word suddenly finds itself part of a couple." Thus, at some level, they "remind us that different significances of a word are potentially in play whenever that word is uttered."[115] Etymological puns have the combined effect of teaching us the root of a word yet also highlighting its duality. We read, therefore, that "No spirit ever brake the band / That stays him from the native land / Where first he walk'd when claspt in clay" (xciii.2–4). The fact of *native* etymologically signifying where one was born becomes prominent through the infant imagery of "where first he walk'd," combined with the contrast of birth and death. When the speaker seems "to fail from out my blood / and grow incorporate" into the churchyard yew tree, *incorporate* becomes a pun between *combined* and *bodiless*. This wordplay may have suggested itself to Tennyson from whatever reading caused him to write in his college notebook "incorpsed, incorporate."[116]

When section xviii is glad that Hallam's bones may lie in English soil "among familiar names ... and in the places of his youth" (7–8), the root of *familiar* tells us that his body rests both in a place well-known to Hallam and that he literally is interred among the grave markers of his family. After an encouraging trance is "cancell'd, stricken thro' with doubt," the speaker returns to a world wrapped in "doubtful dusk," the repetition of *doubt* setting up a resonance between religious uncertainty and visual darkness (xcv.44, 49). Perhaps most pointedly of all, the mourner dreams of boarding a ship, where he meets Hallam again and they sail off together "while the wind began to sweep / A music out of sheet and shroud" (ciii.53–54). An editor's note may tell us that *sheet* and *shroud* refer to types of rope on a ship, but in an elegy, they cannot help but bring connotations of burial garments.

In section xi, Tennyson bridges between the metaphorical and literal to brilliant effect. His repetition of "calm" in describing nature lulls the reader into thinking at first that "dead calm" refers to the sea; when we discover that it describes Hallam's body, the literal side of that expression is thrown into sudden relief. This dark pun

---

[113] Sinfield, *The Language of Tennyson's In Memoriam*, 59.

[114] Empson, *Seven Types of Ambiguity*, 102.

[115] Matthew Bevis, "Tennyson's Humour," in *Tennyson Among the Poets: Bicentenary Essays*, ed. Robert Douglas-Fairhurst and Seamus Perry (Oxford: Oxford University Press, 2009), 240, 238.

[116] Weaver, *Tennyson's Notebook Glossary and Rhyme Lists*, 40.

re-creates the shock of realization that often revisits a mourner after temporarily being distracted from grief. Just as describing an emotional experience from several angles allows a poet to express it fully,[117] a philologically sensitive writer could put to work the multiplicity of possible meanings that can accompany a single word. Such possibilities complicate any apparently confident statement – a useful effect in a composition that has an ambivalent relationship with religion. At the same time, linguistic ambiguity can act as a partial solution for religious doubt, because it evades a fixed doctrine that might inhibit any belief at all.

A creed is an expression of beliefs in fixed, rigid wording – the term itself deriving from the beginning of the Latin statement of Christian doctrine, *credo*: "I believe." Nothing could be more antithetical to Tennyson's approach to religion, which complemented the speculative attitude of many of his friends. For the Apostles, the search for truth was a good in itself, and in fact settling on an opinion for too long was a sign of a calcifying mind. In the words of Apostles historian W.C. Lubenow, "They celebrated the search for truth, with its appreciation for its many-sidedness." In religion, one of the sticking points for a number of Apostles in receiving their Cambridge degrees was the requirement that they affirm the Thirty-Nine Articles of the Anglican Church.[118] Though many eventually took holy orders, Tennyson expressed their collective attitude when he wrote:

> Our little systems have their day;
>   They have their day and cease to be:
>   They are but broken lights of thee,
> And thou, O Lord, art more than they.   (Prologue 17–20)

Even Trench, who eventually proved an orthodox and eminent clergyman, reveled in exploring layers of potential meaning. Two years before he started university, his mother reported, "He wishes much we should purchase a certain Polyglot, and luxuriates in the idea of finding fifteen readings of the same passage in Scripture."[119] This tendency served him well when he wrote *Notes on the Parables of Our Lord* and *Notes on the Miracles of Our Lord*, books of detailed Scriptural interpretation.

From the point of view that "There lives more faith in honest doubt … than in half the creeds" (xcvi.11–12), it is appropriate that *In Memoriam* should demonstrate how Tennyson could use etymology and historical usage to reflect the complexity of his theological thinking. After all:

> If these brief lays, of Sorrow born,
>   Were taken to be such as closed
>   Grave doubts and answers here proposed,
> Then these were such as men might scorn.   (xlviii.1–4)

That is to say, poems that offered pat answers to "grave doubts" – note the pun about questioning the nature of death – would not be worthy of anyone's respect. Fortunately, Tennyson could draw on his philological knowledge to avoid this pitfall.

---

[117] Sinfield, *The Language of Tennyson's In Memoriam*, 6–7, 29.
[118] Lubenow, *The Cambridge Apostles*, 59, 373–385.
[119] Trench, *Letters and Memorials*, 1:xiii.

In the phrase "matter-moulded forms of speech," for example, "both idealist and materialist interpretations find room to manoeuvre," as Angela Leighton writes.[120] In section xli, the speaker worries that he will no longer be Hallam's companion "Though following with an upward mind / The wonders that have come to thee, / Through all the secular to-be" (21–23). The Eversley annotation glosses "secular to-be" as "æons of the future."[121] Per this interpretation, the poem is using *secular* in a sense derived from Latin for an age (that is, a long time). This meaning echoes the Latin version of the Gloria Patri of the church service: "in sæcula sæculorum," to age of ages – that is, forever and ever. But *secular* can also mean – as Tennyson used it later in *Queen Mary* – nonreligious (the *OED* uses Tennyson as an exemplar of these two different meanings of *secular*). This materialist sense remains present, troubling the assurance that the lines seem to offer.

Among the ambiguities usefully created by philology are *In Memoriam*'s speculations as to Hallam's postmortem existence. Tennyson remarked that "Milton's vague hell is much more awful than Dante's hell marked off into divisions," and he took the lesson to heart.[122] In imagining Arthur Hallam's heaven, he considers several potential forms for it, but each is relatively vague, and each remains only a possibility. With the help of philology, he refrains from asserting a particular vision of the afterlife, no doubt feeling that to do so would be untrue both to the reality of that afterlife and to his own uncertainty regarding it.

In particular, the poem repeatedly speculates on the nature of Hallam's soul to try to understand what type of spiritual environment he inhabits. Philology helps multiply this diverse set of possibilities. Indeed, *In Memoriam*'s search for the basis of meaningful articulation, which cannot be located yet undeniably exists, mirrors its attempt to imagine Hallam's unknowable existence. In section xciii, the speaker asks Hallam's spirit to visit:

> from thy sightless range
> With gods in unconjectured bliss,
> O, from the distance of the abyss
> Of tenfold-complicated change. (9–12)

The "tenfold-complicated change" hints at Dante's ten levels of heaven, where Hallam supposedly spends his time conversing with great intellects. With the help of the Dante reference, *complicated* gestures toward its obsolete definition, "folded together," in addition to "complex, intricate." Tennyson had used it the same way in his early poem "Timbuctoo" (223). The "folded together" meaning of *complicated* is also suggested by "tenfold," which Tennyson uses in the sense "Ranged in ten folds, or ten deep." The *OED* identifies this version of the word as an "isolated" use from Joel Barlow's 1807 poem *The Columbiad*, apparently having missed this Tennysonian appearance. The region is a *range*, which could suggest a vaguely mountainous topography, or refer to the aggregate of beings inhabiting the space, or instead

---

[120] Angela Leighton, "Touching Forms: Tennyson and Aestheticism," *Essays in Criticism* 52, no. 1 (January 1, 2002): 64.
[121] Tennyson, *Enoch Arden and In Memoriam*, 237.
[122] Hallam Tennyson, *Memoir*, 2:518.

represent not a location at all but rather Hallam's movement through an undefined space. *Range* is in a position where it seems that it should define the location of Hallam's spirit, but in fact it gives next to no information.

Tennyson's son recalled that "He dreaded the dogmatism of sects and rash definitions of God."[123] Rather than resort to such definitions – which place limitations on God's being – the poet kept many possibilities active in pondering spiritual matters. In particular, breath, speech, singing, and spirit – with their linked etymological metaphors – have powerful significance in Tennyson's poetry. With regard to the ways that philological multiplicity and punning enhance the poem's uncertainty about spiritual matters, the most profound complexity is to be found in its contemplation of the word *spirit* itself. The etymology of *spirit* reverberates throughout the poem's vocabulary, sometimes expressing the horror of death and sometimes working through the word's metaphorical usages to imagine Arthur Hallam's new state of being.

The Etymology of "Spirit"

The word *spirit* derives from Latin *spiritus*, meaning breath or breathing. The word has long been associated with the idea of breath and descriptions God and God's actions – the latter analogy dating to Hebrew theology and also associated with powerful wind.[124] This etymology was widely known, and it was common to say that the spirit of something breathed through an event or a work. *In Memoriam* makes this gesture in section cv, when the speaker suggests that Christmas not be festive, "For who would keep an ancient form / Thro' which the spirit breathes no more?" (19–20). Through repeated occurrences of the words *breath* and *spirit*, often in close proximity, the poem invites an exploration of different aspects of the word *spirit* – its etymology, its associated religious imagery, its connection to speaking, and the physicality of breath in the body – in order to come to the conclusion that *spirit* must include all of them.

We need only look to section xvii for an example confluence of various usages and images associated with breathing, speech, spirit, and wind. The speaker addresses the ship carrying Hallam's body:

> Thou comest, much wept for: such a breeze
>   Compell'd thy canvas, and my prayer
>   Was as the whisper of an air
> To breathe thee over lonely seas.
>
> For I in spirit saw thee move   (1–5)

The next section expresses the speaker's desire for the ability to breathe life back into Hallam's body, with an uncomfortable physicality that becomes figurative and spiritual in the stanza's final line:

---

[123] Hallam Tennyson, *Memoir*, 1:311.
[124] Lloyd Rudolph Neve, *The Spirit of God in the Old Testament* (Tokyo: Seibunsha, 1972), 7–13.

> Ah yet, ev'n yet, if this might be,
>   I, falling on his faithful heart,
>   Would breathing thro' his lips impart
> The life that almost dies in me.   (xviii.13–16)

Here and throughout *In Memoriam*, Tennyson plays off the tension between breath as physical and metaphysical.[125] Section xiii mourns the fact that Hallam is now "a Spirit, not a breathing voice" (12). Yet, by reinforcing the idea of spirit as breath and vitally fused with the body, as happens at various points, the poem raises potentially terrible implications in the fact that Hallam's chest "heaves but with the heaving deep" – that is, is not breathing at all (xi.20). To the extent that breath is physical, it is psychologically threatening to the speaker, because Hallam is not breathing with his lungs.

One of the many possible interpretations of Hallam's death with which the speaker must grapple is that, if spirit equals breath, and there is no breath, there may be no spirit, either. Hence Nature's great materialist threat is, "The spirit does but mean the breath: / I know no more" (lvi.7–8). Personified Nature exclusively asserts the literal (physical) etymological meaning of *spirit*. In doing so, she expresses *In Memoriam*'s central worry: we cannot know the nature of the spirit, or whether it exists at all. Her threat relies on the old idea that etymology reveals the truth of a word. However, Tennyson took full advantage of the historic link between the words *breath* and *spirit* to both consider and reject Nature's simple etymological stance and favor the solution offered by the historic metaphors attached to those words. In this, he also takes a position on the proper use of philology. Its goal is not to find literal truth in word fragments but rather, as Trench would later describe, to illuminate internal metaphors. Donald S. Hair writes that "*In Memoriam* tells the story of the word 'spirit,' from its 'matter-moulded' origin to its full meaning in Tennyson's actual experience,"[126] but it is not a linear progression. Instead, the elegy repeatedly considers the relative physicality of the spirit in a search for its essence.

Certainly, the poem illustrates abundantly the metaphor of *spirit* through its imagery. Breath is essential to speaking, and Tennyson employs a common substitution of the verb *breathe* for *speak*, as when we read of "lesser griefs that may be said, / That breathe a thousand tender vows" (xx.1–2), or when the speaker says he must "breathe my loss" despite the censure of others (lxxvii.15). Hair argues that "The voice with its life-giving breath seems to be for Tennyson the chief manifestation of the spirit."[127] He overstates the case somewhat; it is Tennyson's exploration of both the literal and metaphorical versions of breath that expresses his struggle to imagine Hallam's afterlife. With the history of *spirit* in mind, we can see a wordplay in section xcii, in which the speaker says he would not believe a vision of Hallam were real even if he saw it. No matter what evidence the likeness might provide, "I might but say, I hear a wind / Of memory murmuring the past" (7–8). It might be a false, murmuring wind, not a true spirit. Connor observes that in general "Voice is …

---

[125] It is a tension that emerges elsewhere in Victorian poetry through the frequency of rhyming *breath* with *death*.
[126] Hair, *Tennyson's Language*, 12.
[127] Hair, "Soul and Spirit in 'In Memoriam,'" 187.

identified as pure air in motion; paradoxically, when the noise of voice is removed from the breath, when, that is, we actually hear that breath as mere blind passage of air, this pure and unadulterated current starts to be heard as a kind of noise."[128] Hence *In Memoriam*'s speaker expresses an anxious desire to hear Hallam's voice again, not just the noise of wind.

More directly engaging with the etymology of *spirit* are the moments when *In Memoriam* describes the afterlife in terms of breathing. The phrase "look on Spirits breathed away" (xl.2) recalls the etymological meaning but also attaches motion to Hallam's soul. It transforms the action of dying – a moment intuitively understood as cessation of breath – into transportation: to die is to be "breathed away" (that is, expire, an oblique etymological pun). Similarly, Hallam possibly "breathes a novel world" as his spirit moves on to another realm (lxii.9). Another section declares we must "trust that those we call the dead / Are breathers of an ampler day" (cxviii.5–6). In blurring the lines between ideas of breath, spirit, voice, and wind, Tennyson explores the connotations of the *spirit* metaphor. He bridges between these categories, as when he writes that "The slightest air of song shall breathe / To make the sullen surface crisp" (xlix.7–8). In this instance, *air* puns between a type of song and a puff of air, and *breathe* could work as singing or gentle blowing of wind.

Section xcix describes dawn on the second anniversary of Hallam's death, a day "loud with voices of the birds" and "thick with lowings of the herds" (2–3), a day that "murmurest in the foliaged eaves" (9). In this highly vocal context, "meadows breathing of the past" obviously speak memories, but the natural setting also suggests a wind blowing in the meadows. Likewise, if the reader is aware of the packed meaning of *spirit*, then the line "[Love] breathed the spirit of the song" (cxxv.10) fuses breath, voice, and spirit in a way that exemplifies what Tennyson does with these ideas throughout the poem. The poet asks us to hold available a wider set of possibilities than the simple etymology offered by materialist Nature. The word *spirit* is an example of Trench's principle that "Many a single word … is itself a concentrated poem, having stores of poetical thought and imagery laid up in it."[129] Or to use Empson's phrase, Tennyson insists that his theological words must be considered poetically.

Glooms and Gleams

While recognizing *In Memoriam*'s masterful use of ambiguity, we should not overlook the presence of philological techniques described in earlier chapters. As elsewhere in the corpus, Tennyson makes manifest etymological, historical, or alternative meanings through context, as in the prologue when he desires that "mind and soul, according well, / May make one music as before" (27–28). The musical reference draws out the alternative sense of the verb *accord*, meaning to tune an instrument or to play in harmony, further aided by the auditory pun of (musical) chord within *accord*. Section lxi presents the paradox of being "blanch'd with darkness," with a literal-etymological meaning of "whitened with darkness" (8). The Eversley

---

[128] Connor, *Beyond Words*, 39.
[129] Trench, *On the Study of Words*, 5.

Edition glosses *In Memoriam*'s "crescent prime" as "growing spring,"[130] revealing that the poem uses the literal Latin sense of the adjective, derived from *crescere*, to grow. The use of *prime* to mean *spring* is markedly obsolete, barely attested after Shakespeare – but Shakespeare is more than enough authority for Tennyson.

Patrick Greig Scott describes how investigating the etymology of Tennyson's compositions can reveal a "lively metaphor" where a passage may have seemed vague or inflated, giving as an example "branding summer suns" in section ii, which addresses the churchyard yew tree:

> O not for thee the glow, the bloom,
> > Who changest not in any gale,
> > Nor branding summer suns avail
> To touch thy thousand years of gloom.   (9–12)

Scott points out that for the word *branding* in these lines, the Anglo-Saxon meaning of *scorching* is the closest fit.[131] Indeed, Tennyson had used the word in the same sense in "St Simeon Stylites" (composed 1833), the would-be martyr saying he has been "twice / Blacked with thy branding thunder" (75–76). Some twenty years later, the speaker of "Maud" calls the stars "Cold fires, yet with power to burn and brand / His nothingness into man" (I.637–638).

Scott's example gains further support if we observe the use of *gloom* in the subsequent line of the stanza. The gloom most simply reads as the unchanging foliage of the yew tree, with an obvious pathetic fallacy in attendance. However, a philological reading offers an additional layer of potential reference. Richardson's *New English Dictionary* (1836–1837), which was a resource for Tennyson, took its history of *gloom* from John Horne Tooke (the influential if imaginative eighteenth-century etymologist), who traced it to Anglo-Saxon for "to irradiate, to enlighten. *Gloom* is that which is *gleamed* or enlightened … the darkness *gleamed* or enlightened, through which the light penetrates, or by which it is overshadowed."[132] Here, to borrow Trench's metaphor again, the "tiny dewdrop" of word choice and the "mighty ocean" of the larger statement support each other. The tree's gloom is something which should be illuminated by the "branding summer suns" but instead proves impenetrable.

As Chris Jones has observed, *gloom* "is an etymological paradox" that Tennyson exploits when *In Memoriam* compares life to "iron dug from central gloom / And heated hot."[133] That paradox seems to have intrigued Tennyson throughout his career. The concordance of his works shows that *gloom* was a word he returned to frequently, occurring twelve times in *In Memoriam* alone.[134] Across the span of his corpus, Tennyson explored the word for its every echo. In fact, he provides *OED* quotations for four senses of *gloom*:

---

[130] Tennyson, *Enoch Arden and In Memoriam*, 261.
[131] Scott, "Flowering in a Lonely Word," 378–379.
[132] Richardson, *A New Dictionary of the English Language*, 1836, 1:908.
[133] Jones, *Fossil Poetry*, 267.
[134] Baker, *Concordance*, 263.

- To make dark or sombre: "A black yew gloom'd the stagnant air" ("The Letters" [1855] 2)
- The figurative of the same definition: "Such a mood as that, which lately gloom'd / Your fancy" ("Merlin and Vivien" [1859] 323–324)
- The derivative adjective: "Would that my gloomèd fancy were / As thine, my mother" ("Supposed Confessions …" [1830] 68–69). This is the only example of this adjective in the *OED*.
- The noun for a deeply shaded or darkened place: "Full of long-sounding corridors it was, / That over-vaulted grateful glooms" ("Palace of Art" [1832] 53–54)

He used more meanings than these, but the fact that he could help define these four demonstrates how he investigated the various ways to employ the word. Often that process involved playing with the supposed duality of its etymology in relating to both darkness and light.

Tennyson explores the etymological double-sidedness of *gloom* as supposedly related to *gleam* in several poems. Most strikingly, a "Song" from 1830 begins, "I' the glooming light / of middle night," confronting the reader with an apparent contradiction in "glooming light" (1–2). The water in "The Brook" (1855) speaks: "I slip, I slide, I gloom, I glance" (174). In "The Holy Grail" (1869), lightning flashing in a storm does so rapidly: "every moment glanced / [Galahad's] silver arms and gloom'd" (492–493). The pairing "glanced … and gloomed" could describe alternating flashes of light and followed by a return to darkness, or the words could be synonyms for the flash of light (that is, glanced and gleamed).

At sunset, the characters of "The Princess" (1847) walk 'thro' the ambrosial gloom" – which could mean the general darkness, but in context suggests twilight, a sense the *OED* calls obsolete and rare, giving only one example (IV.6). The case for *gloom* as twilight is yet stronger in *In Memoriam* lxxxvi: "Sweet after showers, ambrosial air, / That rollest from the gorgeous gloom / Of evening" (1–3). The phrase "gorgeous gloom" carries very different connotations than the gloom of the yew-tree. Similarly, in "Gareth and Lynette" (1872), while riding "under cloud that grew / To thunder-gloom," the title characters and Lancelot see "A huge pavilion … Sunder the glooming crimson on the marge, / Black, with black banner" (1,324–1,331). The first quotation uses *gloom* to mean dark as in a thundercloud; the second use of *gloom* refers to the light of sunrise, which is sundered by the black pavilion (Tennyson's notes gloss "glooming crimson" as sunrise).[135] The same combination of word and imagery appear in "The Ancient Sage" (1885) when the speaker recalls how, as a boy, he would feel "desolate sweetness" at "The first gray streak of earliest summer-dawn, / The last long stripe of waning crimson gloom" (220–221). These uses of *gloom* for the first and last light of the day may have suggested themselves from *gloaming* (a word of Old English origin). The *OED* marks the noun *gloaming* for twilight as "poetic" and has only three examples to offer: Tennyson's "The Gardeners Daughter" (written 1833–1834, "the balmy gloaming, crescent-lit" [258]); William Morris's *Sigurd the Volsung*, a poem whose language was studiedly archaic;

---

[135] Tennyson, *Idylls of the King*, 1908, 467.

and an excerpt from Trench's poetry. Notably, all three of these writers knew a good deal about philology.

Tennyson's use of the many facets of *gloom* is representative of the way he engaged with the meanings that reside inside his words, especially in *In Memoriam*. The poem also engages with poetic history. It does so not only in moments such as when it uses *grides* to mean *grates* (cvii) – a meaning for which the *OED* cites only Tennyson and Shelley – but in the very fabric of the elegiac project. Tennyson's work is absolutely of its own time, but it has a kinship with Old English elegy, just as nineteenth-century English has a kinship with Old English itself.

Old English Elegy

On a large scale, this poem of anguish and attempted reassurance drew from a native literary tradition to express a contemporary manifestation of grieving. Tennyson knew his classical literature well, but for all its poetic predecessors, *In Memoriam* was a new kind of elegy, "a form of anti-pastoral" that resists the comfort that is usually provided by steadily distancing oneself from grief.[136] Given his early reading of Old English poetry, it may have pointed the way to Tennyson's version of elegy. In the Anglo-Saxon elegies' tension between howling despair and sapiential reflection, he would have found a template for his own conflicted journey. Alan Sinfield finds *In Memoriam* to be a combination of the Romantic urge to express personal experience and an Enlightenment faith in general truth;[137] but a version of the same duality existed in medieval elegy. As Damian Love writes, "clearly Tennyson [had] an imaginative grasp of Old English elegy … He found in [these poems] a bleakness, a refusal to make easy claims to consolation, and a deeply ingrained sense of the cosmic processes as something inscrutable."[138]

In general, Anglo-Saxon poetry is noted for its wistful attitude toward the past. In the words of S.B. Greenfield, "Much of Old English poetry is imbued with an elegiac spirit, a compound of Teutonic melancholia and Christian utilization of the *ubi sunt* motif."[139] The poignant tone is especially pronounced in certain poems of the Exeter Book, some of which would have been familiar to Tennyson. Kemble's 1833 edition of the *Beowulf* text, for example, included a poem from the Exeter Book which he called "The Traveller's Song" (now known as "Widsið"). Even before that publication, J.J. Conybeare's *Illustrations of Anglo-Saxon Poetry* (1826) included a poem he labelled "The Exile's Complaint" (now called "The Wife's Lament") as an example of "compositions of an elegiac character." Conybeare interpreted the poem as a man lamenting his dead lord; *In Memoriam* repeatedly depicts Hallam as the speaker's superior, the intellectual equivalent of his Anglo-Saxon lord and – through his engagement to Emily Tennyson – his kinsman.

Anne L. Klinck makes the case for Old English elegy as a genre distinct from the classical or pastoral types – but "the Old English poems," she writes, "do have a

---

[136] Sacks, *The English Elegy*, 173.
[137] Sinfield, *The Language of Tennyson's In Memoriam*, 19–31.
[138] Damian Love, "Hengist's Brood: Tennyson and the Anglo-Saxons," *The Review of English Studies* 60, no. 245 (June 2009): 474.
[139] S.B. Greenfield, "The Old English Elegies," in *Continuations and Beginnings: Studies in Old English Literature*, ed. E. G. Stanley (London: Thomas Nelson and Sons, 1966), 142.

kinship with later English elegies ... and even with Tennyson's *In Memoriam*, which, though far longer than the Old English poems, resembles them in consisting of rather various reflections prompted by the need to come to terms with a sense of loss."[140] Broadly, Old English elegiac poems consist of "a relatively short reflective or dramatic poem embodying a contrasting pattern of loss and consolation, ostensibly based upon a specific personal experience or observation, and expressing an attitude towards that experience."[141] The characteristic imagery comprises "the sea with cliffs, hail, snow, rain, and storms, plus the meadhall of heroic poetry with its lords, warriors, hawks, horses, and precious cups."[142] It is not hard to find the parallels in Tennyson's work.

At a high level, Old English elegy may have provided a model for gesturing at large grief through intimate lyricism. The similarities become apparent through comparison with one of the most famous poems in Old English, "The Wanderer" – a first-person lament for the woes of one who has buried his lord and wanders friendless through the world. Elaine Treharne's description exposes some of the parallels with Tennyson's text:

> If this text is viewed as an extended interior monologue, one can see the progression of the *anhaga* [solitary man] from the misery and loneliness of his personal story ... to a general reflection on the transience of temporal things ... and the need to reflect on virtuous and heroic behaviour ... in order to achieve heavenly comfort.[143]

The Victorian poem explores "the transience of temporal things" through the lens of geology and biological extinction, but the journey is much the same.

As Klinck describes, "the elegiac themes [of Old English poetry] are present in a lyrical-reflective mode with characteristic features such as monologue, personal introduction, gnomic or homiletic conclusion, and the ordered repetition of words and sounds, amounting occasionally to refrain or rhyme." None of these features is exclusive to elegy, but their combination makes for a discrete genre in the hands of Anglo-Saxon poets.[144] Most of these features apply equally to Tennyson's work. In this context, section cvii takes on a new dimension:

> It is the day when he was born,
> A bitter day that early sank
> Behind a purple-frosty bank
> Of vapour, leaving night forlorn.

---

[140] Anne L. Klinck, *The Old English Elegies: A Critical Edition and Genre Study* (Montreal: McGill-Queen's University Press, 1992), 11.
[141] Greenfield, "The Old English Elegies," 143.
[142] Herbert Pilch, "The Elegiac Genre in Old English and Early Welsh Poetry," *Zeitschrift Für Celtische Philologie* 29 (1964): 211; Quoted in Klinck, *The Old English Elegies*, 11.
[143] Elaine M. Treharne, ed., *Old and Middle English, c.890–c.1450: An Anthology*, 3rd ed., Blackwell Anthologies (Chichester: Wiley-Blackwell, 2010), 54.
[144] Klinck, *The Old English Elegies*, 11.

> The time admits not flowers or leaves
>   To deck the banquet. Fiercely flies
>   The blast of North and East, and ice
> Makes daggers at the sharpen'd eaves,
>
> And bristles all the brakes and thorns
>   To yon hard crescent, as she hangs
>   Above the wood which grides and clangs
> Its leafless ribs and iron horns
>
> Together, in the drifts that pass
>   To darken on the rolling brine
>   That breaks the coast. But fetch the wine,
> Arrange the board and brim the glass;
>
> Bring in great logs and let them lie,
>   To make a solid core of heat;
>   Be cheerful-minded, talk and treat
> Of all things ev'n as he were by;
>
> We keep the day. With festal cheer,
>   With books and music, surely we
>   Will drink to him, whate'er he be,
> And sing the songs he loved to hear.

The landscape of *In Memoriam* can be as hostile as in the Old English elegies, the pathetic fallacy dwelling on the harshness of winter, which parallels the poem's grief. In response, the speaker turns his attention to the warmth of a large fire, cheerful conversation, and music – elements equally common in depictions of an Anglo-Saxon hall.

In fact, this lyric has strong parallels with a passage from the account of the conversion of King Edwin as told by the medieval historian Bede and then again by Sharon Turner at the turn of the nineteenth century. As Chapter 2 shows, Tennyson not only knew the story, he was working on a project to tell it himself. One of Edwin's ealdormen offers the following case for Christianity:

> The present life of man, O king, compared with that space of time beyond, of which we have no certainty, reminds me of one of your wintry feasts ... The hearth blazes in the middle, and a grateful heat is diffused around, while the storms of rain and snow are raging fierce without.

In the midst of this "chilling tempest," a sparrow flies in through one door and out the other. The sparrow, explains the ealdorman, is safe from the storm for the length of its flight through the hall, but then it must return to the "dreary scene" outside. The parable of the sparrow in the banqueting-hall serves to advise the king to take up Christianity if it can offer any information regarding what happens before or after one's life on earth.[145] The ealdorman's practical advice matches Tennyson's: we choose to believe because doing so makes sense of mortal life by putting it into a larger framework. *In Memoriam* admits that we can only trust that "not a worm is cloven in vain; / That not a moth … Is shrivell'd in a fruitless fire" (liv.9–11). At the same time, life must be lived in the house (the hall?) while it lasts.

Other affinities appear in imagery such as paths and binding. The Victorian poet refers to the bounding ocean and bounding sky as he struggles to see beyond the physical world. Indeed, the sea is itself a highly connotative symbol for both Tennyson and his literary forebears. *In Memoriam* is preoccupied with the ocean, imagining the ship bringing Hallam's body back to Britain and the body being buried within hearing of the wave. The speaker dreams of meeting Hallam onboard a ship and sailing toward a further shore. Another instance of rhetorical echo originates in "The Wanderer," which refers to Sorrow as a companion, implied to be replacing dead friends:

> Wat se þe cunnað
> Hu sliþen bið sorg to geferan
> þam þe him lyt hafað leofra geholena;   (ll. 29–31)[146]

This translates to:

> He knows who has experience
> How cruel is sorrow as a companion
> To him who has few dear friends.

The same idea appears in the beginning of section iii of *In Memoriam*:

> O Sorrow, cruel fellowship,
>   O priestess in the vaults of Death,
>   O sweet and bitter in a breath,
> What whispers from thy lying lip?   (1–4)

Sorrow gives her cruel answer appositively:

> all the phantom, Nature, stands –
>   With all the music in her tone,
>   A hollow echo of my own, –
> A hollow form with empty hands.   (9–12)

By tinting *In Memoriam* with shades of Old English elegy, Tennyson enhances his poem's sense of universality – something the older poems have in abundance.

Yet the comparison also shows the extent to which Tennyson wrote about a nineteenth-century experience with the help of the past, not in imitation of it. Anglo-Saxon elegies emphasize that the physical world is crumbling and then contrast it with the eternal nature of God's heavenly kingdom. For Tennyson, science had given

---

[145] Turner, *History* (Tennyson's copy), 2:439.
[146] Mitchell and Robinson, *A Guide to Old English*, 272.

a potent new urgency to the sense that the universe was failing (for example, the "murmurs from the dying sun" in section iii), while it also threatened to take away the contrasting heavenly world that had balanced the sadness of the Old English texts. Bereft of orthodox solace, the speaker must feel out his own version of grand consolation. Similarly, where "The Seafarer" proposes that earning good repute is one guard against oblivion, Tennyson's mourner has the added anguish that Hallam did not fulfill his promise in this respect. *In Memoriam*'s speaker cannot mourn like an Anglo-Saxon, because his understanding of the physical and spiritual worlds is different; but he can draw on the native elegiac tradition to write his own elegy.

Alliteration

When Klinck identifies a major feature of Old English elegy as "the ordered repetition of words and sounds," she could easily be describing Tennyson's poetry generally, and *In Memoriam* in particular. *In Memoriam* consists of 2,896 lines, of which a staggering number contain alliteration on stressed syllables. In fact, it is difficult to find many consecutive lines that lack this trait; the longest such run is ten lines of section viii (14–23). Even within these seemingly alliteration-free passages, a phoneme will occasionally link across line breaks, meaning that the ear still detects patterns of sonic repetition. What follows is an analysis of this stylistic element within *In Memoriam*.

For the most part, I assessed each line according to the phonemes that fall on its stressed syllables, which enhance how strongly their similarities strike the ear. Assigning where stresses fall in poetry admittedly can be subjective, but *In Memoriam* insists on the regularity of its "measured language." I have therefore assumed the dominance of the iambic tetrameter template in most cases. However, I have included instances in which there is strong evidence for assigning the stress (and therefore alliteration) elsewhere. For example, "Leaving great legacies of thought" (lxxxiv.35) must be read with the first accent on *leaving*; "Week after week: the days go by" has been numbered among the alliterative lines because of the overwhelming spoken rhythm of "wéek after wéek" (xvii.7). Or again, the line "sick for thy stubborn hardihood" strongly suggests the prominence of *sick* and *stubborn*, even in isolation. The extended *s* sound in the surrounding lines reaffirms this inclination: "And gazing on thee, sullen tree, / Sick for thy stubborn hardihood, / I seem to fail from out my blood" (ii.13–15). Accordingly, the line has been counted as doubly alliterative thanks to the pair *sick* and *stubborn* and the *h*'s of *hardihood*. In addition, sometimes the initial sound of a line or word, even if definitively unstressed, still contributes to an alliterative impression, as in "Survive in spirits rendered free" (xxxviii.10) and "For fear divine Philosophy" (liii.14). As with Old English verse, I have considered all initial vowels to alliterate with each other.

Read this way, *In Memoriam* contains 1,117 alliterative lines, forming nearly 40 percent of the entire poem. Within this number, categories may be distinguished according to where the alliterating sounds fall (see Table 6). For convenience, I have labelled them Types A through G, but these should not be confused with the Sievers Types that categorize stress patterns in lines of Old English poetry. Old English prosody would have included types B, D, and some of G, a significant portion of the lines categorized here, though by no means the dominant schema. Tennyson evidently had no prescriptive agenda for re-creating the patterns of Anglo-Saxon sonority; he employed no such firm rules even when he directly adapted Old English texts (see Chapter 2). What is clear is that there is a layer of patterning overlaid on the famous "*In Memoriam* stanza," and it may have gained strength from Anglo-Saxon examples.

Table 6   Alliteration patterns in *In Memoriam*.

Type	Pattern	Example	# of Lines (% of Poem)
A	1, 2, _, _	Thou madest man, he knows not why (Prologue 10)	175 (6%)
B	1, _, 3, _	Thou madest Life in man and brute (Prologue 6)	180 (6.2%)
C	1, _, _, 4	A hollow form with empty hands (iii.12)	118 (4.1%)
D	_, 2, 3, _	Forgive these wild and wandering cries (Prologue 41)	156 (5.4%)
E	_, 2, _, 4	O sweet and bitter in a breath (iii.3)	163 (5.6%)
F	_, _, 3, 4	Thy creature, whom I found so fair (Prologue 38)	193 (6.7%)
G	More than two: 3 x same sound	For merit lives from man to man (Prologue 35) Thy roots are wrapt about the bones (ii.4)	132 (4.6%)
	interlaced	But all he was is overworn (i.16)	
	nested	And silent under other snows (cv.6)	

Among Types A through F – that is, the types that are composed of two alliterating stresses – the least common by a clear margin is Type C, which places the matching sounds on maximally distant stresses (the first and fourth). From this, we might conclude that Tennyson preferred to place his alliteration on adjacent stresses, and it is certainly most forcibly noticeable as such. However, Type D, which nests adjacent alliterations in the center of the line, is significantly less common than the types that place them either in the first or second half. Clearly, it is not mere proximity but some other factor that influences their positioning.

In search of this other factor, possibly linked to the subject matter handled in each line, I charted the appearance of each type across the poem's sections. However, simply marking the number of, say, B-type alliterations in each section would be a poor gauge, for some sections consist of only a few stanzas, while the Epilogue dwarfs all that came before. Therefore, to create an accurate comparison of relative density for each type per section, I took the average – that is, the number of each type of alliteration line in a given section, divided by the total number of lines in that section. With this information, it becomes plain, for example, that after a dearth of lines containing more than two alliterations, the frequency spikes in sections lvi and lvii, and in sections lxiii and lxiv. In the first of these sequential pairs, Nature offers her brutal take on "life as futile … as frail," to which the following section responds with peaceful resignation: a moment of crisis excites exuberant sensory recurrence, after which the poem employs repetition for soothing effect. The second pair of sections ponders how Hallam might think of his earthly life and those he left behind, the idea of his lofty existence contrasting with aural sensuousness of style.

Tracing these patterns not only illuminates the tendencies of the work as a whole, it helps identify the contours of individual sections. Section cxxx, in which the speaker senses Hallam's presence "mix'd with God and Nature," is a good example:

> Thy voice is on the rolling air;
>   I hear thee where the waters run;
>   Thou standest in the rising sun,
> And in the setting thou art fair.
>
> What art thou then? I cannot guess;   (5)
>   But tho' I seem in star and flower
>   To feel thee some diffusive power,
> I do not therefore love thee less:
>
> My love involves the love before;
>   My love is vaster passion now;   (10)
>   Tho' mix'd with God and Nature thou,
> I seem to love thee more and more.
>
> Far off thou art, but ever nigh;
>   I have thee still, and I rejoice;
>   I prosper, circled with thy voice;   (15)
> I shall not lose thee tho' I die.

The section opens with a subtle Type E ("on … air"), with the interposing adjective *rolling* to extend the phrase. This is followed by an internal rush of Type D ("where the waters"), immediately counterbalanced by a line that opens the maximum space between the alliterating sounds ("standest … sun"). The relative stasis of this line's alliterative distance mirrors the peace of "standing" in the calm of dawn. The fourth line's resolution results from hearkening back (literally listening back) to the previous line's sound with *setting*, which is the opposite of the sun's rising. Two lines thus embody in their acoustics the breadth of Hallam's mysterious presence: from sunrise to sunset, from first poetic stress to last and a little beyond. The second stanza begins with a simple enough contrast, followed by an acceleration through the central Type D alliteration of line 6 ("seem in star"), which is continued by *flower* priming the reader for the next line's evenly dispersed *f* sound ("feel … diffusive"). The stanza's final assertion comes to an emphatic end-loaded alliterative conclusion: "I do not therefore love thee less." The following stanza dwells on repetitions of *love*, line 9 matching its sense ("My love involves the love before") by enfolding its key word evenly within the line. After this, alliteration subsides, except for line 12's "more and more."

It is important to note that these patterns are sometimes formed by repeating the same word, or nearly the same word. Hence the following lines:

"By faith, and faith alone, embrace" (Type A, Prologue 3);
"And thou hast made him: thou art just" (Type B, Prologue 12);
"And common is the commonplace" (Type B, vi.3);
"And all the place is dark, and all" (Type C, viii.7);
"Or dying, there at least may die" (Type C, viii.24);
"If any calm, a calm despair" (Type D, xi.16);
"To find me gay among the gay" (Type E, lxvi.3);
"Let knowledge grow from more to more" (Type F, Prologue 25);
"Spirit to Spirit, Ghost to Ghost" (Type G, xciii.8);
"'The dawn, the dawn,' and died away" (Type G, xcv.61).

Alliteration is already a device that depends upon the return of sound to measure the progress of speech. *In Memoriam* loops back on itself so frequently that it makes alliterative connections that are, in fact, self-referential. Like the "no rhyme" at the start of "The Lotos-Eaters" (land/land), which uses stylistic inertia to hint at thematic inertia to come, these alliterations threaten to halt progress altogether and leave the reader in perpetual mourning. These alliterative patterns form an essential part of *In Memoriam*'s soundscape. They invoke the past by calling upon the sound and structure of Old English poetry to complement the poem's reworking of elegy.

"A new and legitimate combination"

In his review of *Poems, Chiefly Lyrical* (1830), Arthur Hallam wrote of Tennyson's ability to blend the past into the present: "The author is well aware that the art of one generation cannot *become* that of another by any will or skill; but the artist may transfer the spirit of the past, making it a temporary form for his own spirit, and so effect ... a new and legitimate combination."[147] This chapter has argued that Hallam summarized quite well Tennyson's general approach to his language. Although other poets of the period were also invested in the past of the English people and their language, Tennyson took an uncommonly balanced view of the changes that English had undergone. Some contemporaries, like Morris or Barnes, tried to preserve or revive the past wholesale. Thomas Hardy, like Tennyson, aimed to "show the manifold ways in which history interpenetrates present thinking and feeling," which led him to construct his verse with words from every stratum of the English language. However, "Hardy insists on the gap between the current and historical,"[148] whereas Tennyson increasingly tried to collapse that distance. Hence he wrote that he would not have used *red-cap* for *goldfinch* had he known it to be "purely provincial."[149] Although dialect was commonly considered more authentically Anglo-Saxon than "schoolmaster" English, Tennyson did not wish to place a largely unknown word in his poetry without providing contextual assistance in understanding it.[150] At the time of composition, he must have believed that *red-cap* was unusual but familiar – just different enough to draw attention without alienating his reader.

---

[147] Hallam, *Writings*, 194.
[148] Taylor, *Hardy's Literary Language and Victorian Philology*, 4, 366.
[149] Hallam Tennyson, *Memoir*, 1:451.
[150] Kemble, *Correspondence*, 268.

Tennyson obviously reveled in the abundance of words available – or recoverable – in his native tongue. The poem "Dora" was a rare attempt at Wordsworthian simplicity, and it was a struggle. As the poet reported it, "'Dora,' being the tale of a nobly simple country girl, had to be told in the simplest possible poetical language, and therefore was one of the poems which gave most trouble" in the 1842 collection.[151] The "simplest possible poetic language" evidently meant adhering to a stringently Germanic vocabulary: Not counting the names of the characters, a meager 5 percent of its words can be traced to the Romance branches of English. When not constraining himself to such a fixed program, Tennyson could apply his philological medievalism to different effect depending on whether the poem itself was medievalist.

The simple, regular structure of *In Memoriam* allows words and their etymologies to do poetic work in the voice of a nineteenth-century persona. Because we understand the subject matter to be contemporary in that poem, archaisms do not make the lyrics themselves archaic. In this and many other poems, Tennyson invokes the "echoes from the deserted temples of the past" as found within a Victorian experience. *In Memoriam* remains firmly positioned in modern experience; as such, its uses of archaic language revive old words, impress upon the reader the history behind modern speech, and allow for equivocations between historic senses in order to add nuance to the expression of a contemporary speaker.

In the *Idylls of the King*, by contrast, the laureate wanted to evoke an immersive environment from a mythical past. He uses many of the same techniques as in his elegy, but the result is necessarily different. Even with a vocabulary that remains largely Germanic in origin, any and all archaisms contribute to the construction of a (fictionalized) medieval society. Whereas *In Memoriam* draws upon linguistic and cultural history to say something about the nineteenth century, the poems that comprise the *Idylls* enact a different kind of relationship with the English past through their use of language. Although they, too, are "permeated with a sense of the new philology,"[152] Tennyson privileges specificity of temporal effect. Rather than holding all historic usages in play simultaneously, the words of the *Idylls* retain the aura of the centuries from which Tennyson took them.

Comparing *In Memoriam* and *Idylls of the King* illustrates how Tennyson's exposure to philology exerted continued influence on his writing throughout his career. This comparison also demonstrates that we must pay attention to exactly how he applied his "fine old words," native elegy tradition, and other strategies if we are to make any claims about his style. Words, Tennyson knew, do not contain fixed meanings in a vacuum but are inextricably tied to "all that men have been doing and thinking and feeling from the beginning of the world till now" (as Trench put it).[153] With a knowledge of the ways they have been used in different time periods, a poet can combine them in richly connotative ways.

---

[151] Hallam Tennyson, *Memoir*, 1:196.
[152] Hair, *Tennyson's Language*, 135.
[153] Trench, *On the Study of Words*, 27–28.

Conclusion

Julius Hare's admonition to his students that in literature (as one of them later expressed it) there is "no road to the sense which d[oes] not go through the words" is especially relevant to reading poetry that is conscious of verbal histories.[1] This book has examined how Tennyson's philological sensitivity shaped his poetic decisions, arguing that there is no road to his sense that does not go through his philological medievalism. Placing him in the context of the nineteenth-century fervor for historical linguistics and his wide reading of early literature improves our understanding of how he constructed his diction, and to what purpose. Tennyson was a poet fascinated by the boundaries of language: where it begins to convey meaning, where it might collapse into unsignifying noise, and where the overlap of the two might express more than words or "music" alone. Building upon that curiosity, the Teutonically oriented philology practiced by the poet's friends taught him that his vowels were the souls of his words, tempered his love of alliteration into a measured effect, and encouraged him to assemble a "studied poetic vocabulary."[2] It also showed him how a single word can carry multitudes of meaning, some of them contradictory.

Patrick Greig Scott has rightly argued that "to read Tennyson we have to know ... the whole philological ethos of his age, where 'words contemplated singly' carried the special force and meaning of their often rather conjectural origins."[3] As previous chapters have shown, the reasons for new philology's importance in the nineteenth century were manifold, coinciding as it did with pressing debates over the origin and nature of mankind. As philology became better equipped to provide evidence for arguments in the disciplines of biology, ethnography, and Biblical scholarship, writers on those subjects appropriated the ancient philosophical debate of linguistic essentialism versus conventionalism. Even if linguistic and biological origins cannot be determined, Richard Chenevix Trench expressed the belief of many Victorians when he wrote that, with regard to both men and words, "If we would know what [they] are, we must know what they have been."[4]

What the English had been was Anglo-Saxons, and the desire to know more about that society blossomed alongside philological interest. For Tennyson, Old English existed on the tantalizing boundary between familiar and foreign, much as

---

[1] Maurice, *The Life of Frederick Denison Maurice*, 1:53.
[2] Pyre, *The Formation of Tennyson's Style*, 224.
[3] Scott, "Flowering in a Lonely Word," 380.
[4] Trench, *English, Past and Present*, 194.

the sounds of nature hover between communication and noise. The language of the Anglo-Saxons was difficult to recognize as English, but it structured the expression of contemporary speakers. It could also, I have argued, structure a poet's expression. Tennyson's poetry incorporated traits from Anglo-Saxon language and literature as part of its sonic structure by means of strong verbs and alliteration; as a template for how to express mourning in short bursts that gesture toward larger consolation; and in the construction of the words themselves, in the form of compounds. Germanic stories sometimes garnered direct attention in the poems, but the legacy of Tennyson's early exposure to early medieval literature was his "use of English – in preference to words derived from French and Latin."[5] This characteristic underpinned his style even when he told a tale of classical myth or high medieval chivalry.

Nevertheless, the Germanic portion of the English language was but one resource that its complex history supplied. Tennyson had at his disposal the full depth and breadth of the English lexicon from which to select items that would enrich his verse. His response to the difficulties of linguistic history was not to return to a certain point in history, or even to favor one heritage exclusively over another, but rather to strengthen the connection between past and present. His friend, the pioneering Anglo-Saxonist John Mitchell Kemble, was "little fond of modern Anglosaxon [sic] verses, of modern Latin hexameters or modern Greek iambics," because he felt that it was pointless to write nineteenth-century material in an idiom that had expressed an earlier society's way of thinking.[6] Similarly, when Tennyson looked to older conjugations, older usages, or obsolete words, it was not with an eye to turning back the clock. Instead, he strove to strengthen his readers' connection to the history of their language by reintroducing them to old words or removing the patina of familiarity from current ones. The preceding chapters show that Tennyson's knowledge of language history – acquired through dictionaries, grammars, medieval literature, and the contributions of friends – equipped him to manipulate the nuances of his vocabulary to achieve his desired effects.

William Wilson classifies Kemble, Trench, and their fellow philologists as pessimists who thought language was in a state of decay.[7] This book has argued to the contrary that Tennyson and his friends ultimately felt positive about the state of English. They shared some of the fears of linguistic alarmists – but in response, they insisted on the benefits of linguistic change, and of studying it. In particular, Tennyson's poetry wavers between hope and fear for communication. A number of critics have identified linguistic anxiety in his work and concluded that he fails to drive back that anxiety; I find a more creative, generative point of view emerging from his philological techniques.

The opening chapters of Linda Dowling's *Language and Decadence in the Victorian Fin de Siècle* provide a good example of modern critical interpretations of Victorian philology. In them, she describes language theory's development under the influence of Romanticism into a kind of secular mysticism, and its grudging shift into a more materialist model. Dowling's narrative is one of linguistic theories that,

---

[5] Hallam Tennyson, *Memoir*, 2:133.
[6] Kemble, *The Saxons in England*, 1:366.
[7] Wilson, "Victorian Philology" 34.

even as they took shape, contained the seeds of their own destabilization.[8] In this framework, the popular works of Trench and Müller were attempts at an untenable compromise – desperate efforts to interpret the results of new philology as something that complemented an orthodox, Christian worldview. Dowling's astute analysis provides the larger context for Tennyson and his friends, but it is predetermined by hindsight. Such an arc is all but inevitable to see when tracking the progression of language theory from Biblical exegesis to materialist laws independent of human will; however, it risks losing sight of the perceived legitimacy of any one stage of that trajectory. As Dowling herself explains, Trench and Müller – and through them, much of the population – saw in the new philology better methods for finding the same reassuring lessons delivered in a sermon that elaborated on a word of Scripture. Unstable as they ultimately proved, their hybrid notions promised a morally grounded logic for language change, precisely because they were philosophically located midway between Coleridge's Romantic logos and Saussure's relativism.

Pleased to find laws at work behind linguistic change, Tennyson's philological acquaintances resisted prescriptive responses to it. Kemble found academically constructed standardization an infuriating phenomenon, and Trench was far more inclusive than scholars generally give him credit for. In fact, he forged a compromise between different interpretations of human history as viewed through language history. Some saw the gradual loss of inflections and other grammatical forms as proof of linguistic decay, reflecting cultural decay, the anxiety that Jason Camlot identifies as the "spectre of language raised by philology."[9] Such an interpretation tended to be favored by earlier philologists and was linked to a sense of cultural inferiority to the classical world. Others, in light of archaeological evidence, saw a progressive path of intellectual improvement over human history, aided by and aiding the increasing complexity of speech. Trench, however, described both linguistic processes going forward at the same time. Although his works contain provocative statements that temporarily suggest one perspective or the other, he demonstrates overall a pragmatic understanding of how language will change over time:

> [L]anguage has a life, just as really as a man or as a tree; as a man, it must grow to its full stature, being also submitted to his conditions of decay; as a forest tree, will defy any feeble bands which should attempt to control its expansion, so long as the principle of growth is in it; as a tree too will continually, while it casts off some leaves, be putting forth others.[10]

Trench did not urge a wholesale reversion to earlier English, though some words and expressions were worth reviving. In the end, "it is according to a word's present signification that we must employ it now."[11] Nor do Trench's philological writings concern themselves with rules for coining new words; taking a broad historical view, he acknowledges that time will determine which neologisms will last and which will fade away. Camlot cites Trench's analogy of foreign-word adoption as

---

[8] Dowling, *Decadence*, 48–71.
[9] Camlot, *Sincere Mannerisms*, 110.
[10] Trench, *On the Study of Words*, 132.
[11] Trench, *English, Past and Present*, 191.

political naturalization, but he reads the philologist's work as primarily supporting a narrative of linguistic corruption by foreign agents. In doing so, he entirely ignores Trench's pragmatic take on language history, in which words became naturalized citizens, strengthening the national tongue – and thereby the nation – by augmenting it. For some Victorians, in fact, the mixture of Germanic and Romance made English an ideal language for empire.[12] For example, Joseph Bosworth wrote in the preface to his Anglo-Saxon dictionary about what English had gained from its foreign additions:

> If … we have lost in simplicity, we have gained in copiousness and euphony. In collecting from other languages, the English have appropriated what was best adapted to their purpose, and thus greatly enriched their language. Like bees they have diligently gathered honey from every flower.[13]

He goes on to argue that it is English's very blended nature that makes it a world language, spoken around the globe. Tennyson subscribed to this same idea with regard to the "races" that had settled in Britain and the words that had found a home there.

Dowling identifies Walter Pater as a writer who shaped "a new vision of the writer as a sort of philologist or scholar of words;" this book offers evidence that Tennyson had taken on that role nearly seventy years before Pater articulated the principles of Decadence in his essay on "Style."[14] Indeed, Angela Leighton comments that "the paradox of Tennyson is that he managed to be both Victoria's laureate, official and moral, and perhaps the most powerful, undeclared voice of English aestheticism at the same time."[15] Dowling considers that "there is surely a suppressed humor at work … when Pater describes Tennyson, Victorian Poet laureate and by 1889 a revered institution in his own right, in terms that would apply to a … Euphuist."[16] Nevertheless, Pater was entirely accurate when he wrote, "How illustrative of monosyllabic effect, of sonorous Latin, of the phraseology of science, of metaphysic, of colloquialism even, are the writings of Tennyson; yet with what a fine, fastidious scholarship throughout!"[17] As early as 1833, in fact, a reviewer for the *New Monthly Magazine* had criticized Tennyson for imitating the "most coxcombical euphuisms" of the Elizabethans.[18]

This book argues that Tennyson's philological medievalism led him to a style that shared elements with literary movements yet to come at the end of the century; however, it is important not to assume that he shared *fin-de-siècle* cynicism. His poetry echoes the various worries of his time, but it does not follow that those concerns dominated his style. On the contrary, he retained his faith in the possibility of creating something new with words. He wrote with a sense of the creative possibility available in the history of words rather than despair over their changeability.

---

[12] Dowling, *Decadence*, 47.
[13] Bosworth, *A Dictionary of the Anglo-Saxon Language*, xxxiv.
[14] Dowling, *Decadence*, 111.
[15] Leighton, "Touching Forms," 57.
[16] Dowling, *Decadence*, 110, 124.
[17] Quoted in ibid., 124.
[18] Sherwood, "'Mr. Tennyson's Singular Genius,'" 257.

I therefore disagree with scholars such as William Wilson, who finds that *In Memoriam*'s "swallow flights of song" fail to defeat its anxiety about the impending collapse of language, concluding: "As Tennyson's lyricism fails under the great demands placed upon it, he is returned to his point of departure, the limits of utterance."[19] The poem is certainly preoccupied with the limits of utterance thematically, but Tennyson and his friends were fundamentally optimistic about what philology taught them about language. It was messy, contradictory, and ever-changing, but that was because it was intimately bound up with the lives of millions of humans interacting with each other. The layers of its words, as we have seen, created space for "Faith beyond the forms of Faith" ("The Ancient Sage" 69). At the same time, Tennyson had no objection to those who found it most useful to exercise faith through form; as a friend recalled, "'To him, ... truth is so infinitely great that all we can do with our poor human utterances is to try and clothe it in such language as will make it clear to ourselves.'"[20] The same might be said of his attitude toward his words: the reality that they try to represent surpasses any verbal constructs, but verbal expression is not, for that, a hopeless enterprise.

Ultimately, the philosophical compromise of new philology was to prove unsustainable, prompting some writers to adopt a "Decadent" style that foregrounded the artifice of language. However, locating Tennyson within a larger trajectory does not mean that he shared all the traits of writers at its endpoint. A modern critic may conclude that he failed to stave off the threats of conventional, synonym-fraught English by means of archaism or revived metaphor, but even if we agree with that evaluation, it does not diminish the creativity of those techniques as Tennyson employed them over a nearly seventy-year career. Like his friend Trench, he offered reassurance to subdue philology's more unsettling implications. Alternatively, when it complemented his subject-matter, he could explore linguistic multiplicity to maintain uncertainty of signification. Thus, *In Memoriam*'s lexical ambiguity is a crucial element of its theological and philological success, not a sign of failure. Müller's memorable maxim had it that "The history of a word, if only we could get at it in all its completeness, is always its best definition."[21] *In Memoriam* similarly suggests that in contemplating large spiritual truths, one must hold many ideas possible. Julius Charles Hare was concerned that "hardly a word [in contemporary English] is used for which half a dozen synonyms might not have stood equally well;"[22] Tennyson's elegy uses the many layers of modern words to suggest many imagined forms of life after death. Just as language seems an impossible project that is constantly failing yet somehow blunderingly succeeds despite its flaws, so *In Memoriam*'s mourner fumbles onward, knowing that all he can do is "trust that good shall fall / At last – far off – at last, to all" (liv.14–15).

In his other works, although Tennyson did not attempt to make his words algebraic, he illuminated where they had come from. Seamus Perry writes that "Tennyson's verse does not, at its best, work to obfuscate or distract – although it is

---

[19] Wilson, "Victorian Philology," 30.
[20] Hallam Tennyson, *Memoir*, 1:310.
[21] Quoted in Taylor, *Hardy's Literary Language and Victorian Philology*, 233.
[22] Quoted in Turley, "Tennyson and the Nineteenth-Century Language Debate," 130.

conscious of the possibility of obfuscation and distraction – but works rather to elaborate intricacy."[23] Chapters 3 and 4 explored some of the ways in which the poet's philological acumen manifested in his writing. Conscious of "the possibility of obfuscation and distraction" in words that had come to be used loosely, he sometimes chose to reintroduce historic usage almost undetectably. At other times, he made use of the strangeness of terms that had started to recede from common speech.

In surveying some medievalist philological influences in Tennyson's poetry, this book expands upon the work of critics who have described his language within the contexts of biography, stylistics, philosophy, and contemporary language debates. Naturally, there remain directions for further research. For example, further analysis of Tennyson's notebooks and his poetic corpus could shed light on which periods of literary history he found most verbally attractive. Similarly, there is room for more investigation into the poet's Germanic versus Latinate vocabulary. Future work might calculate the ratios of etymological origins in more of Tennyson's corpus, which might in turn identify moments when one branch or the other predominates, and to what effect. Such a study would benefit from computer-assisted analysis, as would further work on the aural qualities of the poetry. Tennyson constructed philologically informed poetry through individual word choices and through the dense matrices of sonic reverberations that he wove with them. His patterns of alliteration remain a rich vein for future researchers wishing to assess the sound of his verse. For example, mapping *In Memoriam*'s alliteration patterns in more detail might enable scholars to trace how the sound of the elegy fluctuates alongside its varied moods.

However much more detail such inquiries may reveal, reading Tennyson's work in the context of Victorian philology and medievalism makes it clear that he was interested in "the echoes and recesses of words," to borrow Empson's phrase.[24] He drew attention to verbal origins while also appreciating that language was dynamic and subjective. Thus, although he had a philologist's awareness of the fragility of communication, he could retain a hopeful sense of the possibilities latent within English. In revealing vital metaphors and historic uses, in finding the Anglo-Saxon echoes of his own speech and presenting lexical curiosities plucked from many centuries, Tennyson placed himself in a long line of language-crafters. He used philology to make himself, like those who had formed words in the shadows of prehistory, "a poet – a maker, that is, of things which were not before."[25]

[23] Perry, *Alfred Tennyson*, 7.
[24] Empson, *Seven Types of Ambiguity*, 199.
[25] Trench, *On the Study of Words*, 5–6.

Bibliography

Primary Sources

Allingham, William. *William Allingham: A Diary*. Edited by H. Allingham and D. Radford. London: Macmillan, 1907.
Athenaeum. "An Essay on the Origin of Language; Based on Modern Researches, and Especially on the Work of M. Renan. By Frederic W. Farrar, M.A. (Murray)." December 8, 1860.
Athenaeum. "Outlines of Comparative Philology; with a Sketch of the Languages of Europe, Arranged upon Philological Principles: And a Brief History of the Art of Writing. By M. Schele de Vere." February 18, 1854.
Athenaeum. "Poems, (Now First Published) By Alfred Tennyson. London: Moxon." December 1, 1832.
Athenaeum. "Timbuctoo." July 22, 1829.
Bailey, N. *An Universal Etymological Dictionary*. London: E. Bell, J. Darby, A Bettesworth, F. Fayram, J. Pemberton, J. Hooke, C. Rivington, F. Clay, J. Batley, and E. Symon, 1721.
Barnes, William. *An Outline of Rede-Craft (Logic): With English Wording*. London: C. Kegan Paul & Company, 1880.
———. *Notes on Ancient Britain and the Britons* (Tennyson's copy). London: John Russell Smith, 1858. TRC/AT/494, Lincolnshire Archives, Lincoln, UK.
———. *TIW: Or, A View of the Roots and Stems of the English as a Teutonic Tongue*. London: John Russell Smith, 1862.
Bede. *Historiae Ecclesiasticae Gentis Anglorum: Libri V*. Edited by Abraham Wheloc. Cambridge: Roger Daniel, 1643.
Benson, Thomas. *Vocabularium Anglo-Saxonicum*. Oxford: Samuel Smith and Benjamin Walford, 1701.
Bent's Monthly Literary Advertiser, and Register of Engravings, Works on the Fine Arts, Etc. "Supplement for 1835." January 1836.
Bosworth, Joseph. *A Dictionary of the Anglo-Saxon Language*. London: Longman, Rees, Orme, Brown, Green, and Longman, 1838.
———. *The Elements of Anglo-Saxon Grammar*. Harding, Mavor, and Lepard, 1823.
———, and T. Northcote Toller. *An Anglo-Saxon Dictionary: Based on the Manuscript Collections of the Late Joseph Bosworth*. Oxford: Clarendon Press, 1898.
Brookfield, Frances M. *The Cambridge "Apostles."* New York: AMS Press, 1973.
Carroll, Lewis. *Alice's Adventures in Wonderland and Through the Looking-Glass and What Alice Found There*. Edited by Roger Lancelyn Green. London: Oxford University Press, 1971.
Catalogue of New and Standard Works in Circulation at Mudie's Select Library, 1857.

Chaucer, Geoffrey. *Poetical Works of Geoffrey Chaucer in Fourteen Volumes*. Edited by Thomas Tyrwhitt. Vol. 14. 14 vols. Bell's Edition, The Poets of Great Britain Complete from Chaucer to Churchill. Edinburg [sic]: Apollo Press, 1782.

Christian Remembrancer. "Book Review." July 1842.

"Classified Advertising." *Daily Telegraph*. April 15, 1865.

Cockayne, Oswald. *Leechdoms, Wortcunning, and Starcraft of Early England*. Vol. 2. 2 vols. London: Longman, Green, Longman, Roberts, and Green, 1865.

Coleridge, Samuel Taylor. *Essays on His Times in The Morning Post and The Courier*. Edited by David V. Erdman. Vol. 2. 3 vols. The Collected Works of Samuel Taylor Coleridge 3. London: Routledge & Kegan Paul, 1978.

Conybeare, John Josias. *Illustrations of Anglo-Saxon Poetry*. Edited by William Daniel Conybeare. London: Harding and Lepard, 1826.

Cooper, William Durrant. *A Glossary of the Provincialisms in Use in the County of Sussex*. 2nd ed. London: John Russell Smith, 1853.

Cottle, Joseph. *Alfred: An Epic Poem in Twenty-Four Books*. London: Longman and Rees, 1800.

Darwin, Charles. *On the Origin of Species: A Facsimile*. Edited by Ernst Mayr. Cambridge, MA: Harvard University Press, 1964.

———. *The Descent of Man, and Selection in Relation to Sex*. Vol. 1. 2 vols. New York: D. Appleton, 1871.

Doyle, Arthur Conan. "A Study in Scarlet." In *Sherlock Holmes: The Complete Novels and Stories*, 1:1–120. New York: Bantam, 2003.

Earle, John. "On the English Dialects." In *Rhymes and Reasons*, 1–8. London: Joseph Masters, 1871.

Edmunds, R. "Appendix: 'The Calling of the Sea.'" In *A Guide to Penzance and Its Neighbourhood, Including the Islands of Scilly*, by J.S. Courtney, 53–55. Penzance: E. Rowe, 1845.

"Elements of English Grammar, for the Use of Ladies' Schools. By R.G. Latham, M.D." *Examiner*, no. 2178 (October 27, 1849): 677.

Ellis, George, ed. *Specimens of the Early English Poets*. Vol. 1. 2 vols. London: W. Bulmer, 1801.

Elstob, Elizabeth. *The Rudiments of Grammar for the English-Saxon Tongue*. London: W. Bowyer, 1715.

Emerson, Ralph Waldo. "The Poet." In *Essays and Lectures*, edited by Joel Porte, 445–468. The Library of America. New York: Literary Classics of the United States, 1983.

"English: Past and Present." *Notes and Queries* 12, no. 297 (July 7, 1855).

Examiner. "Classical Museum." May 4, 1844.

———. "The Classical Museum." June 24, 1843.

———. "The Discovery of the Science of Languages. By Morgan Kavanagh." May 4, 1844.

———. "Upton's Physioglyphics." September 21, 1844.

FitzGerald, Edward. *Sea Words and Phrases Along the Suffolk Coast: Extracted from the East Anglian Notes and Queries, January 1869*. Lowestoft: Samuel Tymms, 1869.

Gibson, Edmund. *Chronicon Saxonicum*. Oxford: E Theatro Sheldoniano, 1692.

Grimm, Jacob. *Deutsche Grammatik*. Göttingen: Dieterichsche buchhandlung, 1822.

Guest, Edwin. *A History of English Rhythms*. Edited by Walter W. Skeat. Vol. 1. 2 vols. London: William Pickering, 1838.

———. *A History of English Rhythms*. Edited by Walter W. Skeat. Vol. 2. 2 vols. London: William Pickering, 1838.

Gurney, Anna. *A Literal Translation of the Saxon Chronicle*. Norwich: Stevenson, Matchett, and Stevenson, 1819.

Hallam, Arthur Henry. *The Letters of Arthur Henry Hallam*. Edited by Jack Kolb. Columbus: Ohio State University Press, 1981.
———. *The Writings of Arthur Hallam*. Edited by T.H. Vail Motter. Modern Language Association of America General Series 15. New York: Modern Language Association of America, 1943.
Halliwell, James Orchard. *A Dictionary of Archaic and Provincial Words, Obsolete Phrases, Proverbs and Ancient Customs, from the Fourteenth Century*. Vol. 1. 2 vols. London: John Russell Smith, 1852.
———. *A Dictionary of Archaic and Provincial Words, Obsolete Phrases, Proverbs and Ancient Customs, from the Fourteenth Century*. Vol. 2. 2 vols. London: John Russell Smith, 1847.
Hare, Julius Charles. *Guesses at Truth, by Two Brothers*. Vol. 1. London: John Taylor, 1827.
———. *Guesses at Truth, by Two Brothers*. 5th ed. Boston: Ticknor and Fields, 1861.
———. *Guesses at Truth: Second Series*. 2nd ed. London: printed for Taylor and Walton, 1848.
———. *Guesses at Truth, by Two Brothers: Two Series in One Volume*. London: George Routledge & Sons, n.d.
———, ed. *The Philological Museum*. Vol. 1. Cambridge: J. Smith, 1832.
Hopkins, Gerard Manley, *The Collected Works of Gerard Manley Hopkins*. Edited by R.K.R. Thornton and Catherine Phillips. Vol. 1. Oxford: Oxford University Press, 2013.
———, *The Collected Works of Gerard Manley Hopkins*. Edited by R.K.R. Thornton and Catherine Phillips. Vol. 2. Oxford: Oxford University Press, 2013.
Hunt, Leigh. *The Story of Rimini: A Poem*. London: J. Murray, 1816.
"Hydrography." *The Edinburgh New Philosophical Journal* 37, no. 74 (1844): 403–404.
Ingram, James, ed. *The Saxon Chronicle, with an English Translation, and Notes, Critical and Explanatory*. London: Longman, Hurst, Rees, Orme, and Brown, 1823.
Johnson, Catharine Bodham. *William Bodham Donne and His Friends*. London: Methuen, 1905.
Johnson, Samuel. *A Dictionary of the English Language*. Vol. 1. 2 vols. London: Knapton, Longman, Hitch, Hawes, Millar, and Dodsley, 1755.
———. *A Dictionary of the English Language*. Vol. 1. 2 vols. London: Thomas Tegg, 1832.
———. *A Dictionary of the English Language*. Vol. 2. 2 vols. London: Thomas Tegg, 1832.
Kemble, John Mitchell. *Anglo-Saxon Dialogues of Salomon and Saturnus*. 3 vols. Printed for the Aelfric Society, 1848.
———. *Anglo-Saxon Runes*. Pinner: Anglo-Saxon Books, 1991.
———. *A Translation of the Anglo-Saxon Poem of Beowulf*. Vol. 2. London: Pickering, 1837.
———. "History of the English Language, First, or Anglo-Saxon Period." J. & J.J. Deighton, 1834.
———. *John Mitchell Kemble and Jakob Grimm; A Correspondence 1832–1852*. Edited by Raymond A. Wiley. Leiden: Brill, 1971.
———. *John Mitchell Kemble's Review of Jakob Grimm's Deutsche Grammatik: Originally Set for the Foreign Quarterly Review but Never Published*. Binghampton, NY: CEMERS, SUNY-Binghampton, 1981.
———. "On English Præterites," inscribed "Arthur H. Hallam from His Affectionate Friend. J. M. Kemble," 1833. Private collection of Simon Keynes.
———. "Oxford Professors of Anglo-Saxon." *The Gentleman's Magazine*, December 1834.
———. "Review of Analecta Anglo-Saxonica." *The Gentleman's Magazine*, April 1834.
———. "Review of Cædmon's Metrical Paraphrase." *The Gentleman's Magazine*, April 1833.
———. "Specimens from the Chronicle of England by Lajamon, the Monk of Severn," 1832. Kemble Box. Trinity College Cambridge.
———. "Surrey Provincialisms." *Transactions of the Philological Society*, no. 3 (February 24, 1854): 83–84.

———. *The Anglo-Saxon Poems of Beowulf, the Travellers Song and the Battle of Finnesburh*. Vol. 1. London: Pickering, 1835.

———. *The Saxons in England: A History of the English Commonwealth Till the Period of the Norman Conquest*. Vol. 1. 2 vols. London: Longman, Brown, Green & Longmans, 1849.

Levins, Peter. *Manipulus Vocabulorum: A Rhyming Dictionary of the English Language, by Peter Levins (1570)*. Edited by Henry B. Wheatley. London: Trübner, 1867.

Long, William Henry. *A Dictionary of the Isle of Wight Dialect, and of Provincialisms Used in the Island*. London: Reeves and Turner, 1886.

Lyell, Charles. *The Geological Evidences of the Antiquity of Man, with Remarks on Theories of the Origin of Species by Variation*. London: John Murray, 1863.

Madden, Frederick. *The Ancient English Romance of Havelok the Dane: Accompanied by the French Text*. London: W. Nichol, Shakespeare Press for the Roxburghe Club, 1828.

Malory, Thomas. *Le Morte D'Arthur*. Edited by Janet Cowen. Vol. 2. London: Penguin, 1969.

Mann, Robert James. *Tennyson's "Maud" Vindicated: An Explanatory Essay*. London: Jarrold & Sons, 1856.

Maurice, Frederick Denison. *The Life of Frederick Denison Maurice: Chiefly Told in His Own Letters*. Edited by Frederick Maurice. Vol. 1. 2 vols. London: Macmillan, 1884.

Morris, William. *Three Northern Love Stories; The Tale of Beowulf*. Vol. 10 of *The Collected Works of William Morris*. Edited by May Morris. New York: Longmans Green, 1911.

Müller, Friedrich Max. *Lectures on the Science of Language: Delivered at the Royal Institution of Great Britain in April, May, & June 1861*. 5th ed. London: Longmans, Green, 1866.

———. *Lectures on the Science of Language: Delivered at the Royal Institution of Great Britain in February, March, April, & May, 1863*. Vol. 2. Second Series. Longman, Green, Longman, Roberts, and Green, 1864.

Murray, James A.H., and Henry Bradley. *A New English Dictionary on Historical Principles: Founded Mainly on the Materials Collected by the Philological Society*. Vol. 3. Oxford: Clarendon Press, 1897.

Nall, John Greaves. *An Etymological and Comparative Glossary of the Dialect and Provincialisms of East Anglia*. London: Longmans, Green, Reader & Dyer, 1866.

Pall Mall Gazette. "Morris's 'Life and Death of Jason.'" July 25, 1867.

Parish, William Douglas. *A Dictionary of the Sussex Dialect and Collection of Provincialisms in Use in the County of Sussex*. Lewes: Farncombe & Company, 1875.

Petrie, Henry, and John Sharpe. *Monumenta Historica Britannica, or Materials for the History of Britain, from the Earliest Period*. Vol. 1. London: George E. Eyre & William Spottiswoode, 1848.

Philological Society. *Proposal for the Publication of a New English Dictionary*. London: Trübner, 1859.

Plato. "Cratylus." In *Cratylus; Parmenides; Greater Hippias; Lesser Hippias*, translated by H. N. Fowler, 4:3–191. *Plato in Twelve Volumes*. Cambridge, MA: Harvard University Press, 1977.

Publishers' Circular and General Record of British and Foreign Literature: Containing a Complete List of All New Works Published in Great Britain, and Every Work of Interest Published Abroad. "Literary Intelligence." July 16, 1861.

Publishers' Circular and General Record of British and Foreign Literature: Containing a Complete List of All New Works Published in Great Britain, and Every Work of Interest Published Abroad. "New Works Published from the 16th to the 31st of December." December 31, 1861.

Publishers' Circular and General Record of British and Foreign Literature: Containing a Complete List of All New Works Published in Great Britain, and Every Work of Interest Published Abroad. "A Select Glossary of English Words." November 1, 1859.

Pye, Henry James. *Alfred: An Epic Poem, in Six Books*. London: W. Bulmer, 1801.
Rask, Erasmus. *A Grammar of the Anglo-Saxon Tongue*. Translated by Benjamin Thorpe. Copenhagen: S. L. Møller, 1830.
———. *A Grammar of the Anglo-Saxon Tongue* (Tennyson's copy). Translated by Benjamin Thorpe. S. L. Møller, 1830. TRC/AT/1854, Lincolnshire Archives, Lincoln, UK.
Rice, John. *An Introduction to the Art of Reading 1765*. Edited by R.C. Alston. *English Linguistics, 1500–1800* 161. Menston, England: The Scolar Press, 1969.
Richardson, Charles. *A New Dictionary of the English Language*. Vol. 1. 2 vols. London: Pickering, 1836.
———. *A New Dictionary of the English Language*. Vol. 2. 2 vols. London: Pickering, 1837.
Saxo Grammaticus. *The History of the Danes*. Edited by Hilda Ellis Davidson. Translated by Peter Fisher. Vol. 1. 2 vols., 1980.
———. *The History of the Danes*. Edited by Hilda Ellis Davidson. Translated by Peter Fisher. Vol. 2. 2 vols., 1980.
Schmid, Reinhold. *Die Gesetze Der Angelsachsen*. Leipzig: F.A. Brockhaus, 1832.
Scott, Walter. *Ivanhoe*. London: Penguin, 2000.
Shelley, Percy Bysshe. "A Defence of Poetry." In *Shelley's Poetry and Prose*. Edited by Donald H. Reiman and Neil Fraistat, 2nd ed., 509–535. Norton Critical Edition. New York: Norton, 2002.
Sidgwick, Arthur, and Eleanor Mildred Sidgwick. *Henry Sidgwick: A Memoir*. London: Macmillan, 1906.
Skeat, Walter William. *An Etymological Dictionary of the English Language*. Oxford: Clarendon, 1882.
Smibert, Thomas. *Rhyming Dictionary for the Use of Young Poets*. Edinburgh, 1852.
Smith, John Russell. "Choice, Cheap, and Useful Books." *Examiner*. July 8, 1843.
Spectator. "Tennyson's Collected Poems." June 4, 1842.
Tasso. *Godfrey of Bulloigne; or, The Recovery of Jerusalem*. Edited by Charles Knight. Translated by Edward Fairfax. 5th ed. Windsor: Knight, 1817.
Tennyson, Alfred. *Ballads and Other Poems*. Eversley Edition. Vol. 6 of *The Works of Alfred Lord Tennyson*. Edited by Hallam Tennyson. London: Macmillan, 1910.
———. *Becket and Other Plays*. Eversley Edition. Vol. 9 of *The Works of Alfred Lord Tennyson*. Edited by Hallam Tennyson London: Macmillan, 1908.
———. *Enoch Arden and In Memoriam*. Eversley Edition. Vol. 3 of *The Works of Alfred Lord Tennyson*. Edited by Hallam Tennyson. London: Macmillan, 1909.
———. "Harold." In *Queen Mary and Harold*, 207–381. Eversley Edition. Vol. 8 of *The Works of Alfred Lord Tennyson*. Edited by Hallam Tennyson. London: Macmillan, 1908.
———. *Idylls of the King*. Eversley Edition. Vol. 5 of *The Works of Alfred Lord Tennyson*. Edited by Hallam Tennyson. London: Macmillan, 1908.
———. *Idylls of the King*. Edited by J.M. Gray. London: Penguin, 1996.
———. *Poems I*. Eversley Edition. Vol. 1 of *The Works of Alfred Lord Tennyson*. Edited by Hallam Tennyson. London: Macmillan, 1908.
———. *Poems II*. Eversley Edition. Vol. 2 of *The Works of Alfred Lord Tennyson*. Edited by Hallam Tennyson. London: Macmillan, 1908.
———. "Queen Mary." In *Queen Mary and Harold*, 1–206. Eversley Edition. Vol. 8 of *The Works of Alfred Lord Tennyson*. Edited by Hallam Tennyson. London: Macmillan, 1908.
———. *The Complete Poetical Works of Tennyson*. Edited by W.J. Rolfe. Cambridge Edition. Boston: Houghton Mifflin, 1898.
———. *The Harvard Manuscripts: Notebooks 1–4 (MS Eng 952)*. Edited by Christopher Ricks and Aidan Day. Vol. 1. 7 vols. Tennyson Archive. New York: Garland, 1987.

———. *The Harvard Manuscripts: Notebooks 5–15 (MS Eng 952)*. Edited by Christopher Ricks and Aidan Day. Vol. 2. 7 vols. Tennyson Archive. New York: Garland, 1987.

———. *The Harvard Manuscripts: Notebooks 28–39 (MS Eng 952)*. Edited by Christopher Ricks and Aidan Day. Vol. 4. 7 vols. Tennyson Archive. New York: Garland, 1987.

———. *The Letters of Alfred Lord Tennyson*. Edited by Cecil Y. Lang and Edgar Finley Shannon. Vol. 1. Oxford: Clarendon, 1982.

———. *The Letters of Alfred Lord Tennyson*. Edited by Cecil Y. Lang and Edgar Finley Shannon. Vol. 2. Oxford: Clarendon, 1982.

———. *The Letters of Alfred Lord Tennyson*. Edited by Cecil Y. Lang and Edgar Finley Shannon. Vol. 3. Oxford: Clarendon, 1982.

———. *The Poems of Tennyson*. Edited by Christopher B. Ricks. 2nd ed. Vol. 1. 3 vols. Longman Annotated English Poets. London: Longman, 1987.

———. *The Poems of Tennyson*. Edited by Christopher B. Ricks. 2nd ed. Vol. 2. 3 vols. Longman Annotated English Poets. London: Longman, 1987.

———. *The Poems of Tennyson*. Edited by Christopher B. Ricks. 2nd ed. Vol. 3. 3 vols. Longman Annotated English Poets. London: Longman, 1987.

Tennyson, Emily. *Lady Tennyson's Journal*. Edited by James O. Hoge. Charlottesville: University Press of Virginia, 1981.

———. *The Letters of Emily Lady Tennyson*. Edited by James O. Hoge. University Park: Pennsylvania State University Press, 1974.

Tennyson, Hallam. *Alfred Lord Tennyson: A Memoir*. Vol. 1. 2 vols. London: Macmillan, 1897.

———. *Alfred Lord Tennyson: A Memoir*. Vol. 2. 2 vols. London: Macmillan, 1897.

———. "The Song of Brunanburh." *The Contemporary Review*, November 1876.

———, ed. *Tennyson and His Friends*. London: Macmillan, 1912.

Thorkelin, Grímur Jónsson. *De Danorum Rebus Gestis Secul. III. & IV. Poëma Danicum Dialecto Anglosaxonica*. Copenhagen: Rangel, 1815.

Thorpe, Benjamin, ed. *Analecta Anglo-Saxonica: A Selection, in Prose and Verse, from Anglo-Saxon Authors of Various Ages*. London: John and Arthur Arch, 1834.

———, ed. *The Anglo-Saxon Chronicle According to the Several Original Authorities*. Vol. 1. London: Longman, Green, Longman, and Roberts, 1861.

———, ed. *The Anglo-Saxon Chronicle According to the Several Original Authorities*. Vol. 2. London: Longman, Green, Longman, and Roberts, 1861.

Trench, Richard Chenevix. *A Select Glossary of English Words Used Formerly in Senses Different from Their Present*. 2nd ed. London: John W. Parker and Son, 1859.

———. "Books Relating to the Society's Dictionary." In *On Some Deficiencies in Our English Dictionaries: Being the Substance of Two Papers Read Before the Philological Society, Nov. 5, and Nov. 19, 1857*, 24. London: J.W. Parker and Son, 1857.

———. *English, Past and Present*. 2nd ed. John W. Parker, 1855.

———. *Letters and Memorials*. Edited by Maria Marcia Fanny Trench. Vol. 1. 2 vols. London: Kegan Paul, Trench, 1888.

———. *Notes on the Parables of Our Lord*. London: Pickering & Inglis, 1953.

———. *On Some Deficiencies in Our English Dictionaries: Being the Substance of Two Papers Read Before the Philological Society, Nov. 5, and Nov. 19, 1857*. 2nd ed. London: John W. Parker and Son, 1860.

———. *On the Study of Words*. 7th ed. John W. Parker, 1856.

Turner, Sharon. *The History of the Anglo-Saxons*. 2nd ed. Vol. 1. 2 vols. London: Longman, Hurst, Rees, and Orme, 1807.

———. *The History of the Anglo-Saxons*. 2nd ed. Vol. 2. 2 vols. London: Longman, Hurst, Rees, and Orme, 1807.

———. *The History of the Anglo-Saxons* (Tennyson's copy). 2nd ed. Vol. 2. 2 vols. London: Longman, Hurst, Rees, and Orme, 1807. TRC/AT/2238, Lincolnshire Archives, Lincoln, UK.

———. *The History of the Manners, Landed Property, Government, Laws, Poetry, Literature, Religion, and Language, of the Anglo-Saxons.* Longman, 1805.

Walker, John. *A Rhyming Dictionary.* Edited by J. Longmuir. London: William Tegg, 1865.

Warton, Thomas. *History of English Poetry from the Twelfth to the Close of the Sixteenth Century.* Edited by W. Carew Hazlitt. Vol. 1. 4 vols. Reeves and Turner, 1871.

Wedgwood, Hensleigh. *A Dictionary of English Etymology.* 2nd ed. London: Trübner & Company, 1872.

"William Pickering's Publications, 177, Piccadilly, London." In *Bibliotheca Piscatoria: A Catalogue of Books Upon Angling.* London: Pickering, 1836.

"Works Published by Bach & Co. Foreign Booksellers to Her Majesty, 21, Soho Square, London." In *Tutti Frutti*, 2:241–248. London: Bach and Co., 1834.

Wright, Thomas. *Essays on Subjects Connected with the Literature, Popular Superstitions and History of England in the Middle Ages.* Vol. 1. 2 vols. London: John Russell Smith, 1846.

Secondary Sources

Aarsleff, Hans. *The Study of Language in England, 1780–1860.* Westport: Greenwood Press, 1979.

Ackerman, Gretchen P. "J.M. Kemble and Sir Frederic Madden: 'Conceit and Too Much Germanism'?" In *Anglo-Saxon Scholarship: The First Three Centuries.* Edited by Carl T. Berkhout and Milton McC. Gatch, 167–181. A Reference Publication in Literature. Boston: G.K. Hall, 1982.

Alexander, Michael. "Tennyson's 'The Battle of Brunanburh.'" *Tennyson Research Bulletin*, 1985, 151–161.

Allen, Peter. *The Cambridge Apostles: The Early Years.* Cambridge: Cambridge University Press, 1978.

Alter, Stephen G. *Darwinism and the Linguistic Image: Language, Race, and Natural Theology in the Nineteenth Century.* New Studies in American Intellectual and Cultural History. Baltimore: Johns Hopkins University Press, 1999.

Armstrong, Isobel. *Victorian Poetry: Poetry, Poetics and Politics.* Abingdon: Routledge, 1993.

Attridge, Derek. "Beat." In *The Oxford Handbook of Victorian Poetry*, edited by Matthew Bevis, 36–53. Oxford Handbooks of Literature. Oxford: Oxford University Press, 2013.

Bailey, Richard W. "'This Unique and Peerless Specimen': The Reputation of the *OED*." In *Lexicography and the OED*, edited by Lynda Mugglestone, 207–227. Oxford Studies in Lexicography and Lexicology. Oxford: Oxford University Press, 2000.

Baker, Arthur E. *A Concordance to the Poetical and Dramatic Works of Alfred, Lord Tennyson.* London: Kegan Paul, Trench, Trübner, 1914.

Batchelor, John. *Tennyson: To Strive, to Seek, to Find.* London: Chatto & Windus, 2012.

Baugh, Albert C., and Thomas Cable. *A History of the English Language.* 5th ed. London: Routledge, 2002.

Beer, Gillian. "Darwin and the Growth of Language Theory." In *Open Fields: Science in Cultural Encounter*, 95–114. Oxford: Clarendon Press, 1996.

Bevis, Matthew. "Tennyson's Humour." In *Tennyson Among the Poets: Bicentenary Essays.* Edited by Robert Douglas-Fairhurst and Seamus Perry, 231–258. Oxford: Oxford University Press, 2009.

Bliss, A.J. *The Metre of Beowulf.* Oxford: Basil Blackwell, 1967.

Blocksidge, Martin. *"A Life Lived Quickly": Tennyson's Friend Arthur Hallam and His Legend*. Brighton: Sussex Academic Press, 2011.

Borrie, Michael. "Madden, Sir Frederic (1801–1873)." In *Oxford Dictionary of National Biography*, August 10, 2023.

Bradley, Henry, and John D. Haigh. "Bosworth, Joseph." In *Oxford Dictionary of National Biography*. London: Smith, Elder, & co., May 13, 2021.

Bromley, J. *The Man of Ten Talents: A Portrait of Richard Chenevix Trench, 1807–86, Philologist, Poet, Theologian, Archbishop*. London: S.P.C.K., 1959.

Bryden, Inga. *Reinventing King Arthur: The Arthurian Legends in Victorian Culture*. Nineteenth Century. Aldershot: Ashgate, 2005.

Burchfield, Robert. *The English Language*. Oxford: Oxford University Press, 2002.

Burridge, Kate. "Nineteenth-Century Study of Sound Change from Rask to Saussure." In *The Oxford Handbook of the History of Linguistics*, edited by Keith Allan, 141–165. Oxford: Oxford University Press, 2013.

Burrow, J.W. "The Uses of Philology in Victorian England." In *Ideas and Institutions of Victorian Britain: Essays in Honour of George Kitson Clark*, edited by Robert Robson. London: Bell, 1967.

Cable, Thomas. "Kaluza's Law and the Progress of Old English Metrics." In *Development in Prosodic Systems*, edited by Johanna Paula Monique Fikkert and Haike Jacobs, 145–158. Studies in Generative Grammar 58. Berlin: Mouton de Gruyter, 2003.

Camlot, Jason. *Style and the Nineteenth-Century British Critic: Sincere Mannerisms*. Nineteenth Century. Aldershot: Ashgate, 2008.

Campbell, Nancie. *Tennyson in Lincoln: A Catalogue of the Collections in the Research Centre*. Vol. 1. 2 vols. Lincoln: Tennyson Society, 1971.

Campion, George Edward. *A Tennyson Dialect Glossary with the Dialect Poems*. Lincoln: Lincolnshire Association, 1969.

Chandler, Alice. *A Dream of Order: The Medieval Ideal in Nineteenth-Century English Literature*. Lincoln: University of Nebraska Press, 1970.

Cheshire, Jim. *Tennyson and Mid-Victorian Publishing: Moxon, Poetry, Commerce*. London: Palgrave Macmillan, 2016.

Christie, E.J. "'An Unfollowable World': *Beowulf*, English Poetry, and the Phenomenalism of Language." *Literature Compass* 10, no. 7 (2013): 519–534.

Collins, Sarah H. "The Elstobs and the End of the Saxon Revival." In *Anglo-Saxon Scholarship: The First Three Centuries*. Edited by Carl T. Berkhout and Milton McC Gatch, 107–118. Boston: G.K. Hall, 1982.

Connor, Steven. *Beyond Words: Sobs, Hums, Stutters and Other Vocalizations*. London: Reaktion Books, 2014.

Creed, Robert Payson. *Reconstructing the Rhythm of Beowulf*. Columbia, Missouri: University of Missouri Press, 1990.

Crompton, John. "Haunts of Coot and Tern: Tennyson's Birds." *Tennyson Research Bulletin* 8, no. 2 (2003): 101–110.

Davis, John R., and Angus Nicholls. "Introduction – Friedrich Max Müller: The Career and Intellectual Trajectory of a German Philologist in Victorian Britain." In *Friedrich Max Müller and the Role of Philology in Victorian Thought*. Edited by John R. Davis and Angus Nicholls, 1–31. London: Routledge, 2018.

Deacon, Richard. *The Cambridge Apostles: A History of Cambridge University's Élite Intellectual Secret Society*. London: Royce, 1985.

Dickins, Bruce. "John Mitchell Kemble and Old English Scholarship." *Proceedings of the British Academy* 25 (1939): 51–84.

——. *Two Kembles, John and Henry*. Cambridge: The author, 1974.

Distad, N. Merrill. *Guessing at Truth: The Life of Julius Charles Hare (1795-1855).* Shepherdstown: Patmos Press, 1979.

Dowling, Linda. *Language and Decadence in the Victorian Fin de Siècle.* Princeton: Princeton University Press, 1986.

Elliott, Philip L. *The Making of the Memoir.* Tennyson Society Monographs 12. Lincoln: Tennyson Society, 1995.

Empson, William. *Seven Types of Ambiguity.* 3rd ed. London: Hogarth, 1984.

Esmail, Jennifer. "'Perchance My Hand May Touch the Lyre': Orality and Textuality in Nineteenth-Century Deaf Poetry." *Victorian Poetry* 49, no. 4 (2011): 509-534.

Faulkner, Peter, ed. *William Morris: The Critical Heritage.* The Critical Heritage Series. London: Routledge and Kegan Paul, 1973.

Fay, Elizabeth A. *Romantic Medievalism: History and the Romantic Literary Ideal.* Basingstoke: Palgrave, 2002.

Felce, Ian. *William Morris and the Icelandic Sagas.* Medievalism 13. Cambridge: D.S. Brewer, 2018.

Frantzen, Allen J. *Desire for Origins: New Language, Old English, and Teaching the Tradition.* New Brunswick: Rutgers University Press, 1990.

General List of Works, New Books and New Editions, Published by Messrs. Longmans, Green, Reader, and Dyer. London: Longmans, Green, Reader, and Dyer, 1865.

Goulden, R.J. "Smith, John Russell (1810-1894), Bookseller and Bibliographer." *Oxford Dictionary of National Biography*, September 23, 2004.

Gray, Erik. "Introduction." In *In Memoriam*, by Alfred Tennyson, xi-xxvii. Edited by Erik Gray, 2nd ed. Norton Critical Edition. New York: W.W. Norton, 2004.

Gray, J. M. *Thro' the Vision of the Night: A Study of Source, Evolution and Structure in Tennyson's "Idylls of the King."* Edinburgh: Edinburgh University Press, 1980.

Greenfield, S.B. "The Old English Elegies." In *Continuations and Beginnings: Studies in Old English Literature.* Edited by E. G. Stanley, 142-175. London: Thomas Nelson and Sons, 1966.

Griest, Guinevere L. *Mudie's Circulating Library and the Victorian Novel.* Bloomington: Indiana University Press, 1970.

Guthrie, Steve. "Chaucer's Language and Meter." *Chaucer's Troilus and Criseyde: A New Edition by Steve Guthrie, Agnes Scott College.* Based on Corpus Christi College, Cambridge Manuscript 61, 2014. https://agnesscott.edu/english/troilusandcriseyde/language.html.

Hagedorn, Suzanne C. "Received Wisdom: The Reception History of Alfred's Preface to the Pastoral Care." In *Anglo-Saxonism and the Construction of Social Identity.* Edited by Allen J. Frantzen and John D. Niles, 86-107. Gainesville, FL: University Press of Florida, 1997.

Hagen, June Steffensen. *Tennyson and His Publishers.* University Park: Pennsylvania State University Press, 1979.

Hair, Donald S. "Soul and Spirit in 'In Memoriam.'" *Victorian Poetry* 34, no. 2 (July 1, 1996): 175-191.

———. *Tennyson's Language.* Toronto: University of Toronto Press, 1991.

Hall, J.R. "The First Two Editions of Beowulf: Thorkelin's (1815) and Kemble's (1833)." In *The Editing of Old English: Papers from the 1990 Manchester Conference.* Edited by D.G. Scragg and Paul E. Szarmach, 239-250. Cambridge: D.S. Brewer, 1994.

Heaney, Seamus. "Translator's Introduction." In *Beowulf: A Verse Translation.* Norton Critical Edition. New York: W.W. Norton, 2002.

Hirsh, Elizabeth A. "'No Record of Reply': In Memoriam and Victorian Language Theory." *English Literary History* 55, no. 1 (1988): 233-257.

Hughes, Shaun. "The Anglo-Saxon Grammars of George Hickes and Elizabeth Elstob." In *Anglo-Saxon Scholarship: The First Three Centuries*. Edited by Carl T. Berkhout and Milton McC. Gatch, 119–147. A Reference Publication in Literature. Boston: G.K.Hall, 1982.

Irving, Jr, Edward B. "The charge of the Saxon brigade: Tennyson's Battle of Brunanburh." In *Literary Appropriations of the Anglo-Saxons from the Thirteenth to the Twentieth Century*. Edited by Donald Scragg and Carole Weinberg, 174–193. Cambridge Studies in Anglo-Saxon England 29. Cambridge: Cambridge University Press, 2006.

Jones, Chris. "Anglo-Saxonism in Nineteenth-Century Poetry." *Literature Compass* 7, no. 5 (May 1, 2010): 358–369.

———. *Fossil Poetry: Anglo-Saxon and Linguistic Nativism in Nineteenth-Century Poetry*. Oxford: Oxford University Press, 2018.

Jump, John D., ed. *Tennyson: The Critical Heritage*. Critical Heritage Series. London: Routledge & Kegan Paul, 1986.

Kenneally, Daniel F. "Cockayne, Thomas Oswald." In *Oxford Dictionary of National Biography*, September 23, 2004.

Klinck, Anne L. *The Old English Elegies: A Critical Edition and Genre Study*. Montreal: McGill-Queen's University Press, 1992.

Kuczynski, Michael P. "Translation and Adaptation in Tennyson's Battle of Brunanburh." *Philological Quarterly* 86, no. 4 (Fall 2007): 415–431.

Ledbetter, Kathryn. *Tennyson and Victorian Periodicals: Commodities in Context*. The Nineteenth Century Series. Hampshire, England and Burlington, VT: Ashgate, 2007.

Leighton, Angela. "Tennyson's Hum." *Tennyson Research Bulletin* 9, no. 4 (November 2010): 315–329.

———. "Touching Forms: Tennyson and Aestheticism." *Essays in Criticism* 52, no. 1 (January 1, 2002): 56–75.

Lerer, Seth. "Middlemarch and Julius Charles Hare." *Neophilologus* 87, no. 4 (n.d.): 653–664.

Levy, F.J. "The Founding of the Camden Society." *Victorian Studies* 7, no. 3 (March 1964): 295–305.

Love, Damian. "Hengist's Brood: Tennyson and the Anglo-Saxons." *The Review of English Studies* 60, no. 245 (June 2009): 460–474.

Lovelace, John Timothy. *The Artistry and Tradition of Tennyson's Battle Poetry*. New York: Routledge, 2003.

Lubenow, W. C. *The Cambridge Apostles, 1820–1914: Liberalism, Imagination, and Friendship in British Intellectual and Professional Life*. Cambridge: Cambridge University Press, 1998.

Malone, Kemp. "Grundtvig as Beowulf Critic." *The Review of English Studies* 17, no. 66 (April 1941): 129–138.

Man, Paul de. *The Resistance to Theory*. Theory and History of Literature 33. Minneapolis: University of Minnesota Press, 1986.

Marchand, Leslie A. *The Athenaeum: A Mirror of Victorian Culture*. Chapel Hill: University of North Carolina Press, 1941.

Martin, Meredith. *The Rise and Fall of Meter: Poetry and English National Culture, 1860–1930*. 1st ed. Princeton: Princeton University Press, 2012.

Martin, Robert Bernard. *Tennyson: The Unquiet Heart*. Oxford: Clarendon Press, 1983.

McDonald, Peter. *Sound Intentions: The Workings of Rhyme in Nineteenth-Century Poetry*. Oxford: Oxford University Press, 2012.

Mitchell, Bruce, and Fred C. Robinson. *A Guide to Old English*. 6th ed. Oxford: Blackwell, 2001.

Murphy, Michael. "Antiquary to Academic: The Progress of Anglo-Saxon Scholarship." In *Anglo-Saxon Scholarship: The First Three Centuries*. Edited by Carl T. Berkhout and Milton McC. Gatch, 1–17. A Reference Publication in Literature. Boston: G.K. Hall, 1982.

Murray, Alex. "Decadent Histories." In *Decadence: A Literary History*, 1–17. Cambridge: Cambridge University Press, 2020.
Murray, K. M. Elisabeth. *Caught in the Web of Words: James A.H. Murray and the Oxford English Dictionary*. New Haven: Yale University Press, 1995.
Neve, Lloyd Rudolph. *The Spirit of God in the Old Testament*. Tokyo: Seibunsha, 1972.
Nye, Eric W., ed. *John Kemble's Gibraltar Journal: The Spanish Expedition of the Cambridge Apostles, 1830–1831*. Basingstoke: Palgrave Macmillan, 2015.
Palmer, D. J. *The Rise of English Studies: An Account of the Study of the English Language and Literature from Its Origins to the Making of the Oxford English School*. London: Published for the University of Hull by the Oxford University Press, 1965.
Paulin, Roger. "Julius Hare's German Books in Trinity College Library, Cambridge." *Transactions of the Cambridge Bibliographical Society* 9, no. 2 (1987): 174–193.
Payne, Richard C. "The Rediscovery of Old English Poetry in the English Literary Tradition." In *Anglo-Saxon Scholarship: The First Three Centuries*. Edited by Carl T. Berkhout and Milton McC. Gatch, 149–166. Boston: G.K. Hall, 1982.
Perry, Seamus. *Alfred Tennyson*. Writers and Their Work. Tavistok: Northcote House, 2005.
Phelan, Joseph. *The Music of Verse: Metrical Experiment in Nineteenth-Century Poetry*. Basingstoke: Palgrave Macmillan, 2012.
Pilch, Herbert. "The Elegiac Genre in Old English and Early Welsh Poetry." *Zeitschrift Für Celtische Philologie* 29 (1964): 209–224.
Plotkin, Cary H. *The Tenth Muse: Victorian Philology and the Genesis of the Poetic Language of Gerard Manley Hopkins*. Carbondale: Southern Illinois University Press, 1989.
Pratt, Lynda. "Anglo-Saxon attitudes?: Alfred the Great and the Romantic national epic." In *Literary Appropriations of the Anglo-Saxons from the Thirteenth to the Twentieth Century*, edited by Donald Scragg and Carole Weinberg, 138–156. Cambridge Studies in Anglo-Saxon England 29. Cambridge: Cambridge University Press, 2006.
Prest, Wilfrid. "Blackstone, Sir William." In *Oxford Dictionary of National Biography*. Oxford University Press, September 17, 2015.
Preston, Claire. *Bee*. Animal. London: Reaktion, 2006.
Priestley, F.E.L. *Language and Structure in Tennyson's Poetry*. The Language Library. London: Deutsch, 1973.
Pyre, J.F.A. *The Formation of Tennyson's Style: A Study, Primarily, of the Versification of the Early Poems*. Studies in Language and Literature 12. Madison: University of Wisconsin Press, 1921.
Reynolds, Matthew. *The Realms of Verse 1830–1870: English Poetry in a Time of Nation-Building*. Oxford: Oxford University Press, 2001.
Ricks, Christopher. *Milton's Grand Style*. Oxford: Clarendon Press, 2001.
———. *Tennyson*. 2nd ed. Masters of World Literature. London: Macmillan, 1989.
———. *Tennyson's Methods of Composition*. Chatterton Lecture on an English Poet. London: Oxford University Press, 1966.
Robinson, Fred C. *Beowulf and the Appositive Style*. The Hodges Lectures. Knoxville: University of Tennessee Press, 1985.
———. "Two Aspects of Variation in Old English Poetry." In *Old English Poetry: Essays on Style*, edited by Daniel Gillmore Calder, Vol. 10. Contributions of the UCLA Center for Medieval and Renaissance Studies. Berkeley: University of California Press, 1979.
Romaine, Suzanne. "Corpus Linguistics and Sociolinguistics." In *Corpus Linguistics: An International Handbook*. Edited by Anke Lüdeling and Merja Kytö, 1:96–111. Handbooks of Linguistics and Communication Science, 29.1. Berlin: Walter de Gruyter, 2009.
Rowlinson, Matthew. *Tennyson's Fixations: Psychoanalysis and the Topics of the Early Poetry*. Victorian Literature and Culture Series. Charlottesville: University Press of Virginia, 1994.

Sacks, Peter M. *The English Elegy: Studies in the Genre from Spenser to Yeats.* Baltimore: Johns Hopkins University Press, 1985.

Scott, Patrick Greig. "'Flowering in a Lonely Word': Tennyson and the Victorian Study of Language." *Victorian Poetry* 18, no. 4 (1980): 371–381.

———. *Tennyson's Enoch Arden: A Victorian Best-Seller.* Tennyson Society Monographs 2. Lincoln: Tennyson Society, 1970.

Scott, Rosemary. "Poetry in the 'Athenaeum': 1851 and 1881." *Victorian Periodicals Review* 29, no. 1 (Spring 1996): 19–32.

Scragg, Donald. "Introduction. The Anglo Saxons: fact and fiction." In *Literary Appropriations of the Anglo-Saxons from the Thirteenth to the Twentieth Century.* Edited by Donald Scragg and Carole Weinberg, 1–21. Cambridge Studies in Anglo-Saxon England 29. Cambridge: Cambridge University Press, 2006.

———. "The Nature of Old English Verse." In *The Cambridge Companion to Old English Literature.* Edited by Malcolm Godden and Michael Lapidge, 55–70. Cambridge: Cambridge University Press, 1991.

Shannon, Edgar Finley. "The Critical Reception of Tennyson's 'Maud.'" *PMLA* 68, no. 3 (June 1953): 397–417.

———, ed. *Tennyson and the Reviewers: A Study of His Literary Reputation and of the Influence of the Critics Upon His Poetry, 1827–1851.* Cambridge: Harvard University Press, 1952.

Shaw, Marion. "Friendship, Poetry, and Insurrection: The Kemble Letters." In *Tennyson Among the Poets: Bicentenary Essays,* edited by Robert Douglas-Fairhurst and Seamus Perry, 213–230. Oxford: Oxford University Press, 2009.

Shaw, W. David. *Tennyson's Style.* Ithaca: Cornell University Press, 1976.

Sherwood, Marion. "'Mr. Tennyson's Singular Genius': The Reception of 'Poems' (1832)." *Tennyson Research Bulletin* 8, no. 4 (November 2005).

Shippey, T.A., and Andreas Haarder, eds. *Beowulf: The Critical Heritage.* Critical Heritage Series. London: Routledge, 1998.

Shklovsky, Victor. "Art as Technique." In *Russian Formalist Criticism: Four Essays,* translated by Lee T. Lemon and Marion J. Reis, 24. Regents Critics Series. Lincoln, NE: University of Nebraska Press, 1965.

Simmons, Clare A. "'Iron-Worded Proof': Victorian Identity and the Old English Language." *Studies in Medievalism* 4 (1992): 202–214.

———. *Reversing the Conquest: History and Myth in Nineteenth-Century British Literature.* New Brunswick: Rutgers University Press, 1990.

Simpson, Roger. *Camelot Regained: The Arthurian Revival and Tennyson, 1800–1849.* Vol. 21. Arthurian Studies. Cambridge: D.S. Brewer, 1990.

Sinfield, Alan. *The Language of Tennyson's In Memoriam.* Oxford: Basil Blackwell, 1971.

Stanley, E.G. *Imagining the Anglo-Saxon Past: The Search for Anglo-Saxon Paganism and Anglo-Saxon Trial by Jury.* Cambridge: D.S. Brewer, 2000.

———. "J. Bosworth's Interest in 'Friesic' for His Dictionary of the Anglo-Saxon Language (1838): 'The Friesic Is Far the Most Important Language for My Purpose.'" In *Aspects of Old Frisian Philology,* edited by Rolf H. Bremmer Jr, Geart van der Meer, and Oebele Vries, 428–452. Amsterdam: Rodopi, 1990.

Sutherland, Kathryn. "Editing for a New Century: Elizabeth Elstob's Anglo-Saxon Manifesto and Ælfric's St Gregory Homily." In *The Editing of Old English: Papers from the 1990 Manchester Conference,* edited by D.G. Scragg and Paul E. Szarmach, 213–237. Cambridge: D.S. Brewer, 1994.

Taylor, Dennis. *Hardy's Literary Language and Victorian Philology.* Oxford: Clarendon Press, 1993.

Thomas, Daniel. "'Modest but Well-Deserved Claims': The Friendship of Samuel Fox and Joseph Bosworth and the Study of Anglo-Saxon in the Nineteenth Century." *Amsterdamer Beiträge Zur Älteren Germanistik* 78, no. 2–3 (August 30, 2018): 228–261.

Thompson, Michael Welman. "Wright, Thomas (1810–1877)." In *Oxford Dictionary of National Biography*, September 17, 2015.

Tiller, Kenneth. "Anglo-Norman Historiography and Henry of Huntingdon's Translation of 'The Battle of Brunanburh.'" *Studies in Philology* 109, no. 3 (2012): 173–191.

Torrens, H.S. "Conybeare, John Josias (1779–1824), Geologist, Antiquary, and Church of England Clergyman." In *Oxford Dictionary of National Biography*, September 28, 2006.

Tozer, James. "Tennyson's Popularity." *Tennyson Research Bulletin* 10, no. 4 (November 2015): 372–386.

Treharne, Elaine M., ed. *Old and Middle English, c.890–c.1450: An Anthology.* 3rd ed. Blackwell Anthologies. Chichester: Wiley-Blackwell, 2010.

Turley, Richard Marggraf. "'Knowledge of Their Own Supremacy': 'Œnone' and the Standardization of Tennyson's Diction." *Victorian Poetry* 37, no. 3 (October 1, 1999): 291–308.

——. "Nationalism and the Reception of Jacob Grimm's Deutsche Grammatik by English-Speaking Audiences." *German Life and Letters* 54, no. 3 (July 2001): 234–252.

——. "Tennyson and the Nineteenth-Century Language Debate." *Leeds Studies in English*, no. 28 (1997): 123–140.

Turner, James. *Philology: The Forgotten Origins of the Modern Humanities.* Princeton: Princeton University Press, 2014.

Underwood, Ted, and Jordan Sellers. "The Emergence of Literary Diction." *Journal of Digital Humanities* 1, no. 2. Accessed February 15, 2023.

Waller, Philip. *Writers, Readers, and Reputations: Literary Life in Britain 1870–1918.* Oxford: Oxford University Press, 2006.

Weaver, Sarah. "'A love for old modes of pronunciation': Historical Rhyme in Tennyson and Morris." *Tennyson Research Bulletin* 11, no. 4 (November 2020): 305–324.

——. *Tennyson's Notebook Glossary and Rhyme Lists.* Tennyson Society Monographs 17. Lincoln: Tennyson Society, 2019.

Wilson, William A. "Victorian Philology and the Anxiety of Language in Tennyson's *In Memoriam*." *Texas Studies in Literature and Language* 30, no. 1 (1988): 28–48.

Winchester, Simon. *The Meaning of Everything: The Story of the Oxford English Dictionary.* Oxford: Oxford University Press, 2003.

Index

Addison, Joseph   174, 184
Ælfred's Will   87
"Alfred, an Epic Poem"   5–6
Alfred the Great   5–6, 62, 75, 87, 93
Allingham, William   58, 135
Alliteration   99–101, 109
   see also under Alfred Tennyson
Analecta Anglo-Saxonica, ed. Thorpe   67, 85, 88
Angelsaksisk Sproglaere, by Rask   7
Anglo-Saxon Chronicle   96–97
Anglo-Saxon Meteor, The   67, 70
Anglo-Saxonism   97, 115
   church history   3, 61, 84
   law and government   6–7, 74–75, 84, 115
   perception as cultural ancestors   6, 12, 49, 61–62, 66–67, 71, 74–90, 113, 164
   professorships   7–8, 69, 70
   publication of manuscripts
      before the nineteenth century   3–5, 84
      cost   5, 18, 86–87
      during the nineteenth century   2, 6, 7, 21, 34, 63, 69–70, 84–87, 92
      poetry lineation   100
      reproduction of script   4, 5, 83–86, 90, 124–125
   see also Old English, paganism
Antiquarianism   4, 66, 124, 138–139
   Tennyson's word choices   26, 121, 131
   see also under Old English, Society of Antiquaries, under Alfred Tennyson
Apollonius of Tyre   87, 88
Apposition   107–109, 203
Archaeological Association   21
Aristotle   122
Asiatick Society of Bengal   30

Athenaeum, The   18–20, 22, 120, 123, 151, 173

Bagehot, Walter   200
Bailey, Nathan   15, 144, 145, 147, 157, 192 n.75, 199
Ballads and Other Poems (1880)   95
Barlow, Joel   208
Barnes, William
   dialect poetry   21, 132, 135–136
   linguistic nativism   115–116, 149
   on ancient Britain   82
   on roots of English   38, 43
"Battle of Brunanburh, The" (Anglo-Saxon poem)   62, 95–98, 112
Battle of Hastings   113–115
Bayeux Tapestry   76, 114
Bede, Venerable   71–72, 216
Benson, Thomas   16, 98, 127, 144
Bentham, Jeremy   151
Beowulf   203
   as native literature   83
   editions and translations
      Heaney   162
      Kemble   63, 64, 65, 68, 70, 75, 86, 87, 88, 100, 152, 214
      Morris   161, 194
   emendations of the text   64, 66
   excerpted   7, 85
   literary style   106, 150
   Tennyson's translation   90–95, 124
Bible   3, 38–39, 85, 130, 184
   see also Christianity
Blakesley, J.W.   64
Blackstone, Sir William   123
Blackwood's Edinburgh Magazine   124
Book of Golden Deeds, A, by Yonge   80
Bosworth, Joseph
   dialect   134

endows Anglo-Saxon chair   8
language laws   39, 43, 169
linguistic nativism   6, 7, 149, 182,
    183–184, 189–190, 226
metaphysics of language   60
scholarship   15, 70, 87, 96, 98
Browning, Robert   152
Bulwer-Lytton, Edward   76
Butler, Agnata (Mrs. Montagu)   165, 190

Cædmon   66, 85, 88, 89
Cædmon's Metrical Paraphrase of Parts of the Holy Scriptures   88
see also Benjamin Thorpe
Calderón de la Barca, Pedro   163
Cambridge
    Anglo-Saxon studies   7–8
    see also Cambridge Apostles, Oswald Cockayne, John Mitchell Kemble, Henry Sidgwick, *under* Alfred Tennyson
Cambridge Apostles
    attitude toward language   13, 38, 51, 162, 166
        Germanic element of English   183, 184, 193
        linguistic creativity   156–157, 182
    compound words   151, 154
    connection to *The Athenaeum*   18–19
    Hare, Julius Charles, influence of   31, 33–34
    new philology, knowledge of   62–65, 91, 112–113
    Shelley, enthusiasm for   49
    speculative attitude toward truth   26, 200, 205, 207
    see also John Mitchell Kemble, Richard Chenevix Trench
Cambridge Union   63
Cambridge University Press   86
Camden Society, The   21
Cameron, Julia Margaret   197
Cardale, J.S.   87, 88, 94
Carlyle, Jane   1
Carlyle, Thomas   51, 199
Carroll, Lewis   161
Chapman, George   124, 129, 145, 166, 187
Chaucer, Geoffrey
    glossaries of   16, 164
    Latinate vocabulary   127, 184, 195

rhymes   175, 181
source of Tennyson vocabulary   125, 129, 130, 146, 166, 198
    Tennyson reading   2, 124
Christian Remembrancer, The   151, 183
Christianity   38, 42, 78, 214
    see also Bible
Classical studies   13, 21, 36, 89, 133 n.64, 225
    language   3, 5, 7, 33, 103, 145, 169
    literature   31, 33–34, 185, 194, 197, 214
Classical Museum, The   21
Cockayne, Oswald   89
Codex Aurelius   125
Coleridge, Samuel Taylor
    Germanic ideas   33
    language, ideas about   13, 52, 53, 129–130, 143, 186, 225
    likes Turner's history of the Anglo-Saxons   6
    on Tennyson   152
Collen, George William   88
Columbiad, The, by Barlow   208
Commentaries on the Laws of England, by Blackstone   123
Compendious Grammar of Primitive English or Anglo-Saxon, by Bosworth   87
Contemporary Review, The   95
"Complaint, The" by Young   184
Compound words   12, 26, 107, 114, 115–116, 149–150
Concise Etymological Dictionary of the English Language, A, ed. Skeat   15
Conversations on Language by Mrs. Marcet   23
Conversazione Society
    see Cambridge Apostles
Conybeare, John Josias
    Beowulf excerpts and translation   70, 91, 92–95, 100, 109
    "Exile's Complaint, The" ("The Wife's Lament")   214
    scholarship   69–70, 87
    typesetting of works   85
Cooper, William Durrant   136
Corpus Christi College, Cambridge   3
Cowley, Abraham   184
Craik, George L.   23
Cratylus
    changing meaning of words   45

earliest words 22, 37, 42–43
name-makers 49, 52, 156–157
source of meaning in words 36–37, 142
see also Plato
Croker, J.W. 173

Daily Telegraph 23
Dante 208
Darwin, Charles 41–42, 46, 60, 195
De Danorum Rebus Gestis Secul., by Thorkelin 87, 92
de Vere, Aubrey 162–163
Decadence 161–162, 166, 226, 227
"Defence of Poetry, A", by Shelley 49
Descent of Man, The, by Darwin 42, 60
Deutsche Grammatik, by Grimm 7, 30, 34–35, 87, 91, 169
Dialect 21, 58, 132–138
  see also under William Barnes, *under* Alfred Tennyson
Dictionaries 3, 5, 14–17, 38, 84, 127
  see also under Alfred Tennyson
Dictionarium Saxonico et Gothico-Latinum
  see Edward Lye
Dictionarium Saxonico-Latino-Anglicum
  see William Somner
Dictionary of Archaic and Provincial Words, Obsolete Phrases, Proverbs and Ancient Customs from the Fourteenth Century, A, ed. Halliwell 137
Dictionary of English Etymology, A, ed. Wedgwood 138
Dictionary of the Anglo-Saxon Language, A, ed. Bosworth 15, 43, 70, 87, 98, 134, 184, 226
  see also Joseph Bosworth
Dictionary of the English Language, A 15, 141, 144, 145, 147, 157–158, 192 n.75, 199
  see also Samuel Johnson
Dictionary of the Isle of Wight Dialect, and of Provincialisms Used in the Island, A, ed. Long 16, 132
Dictionary of the Sussex Dialect and Collection of Provincialisms in Use in the County of Sussex, A, ed. Parish 15, 132, 134–135, 136
Discovery of the Science of Languages, The, by Kavanagh 21
Diversions of Purley, The
  see John Horne Tooke
Dodsley, Robert 127
Donaldson, John William 42
Donne, William Bodham 51, 166, 182, 183

Earle, John 134
Ecclesiastical History of the English People, by Bede 71
Elegy 26, 204, 214–218
Elements of Anglo-Saxon Grammar, The, by Bosworth 87, 96
  see also Joseph Bosworth
Eliot, George 17
Elizabeth I 3
Ellis, George 96, 101–102, 104, 125, 127, 141
"Eloisa to Abelard" by Pope 184
Elstob, Elizabeth 5, 84
Elstob, William 5, 84
Emerson, Ralph Waldo 41, 42, 49–52, 56
Empson, William 14
"Endymion" 129
English Dialect Society 132
English, Past and Present, by Trench 23, 119, 150, 155, 156, 170
  see also Richard Chenevix Trench
Essay on the Origin of Language, An, by Farrar 20
Essays on Thought and Language, by Smart 23
Essentials of Anglo-Saxon Grammar, by Bosworth 15
  see also Joseph Bosworth
Etymological and Comparative Glossary of the Dialect and Provincialisms of East Anglia, An, ed. Nall 15, 132
Etymological Dictionary of the English Language, An, ed. Skeat 15, 131
  see also W.W. Skeat
Etymology 5, 8, 21, 59, 204
Eversley Edition 55–56, 77, 201
  cites precedent 24, 130, 131, 171 n.13
  defines terms 17, 23, 24, 131, 136, 137, 140, 166, 197, 198, 199
  dialect context 136, 137, 138
  gives etymologies 16, 144, 198, 199
  gives historical sources 1, 66
  gives pronunciation 171 n.13, 172, 180
  glosses phrases 208, 211–212

Evolution   41–42, 48, 60
Examiner, The   18, 20–22
Exeter Book   214

Faerie Queene, The, by Spenser   127–128, 184, 199
Fairfax, Edward   198
Farrar, Frederic W.   20
FitzGerald, Edward   15, 132–133
Forster, Rev. C.   23
Fox, Samuel   66, 88
Freeman, Edward   76
Froude, James Anthony   52
Furnivall, Frederick James   19, 132

Gammer Gurton's Needle   125–127, 197
Gascoigne, George   131
Gentleman's Magazine   8, 66–69
Geoffrey of Monmouth   197
Geological Evidences of the Antiquity of Man, The   41–42, 57
Gibbon, Edward   184
Gibson, Edmund   96
Gladstone, William   148
Goodrich, Chauncey A.   15
Gower, John   125, 181
Grammar of the Anglo-Saxon Tongue, A, by Rask (trans. Thorpe)   15, 85, 88, 92–94, 97, 98, 104, 109, 125
"Green Knight's Farewell to Fansie, The"   131
Grettis Saga   77
Grimm, Jacob
  correspondence with Kemble   39, 40, 69, 74, 75, 81–82, 85–86, 111, 116, 134, 152, 156, 183, 190
  Deutsche Grammatik   7, 30–31, 87, 91, 169
  known in England   19, 34, 66, 69, 91
  lineation of Old English poetry   100
  new philology   12, 30–31, 170
  opinions on typesetting   85–86, 152
  see also Grimm's Law
Grimm's Law   7, 30–31, 34–36, 173
Grundtvig, N.F.S.   66
Guesses at Truth, By Two Brothers, by Hare and Hare   32–33, 122, 142, 205
Guest, Edwin   97, 99, 101–102, 104, 181
Gurney, Anna   96
Gwilt, Joseph   88

Hallam, Arthur   151
  correspondence with Cambridge Apostles   64–65, 119, 123–124
  poems mourning his death   39, 59, 121–122, 201
  promotes Tennyson   20
  reviews Tennyson   128, 154, 190, 221
  sends poetic words to Tennyson   123–124
  subject of *In Memoriam*
    dead body   206, 209–211, 217
    imagined afterlife   208–209, 220
    superior qualities   214, 218
    theme of communication   166, 204
Halliwell, J.O.   137
Hamlet, by Shakespeare   24, 124, 129, 184, 198
Hardy, Thomas   135, 149, 152, 221
Hare, Augustus   32–33
Hare, Julius Charles
  Germanic ideas in his teaching   13, 33, 91
  Germanic origin of English   182, 183
  hyphenated words   151
  language wearing out   55, 142, 227
  Middlemarch, influence on   17
  new philology in his teaching   31–32, 34, 223
  Philological Museum   21
  truth is multifaceted   205, *see also* *Guesses at Truth, By Two Brothers*
Harold, the Last of the Saxon Kings, by Bulwer-Lytton   76
Havelok the Dane, ed. Madden   64
Heaney, Seamus   106, 150–151, 162
Heath, John Moore   65
Henry of Huntingdon   95
"Heroes and Hero-Worship", by Carlyle   199
Hickes, George   4, 70, 103
Historia Anglorum, by Henry of Huntingdon   95
Historical linguistics
  see Philology
History of English Poetry from the Twelfth to the Close of the Sixteenth Century, by Warton   78, 97–98
History of English Rhythms, A   97, 99, 181
  see also Edwin Guest

History of the Anglo-Saxons, The 6, 7, 44, 71–72, 88, 89, 90, 92–94, 96, 106–107, 184
    see also Sharon Turner
History of the Decline and Fall of the Roman Empire, The, by Gibbon 184
"History of the English Language, First, or Anglo-Saxon Period" 34, 59, 65, 115
    see also John Mitchell Kemble
History of the Norman Conquest, by Freeman 76–77
Holmes, Sherlock 46
Homer 124, 129, 145, 187, 203
Hopkins, Gerard Manley 12, 116, 149, 152, 185, 197
Horace 205
Horne Tooke, John 29–30, 36, 212
Hotten, John Camden 15
Humboldt, William 40
Hume, David 184
Hunt, Leigh 20, 124
"Hymn, A" by Thomson 184

Illustrations of Anglo-Saxon Poetry, ed. Conybeare 69–70, 85, 87, 91, 92–93, 214
Indo-European 7, 30, 48
Ingram, James 87, 96
Introduction to the Art of Reading, An, by Rice 179
Ivanhoe 6, 183
    see also Walter Scott

"Jabberwocky, The", by Carroll 161
James, Henry 194
Johnson, Samuel 15, 130, 141, 144, 145, 147, 157–158, 184, 199
Jones, William 30, 31

Kavanagh, Morgan 21
Keats, John 129, 173
Kemble, John Mitchell
    alliteration 111
    Anglo-Saxon manuscripts, work with 3, 64–65
    Anglo-Saxon religion 13, 78, 79, 81–82
    Anglo-Saxon studies, state of 7–8, 66–67
    attitude toward Anglo-Saxons 75, 150
    attitude toward other scholars 63, 66–69 96–97, 98
    Beowulf 94
    compound words 151–152
    dialect 134
    friendship with Tennyson 65–66, 112–113, 119
    Gentleman's Magazine skirmish 66–67, 68
    linguistic nativism vs. variety 156, 182, 188, 190, 224, 225
    new philology, advocate of 12, 29, 31, 34, 43, 66
        anthropological approach 45, 48, 83–84, 116, 150
    origin of language 39–40, 51, 83, 149
    philosophy of language 59
    reading *Deutsche Grammatik* 91
    relationship between Old and Modern English 24, 115–117, 156–157, 169–170
    scholarship 62–71
    typesetting and lineation in works 85–87, 90, 100
    see also The Anglo-Saxon Meteor, Frederic Madden, *under* Old English, "On English Præterites", *The Saxons in England*, Thomas Wright, "Widsið"
Kinloch, George R. 127
King Alfred's Anglo-Saxon version of Boethius, de Consolatione Philosophiæ, ed. Cardale 88
King Alfred's Anglo-Saxon version of the Metres of Boethius, ed. Fox 88
Knowles, James 141

L'Allegro, by Milton 199
Langland, William 130–131, 166, 175
Language
    contains historic thought 30, 40, 46–48, 119, 143
    etymological metaphors and concreteness of early speech 41, 49–51, 83–84, 142–143, 148, 149
    metaphors and similes for 40–41, 44–48, 57
    origin of 28, 29, 37, 38, 39–43, 50
    philosophy and theory of 11, 25, 29–36, 36–49, 59–60, 122
    progress vs. decay 47

Index

roots 21, 26, 38, 43, 45, 50, 60, 113, 147
source of meaning in 21–22, 25, 28, 29, 37–38, 39, 204, 208
true meaning/accuracy in expression 38, 42, 45, 60
Language as a Means of Mental Culture, by Marcel 23
Latham, R.G. 22
Layamon 197
Lecky, W.E.H. 133, 172
Lecture on the Study of Anglo-Saxon, A, by Silver 87
Lectures on the Philosophy of Life and Philosophy of Language, by Schlegel 23
Lectures on the Science of Language, by Müller 23, 35–36, 43
Leechdoms, Wortcunning, and Starcraft of Early England, by Cockayne 89
Levins, Peter 180
Libri Psalmorum versio antiqua Latina, by Thorpe 88
Life and Death of Jason, The, by Morris 194–195
Lives of the Poets, The, by Johnson 184
Locke, John 29, 184
Long, W.H. 16
Longfellow, Henry Wadsworth 77
Longmuir, John 174
Lye, Edward 5, 16, 70, 98, 127, 144
Lyell, Charles 25, 40, 41–42, 45, 46–47, 57, 60
Lyrical Ballads 186

Macaulay, Thomas Babington 52
Machin, Lewis 128
Macpherson, James 83
Madden, Frederic 19, 64, 69, 97, 98
Magnusson, Eirikr 77
Malory, Thomas 197, 202, 203
Manipulus Vocabulorum, by Levins 180
Mann, Robert James 148
Manning, Owen 87
Marcel, C. 23
Marlowe, Christopher 178
Maurice, F.D. 19, 31, 191
Medievalism
performative 1, 23–24, 25, 120–121, 168, 196–200

philological 1, 23, 139, 168
Menologium, seu Calendarium Poeticum, ex Hickesiano Thesauro, by Fox 88
"Merlin" 197
Middlemarch 17
Milton, John
alliteration 110
compound words 149, 155
linguistic authority 130, 156, 171 n.13, 183, 184, 190, 199
source of Tennyson's words and usages 9, 121, 129–130, 166, 191, 199
style similarities in Tennyson 9, 121, 165, 147–148, 203, 208
Mone, Franz Joseph 88
Morning Post, The 158
Morris, William 12, 77, 161, 194–195, 221
Morte D'Arthur, by Malory 197
Moxon, Edward 18, 20, 21, 22
Mudie, Charles Edward 22
Mudie's Select Library 18, 22–23
Müller, Friedrich Max
linguistic laws 44
linguistic roots, importance of 43, 60, 113
past word usage 139, 227
poetic view of language 205
popularizer of new philology 23, 35–36, 45–46
rejects evolutionary linguistic theory 42, 162, 225
thought and language inseparable 40
Murray, J.A.H. 16, 52, 53

Nall, John Greaves 15
Nationalism 61, 84–85, 108–110, 194
see also nativism, linguistic
Nativism, linguistic 7, 10, 61, 115–116, 150, 169, 182–184, 194–195
see also nationalism
New Cratylus, The, by Donaldson 42
New English Dictionary, A, ed. Richardson 15, 63, 144, 145, 147, 155, 159, 165, 192 n.75, 199, 212
New English Dictionary on Historical Principles, A, ed. J.A.H. Murray
see Oxford English Dictionary (OED)
New Monthly Magazine 226

New philology
  anthropological insights   28, 30, 39, 43–49, 61, 94, 115, 118, 119, 120
  fact-first methodology   30, 53
  German scholarship   2, 19, 30, 31, 33, 34, 47, 62, 63, 66–69, 91
  origins of   29–31
  popularization in England   7, 18, 31, 34, 35–36, 45–47, 98
  readership   17, 19–23
  supports many perspectives   2, 60
  see also Jacob Grimm, Julius Charles Hare, John Mitchell Kemble, Friedrich Max Müller, Henry Sweet, Benjamin Thorpe, Richard Chenevix Trench, Thomas Wright
Norman Conquest   6–7, 25, 61, 62, 74, 76–77, 78, 113–115, 183, 191, 194
Notes on Ancient Britain and the Britons, by Barnes   82
Notes on the Miracles of Our Lord, by Trench   119, 207
Notes on the Parables of Our Lord, by Trench   119, 142, 207

Odyssey, The   185, 187
Old English
  dictionaries and grammars   4, 5, 6, 7, 67, 70, 87, 98, 104
  study of   4, 7, 18, 34, 49, 61, 66–70
  typesetting of   5, 83–90, 121, 127
Old English Drama, The   125
"On English Dialects", by Earle   134
"On English Præterites", by Kemble   21, 64
On Some Deficiencies in Our English Dictionaries, by Trench   22, 119
On the Authorized Version of the New Testament, by Trench   120
"On the Names of the Days of the Week", by Hare   33
"On the Shortness of Man's Life", by Cowley   184
On the Study of Words, by Trench   17, 22, 23, 42, 119
One Primeval Language, The, by Forster   23
Onomatopoeia   21, 54–56, 164
Origin of Species, The, by Darwin   41
Outline of English Speech-Craft, An, by Barnes   116

Outline of Rede-Craft (Logic), An, by Barnes   116
Outlines of Comparative Philology, by Schele de Vere   19–20
Outlines of the History of English Language, by Craik   23
Oxford English Dictionary (OED)   191, 199, 200, 208, 212–213
  definitions and quotations   2–3, 124, 129, 130, 131, 139, 140, 147, 159, 164, 165
  history   19, 86, 119
  Tennyson's relationship with   16, 52–53
  first or only example of a definition   157, 158, 159, 132, 155
  illustrates a definition   159, 172, 52–53, 131, 136, 139, 146
  usage not in the *OED* or earlier than its first quotation   157, 158, 159, 166, 139
"Oxford Professors of Anglo-Saxon", by Kemble   67
Oxford University   4, 7, 8, 23, 35, 61, 66, 67, 69–70, 84

Paganism   13, 65, 72–74, 78–82, 83
  see also primitivism
Pall Mall Gazette   195
Paradise Lost, by Milton   184
Parish, W.D.   15
Parker, Matthew   3
Pater, Walter   115, 226
Paul, Jean   49
Percy, Thomas   62
Piers Plowman, by Langland   125, 130, 141
Philological Museum, The   21, 33
Philological Society   12, 19, 52, 86, 89, 119
Philology
  definitions   2
  history of   3
  insight into human origins   2, 28, 39, 46–47
  methods before new philology   3, 28, 29, 45, 67–70
  relationship to other fields   2, 25, 36, 40–41, 44–46, 48
  see also language, new philology
Plato   36, 163, 166
  see also Cratylus

Poems (1832)   108, 120, 151, 159, 160, 173, 185
Poems (1842)   17–18, 22, 109, 131, 151, 158, 160, 165, 183, 185, 222
Poems, by Trench   193
Poems by Two Brothers   19, 51, 82, 139, 156
Poems, Chiefly Lyrical (1830)   19, 111, 122–123, 128, 156, 160, 161, 162–163, 173, 190, 221
Poems of Rural Life in the Dorset Dialect, by Barnes   21, 132, 135
Poet as language maker   49–53
   see also under Richard Chenevix Trench
Poetic Endings, by Trusler   175
Pope, Alexander   121, 129, 174, 175, 184, 191
Press, The   158
Price, Richard   97–98
Primitivism   25, 61, 72–83, 84, 89
   see also paganism
Publishers' Circular   36

Quellen und Forschungen zur Geschichte der Teutschen Lit. und Sprache, by Mone   88

Ralph Royster Doyster   125–127
Rask, Rasmus   66, 182
   compound words   151
   grammar of Old English   7, 88
      Anglo-Saxon script   85, 124–125, 127
      Tennyson's engages with   15, 92–93, 97
   Old English poetry   100, 104, 109
   sound changes   34
Rawnsley, T.H.   165
Reed, Isaac   127
Reliques of Ancient English Poetry, by Percy   62
Rhymes, historical   173–181
   see also archaic pronunciation *under* Alfred Tennyson
Rhyming Dictionary, A, by Walker   174–175, 178, 179, 180
Rhyming Dictionary for the Use of Young Poets, by Smibert   178
Rice, John   179
Richardson, Charles
   see *A New English Dictionary*
Ritson, Joseph   127

Robertson, William   184
Roman de Rou   76
Romanticism   9, 30, 47, 52, 214, 224, 225
   see also Samuel Taylor Coleridge, Percy Bysshe Shelley
Roxburghe Club   86
Rudiments of a Grammar of the Anglo-Saxon Language, by Gwilt   88
Rundle, Miss   165
Runes   5, 63, 64, 65, 75, 84
Rural Fete, The   132
Ruskin, John   52

Samson Agonistes, by Milton   148
Saussure, Ferdinand de   225
Saxo Grammaticus   65
Saxons in England, The, by Kemble   13, 71, 74, 75
Schele de Vere, M.   20
Schlegel, Friedrich   23
Schmid, Reinhold   66
Scott, Walter   6, 52, 130, 166, 183, 187
Sea Words and Phrases Along the Suffolk Coast, by FitzGerald   15, 132–133
"Seafarer, The"   218
Select Collection of Old Plays in Twelve Volumes, A, ed. Reed   127
Select Glossary of English Words Used Formerly in Senses Different from Their Present, A, by Trench   47, 119
Shakespeare, William
   OED citations   123, 212
   source of vocabulary and diction   124, 129–130, 147
   language admired   149, 156, 165, 183, 184, 190
   subject of essays   32
   Tennyson cites for word usage   121, 171 n.13
   see also *Hamlet*
Shelley, Percy Bysshe   49, 52, 129, 149, 152, 163
"Shepherd's Calendar", by Spenser   129
Sidgwick, Henry   112–113
Silver, Thomas   87
Sisson, J.L.   87
Skeat, W.W.   15, 19, 89, 131, 147
Slang Dictionary, The, by Hotten   15
Smart, B.H.   23
Smibert, Thomas   178

Smith, John Russell   21
Society of Antiquaries   3
Somersby   58, 140, 151
Somner, William   4, 16, 84, 98
Southey, Robert   52
Specimens of the Early English Poets, ed. Ellis   96, 125, 127, 141
Spectator, The   122, 160, 173, 184
Spenser, Edmund
  historical rhymes   181
  linguistic authority   184, 199
  source of vocabulary   129, 158, 165, 166, 199
Spring Rice, Stephen   65
Stephen, Leslie   29
Sterling, John   19
Story of Burnt Njal, The   77
"Story of Justin Martyr, The", by Trench   193–194
Story of Justin Martyr, and Other Poems, The, by Trench   193
Story of Rimini, The, by Hunt   124
Strangeness (defamiliarization)   5, 118, 120–132, 149, 159, 161, 197, 228
Strong verbs   169–171, 189, 200
  see also archaic verb conjugations *under* Alfred Tennyson
"Study in Scarlet, A", by Conan Doyle   46
Sweet, Henry   19, 89, 98, 101–104
Swift, Jonathan   184
Swinburne, Algernon Charles   194
Symons, Arthur   161
Synonyms of the New Testament   119

Tale of a Tub, A, by Swift   184
"Tale of Florent, The", by Gower   125
Tasso   198
Tennant, R.J.   63, 91
Tennyson, Alfred
  at Cambridge   182
    Chancellor's Gold Medal   146
    dialect   136
    friends discuss language   11, 12–13, 33, 119, 123, 130, 156, 182
    new philology, exposure to   31, 33–35
    studies Old English   90–91, 124
    see also Cambridge Apostles, John Mitchell Kemble, notebooks (below), Richard Chenevix Trench
  books owned by   98 n.158
    Anglo-Saxon   70–71, 85, 92–93, 96, 98, 100, 184
    anthologies   96, 97
    by Cambridge friends   65–66, 71, 119
    Celtic subjects   82
    dialect   132–133, 134–135, 136, 137
    dictionaries   15–16, 63, 174
    sagas   77
  Celtic topics, interest in   13, 72, 82, 133
  knowledge of Anglo-Saxon language and literature   5, 10, 12, 24, 62, 70–72, 90–106, 113, 124, 164, 201
    planned poem on Anglo-Saxons' conversion to Christianity   71–72, 216
    translates Old English   25, 90–106
    see also under notebooks (below)
  knowledge of earlier forms of English   23, 26, 123–130, 133, 224
  linguistic themes in his poetry
    communication failure   25, 26, 38, 39, 59, 204
    limits of language   204, 208, 227
    sound and meaning   25, 53–59, 223
    sounds of nature   56–59
  notebooks
    Beowulf translation   92–95, 100–101
    draft poems   35, 57, 108, 145, 164, 168
    glossary of Old and Middle English   5, 15–16, 33, 90, 96, 98, 124–129, 134, 141, 145, 158, 171, 187, 197, 198
    language notes   34–35, 124, 130, 197, 206
    nursery rhymes   80
    rhyme lists   123, 136, 172, 175–176, 178, 180
  poet laureate   18, 25, 76
  prosody
    alliteration   131, 202–203, 110–112, 218–221, 224, 228
    Anglo-Saxonist style   12, 80–81, 113–114, 201–203
    translating Old English poetry   95, 98–101, 103–105
  readership   11, 17–23, 148, 165
  reading   16, 34–35, 92–93, 110, 124–128, 164, 166

reviews of his writing   17, 19, 20
  accusations of affectation   160–163
  compound words   151
  unusual word usage   23, 120, 128, 158, 159, 165
  use of old words and old pronunciation   122–123, 171–173, 181
source for dictionaries   14, 52–53, 131, 138
word uses based on philology   52
  ambiguity   10, 14, 24, 26, 48, 168, 205–211, 227
  archaic pronunciation   26, 118, 120, 171–181
    see also rhymes, historical
  archaic verb conjugations   170–171, 189, 200, 224
  archaic words
    aesthetic effect   9, 23–24, 26, 90, 118, 120–123, 161, 168, 198, 223
    critical dislike of   128, 151, 160–161
    response to concerns about language   142, 163–164, 166–167, 224
    sources   13, 123, 128–131, 212
    see also glossary of Old and Middle English *under* notebooks (above) and reviews of his writing (above)
  compound words   80, 118, 120, 151–155, 159, 164, 168, 202, 203, 224
  dialect   106, 121, 133, 135–137, 187, 221
    see also Dialect
  etymological metaphors   9, 13, 26, 48, 53, 118, 142–149, 165, 210, 211–212
  Germanic vs. Latinate   26, 44, 45, 114–115, 165, 168, 182–195, 200, 203, 222, 224, 227
  historical meanings   11, 13, 14, 16, 25, 118, 138–142, 163–164, 199, 204–205, 214, 224
  innovation   13, 14, 53, 118, 120, 155–159, 163–164, 166, 199–200
Tennyson, Charles   64
Tennyson, Emily (Lady Tennyson)   1
Tennyson, Emily (poet's sister)   214

Tennyson, Hallam
  controls father's legacy   11, 65, 79, 156
  Eversley Edition notes   66, 130–131, 140
  Old English translation   95, 99 103–104
  reading   66
  reports father's conversation   77, 99, 123, 148, 183
  subscriber of dialect dictionary   16, 132
Thomas, Timothy   16
Thomson, James   184
Thorkelin, Grímur Jónsson   87, 92
Thorpe, Benjamin   109
  depicts of Old English script   85–87, 125, 127
  new philology   66–67
  on Anglo-Saxon compounds   151
  publications   15, 88
  Tennyson engages with his work   15, 92–94, 97–98, 127
Times, The   77
TIW, by Barnes   43, 135
Transactions of the Philological Society   22, 134
Trench, Richard Chenevix
  archaic language   30, 156, 166, 199
  compound words   149–150, 154–155
  correspondence with Cambridge Apostles   19, 64, 182
  friendship with Tennyson   13, 119
  language as archive   40, 47, 222
  linguistic nativism   150, 183, 187, 188
  linguistic precision   38, 44, 142, 205, 223
  meaning inherent in words   39, 49, 143, 162, 164
  metaphors for language   26, 44–45, 47, 223, 225
  optimism about language   45, 166, 224–227
  origin of language   42, 57
  popularizes philology   12, 17–18, 33–34, 36, 45–46, 118–120, 224–227
  publications   22, 23, 119, 193
  religious attitude   56, 207
  revitalizing language   122, 142–143, 166, 210
  role of the poet   12, 25, 50, 51–52, 120, 121, 132, 138, 157, 162
  strong verbs   170–171
  words as poetry   49, 143, 205, 211

writes poetry   163, 182, 193–194, 213–14
  see also Cambridge Apostles
Trevelyan, G.M.   19
Trinity College, Cambridge
  language discussed at   13, 119, 130, 151, 156–157, 182
  new philology, early adoption of   31, 33, 91
  philologists studied at   42, 67
  Whewell, William   38
  see also Cambridge Apostles, Julius Charles Hare, *under* Alfred Tennyson
Troilus and Criseyde   130
Trusler, John   175
Turner, Sharon   81, 88
  excerpts Old English texts   7, 216
    lineation   100
    original texts   89, 92–93
    translations   89, 92–93, 94, 96, 102, 104
  opinion of Anglo-Saxon poetry   90, 106–107, 151
  opinion of Old English   115, 150, 184
  popularizes Anglo-Saxons as cultural ancestors   6, 71, 74
  Tennyson interacts with his work   71–72
  theory of language history   29, 44, 140
Tyrwhitt, Thomas   16, 127, 164

"Über den Ursprung der Sprache", by Grimm   40
Universal Etymological English Dictionary, An, ed. Bailey   15, 144, 145, 147, 157, 199

Upton's Physioglyphics   21
Urry, John   16

Verbs, strong
  see Strong verbs
Virgil   203
Vocabularium Anglo-Saxonicum, ed. Benson   16, 98, 127

Walker, John
  see Rhyming Dictionary, A
"Wanderer, The"   215, 217
Warton, Thomas   78, 97
Watts, Walter, Theodore   137
Webster, Noah   15
Wedgwood, Hensleigh   138
Weld, Charles Richard   13, 82
Westminster Review, The   111, 122–123, 160, 161, 173
Wheeler, Charles Stearns   51
Wheloc, Abraham   96
Whewell, William   38, 44
White, Robert Meadows   66
Whitman, Walt   51
"Widsið"   214
"Wife's Lament, The"   214
Wilde, Oscar   161
William the Conqueror   76–77, 182
Wordsworth, William   6, 52, 161, 163, 173, 186, 222
Wright, Thomas   19, 21, 67–69, 78, 83, 106, 107, 134

Yeats, William Butler   161
Yonge, Charlotte M.   80
Young, Edward   184

Tennyson Works Cited

Adeline   57
Amphion   128
The Ancient Sage   213, 227
The Ante-Chamber   128
Antony to Cleopatra   181
Aylmer's Field   53, 107, 130, 171 n.13

Babylon   180
The Battle of Brunanburh   10, 62, 95–106, 171
Becket   53, 72
Break, break, break   14
The Brook   136, 213
Buonaparte   110

The Captain   139
Claribel   58
The Coach of Death   191
The constant spirit of the world exults   47–48, 94, 140, 144, 167
Crossing the Bar   129, 180–181

The Day-Dream   24, 158, 181
The Devil and the Lady   121, 123, 146, 191
A Dirge   58, 130, 136
Dora   222
The Dying Swan   164, 172

Edwin Morris   57
Eleänor   57
Enoch Arden   53, 128, 138
The Exile's Harp   82, 165

The Fall of Jerusalem   139, 180
A Farewell   58

The Gardener's Daughter   57, 177, 213
Godiva   66
The Golden Year   55

The Goose   157, 158

Hail Briton!   74
Harold   25, 53, 76–79, 113–114, 116
The Hesperides   53, 154
The "How" and the "Why"   54

Idylls of the King   1, 18, 25, 26, 35, 53, 56, 58, 76, 128, 130, 131, 136, 143, 148, 165, 166, 168, 171, 172, 195–203, 213, 222
In Memoriam   9, 17, 24, 25, 26, 39, 42, 53, 58, 59, 60, 107, 108, 121–122, 123, 130, 131, 132, 139–140, 141, 145, 147, 165, 166, 168, 171, 172, 177–179, 180, 196–197, 198, 200, 202, 203, 204–221
In the Children's Hospital   139, 180
Inscriptions by a Brook   157
Isabel   128

The Kraken   172

Locksley Hall   137, 180
The Lotos-Eaters   129, 145, 180, 185–192, 195, 205, 221
Love and Death   130
Love thou thy land   78, 109, 116, 118, 180
The Lover's Tale   15, 140
Lucretius   35

Mariana   111–112
Maud   53, 139, 141–142, 144, 146, 148, 158, 171, 177, 180, 185, 192–193, 195, 212
The Miller's Daughter   165
Morte d'Arthur   201

The Letters   213

My life is full of weary days   128

The New Timon, and the Poets   79
The Northern Cobbler   133, 135
Northern Farmer, New Style   35, 58
Northern Farmer, Old Style   135, 138

O Bosky Brook   145
Ode on the Death of the Duke of Wellington   75, 180
Ode Sung at the Opening of the International Exhibition   180
Ode to Memory   137, 179
Œnone   10, 58, 130, 171, 172, 205
The Old Chieftain   51, 83

The Palace of Art   10, 14, 140, 144, 157, 164, 213
The Poet   180
The Poet's Song   58
The Princess   10, 53, 57, 128, 130, 131, 136–137, 171, 200

Queen Mary   45, 76, 156, 208

Recollections of the Arabian Nights   128, 129, 154
Riflemen, Form   180
The Ring   137

The Sailor-Boy   137
Sea Dreams   158, 191
Sense and Conscience   57
Show-Day at Battle Abbey, 1876   113–114
The Skipping Rope   53, 174, 175
The Sleeping Beauty   146

Song   213
The Spinster's Sweet-Arts   180
St Simeon Stylites   193–194, 212
Supposed Confessions of a Second-Rate Sensitive Mind   129, 157, 213

The Talking Oak   11, 23
The Throstle   56
Timbuctoo   19, 146–147, 155, 208
Tiresias   147
Tithon   141
Tithonus   11, 140–141, 191
To J.S.   172, 179
To Poesy   179
To the Reverend F.D. Maurice   191
The Two Voices   14, 58, 179–180

Ulysses   11, 108, 200

The Victim   80–81, 171
The Vision of Sin   59, 156
The Voyage of Maeldune   133

What Thor Said to the Bard Before Dinner   79–80, 152
Whispers   39, 56
Will Waterproof's Lyrical Monologue   131, 172
The Window   58
Woe to the double-tongued, the land's disease   108

You ask me, why, though ill at ease   139
Youth   139

Medievalism

I
Anglo-Saxon Culture and the Modern Imagination
edited by David Clark and Nicholas Perkins

II
Medievalist Enlightenment: From Charles Perrault to Jean-Jacques Rousseau
Alicia C. Montoya

III
Memory and Myths of the Norman Conquest
Siobhan Brownlie

IV
Comic Medievalism: Laughing at the Middle Ages
Louise D'Arcens

V
Medievalism: Key Critical Terms
edited by Elizabeth Emery and Richard Utz

VI
Medievalism: A Critical History
David Matthews

VII
Chivalry and the Medieval Past
edited by Katie Stevenson and Barbara Gribling

VIII
Georgian Gothic: Medievalist Architecture, Furniture and Interiors, 1730–1840
Peter N. Lindfield

IX
Petrarch and the Literary Culture of Nineteenth-Century France:
Translation, Appropriation, Transformation
Jennifer Rushworth

X
Medievalism, Politics and Mass Media:
Appropriating the Middle Ages in the Twenty-First Century
Andrew B. R. Elliott

XI
Translating Early Medieval Poetry: Transformation, Reception, Interpretation
edited by Tom Birkett and Kirsty March-Lyons

XII
Medievalism in A Song of Ice and Fire *and* Game of Thrones
Shiloh Carroll

XIII
William Morris and the Icelandic Sagas
Ian Felce

XIV
Derek Jarman's Medieval Modern
Robert Mills

XV
François Villon in English Poetry: Translation and Influence
Claire Pascolini-Campbell

XVI
*Neomedievalism, Popular Culture, and the Academy:
From Tolkien to* Game of Thrones
KellyAnn Fitzpatrick

XVII
Medievalism in English Canadian Literature: From Richardson to Atwood
edited by M. J. Toswell and Anna Czarnowus

XVIII
Anglo-Saxonism and the Idea of Englishness in Eighteenth-Century Britain
Dustin M. Frazier Wood

XIX
Subaltern Medievalisms: Medievalism 'from below' in Nineteenth-Century Britain
edited by David Matthews and Michael Sanders

XX
*Medievalist Traditions in Nineteenth-Century British Culture:
Celebrating the Calendar Year*
Clare A. Simmons

XXI
Old English Medievalism: Reception and Recreation in the 20th and 21st Centuries
edited by Rachel A. Fletcher, Thijs Porck and Oliver M. Traxel

XXII
International Medievalisms: From Nationalism to Activism
edited by Mary Boyle

XXIII
*Old English Scholarship in the Seventeenth Century:
Medievalism and National Crisis*
Rebecca Brackmann

XXIV
*Medievalism in Nineteenth-Century Belgium:
The 1848 Monument to Godfrey of Bouillon*
Simon John

XXV
National Medievalism in the Twenty-First Century: Switzerland and Great Britain
Matthias D. Berger

XXVI
Reinventing Medieval Liturgy in Victorian England: Thomas Frederick Simmons and the Lay Folks' Mass Book
David Jasper and Jeremy J. Smith

XXVII
Medievalisms in a Global Age
edited by Angela Jane Weisl and Robert Squillace

XXVIII
The Middle Ages in Computer Games: Ludic Approaches to the Medieval and Medievalism
Robert Houghton

XXIX
Medievalism and Reception
edited by Ellie Crookes and Ika Willis

Printed in the United States
by Baker & Taylor Publisher Services